What people are

The End of the ~~...~~

"The topic could not be more important. A very valuable and surely timely contribution."
—**Noam Chomsky**, Massachusetts Institute of Technology/ University of Arizona

"A must read for everyone rising against the system that is destroying life on earth and our future."
—**Vandana Shiva**, World Future Council, founder of Navdanya

"A fascinating new take on the parts of human history that got us where we are today. It's a disturbing story, but it offers some clues on the way out of our box canyon".
—**Bill McKibben**, founder of 350.org, author of *Falter: Has the Human Game Begun to Play Itself Out?*

"This book, a sensation in Germany when it was first published, challenges us to seek a new path for our and the planet's survival. It tells the backstory of the failed promises of economic globalization and market capitalism and shows that the current social and ecological crises have their roots in thousands of years of war, domination and destruction of the natural world."
—**Maude Barlow**, Chairperson of the Council of the Canadians

"A brilliant book, that couldn't be more topical. We owe the author our gratitude, solidarity and a great deal of admiration."
—**Jean Ziegler**, Advisory Committee to the UN Human Rights Council

"A highly original and fascinating book. It helps us to understand and overcome the global Megamachine that is threatening our future."
—**ERNST ULRICH VON WEIZSÄCKER**, World Future Council, Co-President of the Club of Rome (2012–2018)

"What a brilliant achievement—a wonderfully coherent, cogent and gripping story of the historical origins of the political, economic, social and ecological crises of our times. You can't be a serious activist committed to creating a new world if you haven't read this."
—**FIROZE MANJI**, Carleton University, founder of *Pambazuka News*

"A fascinating book, delightful to read in spite of the grim topic. This is an excellent reflection on the terror/hope that we are living."
—**JOHN HOLLOWAY**, Autonomous University of Puebla, Mexico

"*The End of the Megamachine* exposes the slide into a near complete loss of memory of who we are as humans and how we ought to live together. Scheidler weaves a potent tapestry of how we subvert ourselves through reckless exploitation of nature and the piling of socio-ecological harms on human communities. This book is a loud alarm that must not be ignored."
—**NNIMMO BASSEY**, Health of Mother Earth Foundation, Nigeria

"An extremely good read!"
—**THE GERMAN DAILY** *Taz. Die Tageszeitung*

"In this fascinating and rich synthesis, Scheidler tells us the whole story of the Megamachine, this giant creature that eats minerals and spawns armies, from the very beginning of the mining age, to the current wholesale destruction of the Earth's crust."
—**UGO BARDI**, Club of Rome, author of *The Limits to Growth Revisited* and *Extracted*

"An eye-opener for social activists. A history of Western civilization in only 300 pages: no wonder the book is such a great success! Fabian Scheidler brilliantly succeeds in highlighting the rupture points in this process."
—WOLFGANG SACHS, editor of *The Development Dictionary*

"Fabian Scheidler's book paints a uniquely complete picture of the historical roots of capitalism. It is a profound mirror for the Western world, which prides itself so much on values, peace and democracy. For me, the book is more valuable than everything I learned about history at school."
—CHRISTIAN FELBER, author of *Change Everything: Creating an Economy for the Common Good*

"*The End of the Megamachine* is an informed and clearly written chronicle of how societies have reached the dire situation we now face. Going on from our perch on the precipice, do we accumulate ourselves into barbaric death under the rule of the Megamachine? Or do we cooperate ourselves into civilized life by ending the Megamachine, and not ourselves? Scheidler offers historical insights meant to fuel the liberating outcome."
—MICHAEL ALBERT, founder and editor of *Z Magazine*

"This book tells us more than a hundred other books put together. It should be required reading in every school."
—MILO RAU, author, artistic director, City Theatre of Gent

"Top 10 of non-fiction books."
—ROBERT JUNGK Library for Future Studies

"The book makes us understand how today's madness came to be. You do not feel confused and powerless anymore, but ready for a new start."
—THE GERMAN WEEKLY *Der Freitag*

The End of the Megamachine

A Brief History of a Failing Civilization

The End of the Megamachine

A Brief History of a Failing Civilization

Fabian Scheidler

Winchester, UK
Washington, USA

JOHN HUNT PUBLISHING

First published by Zero Books, 2020
Zero Books is an imprint of John Hunt Publishing Ltd., No. 3 East St., Alresford,
Hampshire SO24 9EE, UK
office@jhpbooks.com
www.johnhuntpublishing.com
www.zero-books.net

For distributor details and how to order please visit the 'Ordering' section on our website.

Text copyright: Fabian Scheidler 2019
www.end-of-the-megamachine.com

The German edition was first published in 2015 by Promedia Publishers, Vienna (Austria).

Translation: Bill C. Ray
Translation of the Afterword: Penelope Pinson
Copy editor of the German edition and the English translation: Manfred Froh-Hanin

ISBN: 978 1 78904 271 9
978 1 78904 272 6 (ebook)
Library of Congress Control Number: 2019905183

Design: Stuart Davies

UK: Printed and bound by CPI Group (UK) Ltd, Croydon, CR0 4YY
US: Printed and bound by Thomson-Shore, 7300 West Joy Road, Dexter, MI 48130

We operate a distinctive and ethical publishing philosophy in
all areas of our business, from our global network of authors to
production and worldwide distribution.

Contents

Introduction   1

The Myths of Modernity   3
The Megamachine   5
Limits of the System   6
Book Structure   8

Part I: The Four Tyrannies   11

1. POWER—The Four Tyrannies and the Roots
of Domination   13

The Three Tyrannies   16
Physical Power   18
Structural Violence   21
Ideological Power   25
The Invention of the Dominating God   27
The Fourth Tyranny   29

2. METAL—Mining, Armament and Power over Nature   33

The Origins of the Military-Industrial Complex   34
Environmental Disasters   36
Playing God: Metallurgy and Power over Creation   40

3. MARKETS—Economic Power, Money and Property   43

The Myth of the Market   45
War as the Cradle of the Market   46
The Laurion Mines   49
The Roman Silver Empire   51
The First Corporations   52
Ownership as Complete Power of Disposition   54

4. POWERLESSNESS—The Trauma of Power and
the Origin of Apocalyptic Thinking 59
What is Trauma? 61
Apocalypse as a Response to the Trauma of Power 65
The Destruction of Heaven and Earth 67
Heavenly Jerusalem and the Sulfur Lake 68
Shattering the Present 70
Objections to the End of the World: The Jesus Movement 71

5. MISSION—The Origins of Western Universalism 75
The Great Reinterpretation 76
Mission and Power 78
The Destruction of the Other 79

Part II: The Megamachine 83
6. MONSTERS—The Re-formation of Power and the
Emergence of the Modern World-System (1348–1648) 85
The Epoch of Fear 86
The Great Crisis 91
The Arsenal of Venice 94
The Reinvention of War 99
Resurrection of the Metallurgical Complex 104
The Role of Banks 110
Unleashing the Monster 112
Crushing Egalitarian Movements 117
The Invention of the Joint-Stock Company 124
Power and Powerlessness in the Global World-System 130

7. MACHINE—Mechanistic Sciences, State Apparatuses
and the Disciplining of Man (1600–1800) 135
The World as Machine 136
The Role of the Sciences 138
Redefining Reality 142
The Legibility of the World 149

Urban Planning as Counterinsurgency   155
The Human Machine   159
The School as Disciplinary Institution   162
The Invention of Work   166

8. MOLOCH — Coal Power, Total Market and Total War
   (1712–1918)   173
   Coal: The Third Revolution of the Metallurgical Complex   173
   The Total Market   179
   Uprooting, Social Trauma and Resistance   182
   The Invention of the Nation   184
   The Great Expansion   188
   "Civilization": The New Missionary Project   189
   The Devastation of Africa   192
   India: The Invention of the Third World   195
   The Destruction of China by Western Colonial Powers   199
   The Path to Total War   202

9. MASKS — Governing the Great Machine and the Fight
   for Democracy (1787–1945)   207
   USA 1787: The Filter of Representation   211
   France 1789: The Filter of Money   213
   Haiti 1804: The Filter of Debt   215
   The Filter of "Public Opinion"   217
   The Issue of System Control   221
   Russia 1917   224
   The "Guided Democracy"   227
   The German Revolution of 1918–19   232
   The Fascist Option   233

10. METAMORPHOSES — The Post-war Boom, Resistance
    Movements and the Limits of the System (1945–…)   239
    The Trente glorieuses   241
    Independence Movements in the Global South   248

"Development" as Internal Colonization   249
The World Revolution of 1968   255
The Great Rollback   263
The Power of Debt   270
The Limits of the System   274
The Ultimate Limitation: The Planet   280

11. POSSIBILITIES — Exit from the Megamachine   287
Revolution Without a Master Plan   290
Breaking Away from Capital Accumulation   293
Shrinking the Metallurgical and Fossil Fuel Complex   296
The Rediscovery of the Commons   300
The Search for True Democracy   308
Demilitarizing Society   311
Giving up Control over Nature   314

11. AFTERWORD — The Shadow of the Hydra: Pandemics
and the Limits of Expansion   317

Appendix
Acknowledgments   331
Endnotes   333
Selected Bibliography   389
Image Sources   399
Timetable A: The Four Tyrannies (Chapters 1–5)   403
Timetable B: Formation of the Global Megamachine
    (Chapter 6)   405
Timetable C: Consolidation, Expansion and Crises
    (Chapters 7–9)   407
Timetable D: The Boom and Limits of the Megamachine
    (Chapters 10–11)   411
Index   415
About the Author   427

Introduction

A few days after the inauguration of US President Donald Trump in 2017, two things happened simultaneously. For the first time in its history, the Dow Jones Index reached the threshold of 20,000 points to the frenetic cheers of traders and stockholders. At the same time, the hands of the so-called "doomsday clock" advanced to two and a half minutes before midnight. This was the closest it had come since 1953, after the first hydrogen bombs had been detonated. The clock reflects the assessments of leading scientists concerning the imminent dangers posed by nuclear war, environmental havoc and high-risk technologies. As of 2020, there are only 100 seconds left on the clock.

The ecstasy of the stockholders and the approaching midnight of humanity—the fact that our current economic system is on a collision course with the Earth and its inhabitants could hardly be expressed more clearly. The cheers at the stock exchange are for our doom.

We are witnessing how the entire planet, which took four billion years to develop, is being used up by a global economic machinery that produces vast quantities of goods and mountains of garbage at the same time, insane wealth and mass misery, massive overwork and forced inactivity. A visiting alien would consider this a completely crazy system, but there is indeed a method to this madness. At the core of it all is the unrelenting increase of wealth stored in the bank accounts of a relatively tiny number of individuals. Today, 42 men possess the equivalent of that owned by the poorer half of the world's population.[1] It seems that the only remaining goal of the global Megamachine is to incinerate the Earth for a small clique of the absurdly super-rich and add endless rows of zeros to their bank accounts.

At heart, everyone realizes how destructive this system is; that it is sick and also makes us sick. In Germany, for example,

1

88 percent of those surveyed would prefer some other economic system.[2] Likewise, in Great Britain and the USA, approval of the capitalist economic system is rapidly dwindling, especially among the younger generation.[3] Long gone are the days of market euphoria and an enthusiastic belief in progress. Whether conservatives, left-wingers, environmentalists, young or old, almost all the people with whom I have spoken in the last 10 years no longer believe in the future of the system—that is, if they are honest and willing to remove their professional masks. At the same time, however, there is an oppressive sense of being at a loss. Although clearly pathological and destructive, the spinning wheels seem to be unstoppable. After the fiasco of decades of climate negotiations that have produced no binding reduction targets, fruitless World Food Summits and, at best, only cosmetic repairs to a highly dangerous world financial system, there is hardly anyone left today who is seriously expecting governments to reverse global trends. Although knowledge of the disastrous consequences continues to grow with each passing day, the captains of the Great Machine steadfastly set sail toward inevitable shipwreck.

This is all the more peculiar because there is no lack of alternatives, despite claims to the contrary. Almost every sector of our society and economy could be reorganized in a completely different way. For instance, all of the world's agriculture could be converted to organic farming in just a few years, which would eliminate a considerable amount of greenhouse gas emissions.[4] A money system serving the common good could replace the current financial "casino." And for decades, there have also been concepts for decentralized renewable energy, intelligent public transport systems, fair division of labor and regional economic cycles.[5] All this would be possible if—yes, if what? Who or what is actually standing in the way, and why? Why is it that a civilization that presents itself to the world as the bearer of reason and progress is incapable of changing direction from this obviously suicidal path?

This book attempts to answer these questions by telling a story. Sometimes, if we can't explain a person's behavior, when we think they are crazy, then it can help to tell their story. People rarely do something without a reason. However, these reasons are often not to be found in the immediate present, but rather in the past, where the patterns of behavior were first formed. Only those who know their own history can change it. And the same holds true for social systems, as they are also made up of people.

The Myths of Modernity

The blame for leading us on this wrong-headed and deadly path often falls at the feet of neoliberal politics, which in recent decades has led to increased social inequality and environmental devastation. This book asserts, however, that the causes lie much deeper. Neoliberalism is only the most recent phase of a much older system that, from its inception roughly 500 years ago, was founded on predatory exploitation. We will delve into the history and prehistory of this system and its unprecedented expansion around the globe, which by now is reaching its limits.

This story can be viewed in very different ways. The standard version — the myth of Western civilization — tells the tale of hard-won progress that, despite all its adversities and setbacks, has ultimately led to more prosperity, more peace, more knowledge, more culture and more freedom. Wars, environmental devastation and genocide are, in this version, just setbacks, slip-ups, relapses or the undesirable side effects of an otherwise broadly beneficial process of expanding civilization.

Every society cultivates its myths to establish and justify its own unique organization. The problem with such myths, however, is that they not only give us a distorted picture of the past, but they also reduce our ability to make the right decisions for the future. If I believe that I have been walking on the right road for a very long time, one that will eventually lead me to ever greener pastures, then I will continue to do so. I will continue on, even if the road becomes potholed, devastation occurs all around me and my water supply runs out. At some point, however, I will inevitably wonder whether my maps are right, if I have interpreted them correctly and whether or not I really am on the right road. That is where we find ourselves today. Admitting that we have lost our way can lead to a decisive moment when we have to pause, reflect and take a critical look at the maps, to redraw them where they are obviously misleading, and to redefine the situation for ourselves. This book aims to contribute to that effort.

A reorientation begins by changing the point of view of the observer. Tales of progress always make sense from the point of view of history's winners, who usually include those who write the history books. While writing this book, for example, I am sitting in a heated room, drinking coffee and gazing at the autumn leaves outside my window, while my daughter is playing in a pleasant daycare facility around the corner. The world seems to be in order, at least within the small fragment of time and space I can observe at this moment.

But as soon as I enlarge the field of vision and change the point of view, I am presented with a completely different picture. Take, for instance, the security guard in Iraq who watches over the pipeline through which my fuel oil flows, and who has lost half his family to war. He sees a very different slice of the world, and he has experienced a different history. So the victory march of the system I write about has a completely different meaning for him. The same goes for the coffee farmer in Guatemala, or the coltan miner in the Congo who extracts minerals from the earth without which my computer could not function. I am connected to all these people, although I do not know them; and if I want to tell a realistic story of the system in which I live, then I have to include their stories and the stories of their ancestors. In other words, I have to leave my cocoon and look at the world through the eyes of people whose voices are usually drowned out by the megaphones of power.

When the perspective changes this way, we see the last 500 years of European expansion as a history that for most of humanity was associated with expulsion, impoverishment, destruction of environments and massive violence—including genocide. This violence is not a thing of the past, and not just a sign of early "growing pains" in the system, but one of its permanent structural components. Current testimony to this is provided by the pending destruction of the livelihoods of hundreds of millions of people as a result of climate chaos.

The Megamachine

But how do we substantiate the idea that we are dealing with a global *system* and not just a collection of institutions, ideologies and practices? A system is more than the sum of its parts; it is a functional structure in which all components depend on each other and cannot exist independently. Obviously, there is such a thing as a world financial system, a global energy system and a system for the international division of labor that are all closely intertwined. However, these economic structures cannot function independently. They rely on the existence of states that are able to enforce property rights, provide infrastructure, militarily defend trade routes, absorb economic losses and control resistance to the impositions and injustices of the system. Militarized states and markets, as we will see in the course of this book, are not opposites, but have co-evolved and remain inextricably interconnected to this day. The popular confrontation between the state and the "free market" is a fiction that has nothing to do with historical reality.

The third supporting pillar—alongside economic and state structures—is ideological. The violent expansion of the system and the injustices it inevitably produced were justified from the outset by the claim that the "West" was undertaking a historical mission that would bring salvation to the world.[6] While the Christian religion first made this claim, it was later replaced by supposedly superior "reason," "civilization," "development," and the "free market." In close connection to the military and economic levers of power, schools, universities, the media and other ideologically influential institutions played a decisive role in elaborating and disseminating this mythology—despite important emancipation movements that continually arose within these institutions during modern times.

The interaction of these three spheres of power as part of a global social system has been comprehensively analyzed since the 1970s by Immanuel Wallerstein, Giovanni Arrighi and others. Wallerstein has called this functional structure the "modern world-system." I have labeled it with the metaphorical term "Megamachine," a reference to the historian Lewis Mumford (1895–1990).[7] In this case, "machine" does not mean a technical apparatus, but a form of social organization that seems to function like a machine. I expressly say "seems," because despite all systemic constraints, the machinery is actually made up of people. They re-create the Megamachine every day, and, at least under certain conditions, also have the power to stop it.

Limits of the System

A central thesis of this book contends that during the twenty-first century, the Megamachine will run into two limitations that will be insurmountable when combined. The first is inherent in the system itself. For about four decades, the global economy has been headed toward a structural crisis that can no longer be explained away by the usual economic cycles. This crisis has been temporarily veiled by the steadily growing indebtedness of all actors; by financial bubbles that burst into ever deeper economic crashes (see Chapter 10). At the same time, the system has been offering fewer and fewer people a secure livelihood. Although the 200 largest corporations in the world account for 25 percent of the gross world product, they employ only 0.75 percent of the world's population.[8] More and more people are being dropped from the economic system, not only on the periphery, but also in the centers of accumulation. Some of the most recent examples of this are the decay of the middle class in the USA and the ruin of southern European countries. This structural crisis is accompanied by a transformation of many states, which, after a relatively short welfare-state intermezzo, have regressed to repressive military and police structures from earlier phases of the system. As the ability of the Megamachine to offer people a perspective for the future fades, the belief in its mythology is also disintegrating. Ideological cohesion, referred to as "cultural hegemony" by the Italian philosopher Antonio Gramsci, is starting to fray.

The second and even more important limitation is that the Megamachine belongs to and is dependent upon a larger, comprehensive system—the biosphere of planet Earth. We can already see how the explosive growth of the Great Machine is starting to approach the limits of this overarching system. While there is some flexibility to these limits, it is not infinite.

The combination of ecological and social upheaval brings with it an extremely complex and chaotic dynamic, and no one can predict where it will lead. Clearly, however, a far-reaching, systematic upheaval is inevitable, and in some cases it has already begun. It is about much more than overcoming neoliberalism or changing out certain technologies (even if both steps are necessary). It is about a transformation that reaches right down to the foundations of our civilization. The question is not *whether* such a transformation will take place—it will whether we want it to or not—but *how* it will occur and in which direction it will develop.

The Megamachine is not the first system in human history to fail, but it is by far the largest, most complex and most dangerous. It has created an arsenal of weapons with overwhelming destructive power and is in the process of undermining the Earth's great life-supporting systems, devastating flora and fauna, soils, forests, oceans, rivers, aquifers and the climate system. Industrialized civilization has already triggered the greatest species extinction since the disappearance of the dinosaurs 65 million years ago. At the same time, the growing climate chaos threatens to make entire regions of the Earth uninhabitable, which throws more fuel on the flames of conflict. Therefore, the question of how and where this transformation will take place and where it will be heading is actually a matter of life or death for large parts of the world's population. The nature and direction of this systemic upheaval will determine what kind of world we and our descendants will live in during the second half of this century. Will it be a world that is even more miserable and violent than the present one, or one that is freer and more livable than it is now? The increasing instability of the global system creates an extraordinary situation in which even relatively small movements can have a major impact on the overall process and its outcomes. This can be both good and bad news. The rapid rise of right-wing extremism and police-state repression shows that totalitarian forces can also take hold of crumbling economic and political structures. In this situation, it is up to all of us to act. Remaining a passive bystander to the unfolding drama is not an option, as choosing to do nothing is also a decision that can determine the outcome of history.

Book Structure

In order to understand the origins and functioning of the Great Machine, one must also examine its prehistory. Therefore, the book follows two different timelines. The first part (chapters 1 through 5) covers a period of 5000 years; the second part (chapters 6 through 11) concentrates on the last 500 years.

Chapter 1 traces the development of military, economic and ideological power back to its roots in Mesopotamia. Chapter 2 examines the special role of the "metallurgical complex" in spawning the arms industry and the first monetary systems. Chapter 3 is devoted to the emergence of the first market economies. Contrary to the myth, it reveals that the market and money economy did not grow out of free exchange, but from the logic of war and slavery. Chapter 4 deals with the effects of power on social life and the collective imagination. The emergence of Christianity and apocalyptic thought, which was to significantly shape Western civilization, is viewed from the experience of powerlessness and subjugation to which the majority of people in ancient empires were subjected. Chapter 5 explores the origins of Western missionary ideology, from Apostle Paul to the Crusades.

The second part of this book relates how the modern world-system was formed as a response to the massive egalitarian movements that spread throughout Europe during the late Middle Ages and the early modern period (Chapter 6); how the first highly militarized corporations emerged; how the accumulation of money in the financial centers of Genoa, Augsburg, Amsterdam and London became the motor for colonial expansion; how this colonization ultimately led to genocide in America (Chapter 6); how space, time and people were gradually subjected to the penetrating gaze of the state and the accumulation of capital; how the disciplinary institutions of the military, the school and alienated labor emerged (Chapter 7); and how the development of fossil fuels gave the system an explosive shot of energy for expansion that (temporarily) broke through ecological boundaries (Chapter 8).

The question of democracy also occupies a crucial place in this history. According to the central thesis of Chapter 9, the inner logic of the Megamachine is fundamentally incompatible with true democracy, understood as self-organization. Therefore, to date, it has only permitted limited forms of participation in collective decision-making processes. The search for forms of democracy that go beyond these boundaries is a key systemic question that can be traced to the European revolutions, the struggles for freedom in the colonies, the "world revolution of 1968" and to the present day (Chapter 10). The exit from the Megamachine and thus from the logic of endless capital accumulation is inextricably tied to the question of democratic self-organization (Chapter 11).

The issues covered in this book involve a specialized selection of source material and the choice of a geographical framework. While the prehistory concentrates on the Near East and the Mediterranean, the second part follows the expansion of the modern world-system out of Europe and across the globe.

Hence this book does not aim to be a history of humankind, but the story of a specific social system. Seen from a broader perspective, it represents only a small fragment. Assuming that we have a future, the Megamachine may end up appearing as only a brief interlude within human history's span across the millennia.

Part I

The Four Tyrannies

Chapter 1

Power

The Four Tyrannies and the Roots of Domination

It's good to be ruler!

INSTRUCTIONS FOR THE COMPUTER GAME CIVILIZATION IV

Let us imagine the time span from the first archaeologically documented appearance of Homo sapiens about 200,000 years ago up to the present. Now, picture it as just a single day. The time during which humans were exclusively hunters and gatherers would have lasted almost 23 hours. On the other hand, the 10,000-year period since the beginning of agriculture—the "Neolithic Revolution"—covers only the last hour. Hunters and gatherers had always lived in small groups that were relatively egalitarian, as cooperation was crucial for survival.[1] The transition to sedentary lifestyles and agriculture, however, allowed for more expanded forms of organization and, under certain circumstances, also enabled individuals to accumulate greater wealth. This was hardly possible for hunting and collecting nomads, since their property had to be easily transportable. The transition to sedentary lifestyles is commonly regarded as a prerequisite for social stratification and class formation; however, it was by no means the only factor, and perhaps not even the decisive one. Until the beginning of the Bronze Age between 4000 and 3000 BC, archaeological sites revealing predominantly sedentary lifestyles show few traces of major social differentiation or hierarchical organization.[2] Even in the largest Neolithic settlement discovered to date, Çatal Höyük in Anatolia, which around 6000 BC had roughly 3000 inhabitants, all houses were about the same size. Palaces or central temples were non-existent, and there are no signs of large-scale military defenses.[3] Also in the Persian Gulf region, more than 4000 years after the beginning of permanent settlements, people were still living in relatively egalitarian conditions in the Tigris and Euphrates delta. Their diet was based on a mixture of hunting and gathering with limited domestication of crops and animals.[4]

However, this situation changed with the beginning of the Copper and Bronze Ages. This fork in the road is illustrated, for example, by the pile-dwelling culture on Lake Constance in southern Germany. The earliest inhabitants of these structures all had the same easily accessible wood and stone technologies at their disposal. Then, with the early use of metals, especially bronze, their society split into those few who were able to acquire and process bronze and those who could not. Only select people were buried in elaborate bronze armor, while others were interred more modestly. While pre-Bronze-Age food remnants of the pile dwellers indicate that everyone ate more or less the same food, there was a considerable change during the Bronze Age. The majority had a diet based predominantly on grains, while others (the metal owners) also ate large quantities of fish. Similar inequalities emerged wherever a transition to the Bronze Age took place. This can be seen in Mesopotamia and Egypt as well as nearly a thousand years later in Central Europe and along the Yellow River in China.[5]

Between the comparatively egalitarian phase, which covers the largest part of human history, and the emergence of social stratification and hierarchical relationships, there were far-reaching changes beyond those brought about by metal processing. In the transition to the Bronze Age, the foundations of what we now call "civilization" were laid. In Sumer, which is the southern part of Mesopotamia on the Persian Gulf, the first writing systems developed from cylindrical seal markings around 3200 BC.[6] At the same time, the first cities and also the first states emerged in this area. While Çatal Höyük was still a large village with a few thousand inhabitants, Uruk, with 50,000 inhabitants, was already a city with a complex division of labor and municipal administration. At the center of these first cities were large temples, whose administrators organized agricultural and handicraft production with the end products being distributed back to the inhabitants. In contrast to the region's earlier sedentary culture, nutrition was mainly based on grains. As anthropologist James C. Scott has shown, cereal-based agriculture, unlike the mixed diet of those living in wetlands, is well suited to the establishment of taxation systems and centralized state power.[7] Within a few centuries, other crucial structures developed parallel to the temples—the rulers' palaces. By 2800 BC, all Sumerian city states—Eridu, Uruk, Nippur, Lagash, Kish and Ur—had transformed themselves into kingdoms ruled by a *lugal* who increasingly accumulated despotic power.

Ruler of Uruk with bound prisoners (ca. 3000 BC)

The lugal were originally commanders who assumed military leadership roles during the numerous conflicts among the city states. These conflicts increased as natural resources and precious metals accumulated in the storehouses of temples and palaces behind the walls of fortified cities. At first, the lugal were deployed for short periods, either defending their city's possessions or appropriating them from others. Little by little, however, they succeeded in leveraging their authority to become long-term rulers. The temple, with its distribution of goods, eventually merged with the military dictatorship to form the first authoritarian state. Now, for the first time in human history, the state was able to exert *coercive power* over its inhabitants, most overtly through the monarch's authority to pronounce death sentences. One of the earliest texts to talk about this imperious power is the Gilgamesh epic from the twenty-fourth century BC. It deals with one of the early kings of Uruk, who was supposedly "two thirds God, one third man":

> *Gilgamesh lets no son go free to his father.*
> *By day and by night his tyranny grows harsher.*
> *It is he who is shepherd of Uruk-the-Sheepfold,*
> *but Gilgamesh lets no daughter go free to her mother.*
> *He lets no girl go free to her bridegroom.*
> *He has no equal when his weapons are brandished.*
> *The young men of Uruk he harries without warrant.*[8]

The Three Tyrannies

How did this radical social change come about that has shaped history to this day? Why did the majority of people *allow* elites to emerge and rule over them and to take portions of their wealth as taxes for financing armies and building massive palaces? Why have people allowed such elites to regulate their relationships with each other and have power over their lives? In other words, how and why did people learn to become *obedient*? Before the establishment of authoritarian states and armies, and before the introduction of forced labor and slavery, there were no societies based on the mechanism of command and obedience. While the elders of a hunter-gatherer society did indeed have prestige and influence, and some may have tried to impose their will, they nonetheless had no *power* and could not give *commands*.

The British sociologist Michael Mann points out in his book *The Sources of Social Power* that the emergence of a "civilization," and subsequently of power and domination, is by no means a natural, inevitable development. Historically, it is actually an astonishing exception.[9] In practically all non-state societies there are mechanisms to put a stop to such clusters of power. The limits that even the early Sumerian city states imposed on the power of the lugal are evidence of such efforts.

Why did this resistance break down? How could command, and with it power, prevail? Or asked asked conversely, what does it take for people to end up in situations where they must obey orders?

In principle, there are three types of reasons that can cause a person to follow an order. The first, and most obvious, is fear of physical violence, including humiliation, pain and ultimately physical injury or death. The second category of reasons includes the fear of economic harm or social degradation to the point of losing one's livelihood. This also works conversely, with the desire for social advancement and recognition being a motivator. The third set of reasons for obedience is based on the assumption that it is *right and necessary* that there are people who command and others who obey, either because the commanders have a higher knowledge, or because there is a natural, God-given plan for such hierarchies.

The counterpart to these three reasons for obedience are the three types of power, which I call the three tyrannies:

1. Physical power, especially in the form of armed violence. Throughout history, this has been especially concentrated within militarized states.

2. Structural violence, especially in the form of socio-economic power. The exercise of this kind of power is based on the systematically unequal distribution of rights, property, income and prestige. For these inequalities and the kind of power they yield to be accepted, both ideological power and physical power are

necessary. Ideology provides justification, and physical force can be used to intervene if needed.

3. Ideological power. This form ranges from the exclusive mastery of writing to the codification of religious, moral and scientific ideologies, all the way to modern "expertocracy" and control of the mass media. It can legitimize the first two forms of power or even make them invisible by defining what is "true," "normal," "relevant" and "real."

Through their interaction, these three forms of power add up to what the sociologist Max Weber called "domination," a relationship between people in which a commander can expect obedience.[10]

Physical Power

Physical violence exists in all human cultures, albeit to extremely varying degrees. However, it only becomes physical *power* when the violence is exercised systematically. This happens when people are able to pressure others to do their bidding by the threat or actual use of physical force.

Physical power is so common today that it almost seems natural. Societies without prisons and armies, for example, sound utopian to us. Early modern state theorists such as Thomas Hobbes claimed that the physical power of the state is needed to tame the "war of every one against every one" that constitutes the "state of nature." Therefore, according to this argument, it is reasonable for everyone to accept the state's monopoly on the use of force.[11] But such social contract theories have a catch: no one has ever observed the formation of a state that was actually based on such concepts. Nor has a "state of nature," with everyone at war with each other, ever really existed in the history of humankind. The reality is that the systematic use of force does not decrease with the emergence of state power in the form of armies and police forces—it increases. Michael Mann writes about this:

> Comparative anthropology shows that the frequency of war, its organization, and its intensity in lives killed, increase substantially with permanent settlement and, then again, with civilization. Quantitative studies reveal that half the warfare of primitive peoples is relatively sporadic, unorganized, ritualistic, and bloodless. [...] But all civilizations of recorded history have engaged routinely in highly organized and bloody warfare.[12]

Of course, states and their armies are not the only institutions in which physical power is established. Additionally, there are gangs of robbers and mafias from which states can also emerge. Authoritarian family structures, like those in the Roman Empire, belong here as well, with the patriarchs even assuming the power to make life-or-death decisions over other family members.[13] Those subjected to any of these forms of power are never asked for their consent. On the contrary, physical power is defined precisely by the fact that it is exercised against the will of the subject. But how could systematic physical power over people take hold and spread in the first place? What were its origins?

If we return to the pile dwellings in southern Germany and the possession of bronze armor, it seems that the origin of physical power lies in superior weapon technology that was gained by processing metal. There is no doubt that bronze technology allowed some humans to socially dominate others. Because not everyone had equal access to metals and their processing, the technological divergence could develop into a power divide. Initially, however, the advantages won from such technologies remained limited, both within communities and externally. In small communities, it was difficult to permanently monopolize technology, especially if the community had social mechanisms with which to break up the concentration of power. Even when monopolization occurred, those with inferior weapons could always retreat to other areas (at least where population density was low) to escape permanent domination. Today, we see many indigenous groups still using this strategy of withdrawal to escape domination by falling back to ever more remote forests and mountainous regions. Of course, for sedentary communities, the freedom to leave was limited. This was especially so in the alluvial plains of the Euphrates, Tigris and Nile river valleys. With their extraordinary fertility and a much less attractive wilderness around them, there were good reasons to stay. Michael Mann calls such reasons "cage factors." They are at the core of why humans have ultimately allowed themselves to be controlled by others. As recent research shows, the Persian Gulf also experienced drastic climate change. Thousands of years of predominantly wet weather were followed by a dry spell in the period from 3500 to 2500 BC. The sea withdrew; the wetlands, which until then provided diversified nourishment and a relatively egalitarian way of life, disappeared. As people became concentrated in ever larger settlements, with a diet of mostly irrigated grains, ideal conditions for usurping these structures were established.[14]

The ability to *organize* physical violence also played an important role. The emergence of large, centrally-administered societies, which made irrigation schemes and the mass production of goods possible, also provided the organizational know-how for developing armies. While the reach of this power was confined at the beginning of early civilizations, it continued to expand through the late Roman Empire. The army of the first ancient imperium, the Akkadian Empire (around 2300 BC), consisted of only 5000 men. By contrast, the Roman troops of the imperial period (first to fourth century AD) were comprised of hundreds of thousands of soldiers. With the proliferation of firearms at the beginning of modern times, the spread of physical power surged to a level that was to change the entire world order. Since then, the means for physically controlling and destroying human beings have multiplied in (literally) an explosive manner. Today, there are 16,000 atomic warheads in existence, each with umpteen times greater destructive power than the bomb that devastated Hiroshima. These weapons give the rulers of atomic states the power to decide on the existence or non-existence of all humankind.

Structural Violence

The emergence of economic and social power is more difficult to grasp, because it functions indirectly and sometimes even slips into invisibility. Today, we are often unaware of it. For example, those who work for wages to pay their rent do not necessarily see themselves as subjected to tyranny, and may even feel that they have reasonable freedom of choice. After all, the work is voluntary—you can quit any time—and the rent is based on a voluntary contract between partners, which can also be canceled. No one physically threatens the tenant or wage earner. And yet, workers and employees obey the boss's instructions even if they are extremely reluctant to do the work, or when they find the instructions absurd. Why are these restrictions on self-determination accepted? Because otherwise, you lose your job. This may not happen with the first contradiction, but certainly by the second or third. And without work, it is no longer possible to pay the rent, so you will have to give up your apartment. But why is it acceptable that as soon as you cannot pay enough, you have to get out? Why is the landlord *obeyed* when he demands that the apartment be vacated? Because otherwise it will ultimately lead to eviction, and any resistance would trigger an escalation of coercive measures.

Even if wage labor and rental relationships seem completely harmless, in a modern constitutional state there is physical violence waiting at the end of the chain. While everyone knows about this lurking threat, the chain is long enough that most remain unaware of the violence behind it. The peace and conflict researcher Johan Galtung has called such relationships "structural violence": coercive relationships that do not manifest themselves directly through physical violence.[15]

In order for structural violence to be permanently effective, while keeping the physical violence behind it hidden, cooperation and even a broad consensus from society are necessary. People must accept certain premises as *legitimate*, even if they are opposed to their consequences. For example, it is considered quite all right for wealthy individuals to own thousands, indeed hundreds of thousands of homes, while millions of other people have no property whatsoever; or that it is legitimate for people who cannot pay enough to be put out on the street—by force if necessary. When seen together, these premises suggest that property ownership is not only legitimate, but it also *takes precedence over almost all other rights*.

Historically, enforceable property relationships of this type have developed over thousands of years, along with the ideologies that legitimize them. Once again, the origins trace back to Sumer. In the absence of written evidence, little is known about ownership structures in prehistoric times. The archaeological discoveries from early settled cultures, such as in Çatal Höyük, reveal largely egalitarian conditions at construction and burial sites. One might draw the conclusion that land ownership had not yet been concentrated in the hands of a chosen few.[16] Certainly there was no concept of property in the modern sense.[17] It is likely that fields, pastures and forests were used jointly, or that the distribution of land usage rights was decided by the community. In neither case would land be sold or lent. Similar economic forms can still be found today, both in traditional indigenous communities[18] and in modern commons-based systems. These have been thoroughly investigated by Nobel laureate Elinor Ostrom.[19] This principle was maintained in the early city states of Sumer through the temple, which coordinated the management of large areas and distributed crop yields to inhabitants. At the same time, however, the first forms of private land ownership developed in the hands of selected families. The earliest evidence of actual land purchases in Sumer dates back to the middle of the third millennium BC.[20]

Although the origins of land privatization are still mostly obscure, how it developed during the subsequent millennia is clear. As land turned into a commodity, land ownership became concentrated in the hands of a few. This process reached a pinnacle with the *latifundia*, large Roman estates on which thousands of slaves and landless seasonal workers toiled. During Nero's reign, Pliny the Elder reported that half the land in the African province was in the hands of only six large landowners.[21] As property rights became codified, ownership titles enjoyed protection by the organized physical power of the state.

This wave of privatization had far-reaching consequences. Where the land was privately owned, so were the crop yields. Those with a lot of particularly fertile land could let others, who had no land or poor land, work for them. They were then free to dedicate themselves to other activities, such as trade or administration. The surpluses were also used to buy slaves, who were initially recruited mainly from prisoners of war.

The privatization of land and its earnings also had a knock-on effect which proved decisive for the general expansion of people gaining power over other people—the invention of debt. In *Debt: The First 5,000 Years*, anthropologist David Graeber points out that credit relationships were found in societies across the board, even those that used no money. In non-market societies, such credit relations are part of the social fabric and help create a network of mutual obligations. This differs, however, from commercial credit in that it must not be repaid at all costs, and it is also non-negotiable. Therefore, this kind of loan remains part of a personal relationship, just as loans between friends still are today.[22] When someone exerts force on a friend to pay back their debts, or to sell the debts to a collector, the friendship would likely end. With the privatization of land and the accumulation of assets, however, a different, impersonal form of credit began to spread. Wealthy landowners would lend a portion of their harvest to poorer farmers whose output fell short. The poorer farmer's next harvest was often used as security, and if all went well, the loan could be repaid. If the yield was low again, however, the farmer had to forfeit his land, and even indenture his family and himself. This led to a greater concentration of land in the hands of a few, and more and more farmers became bonded workers or even slaves. This was especially hard on women, who were often used as "collateral" and forced into prostitution. In ancient Sumer, the second most frequently mentioned commodity after grains was slaves. They were traded like agricultural products or farm animals, showing up on lists of goods in the same categories as pigs and other livestock.[23] Anthropologist Guillermo Algaze puts it this way: "The early villagers of the Middle East domesticated animals and plants. The urban institutions of Uruk, on the other hand, domesticated people."[24] One of civilization's dirty secrets is that it is founded upon the systematic introduction of slavery.

Debt is structural violence par excellence, especially if its repayment is enforced *at all costs*. Debt and the associated impoverishment and enslavement became one of the greatest scourges among populations in ancient history. Many revolts were sparked by demands for debt relief, forcing nearly all the potentates of the early empires to regularly forgive debts by way of decree. It was a necessary measure to preserve their power,[25] since armies were not strong enough to constantly put down revolts. This tradition also includes the biblical "jubilee," which celebrated the cancelation of all debts every 49 years and returned landless farmers to their possessions.[26]

Ideological Power

The third form of man's rule over other people took shape in Sumer during the transition from the fourth to the third millennium BC. A class of experts emerged whose members had privileged access to knowledge, as well as an authoritarian religion that developed in parallel with royalty.

In his book *Tristes Tropiques*, the French anthropologist Claude Lévi-Strauss wrote: "The primary function of writing as a means of communication is to facilitate the enslavement of other human beings."[27] This sentence seems disturbing as we usually associate writing with human achievements such as the *Oresteia* by Aeschylus or the *Universal Declaration of Human Rights*. But writing was not created to immortalize literature or ethical principles. Instead, it was a logistical tool.[28] The first bits of writing handed down to us consist exclusively of lists of goods, their quantities and their market value. As we know, slaves were traded as goods, which means that from the start, writing was used as a tool for organizing slavery. Such lists were drawn up by full-time scribes, working in service to the temple, and eventually also to the palace. It was their job to coordinate production and distribution for the centralized economy. The very first schools were for learning to write, and scribes became a privileged class that was soon indispensable to the logistics of rule.[29]

Writing also enabled the documentation of debt on clay tablets, which continued later on papyrus and parchment. These records not only consolidated debt relationships, they also made it possible for promissory notes to become commodities — foreshadowing paper money and modern credit derivatives. The relationship between debtor and creditor became more abstract. While, previously, a personal relationship might have prevented any coercive enforcement of claims, now the holder of a promissory note might not know the debtor and his family at all. This made the path to debt slavery much shorter. It is no wonder that the destruction of debt documentation was often the prime target of revolts during antiquity.[30]

Writing was later used to codify the law as well. The Code of Hammurabi from the eighteenth century BC, the most famous collection of Mesopotamian laws, dealt primarily with property rights and debts. As these rights were codified and guaranteed, the state and its physical power stood ready to enforce property claims. This made the written codification of laws a double-edged sword. Citizens were theoretically protected from arbitrary decisions, and could enjoy a degree of legal certainty. On the other hand, putting laws in writing locked in the relationships of power to be legitimized, systematized, fixed and perpetuated. Therefore, the written word may also lead to the codification of injustices.

Throughout the following centuries, writing took on many other functions, including the recording of myths and epics, which was a way for ruling classes to elaborate their cosmology. Members of literate castes could use the written word to literally carve their concepts of the metaphysical world in stone and give them both permanence and special authority. Oral traditions have a hard time competing with texts carved in stone or pressed into clay, especially when the authors claim divine inspiration. Universal claims to truth, as asserted by some religions, would be impossible without scripture and holy books. The authority for the written word stems not only from its authors, but also from the fact that it can only be interpreted by those who know the Scriptures. Between the experts who debate the meaning of Scripture and the laity who cannot participate, a chasm forms that is characteristic of both theology and modern forms of expertocracy.

Nonetheless, writing has not remained a privilege enjoyed only by the elite. It was also used by the early biblical prophets in their revolts against exploitation and oppression by landowners and kings. Since then, the written word has continued to be contested terrain. Like the printing press and audiovisual media, it can legitimize or strip away the reins of power. So it is no surprise that both state and economic powers still strive to keep a tight grip on these resources. In industrialized states with a liberal tradition, most people can read and write and are fairly free to express their opinions. The distribution of information, however, must pass through the filters of publishers, news agencies, broadcasters and social media networks. A large number of these media are controlled by either large private corporations or by the state—by exactly those actors in whose hands physical and economic power is concentrated.

The Invention of the Dominating God

With the emergence of social hierarchies in Sumer, and soon after in Egypt, there was a radical change to the metaphysical cosmos as well. Without written evidence, we can only make suppositions from archaeological findings about the religious ideas and practices in prehistoric times. Or, we can examine current analogous cultures with comparable lifestyles and assume that they might share similar metaphysical ideas. Despite the uncertainties, we are certain about one thing: there is something *missing* from the prehistoric evidence—the representation of a dominant superhuman being that we would call "God." The idea of a ruling god does not appear in history until earthly forms of domination emerge. From the Paleolithic cave paintings in Lascaux and Chauvet (France) to the finds of Lepenski Vir (Serbia), and the frescoes in Çatal Höyük (Anatolia), there are no depictions of enthroned male rulers who will later populate the pantheons of the gods. Instead, we see animals, dancing figures and various types of female forms, of which the "primordial mother" and the "dolmen goddess" are the best known.[31] When the first states are established in Sumer, however, the situation changes radically. A hymn to the Sumerian god Enlil from the late third millennium describes how the metaphysical world was formed according to the model of earthly rule:

Enlil's commands are by far the loftiest; his words are holy; his
utterances immutable. All gods of the Earth bow down to father
Enlil, who sits comfortably on the holy dais. The gods enter before
him and obey his instructions faithfully.[32]

Like an earthly ruler, a god also has: a kingdom and a throne, his
will is obeyed ("thy will be done"), he decides about existence
or non-existence, he can punish, show mercy and also forgive
guilt or debt. The projection of earthbound courtly life to the
heavenly realm is so strikingly transparent that one wonders
how contemporaries could have taken it seriously. In fact, there
is evidence to suggest that the ruling religion in Mesopotamia
was not very popular. It was celebrated mostly by the elites,
while the broader population stayed with older traditions.[33]
This pattern can still be observed today. The so-called "popular
piety" in Christianity has quite a different character than the
official "high religion." It has preserved many pre-Christian
and even prehistoric references that place less emphasis on
command and obedience. Until these days, with the polemical
juxtaposition of "faith" and "superstition," two very different
types of religiosity can be found under the roof of the great
religions. (In Roman times, the term *religio* referred to official
rituals, especially the emperor's cult, whereas *superstitio* stood
for wild and ecstatic cults that were repeatedly prohibited.) As
popular religion often differs significantly from official dogma,
it cannot be assumed that within a few centuries there was a clear
historical break in the collective imagination. Instead, it was a
process that ran parallel to the increase in worldly dominion.
Over the millennia, the idea of a ruling god penetrated deeper
and deeper until the zenith of worldly dominion was reached in
the Roman Empire. This finally culminated in the notion of the
omnipotent God as found in Christianity and other monotheistic
religions.

Such a shift in the metaphysical reference system is of enormous significance for the collective imagination. Instead of facing forces that people relate to at eye level, such as ancestors, "spirits," "the elements" and the like, now there was a pyramid-shaped system based on the idea of command and obedience and the linear exercise of power.

Such thinking has continued through all secularizations and democratizations as a formative idea of the cosmos up to our present technocratic civilization. As we will see in Chapter 7, during the course of modern times, the ruling God was replaced by the ruling man who tamed the Earth through science and technology. In both the theological and technocratic versions of omnipotence, we find the idea that nature—including human nature—can and must be controlled. Just as the king commands his subjects, and God his creatures, the engineer likewise commands nature to obey his will.

The Fourth Tyranny

The three tyrannies mentioned so far have generated yet another — the tyranny of linear thinking. Linear thinking is based on the assumption that the world functions according to predictable laws of cause and effect and is therefore controllable. An *actio* A produces a *reactio* B in a foreseeable way. This paradigm works well within the world of inanimate objects. A hammer blow will shape metal in a predictable way. One billiard ball striking another will cause movement that we can calculate. The energy that moves ball B is proportionally related to the energy with which it is impacted by ball A. We can also gauge how the orbit of a spacecraft will be changed by a sequence of ignitions, etc.

While this works well for inanimate matter, it can be very misleading when it comes to living beings. I can try to shove human beings around like billiard balls, but I cannot predict how they will react, nor can I truly control their movements (assuming they are alive and awake). The American anthropologist Gregory

Bateson once explained: "When I kick a stone, I give energy to the stone, and it moves with that energy. [...] When I kick a dog, it responds with energy from its metabolism."[34]

The only time that people do behave like billiard balls is when they are given commands. The officer says, "Halt!" and predictably, the recruit will stand still. The foreman says, "Faster!" and the worker speeds up. The teacher says, "Kevin, you stay after class," and the boy will indeed stay. Commands simulate the mechanics of the inanimate world for animate beings. However, people who carry out orders and simulate mechanical behavior are not actually turned into machines. Forcing someone to behave like a machine can lead to unpredictable and unpleasant consequences. If Kevin is constantly forced to stay behind; if the worker is always pushed to work faster; and the recruit is repeatedly ordered to stand still, they may eventually react quite unpredictably and do inexplicable things. When Kevin starts to torment his little sister; and the worker gets hooked on drugs; or if the recruit gets drunk and beats up a homeless person, the teacher, foreman and officer may never see the connection.

Command structures create the false assumption that people can be treated like automatons all their lives without ever retaliating. In his book *Crowds and Power*, Elias Canetti described commands as thorns that poke into those who have to take orders, and that can only be got rid of by passing them on to other people elsewhere.[35] However, this "elsewhere" cannot be seen within the context of linear thinking.

That is why, even though linear thinking is useful in the world of inanimate matter, it blocks the view of reality in the living world. To the extent that the exercise of power produces predictable conduct among those who take orders, inexplicable, "irrational" behavior can erupt that leaves psychologists, sociologists and pedagogues racking their brains.

This applies not only to social life, but also to ecology. I might treat a river like a dead object that I can manipulate, and whose behavior I can foresee and control. I might try to bend it to my will by straightening out its path, shoring up the banks, damming the flow, etc. By trying to bring it under my control, however, it may react more and more uncontrollably and unpredictably, and suddenly overflow with unprecedented flooding.

The application of linear thinking to living systems has left a trail of devastation across the planet, both socially and ecologically. The first three tyrannies—physical, economic and ideological power—can only be overcome if we change our thinking about nature (including ourselves) and transcend the fourth tyranny. We must recognize that the world is alive and therefore unpredictable. Only when we stop trying to dominate nature, can we hope to achieve social and ecological forms of cooperation that will allow this planet to remain habitable for the long run.

Chapter 2

Metal

Mining, Armament and Power over Nature

Far from human dwellings they cut a shaft,
in places untouched by human feet;
far from other people they dangle and sway.
The earth, from which food comes,
is transformed below as by fire.
But where can wisdom be found?
Where does understanding dwell?
THE BOOK OF JOB

In mythology, metal objects are often associated with extraordinary power. From the Saga of the Nibelungs, to the tales of King Arthur and the fantasy novels of J. R. R. Tolkien, magic swords and rings of gold and iron are at the center of the action. Those who possess them gain superhuman powers and can control or destroy both people and nature. Whether the dark Prince Sauron from *Lord of the Rings*, the crafty Hagen from the Nibelungs saga or the savior Arthur with his sword Excalibur, all seek to obtain a metal object that would give them power. Endless variations of this pattern can also be seen in the wonder weapons of science fiction. The extraordinary powers of action figures like Terminator or Iron Man derive from their metallic components.

In some of these myths and fantasy stories, however, there are forces that fight back to destroy this source of power. The sword Excalibur is thrown back into the lake it came from, the Ring of the Nibelung is tossed into the Rhine River and Tolkien's Ring falls into the Cracks of Doom. All of these stories express an awareness of the destructive dynamics of metallurgy.

Left: The sword Excalibur. Right: Advertisement for the XM982 Excalibur artillery shell

In fact, during the past 5000 years, the processing of metals has played a decisive role in the spread and metamorphoses of the "four tyrannies." In both past and present, precious metals have been used as a form of currency—a manifestation of economic power. The minting of gold and silver coins is the origin of our financial system. And, as we will see in the following, this financial system was closely linked to slavery and the economies of war.

The Origins of the Military-Industrial Complex

Throughout history, the production of copper, bronze and iron, and later also aluminum and uranium, has been at the heart of what US President Eisenhower coined the "military-industrial complex" in 1961. Its development can be traced back for more than 5000 years, beginning with the first copper axe on into the rocket age. Those who had advanced metalworking techniques could produce superior weapons and take control over other people or entire populations. New metallurgical techniques were often associated with drastic political and social upheaval. The experience of such upheavals is also reflected in the ancient myth of the five ages, ranging from the Golden to the Iron Age. Referring to the third age, the Greek poet Hesiod wrote:

Zeus the Father made a third generation of mortal men, a brazen race, sprung from ash-trees. They loved the lamentable works of war and deeds of violence; they were hard of heart like adamant, fearful men. Great was their strength and unconquerable the arms which grew from their shoulders on their strong limbs. Their armor was of bronze, and their houses of bronze, and of bronze were their implements.[1]

The beginning of the Bronze Age was indeed a profound break from the past that heralded an era of increasing physical violence. Bronze is an alloy of copper and tin. It is much harder than pure copper and therefore ideal for tools, weapons and armor. Obtaining the raw materials, however, required complex logistics. The Mesopotamians, for example, had to import copper and tin from mining regions thousands of miles away in the Hindu Kush and the Caucasus. Uruk and other city states established colonies for this purpose and created a system of asymmetric trade. Unprocessed raw materials (especially metals) were imported from the periphery into the center, while industrially processed products such as textiles and ceramics were exported.[2] This was the embryonic form of a trading system that today operates worldwide and is based on the power differential between "highly developed" centers and "underdeveloped" peripheries. This also meant that trade routes would require military protection—a self-reinforcing process in which ever more raw materials were needed to produce more and more weapons. The first known organized war in world history was waged in present-day Syria by Uruk against the city of Hamoukar, which was directly on the trade route to the Caucasus.[3]

The second major technological transformation was the Iron Age revolution. Unlike copper and tin, iron is more easily found, accounting for almost 5 percent of the Earth's crust (the share of copper is only 0.1 percent). However, the melting point of iron is more than 1500° C, which is significantly higher than that of copper. Special furnaces and a lot of energy were required to reach these high temperatures, all of which increased the need for more resources.

Pure iron is only a little harder than bronze, but it can be alloyed with carbon to make steel, the ideal material for superior tools and weapons. From around 1200 BC onwards, iron technology spread rapidly from Anatolia. At the time, Assyria became the most aggressive military state of its epoch, with the production of armaments supported by rich iron deposits in the region. One after another, Assyria annexed Mesopotamia, Palestine, Egypt and large parts of present-day Turkey, leaving behind a trail of terror. Numerous passages in the Hebrew Bible bear witness to this, for example in Jeremiah: "Israel is a hunted sheep driven away by lions. First the king of Assyria devoured it."[4]

But even the Assyrian military machine paled by comparison to the iron empire of the Romans. At a nearly industrial level, the mass production of steel provided armor, spears and swords for up to 600,000 soldiers. This allowed Rome to wage war from the Sahara to the North Sea, and from the Atlantic to the Persian Gulf. Twenty percent of all Romans not employed in agriculture worked in metal extraction and processing.[5] The extent of Roman iron production can also be seen from the remains of furnace slag. While the archaeological finds of pre-Roman iron slag are measured in kilograms, Roman finds are measured in hundreds of tons.[6]

Environmental Disasters

Until the "Storm of Steel" in the First and Second World Wars, iron remained the most important raw material of Europe's war machinery. Unlike the manufacturers Krupp or Vickers, however, the Romans used charcoal instead of fossil coals to operate their furnaces. This led to the clearing of an astonishing 25 million hectares of forest,[7] or an area equivalent to twice the size of today's Greece. Together with ship building and house construction, iron production was one of the main causes of deforestation in the Mediterranean region.[8] The consequences of this can still be seen today. For example, if you visit the barren island of Sardinia, it is hard to believe that before the Iron Age it was once shaded by dense beech forests. Large portions of forestation in Spain, Greece and the eastern Adriatic also fell victim to iron production.

It is not just the processing of metals, however, that is strongly tied to violence and the destruction of nature, but also the act of mining itself. Mining ores is the archetype of all extractive industries. Even in antiquity, entire mountains were carted away by the mining of copper, silver, gold and iron — the most radical human activity in the re-shaping of the Earth's surface observed so far. Four thousand years ago, mining as well as slash-and-burn techniques for charcoal production led to landslides and large-scale destruction of the landscape in the Alps.[9] Referring to the Roman gold mines in northeastern Spain, Pliny the Elder wrote of the *ruina montium*, the destruction of the mountains:[10]

This method of obtaining gold surpasses the labours of the Giants even: by the aid of galleries driven to a long distance, mountains are excavated by the light of torches, the workmen never seeing the light of day for many months together. [...] Not unfrequently the earth sinks in, and the workmen are crushed beneath. [...] The mountain, rent to pieces, is cleft asunder, hurling its debris to a distance with a crash which it is impossible for the human imagination to conceive; and from the midst of a cloud of dust, the victorious miners gaze upon this downfall of Nature.[11]

These ruins, hollowed out from the inside and partially collapsed, are still visible today in the mountains of Las Médulas in northern Spain.

Since ancient times, mining has been regarded as a "hell on earth," not least because of the infernal working conditions and the devastation of the landscape. In the fourteenth century, the poet Dante Alighieri carefully constructed the nine levels of Hell in his Divine Comedy exactly like an open-pit mine. According to Dantean mythology, this hellhole was torn into the earth when Lucifer fell from Heaven.

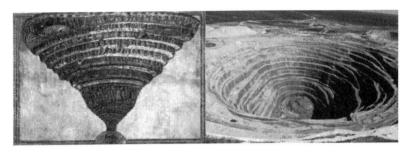

Left: Sandro Botticelli's "Hell" (from Dante's Inferno). Right: An open-pit mine in Russia

In ancient and early modern times, the devastation from mining was caused almost solely by human labor (and in part by working animals). Today, driven by fossil fuels, this destructive force has reached gargantuan levels. Open-pit excavators are the largest machines ever built for use on dry land, and every day, they collectively tear roughly 100 million tons of material out of the Earth's crust, which is then driven, shipped and flown halfway around the globe to be transformed into asphalt, smartphones and skyscrapers. As already mentioned, even the sands by the sea are becoming scarce. The construction industry has already dredged most of the world's beach sand and has now begun to plow through the seabed.[12] The open-pit mining of metals, such as aluminum, copper and gold, leaves behind enormous lunar landscapes and contaminates entire regions with its toxic waste. Millions of people have been driven out of their homes by mining projects. In India alone, this includes at least 2.5 million people[13], most of whom have ended up in big-city slums. In many regions, mining has fueled civil wars, such as in Orissa, India, where hundreds of thousands of people are being displaced so that uranium, aluminum and coal companies are free to mine. Human rights activist Vandana Shiva describes the situation:

> *The government has created private militias called* salva judum *which kill brothers and sisters in order to clear the way for the investors, the miners, the industrialists. That is a war between local people, their rights and the constitution of India on the one hand, and a corporate state and the corporations who for the growth model want to mine the last bit of minerals.*[14]

Places where the mining industry is active often look like war zones. For instance, in the US state of West Virginia complete hilltops have been blown away to uncover the underlying coal, a process that engineers cooly call "mountaintop removal." A local resident says, "We have been a national sacrificial zone. These companies are goin' to strip the whole country."[15] The practice of mountaintop removal has already caused 1200 miles of destruction along affected river systems.[16]

The list of ravages caused by mining is almost endless. Whether gold mining in Ghana, coltan in the Congo, aluminum in Brazil, copper in Chile, tin in Indonesia or uranium in Niger; wherever mining giants like Rio Tinto, Anglo-American, BHP Billiton and the like set foot, landscapes and societies become desolated. Mining—including coal, oil and gas production—is by far the most aggressive and destructive economic sector on Earth. It is also the most powerful, with five out of the world's ten largest corporations involved.[17] It has become the prime symbol of man's power over nature. If humans can change the face of the planet by turning rainforests into deserts and mountains into craters, then aren't they capable of just about anything?

Playing God: Metallurgy and Power over Creation

While the extraction of ores requires brute force and a degree of destruction, their processing constitutes the archetype of the transformation or even creation of matter by human hands. Clay can be shaped into new forms, but its essence remains the same in processing. With its malleability and its potential to form alloys, however, the melting out of pure, shiny metals like copper from raw ore gives the metallurgist an almost god-like creative power. He can devise new substances and design their properties, color, hardness and form according to his wishes. It is no surprise that metallurgy is the origin of medieval alchemy, the secretive science whose goal was to transform base materials into precious metals in the laboratory. As the historian of religion Mircea Eliade has shown, metallurgy and alchemy form the model for the idea of unlimited human domination over the material world.[18] In alchemy, this concept already extended well beyond control over the inorganic world. The alchemical idea of a *homunculus* can be found in modern attempts to artificially produce living beings. In Goethe's drama, the alchemist Doctor Faust has his assistant create an artificial person in a test tube — an act that epitomizes mankind's hubris.

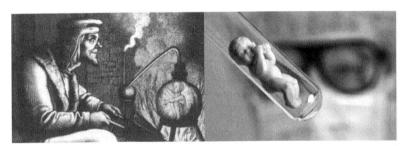

Left: Dr Faust's assistant with homunculus. Right: Vision of a test tube baby

The metallurgical complex and its resultant alchemical worldview have produced a large number of offshoots in modern times. The coal industry is a direct result of iron production,[19] providing human beings with previously unknown possibilities for control over man and nature. Oil refineries and chemical factories have replaced alchemical laboratories. While modern chemistry hardly has alchemy to thank for its modern scientific methods or discoveries, it has nonetheless inherited alchemy's vision of producing new substances and controlling matter down to the smallest particle. Instead of the Philosopher's Stone, the oil and chemical industry has given us the "brave new world" of plastics. Nanotechnologists can even design objects on an atomic scale and produce materials with completely new properties that can migrate through our skin, blood vessels and nervous system.

The heirs of early metallurgists and alchemists have not limited themselves to the inorganic sphere, but penetrate into the biosphere as well. Synthetic biology has already leaped past genetic engineering and the manipulation of individual DNA building blocks to work on creating completely new forms of life. The potential consequences for today's life on Earth are incalculable.[20] The common theme of all these sciences and industries harkens to a line from the biblical Revelation of John, "Behold, I make all things new."[21] The difference, of course, is that today's engineers have replaced the omnipotent God.

Chapter 3

Markets

Economic Power, Money and Property

I'm just a banker doing God's work.

LLOYD BLANKFEIN, former chairman of Goldman Sachs

At first glance, markets appear to be places where something is exchanged. Whether it is the vegetable market or the stock exchange, goods are traded for money, and ownership changes hands. Sometimes markets are loud and hectic, but there is usually no physical violence involved. The general impression is that markets are peaceful places of possibilities and opportunities, in short, freedom. But all of this peace and freedom is actually a matter of perspective. Let us take the most harmless example imaginable, a vegetable market. For those who have enough cash in their pockets, this is usually a great place to go shopping. If you are hungry and have no money, however, things look quite different. The cost of those tempting fruits is a sharp demarcation line that is not to be crossed. And if you simply try to take what you need, in a flash, that peaceful market activity can turn into a scuffle, complete with armed police officers.

Why does one person go home content with a full shopping bag, and the other goes to jail? Why does one person have plenty of that symbolic stuff we call money, and the other does not? To understand, we have to leave the market and take a look at how people earn money, how they sell their labor power, and why one succeeds better than the other. In this broader perspective, the seemingly neutral goods and prices prove to be just the surface of complex social relationships. Consequently, in order to define a market, it is not enough to look only at the place

43

where the exchanges take place. To find out whether markets are institutions of freedom and peace, or conversely, of coercion and violence, we must look beyond location to the overarching structure. It turns out that even an idyllic vegetable market can actually contain various forms of latent or manifest violence that can easily go unnoticed by well-off customers. This is all the more so for large, global markets.

Markets as Masks

Today, the verdict of globalized markets has the kind of significance that God's judgment had during the Middle Ages. If it gives the "thumbs down" to a certain country, its decline is guaranteed. Markets are seen as a force of nature that reward the brave and efficient and punish the weak and slow. Darwinian logic finds this selectivity to be hard but fair, and ultimately indispensable for progress. Otherwise, the world would be condemned to stagnation and mediocrity. And since the markets are like God and nature rolled into one, any objection or resistance to their judgment is not only futile, but unnatural and blasphemous. Furthermore, when the markets become troubled, sacrifices must be made. With ancient gods it was calves and lambs, today it is pensions, wages and social security systems that go up in smoke. Even if they leave behind a trail of scorched earth, the markets must be fed, and they are never really satiated.

Referring to markets as a force of nature obscures their man-made origin and elevates them to a sacrosanct, supernatural sphere. Markets have no name and no address. They are not subject to elections and cannot be held to account—presenting a perfect mask. Lurking behind the disguise, however, are very concrete institutions and individuals with very determined interests. Markets were neither created on some extra eighth day of creation, nor did they evolve all by themselves. Their rules were devised over centuries by people with specific goals in mind. Market players such as public limited companies, central banks and stock exchanges are highly complex creations. To function, they require a wealth of intricate legal regulations (barely manageable by even specialist lawyers) and a state to enforce them, by force if necessary. Today's markets are dominated by just a few hundred corporations with balance sheet totals greater than the gross domestic product (GDP) of entire countries. Although markets do have a long history, there was a time when they did not exist, and for the longest stretch of its history, humanity did just fine without them.

The Myth of the Market

The most widespread explanation for the emergence of markets and currency goes back to the father of modern economic theory, Adam Smith. His assumption was that people had a "natural inclination to barter," and due to this tendency and a desire to gain advantage, they traded goods. This happened at first through direct exchange, and was later mediated by money. Smith believed that this development was then promoted by an increasing division of labor, which grew out of different talents and local conditions.[1] According to this theory, money emerged as a commodity that was initially traded like any other, but, because of its durability, divisibility and transportability, was well suited as an exchangeable unit in barter transactions. Silver and gold had exactly these characteristics, therefore it was natural for them to function as a means of payment. States played a subordinate role in this narrative. While they were capable of promoting or hindering market processes, the emergence of markets obeyed its own natural dynamics.

The problem with this quite logical story, however, is that it is dead wrong. Neither historical research nor comparative anthropology provides any concrete examples to back it up. There have been no societies in which markets and money spontaneously asserted themselves out of a non-market economy. It did not happen all by itself from just the slow spread of barter relationships and the division of labor.[2] Even the "natural inclination to barter," supposedly inherent in all human beings, has not been universally observed.

Instead of bartering, it was actually much more common in non-market cultures for people to manage material and social relationships through offerings, gifts and symbolic acts. When exchange did take place, it tended to be with strangers, with whom closer relationships were neither maintained nor desired.[3] Historically, the transition to a general exchange and money economy has only taken place where the state entered the scene—and with it, organized physical violence. This applies both to the first proto-market economies of world history, such as classical Greece, and to the emergence and expansion of the market system in the modern era.

There is a reason why the tale of a naturally developing market economy is still told again and again. It is to hide the structural and physical violence actually associated with the creation of markets and the money economy that occurred in all historically documented cases. Instead, we hear of a wonderful fairyland in which people follow their natural inclinations and everyone prospers. We are supposed to believe in an innocent, peaceful realm of trade and exchange, which has nothing to do with the heinous crimes of state potentates, their wars and other monstrosities. This story is the foundation upon which the image of "free markets" is built, supposedly as a countervailing force to the despotism of the state. This fable is critically important today for the ideological persuasion it uses to paint the violence of markets and money as natural and legitimate. By contrast, the true story of how markets actually emerged is quite another matter. Here, the decisive roles are played by war and slavery.

War as the Cradle of the Market

We have learned from textbooks that Ancient Greece was the "cradle of democracy." Less well known is that it also produced the first market economy, and that the core of this market economy was the army. Military service was the first and, for a long time, most prevalent form of wage labor.[4]

In the sixth century BC, market relations still played a minor role in Greece, with farmers producing mainly for their own needs.[5] A few large landowners lived in cities and let administrators and slaves operate their farms. Labor markets in which the dispossessed offered to work for market prices were virtually unknown, and trade was looked down upon by the higher classes. Aristocrats used their wealth primarily for display, or for giving generous gifts to gain prestige and political influence. There was no interest in investments, trade projects or even in production facilities. Minted currency was unknown, although precious metals were used as currency in long-distance trading.[6]

With the introduction of coinage in the mid-sixth century, however, the picture changed. The first coins were minted in the kingdom of Lydia in western Asia, the home of the legendary King Midas, who purportedly starved to death because everything he touched turned to gold.[7] It was no coincidence that the oldest Lydian coin was worth 12 sheep. This was exactly the annual wage of a mercenary.[8] Coins then found wide usage in the Greek polis. Starting in the fifth century, the city of Athens used coins to pay city employees and, more importantly, the military.[9] However, the widespread introduction of coins as a means of payment only made sense if officials and soldiers could buy something with them. In other words, they needed markets.

Therefore, the system of state coinage required the commercialization of life in both the city and the country. Instead of just producing goods for personal use, it was now necessary to also produce for markets. In neither antiquity nor in modern times did this happen all by itself. Even during the Roman Empire, most farmers preferred to produce for their own consumption.[10] The decisive step in forcing them to participate in the market was the requirement that taxes and customs duties be paid with coins.[11] Until the introduction of coinage, taxes were levied exclusively in kind, with the state distributing part of the collected harvest to its civil servants and soldiers. When coinage-based taxes were introduced, farmers were now forced to sell part of their produce at markets.[12]

This was an enormous advantage when waging war. Until the establishment of a coin and market economy, there were practically no permanent professional armies. The Greek hoplites (foot soldiers), for example, had to return home for sowing and harvesting and could only be deployed for limited campaigns. In addition, the army had to be paid in-kind, which meant transporting goods to remote bases or allowing looting when on campaign. This also limited the scope and duration of wars. Until the introduction of coinage-based military pay, the maximum range of armies was limited to a 3-day march, because transporting provisions beyond that was not practical.[13] Looting might temporarily increase the range, but large armies quickly exhausted stores taken from their surroundings. In contrast, a market system could ensure that merchants and the local population provided a permanent supply of goods. This way they would also earn coins needed to pay taxes to the state, which in turn paid the soldiers. It was an almost perfect cycle without which neither Greek imperialism, Alexander's empire, the Roman Empire nor the modern world-system would have been possible.

Financed by the new coin economy, it was primarily the naval fleet in fifth century Greece that formed the backbone of Athenian imperialism. As the mint and market system expanded, the size of the Athenian fleet virtually exploded. In the second half of the fifth century, Athens maintained 200 large warships (Triremes) with a crew of 200 each.[14] Little Athens with just 500,000 inhabitants (including Attica) boasted a fleet of 40,000 men. Extrapolated to the current British population, this would correspond to 6 million seamen. Compared to today's United States, it would be the equivalent of 24 million soldiers. The "cradle of democracy" was an extremely militarized society.

The Laurion Mines

The coins used to pay for this undertaking came almost exclusively from a single source located less than 40 miles from Athens, the Laurion silver mines. From the fifth century to Roman times, about 20,000 slaves at a time had been forced to work there. The Athenian state owned the mines and leased them to private entrepreneurs, who often became enormously wealthy as a result. The working conditions were brutal, with miners working 10-hour shifts around the clock in tunnels only 35 inches high.[15] The slaves were branded and many were chained,[16] with most being prisoners of war, either captured directly in battle or bought at slave markets.

Left: Slaves in the Laurion mines. Right: A Lydian coin from the time of Croesus (550 BC)

The Laurion system functioned in an extended perfect cycle. The navy was paid with silver from the mines to enlarge the Greek Empire. Subsequently, the fleet helped capture and enslave more prisoners of war, who in turn mined more silver to finance the ever-expanding war. This three-point system of silver, slavery and war formed the core of the first market economy, which later spread over the entire eastern Mediterranean area with the campaigns of Alexander the Great.

The size of the Alexandrian wars of conquest in the fourth century BC eclipsed the dimensions of the Athenian money-war complex. Alexander needed half a ton of silver a day in order to pay his army of 120,000 mercenaries.[17] This was even too much for Laurion's output. To finance the progress of his offensives, Alexander forced conquered populations to work in their own local silver mines. Furthermore, plundered treasures, in which silver had been hoarded for centuries, also brought in enormous sums of money with which to pay the army. The result was a wave of monetarization, commercialization and militarization in the eastern Mediterranean area. Subsistence and communal economies were increasingly pushed into the background and replaced by markets where soldiers could make purchases with their mercenary wages. The conversion of the tax system from in-kind goods to coinage was once again the decisive lever to force farmers to produce for the market. The army, in turn, ensured that taxes were collected efficiently.

The monetary economy also profoundly changed the political landscape. Now paid on a regular basis, standing armies strengthened the power of rulers in ways previously unknown. Up until the Babylonian era and the advent of permanent mercenary armies, the Mesopotamian kings had been forced to compromise with their populations—often with debt relief— in order to maintain their political power. Now, if rulers had sufficient control over sources of silver, they were able to use brute physical force to assert their will over a population. As the money-military complex became concentrated in the hands of centralized rulers, there was an intensification of both military and economic despotism in the Mediterranean Basin. More and more farmers fell deeply into debt and lost their land to large landowners. The biblical tradition of the jubilee year, in which all debts were canceled and lands were returned to their original owners, was rarely practiced in Palestine during Hellenistic and Roman times. All of this gradually created masses of dispossessed day-laborers who had to sell their labor on the "free" market and were at the mercy of their employers. The numerous day-laborers we encounter in the gospels (such as in the parable of the vineyard) are evidence of this development.[18] Thus, money, military force and the market became a closed circle. Armies were financed with coins, which helped establish markets; and then the armies were used to break down rebellions that resisted the market or demanded debt relief.

The Roman Silver Empire

The tyrannies of the market and military power reached their first high point during the Roman Empire. As was the case in Athens and the Hellenistic empires, a decisive role was played by standing armies, the spread of silver money and the markets.[19] About three-quarters of the Roman state budget was spent on military expenditures. Since the late second century BC, Rome had been waging almost uninterrupted war in the Mediterranean region, financed by silver extracted primarily from the mines of Lyon, Carthage and Spain. Working there was tantamount to a death sentence, and to be penalized in Rome *ad metalla* was considered the second worst punishment after *ad bestias*. The historian Diodorus described conditions in the Spanish mines:

> *The slaves who are engaged in the working of the mines produce for their masters revenues in sums defying belief, but they themselves wear out their bodies both by day and by night in the diggings under the earth, dying in large numbers because of the exceptional hardships they endure. For no respite or pause is granted them in their labors, but compelled beneath blows of the overseers to endure the severity of their plight, they throw away their lives in this wretched manner. [...] Indeed death in their eyes is more to be desired than life.*[20]

Diodorus also mentions that, before the Romans, Carthage had already used the same system to build its mercenary empire:

It was from these mines that they drew their continued growth, hiring the ablest mercenaries to be found and winning with their aid many and great wars. In their wars the Carthaginians never rested their confidence in soldiers from among their own citizens or gathered from their allies. Instead, they subjected the Romans and the Sicilians and the inhabitants of Libya to the greatest perils thanks to the abundance of money which they derived from conquered mines.[21]

Therefore, from the fifth century BC on, the enormous increase in violence in the Mediterranean Basin was caused in large part by the spread of money and market economies.[22] The great imperial crisis in the third century AD shows how critical silver coinage was for maintaining the Roman military empire. After an epidemic in Spain had killed large swathes of the population, including miners, the silver supply dried up. Without pay, the army began to erode. The tax system temporarily reverted to in-kind payments, and the Roman Empire could barely defend itself against external attacks.[23]

The First Corporations

During the Roman Empire, the first forerunners to joint-stock companies were created—the "publicani companies." The Roman state leased the operation of mining companies, army supply contracts and provincial tax collection to private entrepreneurs, the *publicani*, who often formed companies. Shares in these companies were publicly traded.[24] The publicani paid a fixed amount to the state and were allowed a free hand in collecting taxes or operating mines. Because of their brutal and arbitrary actions, the tax leaseholders were hated throughout the provinces. In the gospels, we encounter them as the infamous "tax collectors" or *publicans*. It was frowned upon to share a table with them, and they were the cause of numerous rebellions, including the Jewish resistance against the tax assessment mentioned in the Christmas story.[25]

The publicani corporation is a good example of the interaction of physical violence and economic power. Their markets were first created by the state in order to generate tax revenues and silver with which to pay the army, which also helped selected citizens achieve fabulous wealth. This practice continues today, with states continually creating new markets, most obviously by privatizing war through mercenary companies such as Blackwater or DynCorp. However, as we will see in Chapter 6, the relationship between market and state has tended to reverse itself in recent times. While in antiquity, the state used and created markets to assert its imperial interests, companies today use the state to create *their own* empires. The sovereigns of our time are not emperors or prime ministers, but rather the CEOs and main shareholders of large corporations. As the world-system theorist Immanuel Wallerstein notes, Rome was a world *empire*, but the global system of our time is a world *market*.[26]

There is another reason why publicani corporations relate to the present day. They are the first market players in world history to embrace the principle of endless capital accumulation. Individual entrepreneurs have both a limited life expectancy and only so many opportunities to spend all their money. Until early modern times, successful traders would limit their work to about 6 hours a day and use the rest of the time to enjoy or show off their acquired wealth.[27] So there were certain physical and cultural limits to accumulation, and the heirs often squandered their inheritances instead of increasing them. The publicani companies, however, were immortal and insatiable.[28] As with a modern public limited company, their sole aim was to extract the maximum monetary profit from any economic activity as quickly as possible, and for an open-ended period of time, regardless of the lifespans and specific needs of its shareholders.

Nevertheless, publicani corporations did not become the nuclei of a capitalist system of the modern type. One reason for this was that, over time, they proved very damaging to the Roman state, causing the emperor Augustus to massively curtail their activities and transfer tax collection to state officials. The uprisings provoked by the publicani's brutality and the subsequent loss of revenue were now a threat to the existence of the empire. Consequently, the publicani were replaced during the imperial era by an extensive state-run tax collection bureaucracy. As in the case of Rome, the great bureaucracies of the modern era also originated from the collection of taxes to pay for the military (see chapters 6 and 7). The expansion of market logic and state power went hand in hand in both epochs. Therefore, the popular juxtaposition of "free markets" and "state bureaucracies" is pure fiction. Both in antiquity and in modern times, the creation of markets is inextricably linked to warring states.

Ownership as Complete Power of Disposition

Just as states need markets to facilitate the waging of war, the markets that have prevailed throughout history have also relied on militarized states. As in Rome, this also holds true in today's world. Markets presuppose a certain concept of ownership—you may only sell what you own. But property is more than mere possession. I can steal a Rembrandt from a museum and consequently possess it, but I will have trouble selling it, at least at Sotheby's, because it is not legitimately my property. Ownership means lawful possession. And, lawful means that the state with its concentrated physical power stands behind the ownership, as the earlier example of the evicted tenant illustrates.

States protect property rights, ensure that contracts are respected and punish those who violate them. At first glance, this seems obvious and practical: wouldn't theft, murder and manslaughter spread without the strong hand of the state to ensure law and order? The question, however, is whose law and whose order? Who is defended against whom here? What exactly is meant by ownership?

On closer inspection, today's ownership comprises actually a whole series of different rights, and some of those rights may exclude the rights of others. What can an owner lawfully do with his property? May he simply *use* it—if it is a piece of land, e.g., by walking around on it, or, if it is a cow, by having it draw a cart (Latin: *usus*)? Or may he use the *proceeds* of it— by farming the land or milking the cow (Latin: *usus fructus*)? May the property be altered, damaged or destroyed (*abusus*), for example by mining the land or slaughtering the cow? Are others prohibited from using it? Can it be sold, inherited, rented, given away or mortgaged?

All of these questions have been answered quite differently by different people at different times. The most extreme answer to these questions is that everything is allowed without restriction, and that the owner of the property has total and sole control over it, whether it be things, people, animals, plants, land, rivers, lakes, etc.

The Roman notion of property came fairly close to this extreme position. The central concept in Roman property law is the *dominium*. This term was used to describe the household of a Roman citizen, including wife, children, slaves, cattle, land, house and chattels. The people belonging to such a *dominium* were completely subject to the will of the household patriarch.[29] The father of the family could not only beat his slaves and children with impunity, but he could also sell them into slavery or even kill them. There was no substantial difference between the ownership of people, livestock or land. In contrast to many other ancient societies, where trading land was restricted or forbidden, Roman citizens had unlimited power of disposal over their land and could sell it at any time. With the increasing commercialization of Roman life, the first real estate market in history emerged alongside the slave markets, with a flourishing speculative trade.[30] This unregulated dealing further intensified the concentration of land ownership and accelerated the emergence of a class of dispossessed people who were left searching for work as laborers.

With the decline of the Roman military machinery, this property system also collapsed. In the Middle Ages, with scarce precious metals and few standing armies, the power to control people and land became much more limited. Slavery largely disappeared from Europe,[3] and land was no longer sold freely, but only loaned out as fiefs. With the revival of the money and war economies in the early modern period, Roman property rights were also revived. With them, the concept of total disposal over people and land returned as well.

The fact that today's oil and mining corporations can transform half the planet into lunar landscapes under protection from the state is based on the Roman legal tradition. As "legal persons," everything that these companies acquire and call their property is completely at their disposal.[32] This kind of power is no longer limited to controlling just land and movable goods, but also life itself. Genes and even entire animal and plant species can now be patented and are therefore considered the "intellectual property" of the patent holder.[33]

The history of the social and ecological movements of the last centuries can also be seen as a history of resistance against this kind of dispositional power. The anti-slavery movement opposed the idea that people can be possessed and traded as goods. Women's rights movements have defied men's power of disposition over the patriarchal dominium. Human rights movements demand that states have only limited powers of disposition over their subjects or citizens. Finally, ecological movements have tried to curb the dispositional power of private individuals, states and corporations over the land and living things.

In the twenty-first century, the survival of a large part of the world's population is threatened by the ownership claims of a minority. A relatively small class of global elites, together with several hundred transnational corporations, have taken possession of most of the land, forests, water, food, mineral resources and even the Earth's atmosphere. It is a system of property ownership that, when contested, is enforced by the physical power of the state. As resources become scarce worldwide and conflicts increase, this class seals itself off in gated communities with walls, barbed wire fences and massive security forces to keep out people seeking refuge from their plundered homelands.

Who has what right over which territory? What may or may not a state, a company or a private individual do with that piece of nature they call their property? To what extent may people be barred from using land, water and other existential goods? Must property claims written on a piece of paper be recognized for all time, no matter how deadly the consequences might be? Can someone own a piece of land and all the living things on it, just like owning a pair of trousers or a banana? What can and may be sold or mortgaged, and what is inalienable common property? Who makes these decisions? Today, it is crucial to our existence to ask these questions once again. In the face of the extreme concentration of land ownership at the time, the biblical prophets had also asked these questions, and answered them clearly: the land was nobody's property; it was only on loan to humanity — and in equal parts.

Chapter 4

Powerlessness

The Trauma of Power and the Origin of Apocalyptic Thinking

Night and day among the tombs and in the hills he would cry out and cut himself with stones. [...] Jesus asked him, "What is your name?" "My name is Legion," he replied, "for we are many."

THE GOSPEL ACCORDING TO MARK

The interaction of the money economy, war and metallurgy led to an enormous expansion of people exerting power over other people. This process also has a flip side: powerlessness increased in those who were at the mercy of this power. Historiography makes little mention of this, since history is usually told from the point of view of the victors. The most important source historians draw on is the written word. Those who were able to read and write were usually close to power or were directly employed by it. The written records of this privileged caste were later read as "history," a reconstruction of the past told from the perspective of power.[1] Accordingly, we learn a great deal in our history books about how Caesar, Frederick the Great or Harry Truman saw the world, but little about what those millions of people thought and felt who were crushed under the wheels of their wars. How violence effects the majority of people both psychologically and socially does not appear in the annals. Thus, an image of history as a "struggle of great men" among each other is formed, while the core dynamics and driving forces of world history remain in the dark. Consequently, it is difficult to understand the success of Christianity in antiquity, with its symbolism of suffering and powerlessness and its

59

apocalypticism. Likewise, it is impossible to comprehend the collective epidemic of fear that accompanied the birth of the modern era in Europe, as the historian Jean Delumeau has shown.[2] In order to understand the history of the civilization that today is dominating the Earth, we must tell the story of the *effects of power* and how they have wounded and disrupted people, their imaginations and their social fabric.

What does it mean when, for centuries, a large part of the population is subjected to radical dehumanization, as was the case with slavery? How does a society change when men become part of an imperial military machine whose daily business is torture and murder? What about the survivors on the margins of the empire who had to watch their children, siblings, parents and spouses slaughtered or subjected to a slow torturous death on the cross? What does it mean for families and communities when farmers lose their land through over-indebtedness or land grabbing and become uprooted workers, selling their bodies to a brutal, unregulated labor market? What does it mean to be so absolutely at the mercy of other people's power and whim?

The story of the *demoniac* of Gerasa in the Gospel of Mark is a remarkable testimony to the devastating effects of power:

When Jesus got out of the boat, a man with an impure spirit came from the tombs to meet him. This man lived in the tombs, and no one could bind him anymore, not even with a chain. For he had often been chained hand and foot, but he tore the chains apart and broke the irons on his feet. No one was strong enough to subdue him. Night and day among the tombs and in the hills he would cry out and cut himself with stones. [...] Then Jesus asked him, "What is your name?" "My name is Legion," he replied, "for we are many."[3]

The form of "demonic" possession that Mark recounts would be described in modern psychology as a "dissociative disorder," which can result from violent traumatizing experiences. It is likely that the man from Gerasa had endured a great deal at the hands of the Roman legions, whose practices have been handed down to us from other sources.[4] Around the time of the birth of Jesus, Governor Varus had 2000 people crucified near the city of Sepphoris (a few miles from Nazareth) in retaliation for a previous uprising.[5] Such actions were the rule rather than the exception. While the *Pax Augusta* was celebrated in the central regions of the empire, the Roman troops out on the fringes were notorious for their scorched earth measures. Tacitus, for example, reports the British rebel leader Calgacus as having said: "They have pillaged the world: when the land has nothing left for men who ravage everything, they scour the sea. [...] They plunder, they butcher, they ravish, and call it by the lying name of 'empire.' They make a desert and call it 'peace.'"[6]

The consequences were the traumatization of countless people, even entire societies. It is not by chance that the gospels tell of so many obsessed and psychosomatically ill people. The ancient money-military machine left behind tracks of social and psychological devastation throughout the affected populations. This traumatic process continued centuries later across the entire planet with the spread of colonialism, and continues to this day.

What is Trauma?

The Greek word *trauma* means wound or injury. In its modern meaning, the term has been used since the late nineteenth century for psychological disorders caused by drastic experiences of violence and separation. Combat traumas were first scientifically investigated during the First World War. Trauma researcher Judith Herman describes victims of so-called "shell shock":

Confined and rendered helpless [in the trenches], subjected to constant threat of annihilation, and forced to witness the mutilation and death of their comrades without any hope of reprieve, many soldiers began to act like hysterical women.

They screamed and wept uncontrollably. They froze and could not move. They became mute and unresponsive. They lost their memory and their capacity to feel.[7]

Trauma can occur through the direct experience of violence, the threat of violence and also through witnessing violence against others. The traumatizing experience is associated with a feeling of extreme powerlessness and helplessness. Those affected lose their sense of control, their connection to the surrounding world and their sense of purpose. Judith Herman writes: "Traumatic events call into question basic human relationships. They breach the attachments of family, friendship, love and community. They shatter the construction of the self that is formed and sustained by relation to others."[8] Through feelings of complete helplessness, trauma also destroys the sense of one's self-efficacy and the confidence to manage difficult situations by yourself. The most elementary belief in a meaningful and—in principle— benign world is shattered.

Typical among trauma patients is *dissociation,* or breaking away from the world of emotional feelings. This can extend to the point of mental numbness ("emotional anesthesia") and disengagement from one's own body, which feels removed and foreign. This leads to traumatized people often appearing apathetic and emotionally cold. The apathy alternates with phases in which traumatic situations are re-lived through flashbacks and dreams.

Traumas also produce a series of seemingly paradoxical consequences. These include the famous repetition compulsion. For example, during role-play, children will often reenact situations in which they felt powerless.[9] By re-living the traumatizing situation, they can then experience themselves as powerful in an attempt to erase their feelings of impotence. Thus, experiences of powerlessness often lead to an intensive search for empowering experiences. The famous "identification with the aggressor" also appears paradoxical at first glance. Particularly with repeated traumatizations, "it is vital for the victim to intensively devote his or her mind to the perpetrator, to somehow identify with him, in order to gain a measure of control over a situation that is otherwise characterized by pure powerlessness."[10]

These phenomena: the compulsion to repeat; the search for empowering experiences; the craving for control; as well as revenge fantasies and paranoia, will all be encountered again when we examine apocalyptic thinking.

When traumatic experiences undermine or destroy the relationships and contexts within an entire society, then we call it "collective trauma." Entire societies can be seized by control mania or "emotional anesthesia." Whole cultures can dedicate themselves to re-enacting traumatic experiences or to collective paranoia. Above all, they will seek to regain a sense of power.

The Origin of Apocalyptic Thinking

One of the most striking features of what we call "Western civilization" is its affinity to the Apocalypse. Hollywood, for instance, is clearly obsessed with the idea of Armageddon. However, we have also been permeated by apocalyptic thinking on a much deeper level. Originally, apocalypses did not actually end with the destruction of the world, but were about creating a new one, a Heavenly Jerusalem. The utopian concepts of early modern times, such as Tommaso Campanella's *City of the Sun* and Francis Bacon's *New Atlantis*, were apocalyptically inspired, as were the movements of the Anabaptists, the Protestant Reformation and the early settlers in North America. In the twentieth century, the designs of futuristic cities by Le Corbusier or the early Soviet project of creating a "New Man" were basically permutations of 2000-year-old apocalyptic ideas, even if their creators would have rejected any connection to a religious context. It is no coincidence that the rectangular street patterns and the sky-reflecting glass facades found in modern financial districts fit the description of the New Jerusalem in the Book of Revelation. Apocalypticism has proved to be surprisingly widespread and extremely persistent throughout history. It is as much at home in Christianity as in the atheistic cult of progress. It can be found in the hope of restarting mankind through communism and in the triumphant vision of capitalism in Francis Fukuyama's *The End of History and the Last Man*.[11]

Left: Vision of New Jerusalem (17th century). Right: Le Corbusier's design for a new Paris (1925)

The Apocalypse, however, is not just a province of the imagination. No other civilization in history has managed to produce so many real-life doomsday options, from nuclear war to environmental collapse to the spread of lab-grown, mutated killer organisms. Oddly enough, these real-life scenarios have links to the imaginary ones. It almost seems as if the millennia-long search for a New Jerusalem has helped produce precisely the destructive potential that currently threatens our future. Just beyond the "brave new world" brought to us by the age of consumerism, is a ravaged, burned-out planet. The flip side of controlling nuclear power, which has been linked to the boldest of utopian concepts since the 1950s, is the potential for cataclysmic war. And the creation of artificial life in the laboratory could unleash a catastrophic global pandemic. The aliens who devastate the Earth in apocalyptic films such as *Independence Day* and *Oblivion* are ultimately ourselves.

But where did apocalyptic thinking come from in the first place? What are the origins of the quest for a completely new and different world to replace the old, corrupted one that marks our civilization?

Apocalypse as a Response to the Trauma of Power

Apocalypses are visions of total despair. They emerge from the remnants of imperial devastation, where no human, no earthly help is in sight; where the world appears to be so completely ruined that salvation only seems possible through the total destruction and re-creation of the cosmos. Apocalyptic thinking has always been born out of annihilation. It is therefore no coincidence that apocalyptic literature originated during an epoch of massive economic and physical violence following Alexander the Great's wars of conquest. As we saw in the last chapter, this phase was marked by intensive militarization and commercialization.

The biblical Book of Daniel is one of the earliest surviving apocalyptic texts, written in Palestine around 164 BC. The place and date of its origin are crucial. Probably more than any other region in antiquity, Palestine was subjected for centuries to constant military invasions. But never before had foreign domination been so oppressive and humiliating as under Antiochus IV, who ruled over one of the empires that followed Alexander's reign.

Unlike the Babylonian kings before him, who had granted religious freedom and many other rights to Jews, Antiochus maintained a standing army that he paid with silver coins, which allowed him to impose a much more brutal dominion than his predecessors, both economically and militarily. To pay reparation debts to Rome, Antiochus constantly increased taxes, and repeatedly plundered the temple in Jerusalem. Finally, he put up a portrait of Zeus in the Holy of Holies and forbade the practice of the Jewish cult. His despotic rule did not only desecrate his subjects' bodies, but their metaphysical universe as well.

During the reign of Antiochus, physical violence, economic exploitation and ideological tyranny were consolidated into a totalitarian system. This early peak of absolute power became the incubator of apocalyptic thought, which later proved so formative in the development of Western civilization.

The Book of Daniel testifies to a resistance against succumbing to powerlessness and the effort to regain some measure of self-efficacy. In the episode of the fiery furnace, Daniel and his companions are thrown into a fire pit because they refuse to worship the symbol of foreign rule. But the fire does not burn them, and they remain unharmed.[12]

The seventh chapter of Daniel's prophecy features the actual Apocalypse, taking matters a step further. Now, it is no longer just about salvation, but about retribution. Four empires are described that are symbolized by different animals. The fourth beast was different from the others, "terrifying and frightening and very powerful. It had large iron teeth; it crushed and devoured its victims and trampled underfoot whatever was left."[13] This last beast, representing Antiochus, is brought to justice before a criminal court and condemned by a divine figure to execution by fire.[14]

In contrast to later revelations, here there is no annihilation of the entire universe, but only of the evildoer. But even in the Book of Daniel, the attempt to compensate for powerlessness and humiliation can be clearly seen. An enormous army supports the "Highest," whose power exceeds everything that has come before. The omnipotence of this god both reflects and outperforms the power held by earthly rulers. The tables are turned with respect to the fire that threatened Daniel. In the end, not only has balance been restored, but a final, magnificent triumph has been achieved. It is precisely at this point that the apocalyptic paradigm shifts from hoping for salvation and reparation to an inversion of the traumatic experience. What the victim experienced will now be inflicted on the perpetrator, and with even greater violence. Apocalypticism does not diverge from the principle of power; it amplifies it. In the end, there is no liberation, but the founding of a new kingdom of the "Most High, whom all powers serve and obey." The vision ends with the word "obey," but the author adds, "I was deeply troubled by my thoughts, and my face turned pale."

The Destruction of Heaven and Earth

Written around 90 AD, the most influential apocalyptic text by far is the Book of Revelation (to John), which, by contrast, lacks these feelings of horror and trepidation.[15] The author has absolutely no problem with the logic of annihilation. And this time, it is not just a few tyrants and their henchmen in the balance. Everything is at stake, with the entire universe to be wiped out and recreated. After a nearly endless series of plagues and catastrophes rain down on Earth and humankind, "the beast" and the Devil are to be thrown into a lake of fire to be "tormented day and night for ever and ever."

This radicalization of the apocalyptic vision was a response to the radicalization of domination. The Roman Empire had further perfected the Greek system of a monetary economy combined with slavery and militarism to produce the greatest concentration of economic, physical and ideological violence seen so far. In contrast to Antiochus, whose reign was ultimately overcome by rebellion, the Roman emperor and his legions were practically invulnerable. The emperor's absolute power was inverse to the complete powerlessness suffered by Jews, Jewish Christians and others. Tacitus wrote about the Roman persecution of Christians in the year 64: "Mockery of every sort was added to their deaths. Covered with the skins of beasts, they were torn by dogs and perished, or were nailed to crosses, or were doomed to the flames and burnt, to serve as a nightly illumination, when daylight had expired."[16] Two years later, the Roman military put down a revolt in Judea with a war that ended in the year 70. The Jewish temple in Jerusalem was destroyed, and tens of thousands of Jews were killed, many of them by crucifixion.

These events may have been personally witnessed by John.[17] In any case, the nightmarish attacks on Judea would have been deeply rooted in the collective memory of his contemporaries. The evils of the world were so overwhelming and the lack of power so complete that the only solution seemed to be a heavenly intervention that would destroy and recreate the Earth: "Then I saw a new heaven and a new earth for the first heaven and the first earth had passed away, and there was no longer any sea. I saw the Holy City, the new Jerusalem, coming down out of heaven from God."[18]

Heavenly Jerusalem and the Sulfur Lake

The New Jerusalem is not meant for everyone. It is not a utopian, equitable, peaceful and harmonized "Heavenly Kingdom" as described in the gospels, or by the prophets in the Old Testament. Instead, it is a place where humanity is brutally divided into the chosen and the damned. For those registered in the *Book of Life,* this Heavenly City—the New Jerusalem—has been created, "prepared as a bride beautifully dressed for her husband."[19] Conversely, those who are rejected and not listed in the *Book of Life* are considered worthless and will be thrown into a lake of burning sulfur for all eternity.[20]

Despite all secularizations, this vision has remained formative for Western civilization to this day. As we will see in Chapter 6, with the emergence of a capitalist world economy in the sixteenth century, it experienced both a renaissance and a reinterpretation, especially through the teachings of the Calvinists and Puritans. As the executor of divine will, the market became the divider of humanity into the chosen and the damned. These days, the connection between apocalypticism and capitalism is almost uncannily topical. In modern "global cities," there is often a close proximity between the Heavenly Jerusalem and the lake of sulfur. While the chosen ones sit in glass towers and watch numbers, letters and images flit across their screens, just a few blocks away, those excluded from the global market are buried under mountains of feces and garbage left behind by the privileged. What separates the slum dwellers from those in ascension are the numbers recorded in the present-day version of the Lamb's *Book of Life*— the bank account. In the twenty-first century, if you are not registered in the bank's books, you are surely headed for the sulfurous lake of fire.

Left: A businessman in Houston, Texas. Right: A worker in a sulfur mine in Indonesia

With God no longer sitting on his throne, we now have the market's invisible hand choosing winners and losers. The terrain is split into two radically separate spheres with borders running along the barbed wire fences that have turned Europe and the USA into fortresses, and continue along the walls dividing Israel and Palestine. Connected by high-security corridors, there are networks of "gated communities" and "green zones" springing up all over the world. The winners drive their air-conditioned SUVs on highways that cut across the land of the losers. Left behind is only dust and garbage thrown out of the window. The Heavenly Jerusalem of our time uses police robots and drones to protect against those trying to escape the sulfur lake.

As in the Revelation, today's world is torn apart along a line of abstraction. The Earth's tangible, natural world has been discarded and is mutating into a lake of fire. From Heaven comes a completely abstract, right-angled city "of glass and pure gold" that has been measured off with a golden ruler.[21] It is disturbing how much John's fantasy has become reality today in the city centers of São Paulo, Singapore, Dubai or Houston. God has been replaced by the engineers and architects of the modern world who are working on a second, artificial creation, a world "without death, grief, lament or hardship."[22] But the price for this hubristic project is the destruction of the original creation. It is a bitter historical fact that the vision of gaining total control over creation originally grew out of an impulse to rebel against power.

Shattering the Present

Apocalyptic thinking not only divides space, it also shatters time—more precisely, the present time. For apocalypticists, the here and now is unbearable and cannot be salvaged, as fighting against the impositions of power seems to be a hopeless undertaking. Giving up on self-efficacy, faith is then placed in a higher power that will take care of the powerless in the future. This opens up a completely new concept of time. While the life of an intact (not-traumatized) community follows a pattern of renewal with its recurring rhythms and changes of generations, by contrast, traumatic experiences break that cycle. People are no longer able to see themselves as part of a meaningful and generally benevolent supra-individual context. They become dissociated, torn from natural cycles, their community and the cosmos. Nothing is left with which to defy the present devastation but the vision of a future in which everything will be different. The shattered world of the present will be replaced with an entirely new one.[23] The fixation of Western civilization on the future, whether in Heaven or on Earth, was born out of comprehensive collective trauma. People have been wrenched away from all contexts that define the present—and not just once, but over and over again in different places at different times, right up to the recent past.

The modern cult of progress is a variant of the core concept of the Apocalypse. If the ground beneath your feet is constantly falling away, then you must run forward to reach new, solid terrain. This flight from the present is at the root of what we call *history*. Driven forward by an inescapable, one-dimensional arrow of time, the shattered past is abandoned for a new future. In this race, we try to prevent our own downfall by permanently accelerating, modernizing and erasing all traces of the past. However, this war against time can never be won, since the enemy we fight is actually produced by our own actions.[24]

Objections to the End of the World: The Jesus Movement

Few books are as full of conflicting messages as the New Testament. In many ways, the Book of Revelations contradicts the main goals of the Jesus movement described in the gospels. While the apocalyptics were waiting for a heavenly intervention in the future, Jesus's aim was to heal a traumatized society by taking action in the present.

The gospels are a rare case of early historiography that, at least in part, reflects the views of people other than the elites. It is true that the ecclesiastical canon of gospels emerged decades after the death of Jesus of Nazareth, and none of the authors ever met the central character in their stories. The authors themselves were not farmers, fishermen and day-laborers like Jesus and his followers (most of them illiterate like, possibly, Jesus himself), but scribes and scriptural experts. Further, the texts were strongly shaped by the interests and conflicts of the times in which they were written: the young Christian communities attempted to diverge from competing Jewish groups such as the

Pharisees, and they clearly tried to ingratiate themselves with the Roman occupiers. The legend of the Roman governor Pilate, who listens sympathetically to Jesus and ultimately washes his hands of guilt, is the most striking example of such opportunistic distortion of history.[25]

Despite these revisions, however, the traces of groups who asserted an alternative to the Empire's principles are fairly clear in the gospels.[26] There were many resistance movements against Rome and its vassal authorities at this time. The Jewish historian Flavius Josephus cited numerous factions headed by prophets or peasant kings who were called "the Anointed" (in Greek: Christós, and in Hebrew: mashiach/messiah). Jesus was far from being the only Messiah candidate of his time.[27] Some believers were armed, others relied mainly on the spoken word, and almost all of the leaders were murdered and their movements smashed.[28] The best-known examples are the executions of John the Baptist under Herod and of Jesus under Pilate. The fact that Rome perceived the Jesus movement as an anti-colonial issue is quite evident from the way he was executed. Crucifixion was the typical Roman death penalty for political dissidents found guilty of "seditio" (rebellion) or "crimen maiestatis" (insulting the emperor). According to Josephus, at the height of the Jewish War (66 AD–70 AD), up to 500 people per day were crucified at the gates of Jerusalem. Jesus was not the only one to die this way. Furthermore, part of this punishment was to leave the dead unburied. This was a second trauma for the relatives, since burial was considered a religious imperative. Ultimately, the bodies of the crucified were fed upon by birds and wild dogs. The legend of Jesus being buried and later resurrected was obviously an attempt to suppress this traumatic experience.[29]

Therefore, the gospel stories clearly took place during a time of massive collective trauma. How the Jesus movement responded, however, is visibly at odds with the various later versions of the Christian religion, and also with Christian apocalypticism. Unlike the authoritarian churches that followed, the original movement was based on egalitarian principles. It was not primarily about worshiping an idol named Jesus, but rather a process of individual and collective transformation, whose metaphor was the "Kingdom of Heaven."[30] Unlike the "Kingdom of the Most High" from the Daniel Apocalypse, or the "Heavenly Jerusalem," this project is not associated with a vision of revenge and annihilation.[31] Nor does this concept divide mankind into the chosen and the damned. On the contrary, numerous stories tell of Jesus sharing his table with the outcasts of his time, a sign that this kingdom was open to all.

The gospels spell out that there is no waiting for the Kingdom of Heaven sometime off in the future, but that it has already begun: with concrete actions, such as healing the sick, a primary activity during the travels of Jesus and his followers.[32] The American historian Richard Horsley interprets these healings as an anti-colonial practice and shows this in the history of the demoniac of Gerasa: "If Jesus expels the demon, whose name is 'Legion,' then in reality it is about the expulsion of the Romans, the occupiers of the Jewish people."[33] Healing a possessed individual corresponds on a collective level to liberation from occupation. At the end of the story, a herd of pigs, the "Legion," is sent plunging off a cliff, symbolizing quite explicitly the wish to be rid of the Roman army. The healings associated with the Kingdom of Heaven are about a collective recovery that removes not only the symptoms of trauma but also its causes. This counter-kingdom was, therefore, a strongly political, anti-imperial symbol—one which the Romans understood all too well.

Jesus of Nazareth was not the founder of Christianity. The movement he initiated was an *intra-Jewish* undertaking that invoked deep-rooted traditions of resistance to power, especially by the early prophets. The idea of a hierarchically organized church with written dogma was completely out of line with the practices and goals of his cause.

After the execution of Jesus, the movement lived on, with women often filling important roles.[34] Historically, however, the egalitarian, anti-hierarchical and anti-imperial traditions did not remain in the forefront. Nonetheless, they never completely disappeared and were often rekindled during times of social upheaval, especially at the beginning of the modern era. Over the following centuries, the ideology that was elevated to the level of a state religion and today still shapes the official church had very little in common with the views and practices of the Jesus movement, and in many respects was even its exact opposite. How this came about involves perhaps the most radical and momentous reinterpretation of a story ever.

Chapter 5

Mission

The Origins of Western Universalism

Even if we or an angel from heaven should preach a gospel other than the one we preached to you, let them be under God's curse!
PAUL: EPISTLE TO THE GALATIANS[1]

The idea of *mission* is deeply ingrained in our culture, even beyond Christian evangelization. No action hero can do without a mission. When dropped onto foreign terrain, he fights for the salvation of civilization against the adversities of nature and enemy combatants. Corporations conquer markets on the basis of their *mission statement*, which lays out strategies for global competition. Space missions are meant to conquer outer space, just as the Christian colonizers conquered the Earth.

Similar to earlier evangelization by the Jesuit Order or the London Missionary Society, today the message of the free-market gospel is spread by the International Monetary Fund (IMF) and think tanks like the Mont Pèlerin Society.[2] Like their Christian predecessors, the market's radical preachers push a universalist ideology and claim that theirs is the only way to salvation.

The idea of proselytizing is a historical curiosity. Until the triumphal spread of Christianity, missionary zeal was barely known.[3] One exception is the ancient Zoroastrian religion of Persia, from which Christianity inherited a great deal. This includes: the idea of an eschatological "Last Judgment"; Heaven and Hell; the resurrection of the dead; and the strict division of humanity into the chosen and the damned.[4] It is no coincidence that those religions with a pronounced apocalypticism are prone to aggressively missionize. Without a final judgment and

75

damnation, there is no need to save souls. If there are no sharp lines separating those who possess the truth from the ignorant, pagans, heretics and others who are lost, then there is no point in forcing your beliefs on others. Apocalyptic dualism is a necessary condition of this mission, and it includes the claim that these truths are *universal*.

The Great Reinterpretation

The first to put a universal mission project in writing was Saul of Tarsus, who was also called Paul.[5] Through his letters, Paul had more influence on the development of Christian dogma than any other author. If his confessions are to be believed, Paul first made a name for himself by persecuting the first Christians before becoming an apostle of Jesus.[6] Paul never actually met Jesus, and he took no particular interest in either his life or the contents of his movement.[7] He was exclusively interested in Jesus's death and the story of his resurrection. Merging these elements together with remnants from ancient mystery religions and Old Testament prophecies, Paul forged the myth of the Son of God, who was sacrificed by his Father for the sins of mankind.[8]

This myth is a double-edged sword. On the one hand, it offered an alternative to the Roman emperor cult and put the empire's ideological foundations into question. The emperor was worshiped as God, the "Son of God" and as the "Redeemer" whose words were considered *euangélia* (good news/gospels). By calling a crucified Jewish rebel the "Son of God," and labeling his subversive message a gospel, Paul was being deliberately provocative. His vision of a Christian community based on justice and equality, including women and slaves, was a challenge to the imperial hierarchies.[9]

On the other hand, this mythology stood in sharp contrast to the practices of the Jesus movement. Paul—and even more so the "church fathers" who succeeded him—emphasized belief in the myth, instead of actively trying to change the current reality. They preached a future salvation through the Last Judgment and the Resurrection instead of action in the here and now. By shifting the focus from the practical to the mythical, from the present to the future, and from this life to the afterlife, the Church that developed after Paul turned almost everything that the Jesus movement stood for on its head.

Even more momentous was the claim that this mythology represented a final, indisputable, perfect truth that applied to all of humanity. The mission statement of Paul and his church has four main points:

1. World history follows an inevitable course toward a divine event that will result in the salvation of believers and the damnation of unbelievers.
2. This history is not limited to certain peoples or regions, but is universal. Whether they know it or not, or want it or not, all people are part of this *singular* story. There are no alternatives.
3. There is only one universally valid truth to this story.
4. It follows that whoever knows this truth also has the right and the duty to lead the uninformed onto the right path.

These are the premises that form the foundation of the mission on which stands the entire ideological structure justifying the expansion of Europe during the last two millennia. The label on this mission project might change—from Christianity, to the Enlightenment, to the market economy or simply "Western values." Nonetheless, at its core remains the claim that it is the West that advances progress throughout human history. This narrative forms a continuum that has survived all the great historical disruptions of the last 2000 years. At its center is the idea of radical superiority combined with a mission to convert the whole world. The missionary mandate will not be fulfilled until everyone is like us; when there are no more outsiders; when "the other" ceases to exist.[10] After Paul, Augustine of Hippo (354–430) wrote that the gospel must be proclaimed everywhere and to all peoples until "no land exists where there is no church."[11]

Mission and Power

Missionaries who are not backed by military force are in a very precarious position. Why should anyone believe them? Why would people suddenly toss their own culture overboard and sign on to the authoritarian claims of strangers? Imagine missionaries from the Central African Mbuti nomads showing up in a small Midwestern town to persuade people to follow their way of life. In the town square, they would thunderously insist that all homes should be abandoned, all the superstitious lies that are told in church should stop and people should even get rid of their ungodly clothing. How would the locals react? Who would be convinced?

Most Christian missions that set out to convince people through the power of preaching were in a corresponding situation and often achieved only modest success. Paul must have surely experienced this himself, since he wrote that his message was "a stumbling block to Jews and foolishness to Gentiles."[12] He was often mocked for his unimpressive appearance.[13] From Northeastern Europe to the South Seas, this was the continual fate of missionaries during the 2000 years that followed.

However, this humiliating situation changed radically for missionaries as soon as they received support from the power of the state. Where there had been ridicule and pity, there was now obedience and subservience. Accompanied by men with guns or battle-axes, the missionary's self-esteem and claim to the absolute and universal truth found affirmation, as if by magic. In return, the missionary provided the state with a perfect justification for its expansion. De facto cases of assault, murder and plunder were now presented as part of a higher mission to save souls. The looters felt consecrated, and the missionaries felt themselves filled with God's power.

The Destruction of the Other

The narrative of a mission to save humanity justifies and allows the destruction of other forms of social organization. Depending on the era, such differently organized societies have been labeled as barbaric, pagan, wild, uncivilized, backward or underdeveloped. While their eradication may be painful, the establishment of a more highly developed, progressive society provides a rationalization. The Spanish theologian Juan Ginés de Sepúlveda, for example, justified the genocide and destruction of cultures in the Americas in the sixteenth century by asserting that the indigenous were "barbarians, unlettered, and uneducated, brutes totally incapable of learning anything but mechanical skills, full of vices, cruel and of a kind such that it is advisable they be governed by others."[14]

However, the history of violent missions did not begin during modern times in the so-called New World (which was clearly not "new" to its inhabitants) but much earlier. That which the indigenous peoples of America experienced after the arrival of Columbus had already been endured by the indigenous people of Central and Eastern Europe. In 723, a man named Bonifatius ("the Benefactor") was sent by the pope to missionize the Central European peoples. In present-day Hesse, the population had continually rejected what a chronicler called "the sacred truths of pure faith," and continued unperturbed with their worship of trees and wellsprings. After the missionary's admonitions against these practices had fallen on deaf ears, he sent in troops. Facing vehement protest, he ordered the "holy tree" at Geismar to be cut down and a church to be built from the wood.[15] By desecrating their metaphysical world, Bonifatius traumatized the inhabitants of Geismar just as Antiochus had done to the people of Judea. The annihilation of the symbolic order ultimately aimed to destroy the social fabric that had empowered resistance to the invasion.

Virtually all of northern Germany and the regions from the Elbe River to the Baltic Sea were subsequently subjected to brutal, forced Christianization. Charlemagne's troops waged a 32-year war against the Saxons (772–804), who resisted both his rule and Christianity.[16] It was much the same 250 years later with the Vends, a Slavic group living east of the Elbe who had to suffer through an entire crusade after Christian missionaries failed to convince them. The mission under arms reached its climax at the Baltic Sea in the thirteenth century. After several campaigns by the Teutonic Order, the Old Prussian culture had been largely extinguished.[17] Their homeland became the Duchy of Prussia, and the iron cross design that had adorned the flags of the Teutonic Order was later worn by officers under the German Kaiser and during the Third Reich. Even today, it still serves as a symbol of the German army. Before colonizing the world, Europe itself had been brutally colonized.

With the advent of the modern era, when the four tyrannies re-formed in a new configuration, the Western mission project underwent a series of transformations and changes to its image. The missionary became a preacher of reason, bringing enlightenment to the ignorant. He also slipped into the role of the colonialist, who, as Rudyard Kipling, author of *The Jungle Book*, would have it, took upon himself "the white man's burden" to bring the gifts of civilization to the "new caught, sullen peoples, half devil, half child." The missionary later reappeared in the form of the aid worker, showing the underdeveloped how they can finally become like us. He has also been reborn countless times as a missionary of the free market. Although the content of these different missions varies greatly, they tell a coherent story of the superior role and historical task assumed by Western civilization. This narrative was to become an indispensable ideological pillar for the formation and expansion of the modern Megamachine.[18]

Left: Missionaries with the Ibo people (Nigeria) in the 19th century. Right: A US military mission in Haiti (2010)

Part II

The Megamachine

Chapter 6

Monsters

The Re-Formation of Power and the Emergence of the Modern World-System (1348–1648)

Ever since the world was created there has not been witnessed such lamentation and wailing of people accompanied by such great terror. For us wretched mortals there avails no means of flight, since this monster when advancing slowly far exceeds the speed of the swiftest courser.[1]

Leonardo da Vinci

From the late Middle Ages until the end of the Thirty Years' War (1648), the four tyrannies reorganized to become the basis of our current world-system. The foundations of this system are: an economy that aims for the endless accumulation of capital; competing territorial states with centralized armies, police forces and bureaucracies; and an ideology touting the expansion of this system as a blessing on the history of humankind.

While some of these elements were already present in antiquity, they radically reorganized during the modern period to form a *Megamachine* that spread across the globe with breath-taking speed, devouring everything in its path. Driven by the logic of endless financial expansion, it is a monstrous machine that must continually grow in order to exist. The rapid destruction of the natural world and the elimination of other cultures are not just side effects of the system, nor collateral damage. They are the logical consequences of its core functions.

THE EPOCH OF FEAR

Schoolbooks teach us that the early modern period was an era of illumination when humanity finally woke up and broke free from the servility and superstitions of the Middle Ages. The self-assured individual finally appeared on the historical stage, and an era of humanism, science and enlightenment began. When we think of the Renaissance we imagine light-filled spaces like those in Raphael's painting *The School of Athens*, where man shook off his irrational fears and began to explore the world with serene confidence. By contrast, we still refer to medieval times as the "Dark Ages," branded with religious fanaticism, brutality, torture and inquisition.

It is astounding how this image has been imprinted on our minds, even though it is far removed from the historical reality. In fact, the transition to modern times was marked by monstrosities much greater than those of the Middle Ages. Never before in Europe's already brutal history had there been such a massive outbreak of violence as in the early modern period. This culminated with millions dead in the genocide of America's indigenous peoples and the massacres of the Thirty Years' War, which wiped out roughly a third of Europe's population. This devastation was accompanied by the Inquisition and witch trials, which did not reach their dire climaxes in the Middle Ages, but in modern times. Between 1320 and 1420 there were only 36 witch trials throughout Europe, but in the sixteenth and seventeenth centuries, tens of thousands of alleged witches were burned to death.[2] Sadistic punishments such as the wheel and quartering also spread rapidly in the early modern period and continued up until the nineteenth century.[3] Torture became a legal method of interrogation in the sixteenth century, and its use steadily expanded.[4]

As the historian Jean Delumeau illustrates with great detail in his book *La Peur en Occident*, the early modern era was also plagued by widespread collective anxiety disorders. Social and economic realities as well as the collective imagination all turned profoundly gloomy at the beginning of the modern era. From the fourteenth century on, apocalyptic expectations of the end of times condensed into a mass epidemic of anxiety, which was only surpassed by a similarly spreading fear of the Devil. In early medieval church paintings and texts, representations of the Last Days, the Devil and Hell had been of secondary importance. However, with the late Middle Ages and the transition to modern times, dreadful depictions proliferated, which ranged from the visions of Hell on the "Camposanto" in Pisa, to Albrecht Dürer's woodcuts of the Apocalypse, to the phantasmagorical paintings of Hieronymus Bosch.[5] Preachers criss-crossed Europe to announce the imminent end of the world, while lavish theatrical performances detailed the horrors of Hell and the Last Judgment. Martin Luther made predictions of the Apocalypse several times, including for the years 1520 and 1532. Through the fifteenth century invention of the printing press, his end-of-time prophecies reached a wide audience.[6]

Left: Hans Memling's vision of Hell (1470), Center and Right: Hell by Hieronymus Bosch (1500)

With such a gruesome record, why does the early modern period come across as the new era of progress and humanism, and as a step into the light (perhaps with some occasional black marks)? Since every epoch promotes its mythology to justify and glorify itself, modernity also needs its Dark (Middle) Ages to provide contrast to the bright, modern age of liberation. The reason for cultivating this myth is obvious: it is crucial to the West's narrative of being the bearer of progress throughout the history of mankind. But what if our present system was actually built on a nightmare, born of naked violence and sheer despair?

And, instead of liberation there was actually descent into even deeper subjugation? What if civilization did not make progress but systematized barbarism instead? When we seriously address these questions, the legitimacy of our present situation becomes untenable, and we must thoroughly question the foundations of our economy, our state and much more.

The Incubation Period

But how did the apocalyptic phantasms and the explosion of violence come about in the early modern era? And how is this turmoil related to the emergence of the modern world-system that has since spread across the entire planet?

To answer these questions, we must take a step back. With the collapse of the (Western) Roman money-military complex, larger cities gradually disappeared from Central Europe. The ancient money and market economy reverted to a subsistence and commons-based economy.[7] What many historians regard as a descent into the "Dark Ages" actually provided relief for much of the population. The lower classes were freed from extreme exploitation and humiliation as the excessive wealth and power of the upper classes evaporated. The peasants no longer had to finance large armies, bureaucracies and courtiers, but only support their local landlords, which correspondingly lowered the tax burden. Slavery largely disappeared from Europe (with the exception of Spain). The central military power of the empire had collapsed, and with it the ability to enforce taxation and suppress resistance. Since kings and liege lords could no longer command their subordinates at will, as in the Roman Empire, they were forced to make compromises. An example from the early Middle Ages is the Frankish king Chilperic I, who wanted to collect taxes from the citizens of Limoges in 579. However, the citizens decided to burn the tax files, and Chilperic had to promise never to collect taxes again.[8] Such an outcome would have been unthinkable during the Roman Empire, the citizens of Limoges would simply have been crucified. The dispute over taxes and *corvée labor* was the subject of bitter legal disputes between peasants and landlords throughout the Middle Ages.[9] Because landlords did not have convincing force with which to arbitrarily increase levies, they attempted to manipulate weights and measures. This too met with vehement resistance.[10] These disputes, which were by no means always won by the lords, illustrate not only the defiance of the peasants, but also the limited power of the landowners.

The relationship to land and property also changed dramatically. The wealthy could no longer simply buy up land or foreclose on deeply indebted peasants. Land was largely withdrawn from the market and portioned out as fiefs instead. The descendants of Roman war veterans, who had received land for their service, formed a nucleus of the later knighthood and landlords of the Middle Ages. They too were unable to exercise the same level of control over their dependent farmers in the way that Roman landowners or mine operators had been able to subjugate their slaves. Indentured peasants and even serfs worked their plots of land independently, producing for subsistence and paying their loan fees in-kind and with services rendered. In the Middle Ages, Europe was by no means a peasant's paradise. Compared to the era that preceded and the era that followed, however, it was a period during which the power of man over man, and man over nature was relatively limited.

From the tenth century onwards, Europe's agricultural output increased, the population grew rapidly and the standard of living rose for large portions of society. In addition to innovations in agricultural technology, a relatively warm climate, the so-called Medieval Warm Period, had a favorable effect. In many countries, especially in Italy, the culture of independent craftsmanship, organized in guilds, developed in urban areas. The guilds would impose price controls and regulate working conditions. The great Gothic cathedrals are lasting symbols of the prosperity and highly skilled craftsmanship of this era.

During this period of growth, however, there were already signs of increasing social divisions. As we will see later, the gradual re-introduction of the money economy played a role. Furthermore, higher agricultural productivity enabled the landlords, which included the church, to reap disproportionate profits, and to finance luxurious lifestyles to levels unknown in previous centuries. In many areas, the extravagant wealth of high-level church officials was especially galling when contrasted with the poverty of the apostles. A wave of protest movements developed, striving for "apostolic poverty." The central figure in this cause was Francis of Assisi, famous not only for his lack of possessions but also because he talked to birds and had a sibling-like regard for animals. His criticism of hierarchies also extended to his rejection of the fundamental Western concept that man was born to rule over nature.[11] The *spirituali* and the *fraticelli*, for example, who play a prominent role in Umberto Eco's novel *The Name of the Rose*, reference back to Francis. The *fraticelli* attacked not only the church, but also the rich merchants who had seized power in the cities. They were inspired by the apocalyptic teachings of Joachim of Fiore, who had predicted the dawn of a new era for the year 1260.[12] Resistance movements, including the Waldensians and Cathars, also sprang up elsewhere. The subsequent response by secular and church authorities was brutal. The Albigensians in southern France, a branch of the Cathars, were virtually exterminated in a 20-year crusade (1209–29). Subsequently, the pope and the emperor institutionalized the Inquisition and its practice of torture. The line between orthodox believers and heretics was more clearly drawn than ever before, with heresy systematically being defined as teachings that questioned the wealth and power of elites.

The Great Crisis

Growth during the High Middle Ages suddenly ended at the beginning of the fourteenth century. The Warm Period was followed by cold spells, continuous rain and ultimately crop failures. The resulting catastrophic Great Famine from 1315 to 1322 became deeply inscribed in the collective memory. The extent of the famine is shown by the fact that many parents were no longer able to feed their children and abandoned them in the wilderness. The fairy tale of Hansel and Gretel, who were similarly left to starve in the forest, can possibly be traced back to this period. Crime ran rampant, social cohesion became severely frayed and between 10 and 25 percent of the population of Central Europe was wiped out. During the following decades, agriculture was slow to recover and continuing cold spells weakened the population further. This was the situation in which the first horrifying reports emerged of a disease that was to become one of Europe's greatest traumas—the Plague.

From the ports of Venice and Genoa with their connections to international trade, the Black Death spread rapidly across Europe starting in 1348. This epidemic, which eradicated about a third of Europe's remaining population, represented a profound rupture in Western history. Not only the decline in population, but also the collective trauma of plague survivors fundamentally changed European society. Jean Delumeau quotes survivors from the epidemics that afflicted Europe during those years: "While the bodies lay here and there at people's feet, or in houses, always in view, turning the city into a single huge field of corpses, there was something much uglier and much sadder in the mutual anguish and rampant, monstrous suspicion. Not only neighbors, friends and guests were cause for suspicion, but terror was also sparked by husbands and wives, fathers and sons, brothers and sisters."[13] Another eyewitness speaks of the "chaos of the dead and dying, the suffering and the screams, the roar, the horror, the pain and the fears, the loneliness, the imprisonments and the punishments." Delumeau concludes that "the epidemic left survivors with psychological trauma."[14]

Despite the devastation and mental anguish, there was a positive side for peasants who survived the Black Death. To the detriment of the feudal elites, the balance of power in Europe had been radically changed. The landlords' income was directly dependent on agricultural yields, which now melted away due to depopulation and the deterioration of properties. The surviving peasants now had much greater bargaining power over the landowners. Whereas before there had been too many workers for too little land, now there were too few workers for too much land. Strengthened by this new situation, peasants united against the landlords more effectively and with more self-confidence. A renewed and much more massive wave of popular uprisings swept through Europe that aimed for a class-free, egalitarian society.[15] In Flanders (present-day Belgium), as early as 1323, peasants and craftsmen became allies, wresting the city of Bruges away from the hands of wealthy merchants and occupying it for several years. In the 1370s, the rebels succeeded in conquering the city of Ghent and almost the entire county of Flanders. At the time, it was the richest region in Europe after northern Italy. In Florence, rebel textile workers were able to temporarily take over the government in 1378, which sent a shockwave through the ruling class. In England, the Peasants' Revolt was the largest of its kind in the country's history. At first, the protests were only against war taxes and the landlords' attempts to lower wages to pre-plague levels. But as the movement gained momentum, culminating in the occupation of the Tower of London in 1381, the demands also expanded. Now there were calls for the abolition of serfdom, the right to local self-administration and for the complete abolition of secular and ecclesiastical authorities. Because the peasants had the upper hand, the English king agreed to many of their demands—but only until he could muster enough soldiers to brutally crush the uprising. Some decades later, the Bohemian Hussites, invoking the name of Jan Hus, who had run afoul of the Inquisition, set out to create an egalitarian community. They founded the town of Tábor in 1420 and assumed control over large portions of Bohemia and Silesia for more than 10 years. The state and the church needed five crusades to suppress this uprising. There were similar rebellions in northern France (1358), which could only be put down with difficulty using massive force.[16] Europe had never experienced such a wave of revolts that swept across the continent to envelop the primary centers of economic and political power.[17]

The Birth of the Monster

The feudal elites were confronted with a double threat, massive uprisings on the one hand, and the loss of feudal income on the other. Shocked by the force of egalitarian movements, they frantically sought ways to hold on to privileged positions. Their desperation must be taken into account in order to understand the emergence of the modern world-system, which today operates under various labels ("Western civilization," "modernity," "capitalism," etc.). Contrary to what the myth of modernity would lead us to believe, this system did not unfold from an innocent thirst for knowledge and adventure. Nor was it about "explorers" and "pioneers" who wished to shake off the narrow-mindedness of the Middle Ages. It was an endeavor by elites to stifle emerging egalitarian aspirations.[18] For this, however, there was no master plan. No one, not the bankers, the church, the landed gentry, nor the sovereigns could foresee the new order that emerged after 3 centuries of social struggle and eventually conquered the world. Countless individual steps had finally converged to forge a single system that would produce the monsters of modernity.

The Arsenal of Venice

It was the Italian maritime republics, especially Venice and Genoa, that provided fertile soil for germinating the four tyrannies.[19] After the collapse of the Western Roman Empire, Europe was left on the periphery of the medieval world trade system. The major centers had shifted back to the East: to Constantinople, Alexandria and Aleppo, and later to Baghdad and Cairo. From these focal points, goods were exchanged with China, India, Persia and North Africa.[20] Arab traders used highly developed accounting techniques and financial instruments long before the Europeans, including cashless payment transactions by check (Arabic, "saqq").

However, because the goods traded were mainly luxury items for the wealthy, this international trading system was not yet a world market in the modern sense. Trade in basic foodstuffs was not profitable, as the means of transport were slow and expensive. Only high-quality goods with a low weight-to-value ratio, such as precious metals, silk, pigments, spices, porcelain and glass, were lucrative. There was practically no international division of labor, as in modern times, and most medieval populations remained outside the market.

Initially an outpost of the Byzantine Empire, Venice had participated in this system from the tenth century on. Later, Genoa also joined. The profits from Oriental trade soon made the Venetian and Genoese merchants the richest people in Europe— wealthy enough to loan money to kings and emperors.[21] For such small city states, Venice and Genoa had concentrated a remarkable amount of economic and military power within a very narrow social stratum. These independent cities did not have to answer to any superior central power; neither the pope, emperors, kings nor bishops. The merchants themselves formed the government, leaving everyone else in these "republics" with little political say. The main foundation for Venice's and Genoa's concentration of political power was the military. Their merchant fleets were also their navies, and each trading voyage was accompanied by a massive military presence. With its shipyard, called the "Arsenal," Venice created Europe's largest industrial complex up until the Industrial Revolution. Three centuries before the invention of the modern factory, mechanical assembly lines were already being employed in a three-shift system around the clock.[22] At its peak, the Arsenal produced a fleet of more than 3000 ships of varying tonnage, and Venice, with a population of about 150,000, maintained a navy of 36,000 sailors.[23] Those who controlled this massive military might also held the reins on trading capital. There was virtually no difference between military and economic power.

This point was decisive for the history that followed and also for how we regard the prevailing narrative about the spread of "free markets." Those who cultivated European market expansion at the threshold of modern times were not peaceful merchants seeking to avoid state interference. In reality, they were the grandees of highly militarized city states, who, from the outset, used swords and cannons to assert their commercial interests.[24] For Arab merchants, by contrast, it was quite a different story. Although their commercial culture in the Middle Ages was more advanced than the European trading system, it did not resort to the exertion of physical force and, in general, was kept at a remove from state power.[25]

Combining economic and military power with missionary ideology, the crusades also played an important role in the rise of the maritime republics. Both Venice and Genoa provided massive military and financial support for these expeditions, which the weaker emperors and popes could not finance by themselves. The fact that sovereigns depended heavily on private capital already suggests where the new centers of European power lay. In return for their support, the Genoese and Venetian merchants were granted trade bases, monopolies and other privileges in the eastern Mediterranean, especially in Syria and Palestine.

Genoa's engagement included the first crusade and the conquest of the port city of Acre in Galilee in 1104, for which it received a third of the port's revenues.[26] For centuries after, the Lebanese city of Byblos was completely owned by the Genoese Embriaco family. Anything but a noble courtly adventure, the crusade led to the enormous enrichment of Genoese merchants and was the basis for much of the city's subsequent power. In 1099, William of Tyre wrote an eyewitness account of the massacre at the Al-Aqsa Mosque in Jerusalem:

> *After the other leaders had slain all whom they encountered in the various parts of the city, they learned that many had fled for refuge to the sacred precincts of the Temple. Thereupon as with one accord they hurried thither. A crowd of knights and foot soldiers was introduced, who massacred all those who had taken refuge there. No mercy was shown to anyone, and the whole place was flooded with the blood of the victims.*
>
> *It was indeed the righteous judgment of God which ordained that those who had profaned the sanctuary of the Lord by their superstitious rites and had caused it to be an alien place to His faithful people should expiate their sin by death and, by pouring our their own blood, purify the sacred precincts.*
>
> *It was impossible to look upon the vast numbers of the slain without horror; everywhere lay fragments of human bodies, and the very ground was covered with the blood of the slain. It was not alone the spectacle of headless bodies and mutilated limbs strewn in all directions that roused horror in all who looked upon them. Still more dreadful was it to gaze upon the victors themselves, dripping with blood from head to foot, an ominous sight which brought terror to all who met them. It is reported that within the Temple enclosure alone about ten thousand infidels perished, in addition to those who lay slain everywhere throughout the city in the streets and squares, the number of whom was estimated as no less.*

The rest of the soldiers roved through the city in search of wretched survivors who might be hiding in the narrow portals and byways to escape death. These were dragged out into the public view and slain like sheep. Some formed into bands and broke into houses where they laid violent hands on the heads of families, on their wives, children, and their entire households. These victims were either put to the sword or dashed headlong to the ground from some elevated place so that they perished miserably. Each marauder claimed as his own in perpetuity the particular house which he had entered, together with all it contained. For before the capture of the city the pilgrims had agreed that, after it had been taken by force, whatever each man might win for himself should be his forever by right of possession, without molestation.[27]

The inhabitants of Palestine had just received a taste of what the Americas would later experience to an even greater extent: the tremendous amount of destructive violence produced by the combination of capitalism, militarism and Western missionary zeal. The crusades revealed on a smaller scale what would later expand out into a global system. The fact that William of Tyre describes the massacre in the mosque as "God's righteous judgment" shows how effectively extreme violence was legitimized by the ideology of Christian universalism.

By participating in numerous crusades, Venice was also able to secure critical privileges and trading bases. The Venetians achieved their greatest coup during the Fourth Crusade, for which they provided extensive loans and a fleet of ships. Originally, the Franconian crusaders had targeted Egypt, but they only made it as far as Christian Constantinople, which they plundered in 1204. Political and theological strife served as a pretext to invade the city and loot the vast treasures of silver and gold that Byzantium had accumulated over the centuries. The crusaders murdered and raped thousands, set fire to the famous library and desecrated Christian, Muslim and Jewish sanctuaries alike. Before the raid, the distribution of loot had been contractually agreed to. This included awarding Venetian financiers three-eighths of the Byzantine Empire as a "return on investment."[28] Many of the treasures still viewed by tourists today in the Doge's Palace in Venice originated from this raid, which gave a large boost to the development of early Venetian capitalism. The newly opened trade route to China was now of particular importance. The Byzantine Empire, however, never recovered from this blow and was later conquered by the Ottomans in the fifteenth century.

In the thirteenth century, the rival maritime republics of Venice and Genoa not only controlled the trade routes in the Mediterranean, but also governed numerous colonies stretching from Morocco to the Crimea. From these bases, they could secure their monopolies over corresponding trade routes. Monopolies (or oligopolies) are not only a means of getting rid of unwanted competitors. They are also a basic prerequisite for making profits large enough to sustain a lasting accumulation of capital. Where there is a truly free market, which means unrestricted competition, prices and profits quickly fall to a point where major reinvestments are no longer worthwhile.[29] Monopolies, on the other hand, are made secure by state support, whether by force, as in the case of Venice and Genoa, through patents, or through massive subsidies, as was done in later epochs.

By combining physical and economic violence, powerful Venetian and Genoese merchants were able to accumulate enormous amounts of capital in private hands and seek out ever more investment opportunities. Not only was this capital used for further trading activities, it was also invested in Europe's rapidly expanding business of war. Both the Hundred Years' War and the colonization of America were largely financed by Italian trading capital. It was no coincidence that Columbus came from Genoa.[30]

The Reinvention of War

Just as merchants had to use massive physical force to advance their economic power, conversely, sovereigns needed trading capital to expand their military power. In the modern era, this interdependence eventually evolved into a system where the market and the state were inseparably intertwined, albeit with different roles than in antiquity.

But this was still a long way off. Warfare in the Middle Ages was subject to a number of important restrictions. While free peasants were obligated to serve in the military, princes and kings could only keep them away from their fields for a short time. Otherwise, they would risk crop failures, famine and a loss of their own income. Indeed, most peasants were not free, but tied to feudal lords as *villeins* or serfs. This meant that their military obligations had to be fulfilled by their ruling lords, the knights. The duties of these knights were also limited, with no campaigns in foreign territories allowed and a cap of 40 days active duty per year.[31] Wars of aggression could hardly be fought this way, and for all these reasons, medieval combat usually entailed short campaigns by small armies.

Territorial rulers tried again and again to escape these restrictions by enlisting mercenary armies, but with only sporadic success. With the feudal system in crisis and resistance movements on the rise in the fourteenth century, the search for solutions intensified. Princes and land owners increasingly sought new sources of income by conquering and plundering foreign territories. Simultaneously, larger armed forces were also needed to quell the spreading uprisings. But there were three things missing to build effective mercenary armies capable of coping with these tasks. First, money for wages was needed— more precisely silver, which was chronically scarce in Europe. Second, few people were willing and able to supply the army with food and materials in exchange for silver money, a commodity of little use in a subsistence economy. Third, there was also a lack of people willing to take silver as payment for risking their lives and killing others. Why would farmers and craftsmen who could support themselves and live in fairly secure communities be willing to leave their families and farms to die for the ambitions of a prince? The economy of war not only requires monetization, it also needs a large number of uprooted and desperate people who have no choice but to gamble their lives for money.

To address the first problem, sovereigns and wealthy merchants worked intensively to develop new silver mines. From the twelfth century onwards, significant new silver discoveries ensured a growing cash flow to princes and merchants. But cash was not enough; the army had to have something to spend it on. As shown in ancient times, a very effective way to get people to produce for the market instead of personal use was to switch tax payments from in-kind to coins. For many centuries, most of the taxes in Europe were paid in-kind or through labor for the local landlord. From the twelfth century on, however, taxes were increasingly levied with coinage.[32] Now farmers and craftsmen were contributing to the very war apparatus that had been built to oppress them. With enforced monetization, financing was assured for the standing armies and administrative organs necessary for the effective collection of taxes. This cycle formed the basis for the emergence of the modern territorial state. Having broken down with the decline of the Roman Empire, it took centuries for this process to be restarted, as the peasants resisted it bitterly for good reasons.

Regarding the third problem—mustering a sufficient number of combatants—the princes benefited from a peculiarity of medieval inheritance law. In many regions of Europe only first-born sons could inherit land, while other siblings had to find a livelihood elsewhere. Some ended up as craftsmen in cities or as simple farm workers, but there was always a number of men with no income, especially during times of rapid population growth. Before invading England in 1066, William the Conqueror had recruited just such landless people for his Norman army from across the northern half of Europe. As the historian Erica Schoenberger put it, this campaign was a kind of "crash course in market economy" for the conquered territories.[33] The baggage train and retinue of camp followers, which was often larger than the armies themselves, functioned as a wandering marketplace. Everything was on offer for money, from shoes and weapons to sexual services.

Once begun, such wars feed themselves by destroying livelihoods and creating secondary "armies" of uprooted people. However, William's campaign, considered one of the greatest military operations of the Middle Ages, had an army of just 7000 men. This was still tiny compared to the forces that fought wars in the early modern period.

Mercenary combat reached a new level during the Hundred Years' War between England and France (1337–1453), which transformed Western Europe into a true war economy and enormously increased the tax burden.[34] It was not by chance that the war began during an agrarian crisis when feudal lords increasingly relied on "gangster tactics" and raids to secure their incomes.[35] When the war started, Edward III's mercenary army was financed with 150,000 gold florin by the Florentine banks Bardi and Peruzzi, among others. That corresponds to about $300 million US dollars in today's currency.[36]

The Hundred Years' War radically changed Central European society. Unlike most medieval wars in Europe, in which knights followed rules of combat and the number of dead was limited, there was now a scorched earth policy. The army of the "Black Prince," Edward's son, devastated large parts of southern France in 1355 and left behind countless plundered and burned-out villages. The French also fielded mercenary armies, the so-called Armagnacs, who spread fear and terror with hitherto unknown brutality. During this period, France lost about half of its population to war and the Plague, including as much as three-quarters of the population of Normandy.[37] When the war ended, the situation barely improved as unemployed mercenaries raped and burned their way across the countryside. Ultimately, the French king Charles VII drew on some of these scattered killers to create the nucleus of the first standing army in Europe since the fall of the Roman Empire.[38]

Many of the mercenaries who had served in the Hundred Years' War later moved on to other countries, especially Italy, where combat for hire had developed into a flourishing business.[39] For example, the Englishman John Hawkwood, who had fought under the Black Prince, founded the notorious "White Company" and offered its services alternately to Pisa, Milan, Florence and the pope during their internecine wars. Florence finally commissioned Hawkwood's exclusive service for 130,000 gold ducats (about $20 million in today's currency) and dedicated a fresco to him in a prominent place in the cathedral.

Hawkwood was by no means the only one to get rich in this business. Almost all affluent city states engaged military entrepreneurs, the *condottieri*, whose companies, the *compagnie di ventura*, hired mercenaries for their wars. These Renaissance Blackwater LLCs recruited combatants from all over Europe, including England, France, Flanders, Germany and Switzerland. The mercenary market was one of the first, largest and most lucrative European markets.

Many of the condottieri also pursued political careers. The war entrepreneur Francesco Sforza, for instance, who had waged war for Milan against Venice and then conversely for Venice against Milan, became the founder of the Sforza ducal dynasty, which ruled Milan and Lombardy for almost a century. Some of the most prestigious artists worked at his court. Leonardo da Vinci was in the service of Francesco's son Ludovico for about 20 years and developed military machines for him. Careers like the Sforzas' were typical of the early modern period, and they vividly illustrate how the rise of modern state power was largely due to private companies in the business of mass murder, looting, rape and blackmail. The following inscription is said to have been written on the armor of the German mercenary leader Werner von Urslingen, who fought for Pisa, Florence and other cities: "Duke Guarnieri, head of the *gran compagnia*, enemy of God, mercy and compassion."[40]

This business model reached a high point in the Thirty Years' War (1618–48) with Wallenstein's private army. Responsible for the devastation of large parts of Central Europe, this force of 100,000 men was by far the largest business enterprise in Europe. Until the early twentieth century, there had never been a company that could claim so many employees and so much revenue.[41]

Wallenstein offered to organize a private army for the Catholic emperor, who could not afford his own large military force. Because the sovereign was unable to provide payment until after the conquered territories had been plundered, Wallenstein himself had to fund the campaign up front. The necessary pre-financing was provided by the Dutch banker Hans de Witte (ironically a Calvinist), who found backers in major financial centers such as Nuremberg, Antwerp and Hamburg.[42] Because the Protestant financing of a Catholic war—against Protestants— never became an issue, it is clear that this war was not primarily about religion.

Wallenstein's company also boasted an extensive armaments production facility, located in his Duchy of Friedland, Bohemia, that the emperor had awarded him in return for his investment risk. Wallenstein's goal was to produce all the equipment and food for the mercenaries himself. That way, he could earn from the war in more ways than one. Not only did he pay himself a salary, but much of his fighters' earnings went into his purse as well. They purchased everything they needed from his company: zwieback (Wallenstein's invention), beer (on which Wallenstein had a monopoly), uniforms and, of course, weapons and ammunition.[43] The heart of this military-industrial complex was the production of iron and armaments in Raspenau (today's Raspenava in the Czech Republic), where guns and ammunition were manufactured for the largest army of the early modern era.

Resurrection of the Metallurgical Complex

Fed by the combination of trading capital and mercenaries, the rebirth of the money-war complex required a revival of mining and metallurgy. The soldiers needed armor and weapons, but also money in the form of silver coins. Without large quantities of metal, sovereigns could neither consolidate nor expand their fragile power base. It is therefore no wonder that these rulers promoted mining through a variety of measures, including tax and customs privileges, the granting of monopolies and expropriations, all of which are methods still used today.

But the resurrection of the metallurgical complex was anything but easy. After the collapse of Rome, mining and metal production in Europe had been largely abandoned. In the tenth century, a Bavarian abbot wrote, "We ask you to send some copper, tin and lead, because none of these can be obtained in our country at any price."[44] In particular, precious metals were in chronically short supply in medieval Western Europe. The old mines were exhausted, and the trade deficit with the Orient caused most of the meager silver reserves to flow east. The remainder was taken by plundering Vikings. Only the large silver discoveries in 938 at Goslar's Rammelsberg (Germany) brought relief, forming the material basis for increased monetization during the High Middle Ages.[45] However, medieval mining was burdened by considerable technical difficulties. Deeper excavation meant more flooding in the tunnels. Significant efforts went into the development of new pumping systems, but ore yields still continued to decline. The renewed silver shortage was temporarily improved in 1168 by the epochal discoveries in Freiberg (Saxony).[46] This find not only made the Saxon dukes and kings rich and powerful—in fact the most powerful potentates in Germany—it also triggered a virtual silver rush in Central Europe. This resulted in further large discoveries in Bohemia (Kutná Hora, 1298), Serbia and Bosnia, providing the monetary basis for a massive expansion of the money-war economy.[47]

Armor and Cannons: The Industrialization of Mining

Driven by the growing demand for armor, and later cannons, iron and copper mining also experienced a strong upswing in the late Middle Ages and early modern period. At first, metal production was carried out by self-employed cutters, blacksmiths and farmers for whom mining was a sideline. However, the relative independence of early metallurgists soon came to an end. The deeper that miners had to dig to get the ore, the more expensive the technology became, leading to higher investment costs. Shafts had to be dug several hundred meters deep, which in turn required supporting structures, transport mechanisms, ventilation and above all drainage systems. Such installations could not be achieved by independent miners, but required massive investments, large-scale logistics and complex technical equipment. There was a rapid rise in demand for military equipment, but the supply of metals continued to shrink due to technical hurdles. Feverish efforts were subsequently made to find both financial and technical solutions. This pressure to innovate was ultimately one of the critical driving forces behind the emergence of modern, large-scale technology. For the first time, elevators and rails—centuries before the construction of surface railways—came into use. For water drainage, engineers developed some of the most complex mechanisms of the era, including the water-lifting wheel at Schwaz (in today's Austria), which was regarded as the "eighth wonder of the world." The device replaced 600 water carriers and required only two people to operate.[48] Centuries later, such machines became the model for the first wave of (mainly hydraulic-powered) industrialization in England.

Early on, there were still cooperatives of miners and wealthy monasteries (especially Cistercian) who advanced metallurgical technology and made the necessary investments. But as their financial strength grew insufficient, the mining cooperatives sought fresh money by gradually transforming themselves into corporations under the control of large banks. Thus, the once independent craftsmen gradually became dependent wage earners.[49]

The driving force behind all these changes was the growing demand for silver and armaments. Initially, it was armor in the original, literal sense: the early modern, steel-plated body protection that replaced medieval chain mail tunics. Fully sheathed from head to toe and mounted on their likewise armored horses, the combatants of early modernity looked like a mixture of cyborg and Darth Vader—shiny steel human machines that might have come from another galaxy to colonize planet Earth. This is exactly how they appeared to the inhabitants of Mexico in 1519. As a contemporary reported, they sat on "deer as tall as housetops," completely covered, so that only their eyes could be seen. Moctezuma, the ruler of Tenochtitlán, reportedly believed they were the armies of the god Quetzalcoatl.[50]

Left: Knights in plate armor (16th century). Right: Cyborgs

The manufacture of this armor consumed large quantities of iron. But the real force behind the boom in metal was an invention that radically changed the world's fate—black powder. In his book *A Cultural History of the Modern Age*, Egon Friedell described it as one of the three "Dark Arts" which, along with alchemy and printing, heralded the dawn of modern times.[51] The formula for black powder had come to Europe from China and had been known there since at least the thirteenth century. In the early phase of the Hundred Years' War, firearms were being used on a large scale for the first time. However, it would take another hundred years before cannons were powerful enough to actually break through castle walls. This would spark a momentous revolution not only in warfare but also in the entire political and economic system. In 1450, French guns destroyed 60 English fortresses in just four days, driving the English out of northern France. Three years later, half-ton iron cannonballs, fired from eight-meter-long barrels, bombarded the walls of Constantinople and sealed the fall of the Byzantine (Eastern Roman) Empire.[52]

These events triggered a rapid arms race on a level the world had never seen before. No sovereign could escape this "do-or-die" logic, and those who could not keep pace soon faded out of the picture. Everywhere in Europe new technologies were feverishly developed to hasten the production of larger numbers of better, lighter and less expensive cannons. The mining region in the mountains of Saxony and Bohemia developed into the most important center for metal and armaments production in Central Europe. At the same time, a large military-industrial complex, known as "The Weald," was established in southern England, where iron mines, furnaces, foundries and hammer mills worked around the clock.[53]

Such large-scale armaments production required completely different logistics from the small-scale village mining and forging of the High Middle Ages. A great deal of resources and personnel had to be mobilized, both for the armaments industry itself and for the construction of new fortresses that could withstand cannon fire. It is obvious that this could not work on the basis of the medieval economy where peasants stuck to their land.[54] Similar to the effects of mercenary armies, the armaments industry also became a driving force for the rapid monetization of the economy and the enforcement of wage labor.[55]

The arms race also instigated a financial race. The decisive factor in war was no longer how skilled and motivated the soldiers might be. Instead, it was all about investment in the arms economy.[56] Therefore, if princes and kings wished to survive, they had to focus all their energies on the accumulation of capital within their territories. War and military power became a function of abstract money multiplication.[57]

Deforestation

For both man and nature, the consequences of the armaments boom were enormous. As early as the sixteenth century, mining was responsible for large-scale forced migration. The following testimony is from a hearing on the effects of the iron industry on the area around The Weald:

> *All the inhabitants of the towns and villages shall be driven to seek their living in other places and there utterly to forsake their dwelling, if the mills and furnaces be suffered to remain. Many a thousand not yet born feel with their parents the great hurt and incommodity engendered by their continuance.*[58]

The mining industry itself was responsible for generating many of the uprooted and indigent people who would later have to make a living as industrial wage earners. To operate the blast furnaces, rivers were dammed and diverted to drive the bellows. This caused outrage among farmers who lost their irrigation sources. In 1556, the physician and pharmacist Georgius Agricola summarized the complaints of mining opponents in the most comprehensive book on metallurgy at the time, *De Re Metallica*:

> *Forests and groves are cut down to provide the huge amount of wood needed for buildings, equipment and melting ore. Eradicating*

forests also means the extermination of birds and other animals. Washing the ore poisons streams and rivers, which either kills the fish or drives them away. People living on these lands are caught in a dilemma. It is in exactly these devastated fields, forests, streams and rivers that they must find the things they need to live on. With no wood, they must also spend more to build their houses. It is abundantly clear that mining for ore does more damage than it is worth.[59]

Without changing a word, this description still applies today to the current ecological and social destruction caused by mining in Peru, India or the Congo. After living for a long time in Joachimsthal (Jáchymov, Bohemia), where the largest silver mines in Europe were located, Agricola knew first-hand what he was talking about. It is also where the name "Thaler" and later "dollar" came from. Despite the obvious devastation, Agricola remained a vehement advocate for the mining industry. The arguments he used for justification still sound very familiar today: "Without these metals, people would lead the most horrible and miserable lives among wild animals."[60] He continues: "With precious metals extracted from the ore, many birds, edible animals and fish can be bought elsewhere and brought here to the mountains."[61]

The subsequent history of The Weald shows that this mode of production ultimately destroys its own economic basis.[62] In the seventeenth century, ship building and charcoal manufacture led to the drastic overexploitation of forests, resulting in scarce supplies of wood. This caused charcoal prices to skyrocket, bringing the English arms industry to the brink of collapse. English guns were no longer competitive. As a consequence, Sweden was able to take the lead in cannon manufacture with its large iron and copper deposits and expansive, untouched forests. This industrial complex was also the basis for Sweden's military success in the Thirty Years' War. To further reduce production costs, prisoners of war were sent to the mines as slave labor.[63] Later, it was only the use of bituminous coal as an alternative to charcoal that enabled England to resurrect itself as a great imperial power. Hard coal solved the modern economy's dilemma of ecological overexploitation by postponing it. The boundaries of the natural environment were pushed back by the extraction of resources that had been created underground over millions of years. Today, with looming climate disaster and the limits of fossil resources in sight, it is highly questionable whether industrial civilization will be given yet another respite.

The Role of Banks

The development of finance in Europe was closely linked to both the war economy and mining. Banking was first established in the twelfth century in Genoa, Venice, Florence and Siena, initially as a side business of the large trading houses. It was here that the enormous sums of money generated by merchant magnates and their combat fleets were collected. Founded in 1407, the Banco di San Giorgio in Genoa became the most powerful financial institution of its time alongside the Medici Bank in Florence. As in Florence, one could hardly tell apart the government in Genoa from the bank's board of directors.[64] Some of the Genoese colonies were directly owned and governed by the bank, such as Corsica and the Crimea. The bank became one of the most important lenders to kings, popes and emperors to finance their wars. For instance, the Spanish crown and the German emperor were two such sovereigns who were chronically indebted to the Genoese bankers.

While financing wars was potentially lucrative, it was also a risky business. The Florentine banks Bardi and Peruzzi, the two largest banks of the fourteenth century with branches all over Europe, found this out the hard way. They went bankrupt in 1345, when the English king was slow to service his loans for the Hundred Years' War. Hans de Witte, who financed Wallenstein's private army three centuries later, also miscalculated and committed suicide in 1630 when bankruptcy became inevitable.

Therefore, the cleverest bankers found other ways to benefit from their lending power when dealing with heads of state. In return for loans, they would demand monopolies on spices, wool, silk and especially metals. A master of this strategy was Jakob Fugger of Augsburg, who rose to become the most powerful banker in the world during the sixteenth century. When the Imperial Diet convened in his private residence, it was Fugger who selected the next emperor of the Holy Roman Empire by loaning his favorite royal candidate enough bribe money to buy off the electors. For his financial services, the banker demanded monopoly rights, especially for mining. This enabled him to establish an enormous mining company with control over the entire production chain: from mining, to smelting, to processing and finally the sales of the finished product. In addition to a quasi-monopoly on copper within the empire,[65] Fugger had extensive mining rights for silver. In Tyrol (Austria) he controlled the Schwaz mine, the largest silver mine in the world at the time.[66] The silver produced there was to become the central monetary source for the rise of the Habsburgs as a world-dominating dynasty.

As a combined mining-and-finance concern, Fugger not only loaned the Habsburg emperor Charles V enough money to cover his wars and courtly lifestyle, but he also supplied the copper necessary for producing armaments—again, paid for on loan. From Fugger's point of view, the emperor was like a geyser of money, which magically grew and grew, while the emperor, despite lucrative conquests in America, fell ever deeper into debt.[67] In fact, the early modern war economy can be seen as a system driven by the logic of abstract capital accumulation in the European financial centers—including the genocide in Latin America, which was financed by the banks of Genoa and Augsburg.[68]

Unleashing the Monster

Starting in 1453, European magnates were faced with a problem. Until then, the Asian trade routes had been an important engine for accumulating capital. After the Ottomans conquered Constantinople, however, the routes were blocked or proved to be no longer lucrative, which triggered a feverish race to find a sea route to India and East Asia. The Portuguese had been working at it for a long time and had already built a number of military bases on the coast of West Africa. However, it was not until 1498 that Vasco da Gama finally reached India. Six years earlier, Spain had commissioned a Genoese mercenary, adventurer and pirate named Cristoforo Colombo, alias Christopher Columbus, to seek a western sea route to India. On October 12, 1492, he came ashore at the Bahamas, thinking that he had indeed reached India. This date is still celebrated today as an official holiday in many countries: as Columbus Day in the USA, as Fiesta Nacional in Spain and Día de la Raza in many Latin American countries. Venezuela, by contrast, renamed it "Day of Indigenous Resistance" in 2002. Numerous monuments are dedicated to Columbus all over the world, and he is often portrayed in films as a heroic explorer. For example, the DVD series "Animated Hero Classics" (for children aged 8 and over) presents Columbus as a naive young man whose idealism and childlike spirit of discovery opened royal hearts and helped him find a way across the ocean.

It is no wonder, however, that the film ends just as Columbus reaches the "New World." The producers obviously did not want their young viewers to see what happened next. As the local inhabitants welcomed Columbus with open arms, the Spaniards were harboring devious intentions. Columbus noted in the logbook, "With 50 men, we could overpower the lot and do with them as we please."[69] During the first landings, he already took numerous people captive to extort information about gold deposits. But the people had no information to give. In order to appease his European investors, Columbus kidnapped 500 men to take back to Spain as slaves, of which 200 died during the crossing. To finance a second trip, he promised the Spanish crown and Italian creditors "as much gold and as many slaves as you like." This put him and his crew under considerable pressure to keep this promise at all costs and to generate a return on the capital investment.

The second journey marked the beginning of what was probably the greatest genocide humanity had yet experienced. Because the Spaniards' search for gold had been initially unsuccessful, they ordered all men over 14 on the island of Hispaniola (today Haiti) to deliver a certain amount of gold every three months. Those who failed to do so had their hands cut off and were left to bleed to death. There was little or no gold to be found on Haiti, so the indigenous Arawaks fled to the mountains where the Spaniards hunted them down. Those who were caught were either hanged or burned alive, which ultimately motivated the Arawaks to commit mass suicides. They often even killed their own children to keep them from falling into the hands of the Spaniards. In just two years, half of Haiti's 250,000 people had been annihilated. But that was only the beginning. Since there was so little gold to be collected, the Spaniards decided to put the Arawaks to work on plantations as slaves. Under these conditions, virtually all of them died. In 1515 there were still 50,000 Haitians left; in 1550 only 500.[70]

From Mexico to Peru, it was the same story wherever the Spaniards went. No one will ever know the exact numbers of the genocide, but 150 years after Columbus, an estimated 50 million inhabitants of South and Central America had been reduced to just 3 million. Since the beginning of the *Conquista*, historians have repeatedly tried to deny or trivialize this genocide. The most popular argument is that most indigenous people died unintentionally from imported diseases. Even if this were true for 90 percent of the population (for which there is no evidence), there would still be several million people who were deliberately murdered or worked to death. As the American historian David Stannard correctly points out, the deadly epidemics were often caused by the inhumane living and working conditions that were forced upon millions of indigenous people.[71] The motive behind attempts to play the facts down is obvious. To admit to genocide would destroy the European myth of moral superiority that has been used to justify Western expansion for the last 500 years.

The numbers associated with this genocide cannot fully describe the hell on earth the Spaniards created in the conquered territories. The Spanish Bishop Bartolomé de Las Casas, initially a participant in the Conquista who later became its most famous critic, stresses the unprecedented level of cruelty:

> The Spaniards do nothing save tear the natives to shreds, murder them and inflict upon them untold misery, suffering and distress, tormenting, harrying and persecuting them mercilessly.[72]

Las Casas describes some of the "ingenious methods of torture they have invented" in detail:

> They laid wagers on whether they could manage to slice a man in two at a stroke, or cut an individual's head from his body, or disembowel him with a single blow of their axes. They grabbed suckling infants by the feet and, ripping them from their mothers' breasts, dashed them headlong against the rocks. Others, laughing and joking all the while, threw them over their shoulders into a river. [...]
> They spared no one, erecting especially wide gibbets on which they could string their victims up with their feet just off the ground and then burn them alive thirteen at a time, in honour of our Saviour and the twelve Apostles, or tie dry straw to their bodies and set fire to it. Some they chose to keep alive and simply cut their wrists, leaving their hands dangling, saying to them: 'Take this letter' — meaning that their sorry condition would act as a warning to those hiding in the hills.[73]

The extreme sadism in these descriptions demands an explanation. How could the Spaniards have behaved so monstrously, and not just occasionally but systematically?

We have already seen that the conquistadors were driven by the international money and debt machine. Not only for their own enrichment, but also to pay off their debts and interest to investors in Genoa, Augsburg and Antwerp, they extracted the maximum from the subdued people, used torture to get information about gold reserves and spread fear and horror to force into submission those who resisted. The whole Conquista was based on a chain of indebtedness. Ordinary soldiers went into debt to buy their equipment; commanders like Hernán Cortés were heavily in debt for pre-financing their expeditions; and at the end of the chain was the crown, who was further indebted to the big banks.[74] But this still does not explain it all. To understand the extreme sadism of the Spaniards, we must look at the history of the perpetrators and their society.

Spain had just fought a centuries-long bloody war of conquest—the *Reconquista*—against the Muslim Moors, who had ushered in an era of cultural progress, economic prosperity and relative religious tolerance in al-Andalus, the southern part of Spain. Inspired by a mixture of religious fanaticism and greed, supported by the popes and financed by Genoese banks, the northern Spanish princes fought doggedly until they finally destroyed this culture in 1492. Both Muslims and Jews were expelled from Spain. Having been in a constant state of armed conflict, Spain had turned into a military society in which generations of people were raised on war and knew hardly anything else. We know from other militarized societies that violence penetrates deeply into families and affects the upbringing of children, leaving a lasting mark on personality development. In this context, it is illuminating to note the Spaniards' indignation that the original inhabitants of America refused to beat their children. For example, the Jesuits persistently tried to force indigenous people to publicly chastise their children.[75] The culture of violence that the Spaniards brought with them was anchored at various levels in their economic and political structures and had also left a deeply traumatic impression on their families.

The third decisive reason for the exceptional cruelty of the conquistadors is ideological. The crusade massacre at the Al-Aqsa Mosque had already shown how the Christian claim to universalistic truth could be used to justify violence, both for the perpetrators among themselves and with regard to the victims and the general public. Regardless of how inhuman their deeds may be, believers who receive "authority from on high" and see themselves as part of a worldwide mission are capable of overcoming the last of their scruples. Columbus himself believed that his actions were part of a scheme for apocalyptic salvation — and this belief happened to fit perfectly with the monetary and military goals of his clients.

The main driving force of the Conquista was the enormous demand in Europe for the precious metals needed to expand the money-war complex. The Europeans' thirst for gold is described by an Aztec contemporary as follows: "They lift up the gold as if they were monkeys, with expressions of joy, as if it put new life into them and lit up their hearts. They crave gold like hungry swine."[76] The Spanish conquistador Hernán Cortés himself reportedly said: "I and my companions suffer from a disease of the heart which can be cured only with gold."

For 50 years, the Spaniards devastated half the continent in search of precious metals. Finally, they found a 5000-meter-high mountain in the area of today's Bolivia, which in the following years was to become the largest silver mine in the world: the Cerro Rico. In a short time, the little town of Potosí at the foot of the mountain transmuted into one of the richest cities in the world, growing larger than even Paris, Rome or Madrid. Some streets were actually paved with silver, and more than 600 richly decorated churches and dozens of luxurious gambling houses were built. Behind all of this wealth was the hell of the mines, where tens of thousands of indigenous people were forced to work at digging and smelting.[77] Most of them died at their work due to cave-ins, flooded shafts, mercury poisoning, temperature changes from the glowing heat inside the tunnels and freezing cold outside, and finally exhaustion and emaciation. A monk from the region described Potosí as "the mouth of hell, devouring Indians by the thousands."[78] Perhaps no place on Earth has ever come as close to the image of the inferno as the mines of Potosí. At night, 6000 smelting fires burned on the slopes of the mountain, the poisonous vapors exterminating all vegetation within 20 miles. The Uruguayan journalist Eduardo Galeano estimates a total of 8 million dead after three centuries of mine operation.[79] Agriculture dwindled and entire areas were depopulated. The coastal terraces of present-day Peru, once irrigated and cultivated by the Incas, were turned into a desert that can still be seen today. When almost all the indigenous people had been killed, the Spaniards tried to replace them with African slaves. They too quickly perished. Even the mountain itself collapsed, dropping several hundred meters after a total of 40,000 tons of pure silver had been extracted and shipped to Spain.

The silver did not remain in Spain, however, but immediately flowed through the hands of the crown to its creditors in Genoa, Augsburg and Antwerp, fueling the booming cash economy there. The entire Conquista, including the genocide, had been financed with loans, and it was pressure from creditors that kept the hellfires burning at Potosí.

Crushing Egalitarian Movements

With the stimulation of the money-war complex, European elites could gradually shift the balance of power in their favor and crush egalitarian movements. Well-armed mercenary armies enforced tax collection and suppressed revolts by peasants and craftsmen more effectively than ever. The logic of capital accumulation continued to penetrate further into social structures. In agriculture, money-based leases took the place of in-kind levies and labor services. This was liberating to some farmers, but ruinous for many others who lost their land because of over-indebtedness. The result was a division of the peasantry into wealthy tenants and landowners versus landless laborers.[80] In England, landlords took over common lands by force in order to breed large flocks of sheep for the booming textile production in Flanders. As a consequence of these enclosures, many small farmers, who had depended on the commons, became out-of-work, landless vagabonds. In Flanders, textile traders broke guild rules by creating "special economic zones" outside of cities, where impoverished farmers could earn some extra money by weaving and spinning. Since the merchants controlled the entire supply chain, they could also set wages and prices.

Just at this time, vast quantities of silver came flooding into Europe from Potosí. The result was galloping inflation that hit food prices especially hard, while landlords, merchants and sovereigns held down wages to a bare minimum with the help of their newly won military power. In many regions, real wages fell dramatically by as much as 70 percent between 1500 and 1700. It was not until the end of the nineteenth century that average wages in Europe returned to the level of the late Middle Ages.[81] The result was mass poverty, hunger and misery. This caused a third wave of social revolts to break out, culminating in the German Peasants' War of 1525.

The authorities' response to dissidence and upheaval took various forms, with religious persecution, state repression and war working hand in hand. During the late Middle Ages the church had already persecuted the apostolic poverty movements, who turned against social inequality and founded utopian communities, by defining them as "heretics." The rationale is as simple as it is effective: attention is diverted from the social question to a dispute over religious doctrine. In order to combat "heresy" — i.e., social movements — popes introduced the Inquisition and torture in the thirteenth century. While still limited in the late Middle Ages, these draconian measures reached a peak in the early modern period, especially in Spain.

The persecution of witches, which reached a climax between 1550 and 1700, followed up on the Inquisition.[82] However, it was primarily secular courts rather than ecclesiastical jurisdictions that conducted the trials. The belief in witches was anything but a spontaneous popular movement; it was actually carefully staged and orchestrated by the authorities. The media available at the time played a decisive role as propaganda tools in the creation of collective paranoia through theater performances, sermons, paintings and especially printed books.[83] The infamous inflammatory treatise The Hammer of Witches became one of the most widely printed texts of the period.

The trials were directed primarily against women and especially those who were poor. In England, there was a direct geographical correspondence between witch trial locations and the enclosures of the commons. It was also no coincidence that the high points of the persecutions coincided with times of maximum inflation.[84] The American social scientist Silvia Federici argues that attacking witches was a way to break down social resistance to capitalist modes of production. In fact, the persecutions did have a devastating effect on the peasants' opposition. They divided the population by encouraging mutual denunciations. By demonizing women, they reached deep into families and drove a wedge between husbands and wives.

Finally, the persecution of witches succeeded in destroying the cultural foundations of peasant life, that had long resisted both the church's rituals of submission and wage labor. It was not by chance that the Devil, as illustrated by the church on its walls and printed in countless tracts and sermons, looked much like the shepherd god Pan, a direct symbol of the peasants' independent way of life since ancient times. While the true devils, from the peasants' point of view, were the executioners and torturers found in so many contemporary depictions of Hell, the elites' version of the Devil was a lazy, lecherous faun, who spent his days feasting and his nights hatching conspiratorial plots. The paranoia of property owners, which found its expression in the witch trials, was inspired to a great degree by the fear of uncontrollable peasant activities.

Closely linked to the Inquisition and the witch hunts were the draconian punishments increasingly inflicted on the poor and homeless, who were roving around Europe in great numbers. The first German Penal Code of 1532 legalized cruel forms of execution such as the wheel, quartering and being buried or burned alive for even small offenses such as theft.[85] Poverty became a capital crime. In the chapter on "primitive accumulation" in *Capital*, Karl Marx quotes examples of bloody legislation that had spread throughout Europe since the sixteenth century:

Vagabonds are to be tied to the cart-tail and whipped until the blood streams from their bodies, then to swear an oath to go back to their birthplace or to where they have lived the last three years and to "put themselves to labour." For the second arrest for vagabondage the whipping is to be repeated and half the ear sliced off; but for the third relapse the offender is to be executed as a hardened criminal and enemy of the common weal. (Henry VIII, 1530) If anyone refuses to work, he shall be condemned as a slave to the person who has denounced him as an idler. The master shall feed his slave on bread and water, weak broth and such refuse meat as he thinks fit. He has the right to force him to do any work, no matter how disgusting, with whip and chains. If the slave is absent a fortnight, he is condemned to slavery for life and is to be branded on the forehead or back with the letter S; if he runs away thrice, he is to be executed as a felon. (Edward VI, 1547)

Marx concludes: "Thus were the agricultural people, first forcibly expropriated from the soil, driven from their homes, turned into vagabonds, and then whipped, branded, tortured by laws grotesquely terrible, into the discipline necessary for the wage system."[86]

From the "Bundschuh" uprisings to the German Peasants' War (1525), peasants increasingly joined together in large groups to defend themselves against intensified exploitation, repression and taxes. The reformer Martin Luther played a very ambivalent role during this period. His theses against the sale of indulgences and other church abuses were taken up by opposing sides. On the one hand, they were supported by revolting peasants and other underprivileged people. On the other, sovereigns who wanted to snatch up the church's extensive holdings also nodded approval. When the conflicts came to a head and escalated into civil war, Luther took the side of the authorities. He called for insurgents to be slain without pity: "Therefore let everyone who can, smite, slay and stab the rebels, secretly or openly. It is just as when one must kill a mad dog." And he continued: "Strange times, these, when a prince can win Heaven with bloodshed."[87] In a variety of ways, Luther reiterated Paul's proposition that all authority comes from God and that every man must unconditionally obey. His doctrine became one of the supporting ideological pillars for the establishment of authoritarian structures in Germany and other parts of the world.[88]

In battles that can only be described as massacres, the peasant armies finally succumbed to mercenary troops, who were financed by the merchant and banker Jakob Fugger. The modern money-war complex displayed its asymmetrical superiority near Frankenhausen, where at least 6000 peasants were killed, but only half a dozen mercenaries died. In 1526, when the great slaughter was over, Luther wrote: "I could fairly boast. Since the time of the apostles, no one has so positively written about and praised the authorities and the secular sword as I have."[89] With

Luther's ideological backing, the Protestant princes were finally able to seize the church estates that the peasants originally wished to convert into communal property.

However, the uprisings were not quite over. Starting in Switzerland, the "Anabaptist" movement spread out over large parts of Central Europe. Influenced by freshly-translated versions of the gospels into German, it called for the principles of non-violence, community of goods and self-determination— concepts at the core of the Jesus movement. After the peasant revolts had been put down, the Anabaptists avoided military confrontation and instead sought to build their own communities beyond the state and the church. They were persecuted not only by sovereigns and the catholic church, but also by other reformers such as Huldrych Zwingli, at whose urging many Anabaptists were tortured and executed. With a remarkable argument, Lutherans also participated in the persecutions. They considered the Anabaptists' refusal to serve as soldiers or in other offices associated with violence as a violation of God's will. Even today, Lutheran pastors in many countries are ordained with the Augsburg Confession of 1530, in which there is an explicit passage opposing the Anabaptists' rejection of violence and private property:

> *Of Civil Affairs they teach that lawful civil ordinances are good works of God, and that it is right for Christians to bear civil office, to sit as judges, to judge matters by the Imperial and other existing laws, to award just punishments, to engage in just wars, to serve as soldiers, to make legal contracts, to hold property, to make oath when required by the magistrates, to marry a wife, to be given in marriage. They condemn the Anabaptists who forbid these civil offices to Christians.*[90]

In Münster the conflicts came to a dramatic climax. Part of the city wanted to enforce the Lutheran doctrine (including the

Confession), but a majority of the population was on the side of the Anabaptists. Remarkably, three-quarters of them were women, which is perhaps not too surprising given Luther's misogynistic attitudes. As imperial episcopal troops surrounded the city, the Anabaptists declared property to be communal as it had been in the first Christian community in Jerusalem, then they burned the debt registers in the city archives. At this point, apocalyptic preachers emerged as leaders of the movement to proclaim the imminent appearance of Christ. The Savior, however, did not appear, and instead, the city was overpowered by troops in 1535. The leaders of the movement were publicly tortured and executed. Their tongues and other body parts were torn out with glowing tongs before they were finally stabbed to death. The corpses were hung in iron baskets on the steeple of the church and displayed "to serve as a warning and instill terror in all troubled minds—to not dare to attempt anything similar in the future."[91]

Left: Torture of an Anabaptist (1535). Right: Execution on the wheel (1630)

The Anabaptist takeover in Münster illustrates the tragedy of the egalitarian movements. Like the ancient apocalyptic believers facing superior Roman legions, they too slipped into end-times fantasies when standing powerless before the might of the money-military complex.

Alongside colonial expansion, the second triumph of the monsters of modernity was to smash internal resistance and egalitarian dreams across Europe. It was the birth of what Thomas Hobbes was to call the "Leviathan" more than 100 years later; a monster against whom all resistance is futile.

The Invention of the Joint-Stock Company

The authoritarian state was not the only monstrous institution created during this time. Equally powerful (if not more so) and equally monstrous was a second institution that was closely linked to the first—the joint-stock company, the prototype of the modern corporation.

When examined closely, a joint-stock company is quite a peculiar construction. By law, it is considered a "legal person," in the USA even a "moral person" with constitutional rights otherwise enjoyed exclusively by "natural persons." Unlike other legal entities, such as associations and cooperatives, its sole purpose is to increase the money of its shareholders. Since the joint-stock company cannot die like a natural person, it can, theoretically, exist forever. It is something like a machine with anthropomorphic characteristics whose only purpose is to perpetually produce more and more money. The circuits and gears of this gigantic cyborg are largely made up of humans, but the only functions they are allowed to perform are those that advance the ultimate purpose of the machine. Should their performance fall short, the machine will eject them.

This blueprint has produced the most powerful institutions on Earth, even financially stronger than many states. While they may have conflicts with governments, they are still creatures of the state, as only states and governments can create, preserve and enforce the complex legal constructs that are the core of their existence. They are genetically coded for infinite expansion, because the accumulated capital must be increased still further. They plow through land and sea in search of new ways to invest. If the Arctic is melting due to the greenhouse gases they produce, this does not prompt them to stop and reflect, but instead, to drill for oil in the Arctic as well. The things they produce—cars and medicines, pacifiers and machine guns, cattle feed and electricity—are exchangeable, as they are just a means to the veritable end, namely, money multiplication. Once the demand for products is met, new demand must be created. Thus, in order to continue functioning, it is imperative for them that people be transformed into consumers whose main contribution to social life is to buy things, no matter how superfluous or harmful the products are. Collective considerations about the meaning and purpose of society as a whole have no place in this logic, nor do questions as to what people really need and how they want to live. While the purpose of corporations is abstract, they require concrete input in the way of energy and materials in order to create products to sell for money. So, in the end, these artificial, immortal entities gobble up reality and spit it back out as pure abstraction—a series of digits on a shareholder's account.

But how did the creation of such a strange and destructive institution come about? Until public limited companies were first founded around 1600, only individuals were able to accumulate capital in their pursuit of profits. If someone's desire to increase his personal wealth came to an end—e.g. because he wanted to retire and enjoy the fruits of his endeavors—then economic expansion would come to a halt as well.[92] The situation is different with joint-stock companies, where accumulation is institutionalized, and the people involved are interchangeable.

The independence and abstraction of money multiplication already had a long history before the joint-stock company entered the scene. Then, the pioneers of early capitalism in Venice and Genoa were still adventuring characters who sailed off to sea, fought and sometimes died. They traded in comparatively small quantities of luxury goods, but with high risk and extremely high rates of profit.[93]

With growing trading volumes, greater competition at sea and tighter profit rates, there was a growing need to accurately calculate each transaction. The critical solution came in the fourteenth century with the invention of double-entry bookkeeping, as we know it today. Now income, expenses, profits and taxes could be determined precisely, not only retrospectively, but also with a view to the future.[94] This mathematization of trade was an important step away from the irregular increases in wealth that come from individual trade expeditions or raids. Accumulation could now be calculated and increasingly became an end in itself.

Step by step, the merchant's job description changed profoundly. The seafaring privateer became deskbound, directing employees all over the world from the security of his office. The physical acquisition of material treasures was replaced by the accumulation of an abstract mathematical quantity on paper. This multiplication, however, was not yet fully automated. In addition to the trader's own inclinations and his limited life expectancy, legal restrictions got in the way of limitless accretion. Different kinds of businesses had already been developed during the early Renaissance that allowed investors and traders to merge. However, all of these forms were subject to two restrictions: along with their assets, each investor was liable for potential losses by his partners; and the life span of the company was usually limited to one business trip.[95]

These restrictions were finally removed in 1602 with the establishment of the Dutch East India Company (abbreviated VOC), the first modern joint-stock corporation. It was granted a trade monopoly from the Dutch government that spanned the entire area of the Indian and Pacific oceans. Subsequently, a stock exchange was established in order to trade the company's shares. Not only was the Amsterdam Stock Exchange the first of its kind, it was also the most important bourse in the world for many decades to come.[96] The more that ownership titles became freely tradable, the more fluid, abstract and disassociated from people and places they were. Unlike earlier trading companies, in effect, the VOC had an unlimited life span. It was also the first corporation to limit shareholders' liability to the value of their shares. This innovation, which we take for granted today, was in fact something outrageous. Never before in economic history did investors have a formal right to be free of personal liability for whatever losses and damages they might cause. Conversely, the shareholders had little say in the company's decisions and were not accountable by law for any crimes committed by the company. They simply received a guaranteed dividend of, say, 16 percent, and were otherwise unaffiliated.

In this way, the company radically enforced the process of disembedding the economy from the household (Greek, "oikos").[97] It was detached from all ties to real people, locations, social relationships, human life spans and responsibilities. In other words, it became a kind of metaphysical being, immortal and placeless like angels.

At the same time, the economic power of these unearthly beings could not be asserted without the massive use of physical force. At its founding, the VOC was already allowed to create an army made up of mercenaries who had to swear allegiance to the company. In the course of the seventeenth century, the English East India Company (EIC) was also gradually granted the right to build its own army and to wage war at will. It also minted its own coins, and enjoyed criminal and civil jurisdiction "over all persons who belong to or live under the said company." The trading companies were thus state-like entities with fluctuating territories. They were led by governors who not only had command over their employees, but also over all the people in the colonies conquered by the company. In these organizations, economic and military tyranny were consolidated under one roof.

An example of how these companies operated outside of Europe is the genocide that took place on the Indonesian Banda Islands in 1621. The nutmeg grown there was of keen interest to the Dutch, because it could be sold in Europe for huge profits. The Bandanese, however, were not willing to grant a trading monopoly to the VOC. In response, the company arrived with several thousand mercenaries and committed a massacre on the islands. After a year, the Dutch had their monopoly, but only 1000 of the original 15,000 islanders were still alive.[98] Meanwhile, Amsterdam blossomed into the wealthiest city in Europe, famous for its art and liberality. The company's shareholders did not get their hands dirty while the VOC was rampaging on their behalf in the Pacific. Instead, they moved in sophisticated circles, discussing the merits of painters like Frans Hals or the young Rembrandt and having their portraits painted by them. At the same time, the "golden age" of the Netherlands was surely one of the darkest ages in Indonesian history. The rise of European civilization was directly linked to barbarism on the other side of the globe. For most people, however, this connection had become invisible through the various layers of abstraction that coagulated into the institution of the joint-stock company.

The Chosen and the Damned

The Netherlands had become the new center of the world economy, just as England in the nineteenth century and the USA in the twentieth century would later become. It was not by chance that Calvinism, an ideology reflecting and justifying the new order, also spread in these countries. In Geneva, John Calvin taught that before the creation of the world, people had been separated by God into the chosen and the eternally damned. According to him, no man could change this preordained destiny, by either good deeds or faith. Because no one could be sure to which group they belonged, it was necessary to look for signs. Calvin believed that the clearest sign of belonging to the chosen few was economic success.

Calvinist teaching combines the apocalyptic tradition with the capitalist undertaking. The division of mankind into the chosen and the damned, as proclaimed in Revelations, is projected onto the economic sphere with the divine order and market logic merging into one. In a radical reversal of the gospels, the poor are now rejected by God and irretrievably destined for Hell, while the rich—of whom Jesus reportedly said, "it is easier for a camel to go through the eye of a needle than for someone who is rich to enter the kingdom of God"—slip into the role of the chosen. No earthly power has split mankind in two; it has actually been God's indisputable decision since before the beginning of time. Consequently, it is not only hopeless to try to change the situation, but also blasphemous. The fact that this doctrine spread so rapidly in the centers of heated economic transition was due to the fact that it fulfilled an important purpose—it legitimized social divisions and silenced the debate.

Politically marginalized and facing persecution in England, the Puritans carried these ideas to the North American colonies. Believing that the end of time was near, they also thought that America was where the New Jerusalem would emerge—the "city upon a hill."[99] But like the New Jerusalem, New England was not meant to be a place for just anyone. The indigenous Pequot, for instance, were almost completely obliterated within a few years. The brutal warfare waged by the English aimed at total annihilation of the enemy, including civilians, a cruelty hitherto unknown and incomprehensible to the Pequot, who, militarily and spiritually, were completely unprepared to resist such a brutal assault. In 1637, about 500 Pequots perished in a massacre at Mystic River. An English eyewitness wrote: "It was a fearful sight to see them thus frying in the fyre and the streams of blood quenching the same, and horrible was the stincke and sente there of, but the victory seemed a sweete sacrifice, and they gave the prayers thereof to God."[100]

The Puritans combined their apocalyptic mission with economic ambitions. Colonization was promoted by public limited companies that had been granted control over specific territories by the English crown.[101] The poorer colonists indentured themselves to these companies for seven years as serfs. Their mission was to make profits in the New World for the shareholders in London, by whatever means.

The combination of eschatology and economic expansion gave the project a utopian aura that radiated beyond the harsh realities of the early colonies. The Celestial City would not come from Heaven, but could now be built. The colonization of America was the first step, and to create this New World, the old one would have to be destroyed. The replacement was to come from the hands of the new master of the Earth, the white man, who himself was the tool of a white, male, authoritarian God.

The fusion of profit-seeking and apocalypticism is also reflected by the changing concept of time. The expectation of salvation in the future now coincided with accounting calculations of future profits. This linkage resulted in the modern idea of a beam of time, on which we race irresistibly toward the future. Perception focuses down to a vanishing point, and the present is reduced to a brief moment on the way — to a "not-yet."

Power and Powerlessness in the Global World-System

At the beginning of the modern era, Europeans transformed half the world into a hell on earth in the name of salvation and progress. The money economy, metallurgy and the business of war had coalesced into a powerful machine that was capable of breaking down resistance within Europe as well as gradually subjugating other countries and even entire continents in the outside world. At first glance, the nature of this machinery seems similar to that of empires like Rome, but a closer look reveals that it functioned in a different way.

An indication of the system's novelty is the curious fact that the modern state, unlike its predecessors, started off in debt.[102] It was only with loans from wealthy traders that rulers could pay for mercenaries and weapons with which to gain control over land and people. This is why the balance of power between owners of capital and heads of state is fundamentally different in modern times than it was in antiquity. The overriding goal of the Roman and Chinese empires was to strengthen the central power of the state and to consolidate the empire. In the modern world-system, however, state power is chiefly a means to pave the way for an unimpeded increase in money capital. In both cases, the market and the state are inseparable, but their relationship has been reversed, with far-reaching consequences.[103] Because the system, including the states, is driven by the rationale of endless capital accumulation, there is no final steady state to be attained, just ongoing and infinite expansion.

On the flip side of this new power were large sectors of the population who were subjected to violence, severe poverty and displacement. The period from the outbreak of the Plague up to the seventeenth century was traumatic for the people of Europe in many ways. Wars were being fought on completely new levels, reaching a temporary high point as Europe tore itself apart during the Thirty Years' War. About a third of Central Europe's population was wiped out. A whole generation grew up that knew nothing other than war. Countless children were born into the army's retinue to become part of the war economy.[104] The central driving force behind this war was not a religious confessional conflict, and often it was not even the rulers' desire to conquer. It was driven mainly by the needs of the war economy. The war could have already ended in the winter of 1620–21, but the Bohemian mercenary army demanded to be fed. Its commander, war entrepreneur Ernst von Mansfeld, threatened to turn the army against his clients. After all, he still had to service his debt. So the war continued.[105]

Not only did the war uproot and traumatize people, but the new economic regime did as well. Communal subsistence economies and lifestyles were forcibly destroyed. More and more people were deprived of their livelihoods with the enclosure of the commons, forced taxation in coins and the repression of the poor and homeless. Their only option was to sell themselves into labor and compete with each other on the open market. Cooperative coexistence was gradually pushed back in favor of a ruthless struggle for survival. Over a span of centuries, the social fabric that had held people together had been torn to pieces, leading to a permanent "war of all against all," described by Thomas Hobbes as the "state of nature."

The upheavals of the early modern era are not just a matter of the past. The monsters of modernity still live on in us today, in a society that has elevated the full-out competition of all against all to its supreme principle. The economic-political system that had been created by force at the time has now spread throughout the world. With modifications, it is still the system we live with today.

However, we must ask again the question posed in the introduction. Can we really speak of a system here, as opposed to a mere collection of different institutions, practices and worldviews? If no part can exist without the other, and if all ingredients are necessary components of a larger whole, then yes, we can call it a system. Indeed, the history of the early modern period clearly shows that the economic power of capital could not have developed without the physical violence of the state, and vice versa; that both were (and still are) closely tied to the development of the metallurgical complex; and that expansion was always justified by a universalist ideology, at first dressed up in the garb of Christianity, then later legitimized in the name of "civilization," "reason," "democracy" and the "free market."

For centuries, social movements have defended themselves against the impositions of this system and attacked each of its elements. They have had some success in holding back physical and structural violence in certain places and in fighting for new freedoms. In other places, however, the power of the four tyrannies has broken new ground in unexpected ways, most obviously in the spectacular rise of the metallurgical complex, which today has the capability to extinguish all life on Earth.

Chapter 7

Machine

Mechanistic Sciences, State Apparatuses and the Disciplining of Man (1600–1800)

What is the heart but a spring, and the nerves but so many strings, and the joints but so many wheels?

THOMAS HOBBES, LEVIATHAN

After the great upheavals of the sixteenth century, the newly emerging world-system was able to consolidate in the following two centuries.[1] The conquests and plundering during early colonization evolved into a system of international division of labor. The world was increasingly divided into centers that processed high-value products, and peripheries that were primarily sources of cheap labor and raw materials. Through various waves of globalization, this system has spread to the far corners of the Earth. In the seventeenth and eighteenth century, the Atlantic slave trade between Europe, West Africa and the Caribbean became a mainstay of this system.

In the centers of the world economy, the proliferation of the money-war complex gave rise to state apparatuses with a level of military power that had not been seen since the Roman Empire. These states were able to effectively crush resistance to the new system, subject territories and populations to increasing control, and at the same time promote the accumulation of capital within their spheres of power.

Closely related to these developments was a tremendous ideological clash that continues to shape our civilization to this day. This upheaval has often been portrayed as a conflict between tradition and modernity, religion and science, or superstition and enlightenment. It is a tale of how reason has gradually asserted itself, and led us to today's enlightened, rational and democratic civilization (albeit always under threat from the dark forces of the irrational).[2]

However, this kind of narrative is misleading for several reasons. First there are no such things as "reason, science or religion" as monolithic entities; instead, these are concepts whose definitions and definers have always been hotly disputed. The decisive lines of conflict run *across* these areas, and the dispute is over *what kind* of religion, reason or rationality will prevail. Which traditions are to be rejected or preserved? Which innovations are desirable? In these debates, it is not a question of rational truth versus irrational superstition, but rather a competition among different interests and different ideas for a desirable social organization.

Because the narrative portraying reason's steady advance and modernity's struggle against pre-modernity misrepresents the lines of conflict, it is difficult to see the hidden and often much more important continuities that exist between certain forms of religion and certain forms of "scientistic" and technocratic ideology.[3] The idea, for instance, of a heavenly ruler who has total power over his creatures is structurally similar to the idea of man having absolute power of disposal over nature. Authoritarian religion and technocracy are not opposites, but parts of a continuum. It was not knowledge against belief or rationality against irrationality that triumphed in modernity, but a *certain kind* of rationality. And this rationality was successful because it reflected the functioning of the newly emerging power apparatuses.

The World as Machine

The symbol for this type of rationality was the machine. Long before the Industrial Revolution elevated machines to such a dominant position in Western societies, leading circles in the state, the economy and the sciences were obsessed with the *idea* of the machine. As early as the beginning of the fifteenth century, the Venetian Giovanni Fontana designed a quite popular catalog of partly useful, partly absurd automatons. Along with siege machines, weapons and heavy equipment for mining, he also featured mechanically operated devils, automatic fire witches and rocket-driven birds, fish and hares.[4] A short time later, Leonardo da Vinci developed the first model of a robot, a fully armored knight with a mechanical drive, for his warlord client, Ludovico Sforza, the Duke of Milan. Automatons featuring praying monks, flute players and digesting ducks delighted kings and scholars alike. Fascinated by the functioning of the mechanical wheel clock, invented in the fourteenth century, pioneers of modern science such as Galileo Galilei, René Descartes and Isaac Newton subsequently began to view nature as a great wheelwork. While Galileo and other astronomers examined the planetary system and interpreted it as a gigantic celestial machine, the mechanistic philosophers like Descartes and Thomas Hobbes went a step further. They claimed that even living beings were nothing more than automatons, a radical break from earlier worldviews that perceived nature as a living organism.

By equating life with an apparatus, they established an important ideological prerequisite for the progressive domination of nature and man. If living beings were nothing but automatons, then once their functions were understood, with the proper techniques, they could be utilized to maximum effect. These radical views met with considerable resistance from society, and often from other scientists. Nonetheless, the ideas were ultimately able to assert themselves as the epitome of reason and rationality due to the fact that they fitted perfectly into the political and economic system that was taking form and spreading throughout the world.

Left: Leonardo da Vinci's model of a combat automaton. Right: A modern army

Not only were the bodies of animals and humans regarded as mechanisms, but also society as a whole. Just as a machine is controlled by its user, the social body should be governed by a central authority as well. With the consolidation of the money-war complex, Europe's newly created standing armies served as a model for this concept and were also the tool used for its implementation. The well-drilled soldier was the perfect man-machine, reacting just as reliably and predictably to commands as Leonardo's robot. The army, on the other hand, later set the example for a whole series of social institutions that were also organized according to the machine model, from the factory to the prison to the school. Naked physical violence was increasingly replaced by a variety of more subtle disciplinary techniques meant to ensure that human action and thought fit into the Megamachine as smoothly and efficiently as possible.

THE ROLE OF THE SCIENCES

There is no doubt that the modern natural sciences, as they developed in Europe since the seventeenth century, have considerably expanded the range of human knowledge and understanding. They have provided us with new insights into the structure and history of the universe, and opened unimagined views into the complex organization of matter and life. They have become a sharp instrument for critical thinking, used to distinguish mere claims from testable hypotheses, and they have laid the foundations for remarkable technological developments.

At the same time, however, the sciences were, from the outset, closely linked to military and economic power apparatuses, which decisively shaped their development and exerted considerable influence on the selection of research subjects and methodology. This close association with the powers-that-be led to the emergence of an ideological system that superimposed itself upon and partially permeated the work of scientists, a mythology that, in some cases, tends to obstruct rather than promote an accurate understanding of nature. This ideology was also able to immunize itself against criticism and assert universalist claims to truth, which were inherited in large part from Christian universalism.[5]

Science can have a wide variety of goals and can be used for many different purposes. It can serve, according to Francis Bacon's motto "knowledge is power," to support domination relationships—or dismantle them. And it has been a contested terrain from the very start. What constitutes valid methods, valid data and valid conclusions? What is to be included in the observations, and what should be excluded from the outset? By defining what is real, true and relevant, science not only produces knowledge but also worldviews. On the other hand, scientists do not exist in an ideological vacuum. With every breath, both consciously and unconsciously, they absorb the prevalent views of their times and their milieu. Furthermore, scientists are never free of personal interests. Like other people, they want to earn a living, gain recognition and avoid repression. At the same time, their knowledge inevitably becomes the target of non-scientific actors who are bent on controlling, using or limiting the production of knowledge according to their own interests. In short, the world of science is not an ideal cosmos floating freely above society, but part of a larger social system and inevitably subject to change along with that system. It is therefore no surprise that, with the re-formation of economic and physical power during the early modern period, completely new forms of knowledge production emerged that were closely linked to the logic of the new power apparatuses.

The New Atlantis

The development of the modern natural sciences is closely linked to the name of a man who simultaneously played leading roles in the economic and political systems of his time— Francis Bacon (1561–1621). Voltaire called him the "father of experimental philosophy," and Thomas Jefferson, author of the American Declaration of Independence, considered him one of the three most important people who ever lived. Bacon's life and work exemplify the fusion of apocalypticism, colonialism, the domination of nature, and the pursuit of profit that is so characteristic of what we call "Western civilization."

His contribution to the development of the natural sciences had little to do with inventions or discoveries. Instead, it was his vision of a scientific society that was especially momentous; a foresight of real developments that largely came to pass centuries later. The most famous rendering of this vision is his unfinished novel *New Atlantis*. The title alone implies a variation on the theme of the "New Jerusalem." The world of the New Atlantis is ruled by a small group of patriarchal scientists, the "Fathers of Solomon's House," an allusion to the Temple of Solomon in Jerusalem. The panorama of their inventions reads like a tour of our world today: skyscrapers as tall as the One World Trade Center; laboratories for vivisection and animal experiments; manipulations of nature reminiscent of today's genetic engineering and synthetic biology (production of new animal breeds and plant species, planned modification of their size and shape, their yield, their reproductive capacity, their behavior, etc.); light and sound studios; modern blast furnaces, manufacturing plants and armament factories; devices to deceive the senses to the point of virtual realities; and last but not least, facilities that generate weather phenomena such as thunderstorms, rain and snow that bring to mind today's concepts of geoengineering. For Bacon, the second creation would not come from Heaven, but would be technically produced by man. The omnipotent God was to be replaced by the engineer.[6]

It is not by chance that the story is set on an island in the "New World," which Bacon, like many of his contemporaries, associated with the promise of a new creation. However, Bacon's involvement with the colonization of North America did not take place just in the fantasy world of his novel, but also in real life. Among other things, he was a shareholder and council member of the Virginia Company of London, which laid claim to almost the entire east coast of the future United States as its property.[7] At the same time, he was a senior prosecutor, later appointed attorney general, and a member of parliament who played a leading role in drafting the charter letters granting this corporation monopoly rights, administrative authority and military power.

To some extent, Bacon still held on to the Renaissance philosophy of the cosmos being a living whole. For example, he believed that "love is the overarching law of nature," and that this also applied to atoms.[8] Yet, at the same time, his view of nature was shaped by the perspective of power. It was especially metallurgy and the power of the Inquisition that inspired the development of his methodology. He was convinced that "truth lies hid in deep mines and caves" and advised students to "sell their books and build furnaces."[9] Bacon thus continued an alchemical-metallurgical tradition that saw the mastery of metals as the key to domination over nature.

Bacon's methods of experimental investigation, which had an enormous influence on the modern natural sciences, draw some of their most important ideas from the courtroom—more precisely from "relentless interrogation" supported by torture.

Witch trials and torture were at full throttle in England at the time, and Bacon, as a leading lawyer, was involved in them. So it is no surprise that he applied the methodology of the Inquisition—interrogation in a closed chamber—as a metaphor for the ideal approach to science: "Proteus ever changed shapes till he was straitened and held fast, so nature exhibits herself more clearly under the trials and vexations of art than when left to herself."[10] Bacon's use of the word "trial" connotes both legal proceedings and experiment. In 1660, inspired by Bacon's inquisitorial methods, Robert Boyle conceived the first animal experiments in modern history, which involved sealing mice, birds and snakes inside vacuum vessels to observe their death.[11]

Bacon's language is also full of sexually charged metaphors associated with violence against women: penetrating the mysteries of nature, unveiling them and so on. All these images amount to the fact that nature must be conquered and violated in a sort of battle, until it reveals its secrets and submits completely to the power of humans (more precisely, to the power of men).

Bacon's influence on the development of the sciences was monumental. His fictitious "Fathers of Solomon's House" became the source of inspiration for the founding of the Royal Society in London, which, alongside the French Académie des Sciences, was to become the leading scientific institution in Europe for centuries.

Redefining Reality

Galileo Galilei wrote in 1623 that knowledge of nature ("philosophy") "is written in that great book which ever is before our eyes—the universe. It is written in the language of mathematics, and its characters are triangles, circles and other geometric figures without which it is humanly impossible to understand a single word of it; without these, one wanders about in a dark labyrinth."[12] This famous proposition became one of the foundations of modern science. Considering Galileo's various activities, it made perfect sense. As a physicist and astronomer, he worked on the exact calculation and prediction of parabolic trajectories and planetary orbits, for which mathematics were an obvious necessity. However, his comment becomes highly problematic if one applies it beyond planetary orbits to the entire universe and all spheres of existence. In a pointed form, the statement then reads: "Reality is that which can be described mathematically. Everything else is illusion."

We do not know whether Galileo himself would have gone that far—probably not—but this is beside the point for our story. What is essential is that this conception of reality became increasingly accepted over the course of the following centuries. Measuring and counting gradually took precedence over other forms of knowledge and experience. While the unmeasurable and the uncountable were reduced to mere "subjective impressions," measurements and mathematical explanations achieved the status of "objective truth." In this way, primary human perception was accorded an ever smaller say in the process of understanding and interpreting the world. What a person saw, heard, felt and smelt could no longer be considered truth, or indeed reality. It was only considered real when experts measured it in a controlled, repeatable experiment. Thus, step by step, people were deprived of the meaningfulness of their own perceptions. The behaviorists of the twentieth century, who pushed this ideology to its extreme, even claimed that people's spiritual life does not exist, and that thought was simply subvocal, laryngeal responses.[13] From this perspective, the intellectual history of modern times is not, as is repeatedly claimed, a history of man's emancipation, but on the contrary, a history of his *fading to invisibility*.

Excluding the Unpredictable

The seventeenth-century epistemological shift that accorded the measurable a privileged status of reality at the expense of perception was closely related to the new formation of physical and economic power. The rise of the monetary economy and merchant capitalism had turned counting and calculating into a veritable obsession. From tax collectors to speculators, leading circles were busy making computations about the future of investments. Predictability and calculability became crucial categories of thought and action for both private businessmen and civil servants.

This *Zeitgeist* was also reflected in the work of researchers. For the pioneers of the "classical" natural sciences, predictability and repeatability became decisive criteria for the selection and assessment of the phenomena they examined. Whatever eluded repetition in experiments, and whatever behaved *unpredictably*, was seen as a disruptive factor and excluded from consideration. Therefore, a large part of the living world that is characterized by non-determinability, non-repeatability and spontaneity was ruled out.

However, there was a deeper reason why early natural science turned its attention to the predictable, thereby excluding a large number of phenomena from examination. What is predictable is also controllable. Ilya Prigogine, Nobel laureate for chemistry (1977) and pioneer in the study of non-deterministic systems, wrote: "Any science that conceives of the world as being governed according to a universal theoretical plan that reduces its various riches to the drab applications of general laws thereby becomes an instrument of domination."[14]

The early natural sciences were also very closely in step with the demands of the modern apparatuses of power. Scientists such as Galileo calculated the trajectories of cannonballs and the penetrating power of projectiles. Their astronomical calculations laid the foundations for precise navigation technology at sea, which was indispensable for trade, colonial expansion and naval warfare. The war-and-capital-accumulation machine relied on such inventions, and, conversely, researchers needed the machine to finance their work. Therefore, it is not surprising that those scientists and research projects that best conformed to this system were the ones that prevailed.

The Death of the World

A generation after Galileo, philosophers, mathematicians and natural scientists appeared on the scene to take another decisive step forward. The circle of so-called *mechanists*, which included René Descartes, Marin Mersenne and Pierre Gassendi, and which maintained intensive contacts with Thomas Hobbes, claimed that the principles of mechanical laws also applied to the realm of living things. This amounted to one of the most momentous epistemological errors in human history. Not only did the mechanists exclude the aliveness of the living world from their investigations, they also rejected the notion that there could be anything at all such as non-determinability and spontaneity in nature.

Descartes, for example, claimed that animals were nothing but automatons, as mechanical as a clock, and with the right technology they could be easily replicated. That they might have feelings or a soul was out of the question. He also regarded the human body to be a mechanical clockwork, although explicitly excluding the human spirit.[15] The Cartesian approach holds that the human spirit maintains sovereign rule over the body, much like God controls the spinning cogs of His creation. Thus, Descartes projected the model of centralized military power, characteristic of the absolutism of his time, onto the way that life is organized. The spirit commands, and the body obeys, just as the monarch commanded his army of soldier-machines. And just as the Sun King and his laws controlled the behavior of his subjects, the universally valid natural laws dominated nature.[16] Thomas Hobbes shared Descartes's mechanistic views, but he did not exclude the human spirit. In the introduction to *Leviathan*, he asks, "For what is the heart, but a spring; and the nerves, but so many strings; and the joints, but so many wheels?" Hobbes transferred his mechanical perception of nature to humankind and derived from it the vision of a fully mechanical society based on the principle of total domination.

The mechanists made a radical break from the common medieval and Renaissance concept of a living, meaningful universe that in principle is capable of perception and response.[17] Not only was the sphere of planets and minerals soulless, but animals and humans were thought to be nothing more than mechanisms made up of colliding atoms that produced only an illusion of life. The lifeless became the model of life.

It is remarkable how influential this view would become, given that equating, say, a cat or a bird with the mechanics of a clock must seem absurd to any unbiased observer. If anything is characteristic of living beings, it is precisely the unpredictability and spontaneity of their movements. For this reason, the idea of nature being completely mechanical met with stiff resistance from the very beginning, even by some leading scientists. Isaac Newton, who is usually regarded as the father of the mechanistic view of the world, wrote in the drafts of the third book of his treatise, *Opticks*:

> *Matter is a passive principle and cannot move itself. It continues in its state of moving or resting unless disturbed. It receives motion proportional to the force impressing it. These are passive laws, and to affirm that there are no other is to speak against experience for we find in ourselves a power of moving our bodies by our thought. Life and will are active principles by which we move our bodies and thence arise other laws of motion unknown to us.*[18]

Newton was not the only one with this objection. Throughout modern history, there has been massive opposition to the mechanists' claim to universality. But it was only in the twentieth century that researchers were able to use the language of the natural sciences to express how life is founded on principles that are completely different from the world of classical mechanics. Unlike a set of billiard balls, a pile of stones or a planetary system, living systems are based on self-organization. When I kick a stone, it will move from the force of my moving foot, while a dog will move with the energy from its own metabolism (see Chapter 1).[19] I can precisely calculate the movement of the stone, but exactly how the dog will move is anyone's guess. Maybe he will attack me, or maybe he will walk away growling. Even if I correctly anticipate that he will attack me, it is absolutely impossible to precisely predict his movements. This is not, as the mechanists believed, due to a lack of information on the part of the observer. It is because living systems are based on non-linear processes in which a certain input does not produce a determinable, proportional output.[20] A tiny movement on my part can cause the dog to bite me—or perhaps run away. The glance from one person may cause another to take the most unusual actions, inspiring them to climb mountains or cross oceans; it can trigger rage, or ecstasy; and perhaps on a different occasion, the exact same look will have no effect at all.

Because life is organized by non-linear, non-deterministic cause-effect relationships, it cannot be controlled by the exercise of linear power. A father who beats his child may believe that he can force the child to behave in a certain predictable way, and the harder the blows, the more effective they will be. The child's initial obedience may seem to prove him right. Later, however, the child might end up doing completely "crazy" things, like lighting Daddy's car on fire or slashing his own wrists. Such "side effects" are typical consequences of the attempt to control living systems through the linear exercise of power.

The Objectification of Human Beings

The choice of measurement over perception, predictability over spontaneity, and the idea that life is basically made out of dead matter are all ideological elements of early modern natural sciences that converge at a common vanishing point. They eclipse the self-organizing, self-perceiving, self-dynamic character of living beings, who can elude the control and guidance of an external power. Early on, the Great Machine's ideal person was one who could be objectified, was predictable and who followed orders.

By far, however, not all scientists shared this worldview, and it would be unfair to assign collective blame. The practices of measurement, counting and arithmetic are *in themselves* value-free and can be applied to a wide variety of purposes. The move toward an ideology and an instrument of domination does not lie in the use of these methods, but in the assertion that they, and only they, can produce the complete truth about the world "as it really is." The core of this creed is the belief that measuring and counting produce forms of knowledge superior to all others, and for something to be *real,* it must be verified in repeatable experiments.

By disqualifying personal experience as mere "subjectivity," the modern expert followed in the footsteps of priests and theologians, even though the methods were different. It is not by chance that the word "layman" has been transferred from the religious sphere to the scientific vocabulary. The Greek *laikós,* "he of the people," cannot have a say in either of the two realms when it comes to ultimate truths. Instead, these truths are served up to him from the hands of experts, in professional garb (white coat or cassock), framed with official seals and rituals, in mysterious rooms with special accessories (golden altars or flashing instruments) and in a technical language (Latin or mathematics) that is incomprehensible to the uninitiated. The social function of both the priest and the expert is to define recognized "truths" and "insights" and to disconnect them from the world experienced by human beings. What "really" goes on with a human being and how the world "really" works is not something that person is qualified to say. Only the experts know.

The claim of having exclusive access to knowledge and truth has led to a new version of Western universalism that has supplemented and overlaid the Christian mission project. When we know what *real* reason is, and we know *the* way to truth, and we have *the* methods, then it is only right and proper to impose this gospel on the world. However painful the destruction of other systems of values and knowledge may be for those concerned, it is ultimately a good deed to replace ignorance with knowledge and superstition with reason. With their world-historical consequences in mind, even the morally reprehensible crimes committed in the name of European expansion, from the Conquista to twentieth-century globalization, can now be regarded as "progress."

THE LEGIBILITY OF THE WORLD

The effort toward an all-encompassing penetration, evaluation and control of nature by science went hand in hand with another equally comprehensive project, the penetration of the social world by the state. The emergence of modern states is marked by various myths and legends. Early modern state theorists such as Thomas Hobbes claimed that a state is created on the basis of something like a "social contract" between the government and citizens. It is assumed that the state is an institution that is indispensable for safeguarding the common good, and therefore every rational person must be in agreement with such a contract. It is up for discussion as to whether such a state is conceivable or even desirable; in any case, it has never been a historical reality. Modern states have arisen neither for the benefit of populations nor with their consent, but as the products of physical violence.

At the core of modern state building was the army and its financing, which is made apparent by military budgets. In Prussia and other European countries, during the seventeenth and eighteenth centuries, for example, the military devoured about 85 percent of the state finances.[21] In the first phase of the early modern era, sovereigns were dependent on private war entrepreneurs due to a lack of state resources. The system, however, had serious disadvantages, since the hired warlords were often unreliable and even a danger to their own clients. At any time, they had the option of turning against a state if a higher bidder beckoned elsewhere. For this reason, the establishment of a functioning standing army, including supporting taxation, was the most pressing concern of all European rulers. This was especially fueled by their competition with each other and the existential fear of falling behind in the race.

Under this pressure to compete, Europe experienced an unprecedented militarization during the following centuries. While France's first standing army of the mid-fifteenth century was comprised of 9000 men, in the seventeenth century under the "Sun King" Louis XIV, the army had swelled to 400,000 soldiers. By the beginning of the nineteenth century, with the introduction of compulsory military service, it had even reached 1 million. In Prussia, the number of troops rose from 14,000 in 1646 to over 350,000 in 1815, a 25-fold increase. (The twentieth century was to exceed even these figures many times over. At a high point in the First World War, the German army mustered 7 million soldiers in the field.) Even when population growth and territorial expansion are taken into account, there had been an explosive enlargement of the military complex in practically all of the larger European states. Such an increase clearly indicates that the system that emerged at the beginning of modern times had become consolidated and stable.

Militarized states were necessary prerequisites for the expansion of the new economic system. Nonetheless, the leading economic forces—large landowners, trade magnates, bankers and, later, also factory owners—were somewhat leery of the growing power of the central state, since it was capable of severely limiting their scope of activities. At the same time, however, they also knew that only a centralized state could organize physical violence on a scale sufficient to put down the massive anti-systemic movements and create an institutional framework for the lasting accumulation of capital. As we have seen in the previous chapter, the state was also a crucial driving force of the money economy through its massive funding of armaments and armies. This is why, despite occasional critical rhetoric, the primary economic actors opted for ways to exert influence over the state—and were highly successful in doing so.

This success is not surprising. The state was dependent on capital from these merchants and their loans to finance the building of armies as well as a tax system. In addition, the owners of capital had the upper hand because, from the beginning, they could operate transnationally across state borders. The power of each individual state, on the other hand, was always confined to a territory much smaller than the world economy. Banks and trading houses could easily relocate their investments from one country to another whenever the conditions no longer suited them. This was done again and again; a good example being the massive transfer of capital from Italy to Holland in the seventeenth century, then from Holland to England in the eighteenth century.[22] The competition among states for capital was characteristic of the modern world economy from the outset. It also fundamentally set it apart, for instance, from the Chinese system, which also featured a developed class of merchants, but granted superior priority to the stability of the empire. When the Chinese emperor felt threatened by the merchants' activities in the fifteenth century, he ordered the entire merchant fleet to be decommissioned and scrapped—just as the Roman emperor had once eliminated public companies. This signaled the end of Chinese expansion.[23] The competition among states for capital and military power is one of the decisive reasons why the capitalist world economy originated in Europe and not in China.[24]

Maps and Territories

To build standing armies, the states needed money—a lot of it. A series of state bankruptcies in the early modern period showed that financing the military solely through debt was not a workable plan in the long run. Therefore, regents and their administrations took great pains to set up centralized tax systems. To levy taxes, however, the state first had to know who lived where on its territory, what they owned and earned, and how much it could expect to garner from them. As the enforcement of tax collection was often met with fierce resistance, the state also needed to uncover the whereabouts and activities of troublemakers. So typical of modern times, this is how the states' thirst for information about their citizens first began. The ideal of the emerging military and tax apparatuses was therefore maximum legibility regarding citizens and their environments.

The world that tax collectors actually found, however, turned out to be anything but legible. Roughly 80 percent of the population was comprised of farmers, who, for good reason, were notoriously unapproachable and close-mouthed around strangers. How much land and other possessions they owned, how much of it they used, and how much was collected and paid in levies was all regulated in a complex local system of usage rights. This varied considerably from village to village and was opaque to outsiders. There were no detailed maps or land registries, surnames were largely unknown, and each region had its own weights, measures and its own dialect or language. Towns and cities were also difficult to negotiate for the uninitiated. Without a local guide, strangers were easily bewildered in the labyrinth of winding alleys found in a medieval town, and how would one know if a guide could be trusted? This impenetrability offered local populations considerable protection against access by outsiders. When the police, army or tax collectors approached, the people they were looking for and their possessions were often simply nowhere to be found. Sometimes it was unclear who exactly the sought-after person was, even if he or she was standing right under their noses, and helpful information was not to be expected from the rest of the local population.

To deal with such extreme opacity, states took almost obsessive action against the inscrutability of the world. Such efforts are still in operation to this day and will probably continue for as long as the current world-system lasts. The unprecedented frenzy of data collection by secret services in the twenty-first century is just one example. When it began, the program was primarily concerned with land surveying, property registers, urban planning, standardization of weights and measures, establishment of a national language, assignment of surnames and the like.

The goal of all these efforts is a world in which the eye of a centralized observer no longer meets with resistance; in which everything can be taken in at first glance. A quick look at a map should reveal all one needs to know about a territory and its people. For the central observer, the map and the territory should completely coincide.

To reach this goal, however, it is not enough to just take note of all that is extant. The multi-faceted complexity of the actual world is simply too great to ever be completely captured by a map. For the world to become truly transparent, it must be *turned into* a mapable and recordable entity; it must be transformed into a perfect copy of the map; and it must become as concise and two-dimensional as the map itself.

Militarizing the Forest

A symbolic example of making the world legible is the transformation of the Central European forests since the eighteenth century. Wood was a strategic raw material for the construction industry, ship production and, above all, as an energy source for the metallurgical complex. Not only private investors, but also the treasurers of states with large forested areas recognized that a lot of wood meant a lot of money. Nonetheless, the resultant revenues were subject to extreme fluctuations and nearly impossible to predict. The forests were as wild and inscrutable to forest officials as medieval towns and villages were to tax collectors. In the face of high demand, especially from the arms industry, the irregular harvesting of timber soon led to shortages. To cope with this situation, German forest managers invented a system for registering stocks by meticulously recording tree species, trunk diameters and exact stand locations. Thus, sovereigns could calculate their income for the army, the court and larger building projects with some degree of lead time. In the course of these systematizations, the standard tree ("Normalbaum") was also invented: a set of standard measurements with which to calculate the saleable volume of timber from a given section of forest.[25]

However, mapping the forest was only the start. In a second step, the map became the model for converting the forest itself—for actually re-creating it. In order to be able to measure tree populations more easily, to access the wood more quickly and to increase yields, the undergrowth was cleared and the variety of species radically reduced, right down to monocultures. The transformation of many German forests from mixed woodlands to spruce or pine plantations dates back to this period. As if arranged on a chessboard, the new seedlings, all of the same age and type, stood in straight rows like soldiers at roll call. The forest became readable to the calculating eye, and the standard tree was transformed from an arithmetic unit into a reality.

In fact, this development has many similarities with the new type of army created at the time. Just like soldiers, rows of trees stood at the beck and call of the sovereign, and they were felled in rank and file, just as soldiers were cut down in battle. Furthermore, it was all detailed on the maps of generals and forest officials. In his book *Seeing like a State*, James C. Scott writes, "At the limit, the forest itself would not even have to be seen; it could be 'read' accurately from the tables and maps in the forester's office."[26] To the ruler's eye, the map and the territory became one and the same.

But the price of readability was high, as forestry researchers were to find out after a few decades. Although the yield increases from the first planting cycle were considerable, the following generations of trees showed signs of progressively severe damage. A new German word was introduced that summed it up: *Waldsterben* (forest dieback). The cause of the decline was only slowly and incompletely understood. The creation of monocultures and the eradication of undergrowth had interrupted the complex vital nutrient cycles between fungi, bacteria, insects, mammals and trees. The forest managers had destroyed a system that they did not know had even existed.[27] The price of trying to make the territory an exact replica of the map proved to be the death of the territory. This example is characteristic of the continuing attempts to subjugate complex natural systems to the power of human beings and the principle of profit maximization.

Urban Planning as Counterinsurgency

Making the forest transparent went hand in hand with another project: making human society legible. Not only trees, but also people should be available for utilization according to plan, whether for paying taxes, going to war or for constantly expanding the production of goods. This project took shape in different ways, depending on whether applied in urban or rural areas.

In the countryside, tax collectors and recruiting officers cleared away the dense thicket of obstruction they faced by introducing cadastral registration. As is still the case today in many indigenous societies, local economic relations were determined by a complex system of usage rights that was incomprehensible to outsiders. For example, individual families used certain plots of land, but could neither sell nor lend them, while other tracts were allowed to be shared. In some cases, designated groups had the right to graze certain animals on specific portions of the land at certain times. The use of water resources was also regulated for different people at explicit times. Such regulations were renegotiated when unexpected events occurred, such as extreme weather conditions. Consequently, an official who thought he had the system all figured out might once again be scratching his head the following year. Such a system can be meaningful and comprehensible for the local population, but viewed through the lens of power, it seems chaotic, opaque and inaccessible.

As with the transformation of forests into timber plantations, the first step toward seizing control of the land was to create maps and registers. However, since reality defied mapping here as well, the land was *made* mapable in a second step. The goal was to transform a web of complex socio-economic relationships into a uniformly structured register. Each piece of land was assigned to an owner with comprehensive rights, including sale and mortgaging. This owner could then be taxed and his piece of property was tradable on the open market.

In towns and cities, on the other hand, the state was confronted, above all, with confined spaces and a high concentration of people who were difficult to control. For this reason, the densely complex cities of the Middle Ages were anathema to modern statesmen and generals. How easy to foment an uprising here, and how difficult it was for police and the army to penetrate! Contrary to widespread belief, centralized urban planning, which began in the Baroque period and tended toward simple geometric forms, was not just a symbolic display of absolutist power. It was one of its instruments. The chessboard pattern of many baroque cities such as Turin (Italy) or Mannheim (Germany) is similar to that of Roman garrisons. The Renaissance architect Andrea Palladio is credited with saying that there should be no main street "where armies may not easily march."[28] Karlsruhe, for example, a German city that was drawn up on the model of Versailles, is laid out in a corona of radial avenues with the palace located at the hub for optimized and centralized military control. The layout of Washington DC, designed by the military engineer Pierre Charles L'Enfant, follows a similar pattern.

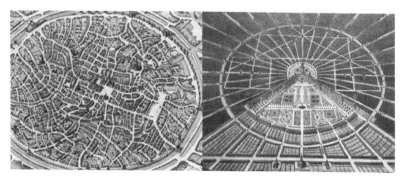

Left: City plan of Bruges, today's Belgium (14th century). Right: The layout of Karlsruhe, Germany (17th century)

However, as long as there were still trouble spots in the old cities, it was not enough to just build new ones. Therefore, the reconstruction of urban spaces according to military requirements became one of the major projects of the modern period, from the Baroque to Le Corbusier, Albert Speer and Ceaușescu. (Today it is often major sporting events, such as the Olympic Games or the soccer World Cup, that are used as a pretext for eliminating urban neighborhoods that are difficult to manage.) In Paris, this kind of reconstruction is linked to the name of George Eugène Haussmann. In the nineteenth century he had some of the hard-to-handle workers' quarters—of which there were not even accurate maps—demolished and replaced with the *grands boulevards*. Performing this kind of "radical surgery" on the structure of a big city was the answer to a series of revolutionary uprisings that Paris had experienced from 1830 to 1848. Barricades had been erected in the streets of Paris nine times during this period, making entire quarters inaccessible to the state. The new boulevards carved out corridors through the city to allow the army quick access when needed.[29] The success of this transformation was demonstrated by the suppression of the Paris Commune in 1871. Backed by the German chancellor Bismarck, the Versailles troops were able to march through the boulevards to ultimately shoot tens of thousands of Communards.[30]

Power's Gaze

These examples show how the mapping of the world became an instrument of domination. The "disenchantment of the world" that Max Weber saw at work in modernity has one of its origins here. The "magic" so painfully missed by the romantics in an all-transparent world is actually the resistance of that world to the gaze of power.

Power's gaze is deadly because it permeates everything and can kill whenever it pleases. It is the drone pilot's view from on high that can precisely locate his target and, when necessary, destroy it with the push of a button. Likewise, it is the view of the investor who strives to extract maximum *return on investment* from every square inch and with every tick of the clock, eliminating every crooked line, every uneven blade of grass, and every inefficient gesture.

The gaze of power creates barrens all around, a "wasteland." A world in which nothing remains unexposed, with no hidden corners, where everything can be seen at a glance, and where everything is utilized to maximum efficiency, starts to take on the qualities of an army barracks or a supermarket parking lot. Indeed, there are more and more places around the world that appear this way. The abject desolation that devastates cities around the globe is caused by the attempt to gain total control over all the world's spaces.[31]

However, the price for complete control is death. If I really want to find out *everything* about a lake, then I must pump it dry and neatly pin down all of its creatures inside a glass case. As knowledge and control are gained, the object itself begins to disappear. If anything is still left alive, then absolute control has not yet been achieved. If everything actually does die, however, there can be no control since no living being is left to be controlled. Instead of true and complete domination, there can be only the illusion of control.

THE HUMAN MACHINE

In order to maintain rapid growth, the Great Machine that was created in the early modern period needed to absorb ever more people into its structures. To be precise, it needed bodies: functioning bodies, whether in the army, in mining or in manufacturing; bodies that did not follow their own impulses and rhythms, but rather the external beat of the machine. First, however, it was necessary to produce such bodies. This meant breaking the mental, spiritual and physical continuum in which humans naturally live. One of the best tools for this was the army.

Besides slavery, an army is probably the most perfect system ever conceived for subjugating human beings. It is a radical attempt to organize human interaction similar to the functions of a machine by following the mechanical principle of cause and effect, i.e. command and obedience. The ideal army is devoid of unpredictability and spontaneity, an environment with no signs of life. The army organizes people according to the model of death even before it has actually killed anyone.

However, a considerable amount of time and physical force is required to train the spontaneity out of people. The sporadically assembled mercenary armies of early modern states lacked the means to accomplish this. Because of their economic dominance, the Dutch were the first to form and train a modern standing army in Europe. It was no coincidence that the groundbreaking Orange army reform, ca. 1600, coincided almost exactly with the founding of the Dutch East India Company (1602) and the Amsterdam Stock Exchange (1612). The aim of this reform, which drew many of its ideas from ancient Roman military writings, was to turn unorganized troops into a large machine capable of responding precisely and predictably to every command.[32] To this end, daily exercises were conducted for hours, both with and without weapons; a sophisticated code for announcing and executing commands was established; and a system of punishments and rewards was meant to ensure the soldiers' unconditional obedience. Subsequently, similar systems emerged in virtually all European countries.

Drilling the Body

Essential for drilling the body, draconian penalties were imposed for any kind of nonconforming behavior. In the Prussian army, for example, the infamous "running of the gauntlet" was used to punish insubordination. Stripped to the waste, the condemned man had to walk slowly through a long pathway created by several hundred soldiers on both sides. Each soldier had to strike the offender's back with a rod, and those who did not hit hard enough risked suffering the same punishment. To prevent the man from walking through too quickly, an officer led the way with a saber pointed at his chest. If repeated, running the gauntlet often resulted in death. This punishment, which was routinely practiced in various forms by the French, Dutch and English armies as well, was based on the *fustuarium*, a form of execution devised by the Romans. The obvious point of this method was not only to punish the condemned, but also to make his comrades accomplices in the punitive violence. By mistreating one of their own, the soldiers subjugated themselves as well.

There was more to military discipline, however, than just these rituals of humiliation and submission. The ultimate goal was to penetrate and harness the soldier's entire motor system;

to control every gesture and glance and integrate them into a precise cadence. In short, the aim was to penetrate the core of the body with the "microphysics of power" (Michel Foucault).

With the rapid growth of the military, more and more European men were subjected to this synchronizing machinery. When the recruitment of volunteers could no longer meet the demand, many countries switched to forced induction. Army press gangs stormed into villages, and forcibly ripped the sons of peasants and craftsmen out of their normal lives and forced them into the army. These manhunts were played out frequently, for instance, in Prussia during the War of the Spanish Succession (1701–14). When this instigated a mass exodus from the countryside, as well as widespread desertions, the state upped the intensity of its coercive measures.

Ever more Europeans were exposed to a combination of military drill and grotesque punishments for even the smallest infractions. This began in the army, but later spread to schools and factories, leading to a profound change in people's body awareness and sense of self during the modern era. The individual's personal impulses and emotions had to be brutally suppressed. In order to become a physically compliant automaton in the hands of another, those taking orders must actively participate in the control and suppression of their own bodies. To prevent rebuke from their commander for improper conduct—perhaps an ill-advised gesture or facial expression— they must become their own *personal commanding officer*.

Nonetheless, the military's training and standardization methods were not only based on fear of punishment but also on the prospect of rewards. In order to create a more agile, faster and more intelligent army than the enemy's, the soldiers' motivation and ambition had to be fueled. A system that only relies on punishment tends to promote various forms of secret resistance, obstruction, sabotage, desertion or even open rebellion. Due to the additional personnel needed to keep subordinates under control, it is also costly. Military experts, like their pedagogical counterparts, soon discovered that it was far more effective to transform the one-dimensional punishment system into a two-dimensional grading system that provided rewards for desirable behavior and sanctions for unwanted behavior. This approach has the advantage of making individuals measurable and comparable, which enables the establishment of a ranking system. In this arrangement, it is not only the supervisors who compare and evaluate, but those under scrutiny are themselves also constantly aware of their position relative to others and will make efforts to be promoted, or at least to avoid demotion. Thus, those being judged become their own supervisors. The final stage of this development is reached when people have internalized this system to such an extent that they believe they are following their own choices. In reality, of course, they are just fulfilling the demands of the system.

The School as Disciplinary Institution

Over the centuries, the organizational features of the military became a model for many other institutions: the prison, the workhouse, the factory, sport and, last but not least, the school. The modern school system also drew on a second source, monastic schools, where rigid time management and physical discipline had already been developed in the late Middle Ages. The school combined Christian asceticism with military drills.

As with the monastery and the army, schools were based on the principle of confinement. Selected groups were isolated from the outside world and housed in closed facilities, which they could not leave without the permission of someone in authority. Inside the school itself, the space was carefully sub-divided, with each pupil assigned his or her place, which, again, they could only leave with permission. As in the case of the modern city and the modern forest, the transparency of the space is of crucial importance here as well. Pupils must be arranged so that the teacher can see them all at a glance, and the aisles between school desks must allow quick access to each individual.

Not only the space, but also the schedule and every single gesture were rigorously regulated. The French philosopher Michel Foucault (1926–84) describes how the bodies of students, in analogy to those of soldiers, were subjected to meticulous discipline through a system of signals:

> *The first and principal use of the signal is to attract at once the attention of all the pupils to the teacher and to make them attentive to what he wishes to impart to them. Thus, whenever he whishes to attract the attention of the children, and to bring the exercise to an end, he will strike the signal once. Whenever a good pupil hears the noise of the signal, he will imagine that he is hearing the voice of the teacher or rather the voice of God himself calling him by his name.*[33]

The so-called Monitorial System of the British pedagogues Lancaster and Bell in the nineteenth century pushed mechanically organized and scheduled time to an extreme:

> *8:45 entrance of the monitor, 8:52 the monitor's summons, 8:56 entrance of the children and prayer, 9:00 the children go to their benches, 9:04 first slate, 9:08 end of dictation, 9:12 second slate, etc.*[34]

Every word became an order that demanded prompt obedience. As in the military, this obedience extended into the fine motor skills, where the synchronization of movement had to be absolute. No deviant gesture was tolerated:

> *"Enter your benches". At the word "enter," the children bring their right hands down on the table with a resounding thud and at the same time put one leg into the bench; at the words "your benches," they put the other leg in and sit down opposite their slates." Take*

your slates." At the word "take," the children, with their right hands, take hold of the string by which the slate is suspended from the nail before them, and, with their left hands, they grasp the slate in the middle; at the word "slates," they unhook it and place it on the table.[35]

The aim of this whole procedure was to create a smoothly functioning learning machine. As the "father of modern education" John Amos Comenius commented in the seventeenth century:

As soon as we succeed in finding the proper method it will be no harder to teach school boys in any number desired than with the help of the printing press to cover a thousand sheets daily with the neatest writing. It will be as pleasant to see education carried out on my plan as to look at an automatic machine of this kind, and the process will be as free from failure as are these mechanical contrivances, when skilfully made.[36]

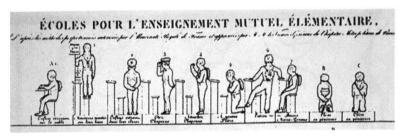

School based on the Monitorial System (France, 1818)

Although some quite grotesque and brutal disciplinary methods have disappeared from schools over the last 200 years, the foundations of that system are still in place to this day. Pupils— at least those beyond primary school—may not choose to speak or move within the classroom without permission from a person of authority. They may not even go to the window on their own initiative to catch a breath of air. They may not communicate with other pupils at the same table, but only along the central axis leading to the teacher, and then, only with regard to the prescribed subjects. Even prisoners in lockup have more rights than pupils in the classroom.

At first glance, it is surprising that this approach has endured all these years. For it has long since been established that the principle of command and obedience hinders rather than promotes learning. People learn better through curiosity than fear, and with interest rather than from externally imposed tasks whose purpose they may not grasp.[37] Despite persistent criticism, however, the fundamental pillars of the school system have changed little since the nineteenth century. The curriculum is still dictated from above and applied indiscriminately to all, the course material is broken down into subjects and hours, pupils are graded, etc. At first this may not seem to make sense, but a closer look reveals the simple reason behind institutional resistance to change. From the very beginning, schools were not mainly oriented toward the learning of *topics*, but had a different, overriding educational goal. School was for practicing a state of mind that would later prove to be indispensable to functioning within the economic world—alienation. Instead of students following their personal interests and developing skills in the service of fulfilling human needs, school was meant to prepare them to complete interchangeable tasks while earning points in an abstract system of penalties and rewards. Practicing this alienation mode is a prerequisite for preparing people to take their place in an alienated economy.

Therefore, people must unlearn the pursuit of their own impulses; they must accept work as the completion of tasks devised by others; and they must orient their lives to earn points that others award or deduct. Only then can they function in a global economy that reduces every work process to criteria for efficiency and utility maximization. The modern economy needs the alienated human being. It replaces curiosity and meaningful experience with payment, an abstract monetary value that is intended to compensate for work that is often senseless or grueling. It is exactly the same in school, where a grade takes the place of a fulfilling learning experience.

The Invention of Work

We tend to think of "work" as something as old as mankind. Did people not always have to "work" to earn a living? No doubt, they had to *do* something to sustain their lives, but for most of human history it was not understood as "work." The Latin word *laborare* (to work) originally means "to sway under a load." In antiquity, labor was exclusively slave labor, drudgery imposed by a foreign will, while the tasks that free people performed were not considered work.

In communities that were subjected to neither slavery nor the market, life was marked by *activities*: repairing a roof truss, washing clothes, harvesting, breastfeeding children, making tools, weaving, preparing a feast day and so on. From today's point of view, we would call some of these undertakings "work," others "housework," or "care work" and still others "leisure activities." But this differentiation is a modern invention. From the point of view of a self-sufficient, self-determined community, these categories do not make any sense, as all of these activities equally serve to provide that which is necessary for life.

When such communities were violently integrated into the Great Machine, the situation changed radically. It was now a matter of subjugating the energy and skills of people to goals that were outside their own motivation and community life. The result of this submission is what we now call "work." Historically, it took two forms. On the periphery of the world-system, slavery and forced labor were predominant for centuries, while wage labor was prevalent in the core regions. Both forms of work aim to make the worker a useful cog in the Great Machine, and both are associated with tremendous violence, albeit in very different forms. While slavery and forced labor were dominated by naked physical violence, wage labor developed over the centuries into a system with increasingly sophisticated forms of discipline that ultimately led to workers participating in their own subjugation.

Slavery

From the sixteenth to the nineteenth centuries, European slave traders abducted about 12 million people from Africa and shipped them to the Caribbean, Brazil and the USA, where they were sold to sugar, tobacco, coffee and cotton producers. As many as 50 percent of those captured died during "death marches" from the interior of Africa to the coasts. Of those who made it that far, another 20 percent died on the ocean crossing. In many ships, the slave decks were built so low that the prone, chained-up men, women and children could not even turn over. People lay in their own excrement for days on end, and many went mad during the voyage.[38]

For the trade in "black ivory" — as the Africans were called by English merchants — a number of joint-stock companies were founded on the model of the Dutch East India Company. These included the Royal African Company, the South Sea Company, the French West India Company and the Senegal Company. Shareholders included such distinguished personalities as John Locke (the "father of liberalism"), Isaac Newton, Daniel Defoe (author of *Robinson Crusoe*) and Jonathan Swift (author of *Gulliver's Travels*).[39]

As in Roman law, the European and colonial legal systems considered slaves to be objects instead of living beings. The *Code noir* of 1685, which the French historian Louis Sala-Molins described as "the most monstrous legal document of modern times,"[40] defined slaves as movable goods ("meubles") who were completely at the mercy of their owner's power.[41] According to this law, even small thefts were punishable by branding and lashing, and more serious cases with death. Escape was punished by cutting off the ears, severing a hamstring, and, after three escape attempts, with death.[42] The *Code Noir* was in effect in French overseas territories—with a short interruption during the Revolution—until 1848.

Slavery was the most radical conceivable attempt to break an individual's cultural and social ties in order to produce an *objectified* human being. Those who became enslaved were torn out of their everyday lives and deported to another continent. Slave traders also made efforts to separate prisoners from others who spoke the same language. Only the slave's pure physicality was to be transported across the Atlantic, isolated and liberated from all social and cultural connections. Nevertheless, many slaves, whether in Brazil, the Caribbean or the USA, secretly managed to continue and develop many of their cultural traditions. For example, despite prohibitions, the Candomblé religion was practiced for centuries in Brazil and played an important role in resisting the white masters.

Slavery contributed considerably to the expansion of the monetary economy. It was a boon to cities such as Liverpool, Bristol, Bordeaux and Glasgow that rose to become rich urban centers through the triangular trade in slaves, cotton, tobacco and sugar. The Caribbean sugar plantations also provided cheap calories for European workers, who, thanks to these imports, could be kept fed on minimal wages. Alongside coal, sugar became the second decisive fuel for Manchester's factories.[43]

Wage Labor

The emergence of wage labor in Europe was closely associated with war. Just as in ancient times, mercenaries were the first wage earners of the early modern period. The hired soldier embodies the principle of wage labor in its purest and most radical form. He kills or lets himself be killed, with money being the only motive. Ideally, he has no loyalties or commitments to a community outside the army that might hinder him in his work, making him as alienated and available as a person can be. However, when combat is over, and the flow of money dries up, the mercenary will fall into a social void. Dismissed mercenaries formed the first armies of the unemployed in history.

Although wage labor was considered to be formally "free" because it was based on a terminable contract between employer and employee, it was nonetheless seen by large sections of the population as a form of slavery. In fact, the free choice involved was very limited. Having been forced by increasing tax burdens, enclosures and expulsions to give up the subsistence and commons-based economy, people had to accept wage labor under almost any conditions. For the poorest of the poor, wage labor was even directly organized as forced labor. In England, France, the Netherlands and Germany in the early seventeenth century, workhouses were set up to intern beggars, vagabonds, unemployed craftsmen and orphans. Life in these institutions was subject to ceaseless disciplinary terror that was intended to be a deterrent. The poor would rather sell their labor for starvation wages than risk landing in the hellish conditions of the workhouse.

However, despite these different forms of structural and physical violence, the enforcement of wage labor and its associated system of discipline have faced considerable difficulties. Over the centuries, employers have never stopped complaining about lazy and unreliable workers. In the early phase of "proto-industrialization," when peasants earned an extra income at home through commissioned work for merchants in the so-called "putting-out system," work discipline could hardly be enforced. The peasants tended to work only when in urgent need of money, otherwise they preferred to pursue a life of self-determination.[44]

The miserable pay was not the only reason for resistance; it was also due to wage labor being forced upon people. As long as farmers and craftsmen were producing primarily for their own consumption and local markets, their economy was working toward satisfying basic needs. This often allowed for considerable freedom in the organization of their daily routine. How and when things were done and what techniques were used was determined by individual preferences as well as cultural customs and rhythms. All of these activities were embedded in a communal life that was not determined by purely economic criteria.

From a capitalist's point of view, all of these customs and rhythms were barriers to investment. For him, the working person is a tool whose "subjective" and culturally influenced preferences—as in the case of slavery—must not play a role. Only the objective requirements of the market count; therefore, home-based work was not enough in the long run. Although it proved to be highly profitable for many merchants, increases in production remained limited. The work processes were still too uncontrollable and inefficient, too deeply embedded in the stubborn structures of the communities.

Therefore, the next step was to extract the work from the home and relocate it to factories, where a supervisor could keep track of the workers' attendance, diligence and skill, even if they were still officially independent. In the beginning, these manufactories were just a collection of workshops gathered under a single roof, and each craftsman still maintained his own workflow from start to finish. To boost productivity, however, the work processes were gradually broken down into individual steps and distributed among various workers.[45] In this way, the activity was not only ripped from the fabric of the community, but also from the hands of the individual worker, degrading him to the level of an interchangeable element in a large logistical system. The late nineteenth and early twentieth centuries pushed this process to an extreme with the "scientific management" of Frederick Taylor, who divided and sub-divided the hand movements of factory workers into ever smaller components, in an attempt to eradicate every wasted millisecond.

With ever more meticulous control over space, time and movement, wage labor became a disciplinary tool similar to the army and the school. People were subjected to the "tyranny of abstract time" (according to the German philosopher Robert Kurz); a dictatorship of efficiency. It was no longer the pulse of the community, the cycles of nature or the idiosyncratic rhythms of different personalities that shaped life, but the monotonous ringing of alarm clocks, time clocks and bells.[46]

The complex structure of meaning in the relationships upon which community life is based was replaced by machine-like chains of command and obedience. The vanishing point of this development is a society striving exclusively for an infinite increase in the production of goods, and in the process, wiping out everything that does not serve this purpose.

Long before the Industrial Revolution, the military, educators, manufacturers and scientists dreamed of such a thoroughly machine-organized society. But they lacked one thing to make this dream a reality—fuel.

Chapter 8

Moloch

Coal Power, Total Market and Total War (1712–1918)

*Moloch whose mind is pure machinery! Moloch whose blood is running
money! Moloch whose fingers are ten armies!*
ALLEN GINSBERG, HOWL

I would annex the planets if I could.
CECIL RHODES

COAL: THE THIRD REVOLUTION OF THE METALLURGICAL COMPLEX

The industrial use of fossil coal ushered in a new era in the history
of planet Earth, which geologists call the *Anthropocene*. In just
200 years, the unleashing of fossil fuel energy has increased the
effects of human activities by a factor of hundreds or thousands
and radically transformed the planet's crust, biosphere and
atmosphere. This has not only triggered an enormous increase
in the production of goods, but has also caused one of the largest
mass die-offs in the Earth's history.[1] Not since the spread of
cyanobacteria more than 3 billion years ago, has a single species
changed the shape of the planet as profoundly as *homo carbonicus*.
However, while cyanobacteria's invention of photosynthesis
made it possible for more complex forms of life to spread on
Earth, the human-carbon culture is in the process of wiping out
large portions of evolution.

In schoolbooks, the history of the Industrial Revolution often
begins with technical inventions. Above all, the steam engine
is credited with the extraordinary increase in production that
has been observed since the nineteenth century. However, while

technical inventions were indeed of great importance, they are less the cause of economic expansion than its result. Therefore, it makes more sense to name this new age *Capitalocene* instead of Anthropocene, as it was not humankind as such who drove this development, but rather the dynamics of endless capital accumulation.

After being a known source of energy since antiquity, why was it precisely in the late eighteenth century that fossil coal suddenly began to be used to an ever greater extent? Why was there a sudden wave of technical inventions that broke at exactly this time—including the steam engine, whose principle had also been known since antiquity?[2] To answer these questions, we have to first set energy and technology aside and focus instead on money.

As we have seen in previous chapters, the money economy continued to spread during the course of the early modern period. In trading houses, banks and corporations, and also among large landowners, war entrepreneurs, slave traders and manufacturers, enormous amounts of capital had accumulated that were waiting for favorable investment opportunities. Other citizens who profited from the new money economy, such as lawyers and civil servants, were also willing to invest their savings. In some institutions, capital accumulation was quasi-automatic, for example, in public limited companies and banks. However, even where institutional automatism did not yet exist, a capitalist culture had developed in which the restless pursuit of profit and permanent reinvestment were no longer considered to be disreputable, but, on the contrary, as the epitome of virtue. States also gave top priority to promoting capital accumulation in order not to fall behind in the global military-economic competition.

Money does not actually increase by itself, even if it sometimes seems to. Over time, to augment financial value, there must be an expansion in the production of goods and services. Furthermore, in order to achieve a reasonably stable profit rate on investments, it is even necessary for output to grow exponentially. At first, this may sound paradoxical, but there is a simple mathematical reason. After every successful investment cycle, there will be more money in the system, which, in turn, will be further reinvested. For example, if I invest $1000 today that generates a return of 10 percent, after a year, I will have $1100. This will be reinvested again to gain another 10 percent return on this higher amount. This mathematical series is called compound interest. In the beginning, the slight exponential increase seems modest, but after 10 years, if the yield is maintained, I will have over $2500. After 50 years it will be $117,000; and after 100 years over 12 million dollars. This is, of course, only a model with an arbitrarily chosen yield. In reality, it is usually not the entire profit that is reinvested, and inflation or an economic downturn can lower the profit rate. Nonetheless, the principle of this arithmetic forms the foundational logic for the modern expanding economy. Incidentally, it is not exclusively restricted to money lending, as some interest rate critics think, but it applies to every economic activity that is based on a permanent cycle of profit-making and reinvestment. This simple arithmetic is the decisive reason why capitalist societies tend to produce exponential economic growth. Without it, they fall into serious crises. In order to expand production, however, work must be done, and energy must be expended.

For as long as the energy available to the system was restricted to wood, water, wind and muscle power (either human or animal), such expansion ran up against natural limits. By the end of the eighteenth century, in the leading economic centers of the Netherlands, England and France, the profitable energy potential had been tapped out. Men, women, children, vagabonds and prisoners were coerced to work through the use of both physical and structural violence. By accelerating the division of labor and mechanization, more output from each working hour was extracted. Livestock were not only used in fields, but also in mills and water-pumping systems. Holland was littered with windmills, and water power was used extensively in England.

Wood presented a special kind of bottleneck, since furnaces for metal production relied on burning charcoal. Here, neither water, wind, cattle nor humans could replace wood as a raw material. Metal production, in turn, was of vital importance for the core functions of the modern world-system. As long as silver and gold formed the basis of currencies, the expansion of the monetary economy and the maintenance of large armies would be impossible without precious metals. Iron, copper and tin were the most important mineral resources for the armaments industry. The expanding metallurgical-military complex swallowed up ever larger quantities of wood and, as a result of this dynamic growth, increasingly brushed up against ecological, social and financial limits. Consequently, prices for wood and charcoal soared. The German economist Werner Sombart even considered the fuel limits that were approaching around the end of the eighteenth century as "the impending end of capitalism," which could only be prevented by switching to hard coal.[3]

Black coal had been known as a fuel since ancient times, but until the Industrial Revolution it was mined only in relatively small quantities and mostly for local use. So much energy was necessary to mine the coal in deep seams and then transport it, that it was barely worth the effort. By the sixteenth century, fossil coal was being used more extensively in England, for instance, for heating buildings. However, technical and financial limits to the depth of exploration and transport remained. Pumping water out of the pits also posed a major problem, since it consumed more energy than that which could be extracted from the coal itself, even at relatively shallow depths.

With the rise in charcoal prices and the simultaneous increase in energy demand, pressure mounted to find a solution to these technical problems. This led to the development of new machines by enterprising inventors who hoped to make a lot of money from their patents. In 1712, the first commercially viable steam engine, developed by Thomas Newcomen, began operation in a coal mine in northern England. The highlight of this machine was that it ran on the coal from the mine itself and thus became part of a positive feedback cycle. The more coal that was mined, the more water that could be pumped out, and consequently, the more coal that could be mined.

However, there was still another hurdle blocking the large-scale use of fossil coal. Unlike wood, coal is concentrated in only a relatively few locations, which poses a need for transport over long distances to smelting works or other production sites. This too costs both energy and money and, over long hauls, was not worthwhile. The solution was provided by an invention that had been developed within the mining industry itself—the railway. Again, the key to its success was that it was powered by the coal it transported. The more coal that was mined, the more coal that could be transported. And with the conversion of blast furnaces from charcoal to hard coal coke, more steel could be produced with the transported coal. This, in turn, allowed for more rails, locomotives and wagons to be produced, with which still more coal could be transported. The coal-iron cycle was a system of several interconnected positive feedback loops. The eventual transport of passengers by rail was initially only an unintended side effect.

The combination of this cycle with the equally self-reinforcing system of endless capital accumulation was precisely the explosive mixture that catapulted the Earth into the Capitalocene and has left us today with a systemic crisis of planetary proportions. Together, capital accumulation and fossil energy form a kind of symbiotic double star system—a *nova*.[4] Only the accumulation of large amounts of capital could finance the enormous investments needed to open new mines, build steel mills and railway lines;

on the other hand, it was only fossil energy that could enable the exponential expansion of production necessary for permanently profitable investments and the continued accumulation of capital. The solar energy that had been stored up in coal for millions of years allowed the economic system to surge past the natural limits it had reached—at least for the time being.

One could describe the consequences of this volatile combination not only metaphorically as similar to the explosion of a nova. If we imagine the Earth's history for the last 200 years as a time-lapse film, then, viewed from outer space, we would see the image of a violent detonation. Starting off in Europe, individual points expand slowly at first, then ever more rapidly, enveloping everything around them. Some of these points also grow upwards to create "global cities," while others bore down to create lunar-like craters (huge open-pit mines). The epicenters then become interconnected by an ever denser network of pathways. In the second half of the film, the points and connecting lines all light up. Jumping forward by a few decades, the Earth would consist only of luminous centers and extinct craters. In the end, however, the centers will also burn out.

Coal Fuels the Vision of a Mechanistic Society

The mechanists of the seventeenth and early eighteenth centuries had dreamed of a machine world, and it was coal that finally provided the energy to turn this vision into a reality. What actually happened in the nineteenth and twentieth centuries, however, surpassed even the wildest dreams of radical mechanists. Like Charlie Chaplin in the famous assembly line scene from the film *Modern Times,* people actually became cogs in the workings of a global Megamachine. The logic of exponential money multiplication merged with the sheer inexhaustible combustive power of coal. The historian Fernand Braudel once calculated that before the Industrial Revolution, Europe's energy capacity was around 13 gigawatts (primarily from animal labor, wood and watermills).[5] Today, in the EU there are more than 1500 gigawatts, greater than a hundredfold increase, with around 85 percent of it produced by fossil fuels. Energy consumption per capita has increased by a factor of 20 over this period.

Capitalists and many socialists have struggled for a long time to improve and expand this machine and to redistribute the goods it produces in one direction or the other. Today, in view of the life-threatening ecological crises, however, we are faced with a completely different question, namely, whether and how we can stop this machine before it devastates most of the planet. It is not, as is often believed, just a question of exchanging energy sources. While quickly abandoning coal and oil is surely indispensable to achieving a sustainable society, it remains more than questionable whether a sufficiently rapid withdrawal is at all possible under the conditions of endless capital accumulation; for a continually growing system tends to need more and more energy, not less.[6] But even if a complete switch to renewable energies were possible in the near future, a solar-powered Megamachine would still plunder the last fishing grounds, the last fertile soils, the last forests, the last ore mines and even the last grains of sand on the beach. The mathematical formula for money multiplication would still have to be satisfied. Consequently, we have to talk about more than just the exchange of individual components. It is about the entire machine.

THE TOTAL MARKET

For the machine to function, work must be done. In the nineteenth century, mechanization and machinization did not save on human labor, but instead led to an enormous increase in the need for a freely available work force. People were reluctant, however, to voluntarily become part of this machinery and make themselves available at any given place for any purpose. As we shall see, a labor market had to be created, and this was done by force.

Industrial production, driven by fossil fuels and the dynamics of capital accumulation, not only needed a market for its output, but also a market for its input of raw materials, machinery, money and, above all, human labor. Creating labor markets involved nothing less than turning human beings into commodities. Although widely accepted as normal today, such markets were considered quite monstrous at the beginning of industrialization. People had to be available for input at any time, like a bale of cotton or a wagon full of coal. In his seminal book *The Great Transformation*, Karl Polanyi described how the commodification of human beings resulted in the demolition of society.[7] As a commodity to be freely traded, people had to be completely at the market's disposal, without ties to places, other people or cultures that might restrict their availability.[8]

In order for large investments in machinery to pay off, it had to be operated continuously, which meant that the supporting supply of manpower could not be allowed to fall off. However, as long as people could still choose for themselves whether to work in a factory or mine, or instead, to live off the fruits of their own land, the supply of manpower could not be guaranteed. It turned out that if people were given the choice, they preferred a subsistent, self-determined existence, even if they could make more money through factory work. Many even preferred living as homeless vagabonds to becoming "wage slaves."[9] In order to propel industrial production, people had to be deprived of this option and forced to be available to the market. The two methods used to accomplish this were the application of direct physical violence, such as slavery and forced labor, and the structural violence of the "free labor market."

Contrary to conventional wisdom, labor markets are not "natural" institutions. They do not form by themselves, but are made. A classic example is the creation of the national labor market in Britain, the pioneer of industrial production. As we have seen in Chapter 6, starting in the sixteenth century, large parts of the rural population were deprived of their subsistence opportunities, forced out by enclosures and compelled to sell their labor, usually on very unfavorable terms; the only other options being begging and stealing. To prevent escalating social unrest, the British state created various forms of support for the poor, including, in 1795, a minimum income. At the same time, employers continued to complain about the poor's lack of will to work. Even when enough workers were available, their motivation and productivity were dismal. Against this backdrop, voices were raised to withdraw state support in order to increase their willingness to work. The British doctor Joseph Townsend made this very clear in his influential essay on the Poor Laws:

> *Hunger will tame the fiercest animals, it will teach decency and civility, obedience and subjugation. It is only hunger which can spur and goad them on to labor. Yet our laws have said, they shall never hunger. The laws, it must be confessed, have likewise said that they shall be compelled to work. But then legal constraint is attended with too much trouble, violence, and noise; creates ill will, and never can be productive of good and acceptable service: whereas hunger is not only a peaceable, silent, unremitted pressure, but is the most natural motive to industry and labor.*[10]

With hunger and death looming in the background, workers were now to be disciplined by the "free market," instead of by operatives of the state. This was a cheaper and more effective solution that made for much less "trouble, violence, and noise." Already popular in the liberal camp, these ideas found expression in 1834 through the infamous New Poor Law, which largely did away with support for the poor. The result was the most massive wave of impoverishment in British history, which was described in detail by the French writer Flora Tristan, by Charles Dickens in his novel *Oliver Twist* and in the writings of Friedrich Engels, among others. During the unprecedented economic boom of the following decades, the hunger of millions of people became an everyday phenomenon. Slums spread in the big cities. A government commissioner described the dwellings of the poor, where ten people often lived in a single room, as "generally, as regards dirt, damp and decay, such as no person would stable his horse in."[11] Without changing a word, many of these descriptions can be applied to today's slums in Mumbai, Manila or Nairobi. Like their successors in Lagos and Lima today, the slum dwellers of London and Manchester did not suffer from general impoverishment and scarcity, but were victims of an unprecedented increase in wealth in the overall system.

Women were exposed to poverty and humiliation in even more extreme ways than men. To escape starvation, the only option left for hundreds of thousands was prostitution. Flora Tristan, who traveled through England as a journalist in 1839, speaks of 80,000 to 100,000 prostitutes in London alone, of whom more than 15,000 "grow sickly and die a leper's death in total abandonment" every year. There were thousands of child prostitutes between the ages of 10 and 15.[12] By threatening death, the "free market" subjected not only factory workers (many of whom were also women) to the regime of machine production; it also condemned women and girls to men's (sexual) power of disposal according to the laws of supply and demand.

Uprooting, Social Trauma and Resistance

The physical misery generated by the unleashing of the total market was only one part of the disaster. The radical uprooting and social disorganization caused by the creation of "free labor markets" was at least as painful. In nineteenth-century Europe—as later in the Global South—people had to separate from their families and cultural roots to sell their physical labor in the anonymity of newly sprouted industrial cities. There was no security or protection whatsoever against either illness or unemployment. The individual was degraded to being a mere object; a production factor; a replaceable cog in a monstrous economic machine. This uprooting has continued all across the planet ever since.

In the long run, it is impossible for people to live in a social and cultural void, and wherever possible they will create new meaningful relationships and social structures. In this sense, the labor movements that emerged in the nineteenth century did far more than just represent the interests of specific economic groups. They were also a response to social uprooting. Trade unions, associations (together with the important club houses), cooperatives and workers' choirs were organizations that offered something akin to a new home, an identity. Instead of atomized individuals competing in the economic arena, there was a form of solidarity, collective decision-making and often internal democracy. When "outside," within the zone of the unbridled economy, one was subject to bourgeois value norms, which were based above all on property, income, formal education and competition; when "inside" self-created structures, however, it was possible for workers to develop their own values, language and alternative concepts of education—their own culture.[13] Now, the workers' trauma of being reduced to an object could be offset by an experience of self-efficacy.

At first, large segments of the workers' movement were not just about securing better wages and working conditions within the system. They also saw themselves as part of a much more fundamental opposition. Many rejected the principle of wage labor out of hand because it destroyed the economic independence of households and their self-organization, leaving workers completely at the mercy of large corporations. The Lowell Mill Girls, for example, an organization of US textile workers who popularized the term "wage slavery," declared in the 1830s:

When you sell your product, you retain your person. But when you sell your labor, you sell yourself, losing the rights of free men and becoming vassals of mammoth establishments of a monied aristocracy that threatens annihilation to anyone who questions their right to enslave and oppress. Those who work in the mills ought to own them, not have the status of machines ruled by private despots who are entrenching monarchic principles on democratic soil as they drive downwards freedom and rights, civilization, health, morals and intellectuality in the new commercial feudalism.[14]

In Europe as well, there was massive resistance to the degradation and subjugation of workers. In England in the 1810s, for instance, the Luddites stormed textile factories and destroyed machines. Later, they were labeled reactionary enemies of technology by leaders of the labor movement, but in fact, that was not their primary concern. The Luddites did not fight against technical innovations per se, but struggled for the preservation of traditional craftsmen's rights and fixed prices. In short, they opposed the logic of the total market.[15] In a brutal response, the "liberal" state deployed a large army contingent against the Luddites. The destruction of machines ("sabotage") was declared a capital crime, and dozens of Luddites were sentenced to death in show trials. Once again, the "free market" had to assert itself through the use of massive physical force.

The Invention of the Nation

The great uprooting associated with industrialization, and the cultural vacuum resulting from it, led not only to the emergence of labor movements and labor cultures, but also to another movement that ultimately turned out to be disastrous— nationalism. As the historian Benedict Anderson put it, the nation is an "imagined community."[16] No Frenchman or Briton ever really gets to know all of his 65 million compatriots; no US citizen can ever meet all the other 320 million other Americans; and no Indian can ever become acquainted with the entire population of

1.2 billion Indians. Yet, even today, many still believe that they belong to a large community of French, German, British, Indian or US citizens; to a community united in sharing the same fate — even if they might be tricked and cheated every day by some of their compatriots. For many people, the abstract concept of the nation substitutes for a genuine, naturally-evolved community, with genuine participation and solidarity. This illusion has been instrumentalized to a great extent in order to divert attention from social conflicts and to mobilize people for the purposes of the Great Machine, even to the point of war.

The term "nation" has been broadly interpreted at different times to mean very different things. In the early days of the French Revolution, it meant a society of citizens with equal rights. The idea of the nation was based on demands for freedom, equality and fraternity; it was to be egalitarian and, in principle, open to everyone. The notion of an ethnically and linguistically uniform "national community" that distinguished itself from others had not yet been established.[17] Traces of this revolutionary concept can also be found in the 1848 Revolution, when democratic hopes, especially in Germany and Italy, were projected onto the idea of founding a consolidated nation that would put an end to small-state rule by despots. But in the 1820s, the German poet Heinrich Heine had already come to the realization that the demand for a unified nation that was inspired by social revolution was increasingly overshadowed by "Teutomania," xenophobia and anti-Semitism.[18]

Thus began the major reinterpretation of the nation as an idea. From a concept that demanded equal rights for all, it transformed into a paradigm that excluded certain groups.[19] The notion of an ethnically and linguistically uniform community that was to merge with the state was especially popular within the petty-bourgeois milieu and with government employees, such as teachers. For a long time, it remained alien to workers and peasants, as their experience was not marked by the antagonism between different "peoples," but much more by their daily conflicts with landlords and employers.[20] The moneyed bourgeoisie and aristocrats had traditionally taken an inter-national view, since their investments and connections were spread halfway across the globe.[21] Over time, however, they were to discover that it could be very useful to promote nationalism and turn it into a state ideology.

The concept of the nation as a family-like community has since become very useful to ruling classes, because it diverts attention away from the struggles for justice and genuine participation that run across all societies. It suggests a unified population in which factory owners and workers, war ministers and soldiers all work together for a higher common purpose. It conveys to the lonely and dejected that they are actually part of a great common project—the establishment of a glorious nation, a kind of superfamily. It also promises that some of the splendor of the nation will trickle down onto the desolate life of the individual. Nationalism became a useful tool for maneuvering considerable portions of the populace that were critical of the system, including those from the working class, toward an illusion that helped stabilize the system and ultimately proved suicidal.

In order to achieve this, the idea of the nation had to be gradually stripped of its social-revolutionary content. Class differences had to be shoved into the shadows, and the commonalities of "the people" highlighted. The rapidly expanding mass media made important contributions to this end. More importantly, however, schools, the military and universities became institutions for indoctrinating people with the concept of the nation. A case in point is the 1914 *Declaration by University Teachers of the German Reich*. Almost the entire German professorship proclaimed that "the spirit that infuses the German army is none other than that of the German people. They are one and the same, and we are part of it."[22] Identification symbols were deliberately created through flags and hymns, resulting in the staging of a quasi-religious cult. Historiography constructed national histories spanning thousands of years, in which old Teutons became "Germans," Gauls "the French" and Anglo-Saxons "Englishmen." In doing so, it spawned national myths and "invented traditions" (Eric Hobsbawm) that were intended to legitimize the artificial edifice of the nation state as something that had evolved naturally. Racism was given a scientific gloss in the form of biological research, fostering the phantom of a "pure," ethnically homogeneous, national community.

On closer inspection, the fact that this strategy could, at least partly, succeed was an astonishing sleight of hand. Throughout the early modern period and well into the nineteenth century, the state was a thoroughly hostile institution for the majority of European populations (not to mention colonized peoples in conquered lands). It collected taxes by force; it swallowed up men for the military apparatus; it enforced debt collection; and it subjugated the poor to draconian laws.[23] How, then, was it possible that, at the end of the nineteenth and beginning of the twentieth century, large masses of people were so enthusiastic about the state that they were willing to go to war for the nation and the fatherland, to kill or be killed?

It is not very surprising that a certain number of civil servants and other beneficiaries of the new system willingly embraced the national myths. Workers, on the other hand, did not buy the propaganda so easily. Their experience was that the state acted primarily as an extension of the employer and worked on behalf of his interests, and for them to identify with these goals was simply not to be expected. This situation only changed when governments began to gradually meet some of the workers' demands: for shortened working hours, the right to vote, health and safety measures, and social insurance.

With these steps, there was a partial merging of both the state's and the labor force's interests. The state took care of "its" workers with protectionist measures against other workers. This enabled the national ideology to find fertile ground in certain segments of the working class. It was a *double movement* of the total market that set the national trap and ultimately made the Great War and the mass movement of fascism possible. On the one hand, the radical uprooting of workers created a social and cultural vacuum that was only partially filled by emancipatory workers' organizations. On the other hand, to those who were uprooted, the pseudo-community of the nation came across as a savior—in a material sense as a kind of rudimentary welfare state, and conceptually with a vision of "the people" as a unified, collective body.

THE GREAT EXPANSION

The epoch from 1815 (the end of the Napoleonic wars) to 1914 is often described as "The Hundred Years' Peace" or "Pax Britannica," a peace brought about chiefly by the triumph of liberalism and free trade. It is true that the number of wars between major European powers decreased compared to previous centuries. It is also true that certain elements of high finance had a (temporary) interest in avoiding wars that would have interrupted the free movement of goods and money. However, with regard to most of the world's population at the time, it is absurd to apply the term "peace" or even "relative peace." During this period, especially in the second half of the nineteenth century, practically the entire planet was overrun by the the European money and war machinery, entire peoples were exterminated and countless cultures destroyed.

In order to survive, the Great Machine must internally expand and deepen its monetary economy ("internal colonization"), while externally, it must integrate new territories and their inhabitants into its structures.[24] Such expansion has come in waves since the emergence of the system in the early modern era. In the sixteenth and seventeenth centuries, North and

South America, including the Caribbean, were incorporated; the Dutch and English East India companies established colonies on the coasts of India and Indonesia, while slave traders set up business on the west coast of Africa. In the late eighteenth century, another wave of expansion began: India and Southeast Asia (reaching to their interiors), Africa (first the West, then the entire continent), the Ottoman Empire (what we now call the Middle East) and Australia were all integrated into the system as peripheral areas. China was able to resist this process for a relatively long period and avoid formal colonization. From the middle of the nineteenth century, however, it was also integrated into the periphery through several wars. The periphery would later be referred to as the "third world."[25]

"Civilization": The New Missionary Project

The expansion of the West has always been accompanied by a civilizing mission to legitimize the massive violence employed, for both the perpetrators and the general public. The Christian mission had been fulfilling this function for centuries, and with a new wave of expansions, the nineteenth century experienced a veritable boom in missionary activities. Even though individual missionaries occasionally opposed the extermination of indigenous populations, on the whole, they contributed significantly to preparing the ground for military and economic occupation. In some cases, missionaries not only paved the way ideologically, but they were also economic actors. For instance, the Livingstonia Central Africa Company (later renamed African Lakes Corporation), which played an important role in the colonization of Central Africa, was first established to support missions in the region. Missionaries and traders often combined both functions, or worked hand in hand in partnership. Sometimes the missionaries even operated as military shock troops and established their own state authority. One example is the colonization of Tahiti by the London Missionary Society, founded in 1795. After an initial wave of only lightly armed missionaries was warmly received by the Tahitian people, but hardly made any converts, the Society reverted to other methods. They turned one of the clan leaders into an alcoholic, supplied him with weapons and drove him into warring against the other islanders. Once all the inhabitants were forcibly converted, the missionaries set up a veritable regime of terror on the island with the help of a newly created mission police force. Even seemingly harmless expressions of island culture, such as singing (with the exception of church songs), dancing or bathing in the sea, were strictly forbidden. For dancing, the punishment was several years of forced road construction, and the practice of their indigenous religion was punishable by death. In order to destroy the economic independence of the Tahitians, the missionaries had the breadfruit trees cut down, which also deprived the population of its main food source. By 1850, the Society had largely eradicated the islanders' independence and culture. James Cook, who had already visited the island in 1769, was to be right with his remark: "It would have been far better for these poor people never to have known us."[26]

Since the late eighteenth century, the Christian mission project had been supplemented and overlaid by a secularized variant: the good news brought by "civilization." Enlightened missionaries claimed that it was not only the West's religion that made it superior to all others, but also its civilized customs along with a superiority in morals, science, economy, administration and technology. In 1798 Napoleon addressed his troops on their way to Egypt, "Soldiers, you are undertaking a conquest with incalculable consequences for civilization."[27] The motto of the British missionary David Livingstone was "Christianity, commerce, and civilization."[28]

The gospel of civilization was inextricably bound together with racism, which was cultivated not only by politicians but also by many of the most venerable scientists of the day. The British mining entrepreneur and chief architect of the British colonial empire in Africa, Cecil Rhodes, had no qualms about linking this racism to concepts of progress and the civilizing mission: "I contend that we are the first race in the world, and that the more of the world we inhabit the better it is for the human race. If there be a God, I think that what he would like me to do is paint as much of the map of Africa in British red as possible."[29]

Racism is not some sort of natural phenomenon that arises out of a general fear of strangers. It is man-made and meant to fulfill a specific function in the modern world-system. As the populations of Africa, the Americas and Asia were forcibly integrated into the global economy, a justification was needed for these people to be subjected to such monstrous disenfranchisement and exploitation. At first, it was the supposedly superior Christian religion that served this purpose. Then, in the eighteenth and nineteenth centuries, an extensive literature developed that divided people into a hierarchy of different "races," with whites in the top position. Voltaire, for example, compared the blacks with monkeys, and the German philosopher Immanuel Kant claimed, "Humanity is at its greatest perfection in the race of the whites." The Indians and blacks, on the other hand, were, according to Kant, "lower, and the lowest are a part of the (Native) American people."[30] Similar expressions came from Hegel, Hume, Darwin and many other luminaries of Western philosophy and science. By the eighteenth century, researchers were measuring people's skulls in order to demonstrate that blacks were less intelligent than whites and thus predestined for menial work. These studies, which were to become the origins of biological anthropology as a scientific discipline, were later continued by the Nazis for their own purposes.

Racism cannot be dismissed as just an aberration of modernity. It is an integral and indispensable component of the Megamachine, and to this day it serves to legitimize the extreme inequalities, without which the modern world-system cannot function. The migration regime is a case in point. Every year, thousands of people from Africa and the Middle East flee homes that have been destroyed by war, poverty and climate chaos, only to die on the borders of "Fortress Europe." Europeans, on the other hand, can travel effortlessly to any country in the world. The same type of Apartheid system applies to those who flee from Central American countries that have been devastated by US interventions for decades. Their search for refuge is met with racist propaganda and a highly militarized border between Mexico and the US. These forms of structural racism are deeply rooted in our institutions.

The Devastation of Africa

As before in the Americas, the colonization of Africa provided an excellent opportunity for combining mission (either religious or secular) and business interests. Founded by Rhodes in 1889, the British South Africa Company was granted a license by the Crown to mine gold, copper (chiefly for the electrification of Europe) and diamonds in southern Africa. In support of this effort, a private army was assembled with which to establish rule over an area that was later named "Rhodesia." Standing between Rhodes and those mineral resources, however, were several hundred thousand local inhabitants who clearly did not agree that it would be best for the world if the English owned everything. In 1893, the Ndebele rose up with about 100,000 men to oppose the company's army. Cecil Rhodes would have undoubtedly deemed it a sign of his superior race and civilization that the British were able to deploy weapons against which the Ndebele were helpless — machine guns.

The machine gun, developed in 1885 by the British inventor Hiram Maxim, fired 500 rounds per minute, and had its first large-scale application during the two Matabele Wars. With less than 2000 men, Rhodes's army was able to crush the resistance, killing a total of 60,000 Ndebele during the two wars. The British, on the other hand, lost only about 500 men, most of whom were local mercenaries. The extreme asymmetry is reminiscent of the Conquista massacres or the Battle of Frankenhausen during the German Peasant War. In each case, the insurgents were powerless against the new weapons of the metallurgical complex. The term Matabele "War" is a euphemism for a genocide that belongs to a long dark line of many forgotten, repressed and covered-up genocides in Africa, including the Herero genocide perpetrated in German Southwest Africa (present-day Namibia) by German colonial rulers.[31]

Thanks to South African copper, the people in London and other European capitals, who had never or only cursorily been informed about these events, enjoyed their newly installed electric lights. They had no idea that the same machine guns that cleared the way to African copper would be turned against them in just a few years.

Left: The Matabele War (1893). Right: The Electricity Pavilion at the Chicago World's Fair (1893)

The Belle Époque and the Extermination of the Other

The decades before the outbreak of the First World War were later referred to as the "Belle Époque" and described as a carefree and pleasure-filled era. However, while corks were popping in the Moulin Rouge, the Savoy and the Adlon Hotel, and marveling visitors were strolling through world exhibitions in Brussels, Paris or Milan, other parts of the world were sinking into barbarity, set in motion by the very European capitals that claimed to be the epitome of progress and civilization. In 1884, Leopold of Saxe-Coburg and Gotha, King of Belgium, laid claim to an area in Central Africa as his private property. The "Congo Free State" was about 20 times larger than Belgium, and all of its inhabitants, mineral resources, fauna and flora were now completely at the king's disposal.

Leopold's presumptions regarding property seemed extreme, crazy and barbaric, especially to the Congolese. Nonetheless, the Western governments at the Berlin Congo Conference of 1884, who divided up Africa among themselves, found Leopold's claim quite reasonable and expressed unanimous approval. Perhaps a little extravagant, it was broadly in line with a long tradition of ownership of entire countries and their populations by private individuals and corporations.

The Belgians were interested in two things: copper and rubber. Rubber experienced a tremendous boom due to electrification, the advent of the bicycle industry and later the automobile industry and was primarily used for tires and insulation. Leopold subjected the Congolese to forced labor in rubber extraction and mining. Rubber production quotas were imposed on every village, and to ensure punctual delivery, the military took women hostage. If the required amounts were not delivered on time, the women were shot. Unimaginably, 10 million people were killed by shootings, inhumane working conditions, imprisonment and evictions.[32]

The horrors of Belgian rule became widely known thanks to the tireless work of journalist Edmund Morel, who launched the first international human rights campaign in history. The American writer Mark Twain also wrote extensively about the atrocities.[33] Regardless, not a single one of the mass murderers was ever brought to justice. The only consequence for Leopold was that he was forced to sell the Congo to the Belgian state in 1908—as if the country and its inhabitants were a sack of flour. The Société générale de Belgique, the largest metallurgical corporation in Belgium, had been a key player in looting the natural resources and committing genocide. After the end of the "Free State," the company continued to conduct business unhindered until merging with the multinational Suez Lyonnaise des Eaux in 2003. This corporation subsequently merged with Gaz de France in 2008 to become the world's second largest energy group.

India: The Invention of the Third World

The physical violence of war and forced labor was only one way to conscript new territories and their inhabitants into the expanding system. An equally important instrument, closely associated with physical violence, was the structural violence of the market. A case in point is the incorporation of the Indian subcontinent into the world economy.

From the mid-eighteenth century on, India had been ruled by the British East India Company, a private state-like entity owned by the company's shareholders. After a rebellion by the company's mercenaries (some 200,000 soldiers), which turned into a dangerous anti-colonial revolt, the British government withdrew administrative and military rights from the corporation in 1858. India was now directly subordinated to the British Crown as a colony, with a viceroy administering rule from Calcutta. Under the direct control of the Crown, Indian agriculture was monetarized at an accelerated pace and integrated into the world market. The means for accomplishing this were familiar. Most importantly, taxes were collected in currency instead of in-kind to force farmers to abandon subsistence production methods and produce for the market instead. Furthermore, peasants were driven into debt bondage, a principle known since ancient times and perfected in colonial times. Small farmers would receive advance payments, which then committed them to deliver a certain quantity at a certain time. If unable to fulfill the contract (due to drought, illness or other reasons), they were subjected to life-long debt bondage, which in some cases was even passed on to their descendants "in perpetuity."[34] The consequence of the forced market integration for the peasants was a creeping disintegration of community-based economic solidarity. This was felt especially at the village level with a widening of the gap between rich landowners and simple peasants, who became increasingly indebted after crop failures and eventually lost their land and freedom.

Meanwhile, financed by taxes from Indian peasants, the British built an extensive rail network across the subcontinent, which made it possible to bring raw materials and agricultural products quickly and cheaply to ports, and thus to the world market. The colonial rulers also touted the railway network as a means of quickly bringing aid to affected areas in the event of famine. When the Great Famine did come, however, the railway in conjunction with the "free market" brought nothing but tragedy and disaster.

In the years 1876–8 and 1896–1902, hunger epidemics of unprecedented proportions swept through India and other parts of the world, including China, Brazil and South East Africa. According to various calculations, between 12 and 30 million people died in India alone.[35] As is so often the case with famine, the simplest and most convenient explanation was the weather. While insufficient monsoon rainfall did play a major role, the extent of the tragedy, according to sociologist Mike Davis in his book *Late Victorian Holocausts: El Niño Famines and the Making of the Third World*, was actually caused by the combination of weather events, market logic and state repression.

During the famine years, a weather pattern was observed over the Pacific Ocean that is known today as "El Niño." This phenomenon, which affects large parts of the Earth's entire climate, leads to severe drought in India, northern China and the Amazon, while causing intense precipitation along the west coast of South America. While the Niños of 1876–8 and 1896–1902 were particularly severe, people did not die in such large numbers solely because there was not enough food. From 1877 to 1878, during the worst years of famine, India actually exported 320,000 tons of wheat to Europe.[36] Many grain stores were full, as traders speculated on the rapidly rising prices, while people were left to starve to death in front of silos that were held under strict militarily guard.[37] Drawn by the magnetism of purchasing power, the railways did not transport the grain to the starving, but hauled it off to the world market.

The dire situation led to increased appeals for Viceroy Lord Lytton to intervene in the market on behalf of the millions facing death. But Lytton insisted on the "prohibition of interference in private trade." Any intervention in favor of the hungry would only distort the infallible balance of the self-regulating market.[38] *The Anti-Charitable Contributions Act* of 1877 even forbade private donations under threat of imprisonment.[39] Lytton also roundly rejected the Indians' urgent requests to suspend tax collection in the hard-hit areas. After all, he needed the money for a military campaign in Afghanistan. To pay the taxes, the highly indebted, starving peasants had to sell the last of their cattle, which usually amounted to a death sentence. Countless people died because they lacked the two cents a day on which to survive, while in London the tills of the wheat merchants were ringing. Local creditors and big landowners were happy to take possession of forfeited livestock and land from the dying. The only "relief measure" the British undertook was to set up labor camps in which completely emaciated workers were given the most backbreaking physical labor and a totally inadequate diet. Although British health officials warned that people were facing certain death under the camp conditions, the administration neither increased rations nor reduced the workload. The combination of heavy labor and chronic malnutrition eventually turned the labor camps into death camps.[40]

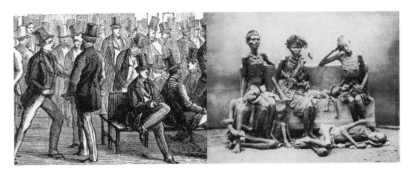

Left: The London Stock Exchange (1873). Right: Starving people in the Indian state of Madras (1877)

What the British did in India was far worse than the mismanagement of a crisis, it was another case of genocide. Nonetheless, historiography still fails to acknowledge this fact, just as it ignores the 57,000 people across the planet who in our times are starving to death every day, although more than enough food is produced. This is because these people are not murdered by volleys of gunfire, but by an economic system that is considered to be an incarnation of nature itself.[41] The fact that this system could only be maintained by massive physical violence during the Great Famine shows just how *un*-natural it actually is. Without the police operations against rebellious starving people who attacked the granaries, the "free market" would have collapsed. How could it be otherwise? How could a social system that extracts obscene wealth and produces deadly misery in such close proximity be maintained without violence?

The Great Famine also reveals a particularly dangerous characteristic of global agricultural markets: they strongly couple weather events with prices clear across the globe. "Suddenly the price of wheat in Liverpool," writes Mike Davis, "and the rainfall in Madras were variables in one and the same vast equation of human survival."[42] As a result, starvation was occurring not only where there were crop failures, but was also being spread epidemically through the mechanism of rising prices. As peasants were forced by colonial governments to produce cash crops such as cotton for the world market instead of food they could live on, they could no longer afford to eat if wheat and rice prices rose too sharply. In today's era of climate chaos, when even more massive and extreme weather conditions are to be expected than the El Niño events of the nineteenth century, the globalized agricultural market may prove to be a deadly trap. Survival in the twenty-first century can only be ensured by prioritizing food sovereignty over the logic of the market.

The Destruction of China by Western Colonial Powers

China's integration into the modern world-system played out differently than in India, but it was no less brutal. As the sociologist Giovanni Arrighi explains, over centuries, China had developed a "non-capitalist market economy" based, unlike the economies of the West, on the separation of state and capital.[43] In this way, the "Middle Kingdom" had become the most prosperous country on Earth. At the beginning of the nineteenth century, however, as European expansion continued to penetrate East Asia, the chronic trade deficit with China was a thorn in the side of the British. To compensate, they attempted to export opium from British India to China. At the time, the British East India Company was not only the world's largest corporation, but also the world's largest drug dealer, smuggling huge quantities of opium into southern China's Guangzhou Province (Canton). However, the Chinese government resisted the illegal trade, just as they had successfully resisted both colonization and creeping integration into the capitalist world market. Foreign traders were subject to considerable restrictions, as were missionaries. To pry open China, the British government ultimately resorted to methods that would plunge the country into chaos and impoverishment and contributed to one of the greatest tragedies in human history. As is so often the case when the victims of a major crime are not Europeans, there are little or no historical accounts of it to be found in our textbooks and travel guides.

British traders in the nineteenth century used South Chinese secret societies, the so-called *triads*, as opium distributors and built them up into powerful mafia-like organizations that profoundly destabilized Chinese society over the next hundred years. In addition to the East India Company, a central role was played by Jardine, Matheson & Co., which today is a multi-billion-dollar global corporation, headquartered in the British tax haven of Bermuda.[44] Later, the Hong Kong and Shanghai Banking Corporation (HSBC), which is currently the second largest bank in the world, also became a central player. The cornerstone for the wealth of these corporations was laid by organized crime. Together with the governments of Great Britain and France, later also the USA and Japan, these companies were the pioneers of global drug trafficking, which today, with a turnover of around $4 trillion (4000 billion), is one of the largest industries in the world economy.[45]

In many ways, governments are still involved in this trade today. During the Vietnam War, for example, the US boosted drug trafficking immensely in the "Golden Triangle" of Indochina to finance its secret operation to bomb Laos. In doing so, powerful mafia organizations were created that continued to flourish even after the war. This resulted in roughly 20 percent of US soldiers becoming addicted to heroin, which was followed by a flood of hard drugs on the American market. A similar pattern was later repeated in Nicaragua and Afghanistan.[46] The global drug drama has largely been the result of Western attempts to destabilize uncooperative governments—a development with its roots in the British invasions of China.

When Chinese authorities arrested British drug traffickers in 1839 and burned more than a thousand tons of illegal narcotics, businessmen William Jardine and James Matheson persuaded the London government to start a war that went down in history as the First Opium War. The British Parliament and traders demanded "satisfaction and reparations" from the Chinese government for daring to apply its own laws against drug gangsters and for deploying war ships to protect the country. The Chinese military could muster only meager defenses against British cannons and the first steam-powered steel ships, called "devil ships" by the Chinese. After capitulating in 1842, a similar incident occurred in 1856, spurring Britain and France to engage in the Second Opium War. The high point of this invasion resulted in the devastation of the Imperial Summer Palace in Beijing. The victorious powers, now joined by the USA and Russia, forced through the so-called "unequal treaties," which legalized the opium business, compelled China to open up to world trade, and gave Christian missionaries a free hand. The result of the invasions and mafia activities was China's spiral into the chaos of a failed state—a situation akin to the results of Western intervention in Iraq and Libya 150 years later. The once flourishing economy began to decay, and the social fabric was in shreds. In 1851, the Taiping uprising had already erupted, which was to become the bloodiest civil war in human history and cost the lives of between 20 and 30 million people. The uprising had its origin in the south, where the Mafia triads, controlled by England and France, did their mischief. Pumped full of Christian apocalyptic ideas by an American missionary, a farmer's son named Hong Xiuquan became the rebel leader and mobilized dissatisfied minorities for an armed struggle against the central government.[47] Although the movement he founded promoted a classless society, it was actually quite authoritarian, repressive and marked by religious fanaticism. The conflict escalated into total war, in which both sides pursued a scorched earth strategy, burning entire stretches of countryside and devastating hundreds of cities. While the civil war had partly internal causes, the British intervention added fuel to the fire. Another result of the Opium Wars was that 20 million Chinese became drug addicts, a macabre symbol of forced dependence on the West. The drugs weakened the population, the military and the leadership of the country and, at the same time, offered an escape from the social catastrophe into the parallel world of intoxication.

After two invasions and a catastrophic civil war, China was shattered. In 1899, a massive revolt against the Western colonizers broke out, known as the "Boxer Rebellion."[48] A coalition of eight states, Germany, Great Britain, the USA, Russia, Japan, Italy, France and Austria-Hungary, responded with yet another invasion. The German Kaiser galvanized his soldiers for a campaign of extermination with the slogan, "No quarter will be given. Prisoners will not be taken." At the same time, the propaganda term "yellow peril" was coined by the West, and is still used today in various forms to arouse opposition to China, although at no time in the last 700 years—since Genghis Khan— has China actually posed a danger to the West.

After the allied troops had defeated the "Boxers" and plundered Beijing for three days, they blackmailed the Chinese government into "reparations" worth billions, which completely ruined the country. In the following decades, the Middle Kingdom fell into the hands of competing warlords and mafia organizations, each of which was supported by different factions of Western powers and Japan.[49] Torn apart by civil war and economically bled out, the country eventually became the prey of Japanese fascists. The interventions of the colonial powers had plunged China into a spiral of devastation known as the "Century of Humiliation"—a historical episode still downplayed or hushed up in Europe and North America.[50]

THE PATH TO TOTAL WAR

By around 1900, virtually the entire globe was participating in the world economy, the first truly global system in human history. The intense competition among colonial powers for markets, raw materials and spheres of influence eventually became one of the primary factors leading to the First World War. As long as Britain was economically and militarily superior to all other countries by orders of magnitude, no one could seriously consider a direct military challenge to her empire. Thanks to its enormous coal and steel industry, however, Germany reached economic parity by 1900 and made moves toward replacing England as the reigning hegemonic power.

Therefore, the fact that the Great War broke out in 1914 is not so surprising. Wars have always been a routine way to assert national interests within the modern world-system. They are considered to be rationally manageable, because those who want to assert their interests usually take almost no personal risk. Regents, arms producers and financiers usually do not step onto the battlefield—neither do generals, for that matter. Wars are always paid for with the lives of common soldiers and civilian victims, and the financial damage is usually spread across the population. This makes war a typical example of a "moral hazard." Those making the decisions risk virtually nothing themselves, and those whose lives are at risk have no say at all.[51]

It was therefore not surprising that the Great War was decided upon by governments, and that they waged it with the utmost lack of scruples. New indeed was the technology that made it the first industrial war of extermination. Millions of soldiers ran into a wall of Maxim machine gun salvos and were mowed down row by row. Elsewhere, the Great Machine continued to hum along, producing new ammunition and using rail transport to send more people to a certain death. The metallurgical complex, catapulted by fossil energy to a new dimension, and driven into a grotesque arms race among competing states, provided a completely new generation of weapons. For their precision and destructive power, human history had never seen anything like the machine gun, the tank, the grenade, the air raid bomb, the armored warship, the submarine or the torpedo.

The chemical industry, which had always been closely linked to the metallurgical complex,[52] also made a major contribution to industrialized killing. Fritz Haber's and Carl Bosch's invention of synthetically produced saltpeter made it possible not only to produce artificial fertilizers, but also to manufacture explosives and gunpowder in previously unimaginable quantities. Without this invention, the war might have ended as early as 1915. During the war, Fritz Haber, who later received the Nobel Prize in Chemistry, also developed various forms of poison gas for the German army.

Another novelty in this conflict was the level of mobilization. A total of 50 million soldiers were drafted into service during the course of the war, 13 million of whom were on the German side alone. When one remembers how difficult it was during the High Middle Ages for sovereigns to assemble just a few thousand men for the greatest military expeditions, the extent becomes clear to which society had been transformed into an enormous machine with the advent of modern times—a machine that could turn half the world into a battlefield overnight if a handful of regents so ordered.

But why were all these people willing to obey? How could they set off for barely familiar lands, to shoot people they did not know, who had done nothing to them, with ultimately nothing to gain but their own miserable death? Could it really be only because of orders given by a group of what the Austrian writer Karl Kraus referred to as "figures in an operetta," somewhere in distant Berlin, Vienna or Petersburg? Which invisible cables and mechanisms induced them to respond like cogs in a machine?

Certainly, part of the answer lies in the 200 years worth of efforts by disciplinary institutions along with nationalistic indoctrination. Yet, something unfathomable remains. With the First World War, the modern world-system entered a surreal and eerie phase. It was no coincidence that this era produced Franz Kafka's descriptions of a world with invisible constraints that deprived people of their freedoms. It was also not by chance that Dadaism and Surrealism emerged at this time. Karl Kraus spoke of the "unreal, unthinkable years, inaccessible to any memory, any waking consciousness, preserved only in a dream of blood."[53] Ten million people died in the First World War, 20 million were injured and countless were severely traumatized — an army of physically and mentally ravaged people.

Chapter 9

Masks

Governing the Great Machine and the Fight for Democracy (1787–1945)

Those who own the country ought to govern it.[1]
JOHN JAY, first Chief Justice of the United States Supreme Court

European democracies have been only partially and sometimes theoretically open. Their regulations were built on a subtle screening of participants and demands.
MICHEL CROZIER: THE CRISIS OF DEMOCRACY. REPORT TO THE TRILATERAL COMMISSION

In the usual narrative touting Europe as the cradle of freedom, democracy and prosperity, the expansion of capitalist production in the eighteenth and nineteenth centuries is seen as a prerequisite for the gradual assertion of democratic rights. This story presents capitalism and democracy as twins, joined at the hip. Even if there were some setbacks and delays after the French Revolution, an enlightened bourgeoisie, so the narrative goes, intrepidly followed the path to democracy, inspired by the ideals of the American Declaration of Independence. The storyline further claims that since the West invented democracy, it has also been summoned to an important historical mission: it should—no, *must*—emphatically continue to spread its achievements; if necessary, by force.

It is remarkable how popular this narrative is, although practically every single assertion in it is wrong. Democracy is not a creation of Europe or North America. It was not invented by either the ancient Greeks, or the French or even the "founding fathers" of the United States. As we have seen in the first chapter, for a very long stretch of human history, until about 5000 years ago, the principle of people dominating other people did not exist at all. It was practically impossible for a minority to impose its will on a majority for an extended length of time. In those times, the customs and institutions created by communities to regulate human relations and negotiate various interests cannot be described as "democracy" in the narrow sense of the word, as there were neither national populations (demos) nor was there formal rule (kratía). In a broader sense, however, the forms of social organization that existed all over the world before the advent of hierarchically structured civilizations were certainly far more democratic than anything that Ancient Greece, modern Europe or North America have produced. Some of these forms still exist today in various indigenous cultures. In these mostly small groups, where individuals may have prestige or influence but no power of command, it is common for collective decision-making processes to include most of the people concerned. Typical examples of this are the South West African Herero, about whom a German colonial official in 1895 noted in horror: "Not only the men, but frequently also the women, and even the servants, join in the discussion and give their advice. Thus, no one really feels like a subject; no one has learned to be subservient."[2] At the height of Athenian democracy, on the other hand, only a minority had voting rights. Democracy meant that property-owning male citizens maintained control over the majority, which included slaves, women and non-citizens. The same can be said about the first modern democracy in the USA and all representative systems in nineteenth-century Europe.

Furthermore, there are still significant sectors within Western representative democracies that are largely devoid of democracy. This includes most corporations, which, as the Lowell Mill Girls pointed out, are basically structured along the lines of absolutist tyrannies. Schools, the military and other disciplinary bodies are also, by and large, bereft of democracy. In fact, the majority of people in modern representative democracies spend a significant amount of their time within completely undemocratic institutions.[3]

If Europe cannot lay claim to be the inventor of democracy, it should receive even less credit for having spread it around the world. Wherever the European trinity of military, merchants and missionaries set foot, sooner or later, it laid waste to egalitarian forms of social organization. Under European colonial rule, the peoples of Africa, the Americas and large parts of Asia were subjected to tyranny and foreign rule, which in places extended into the 1970s. Many countries are still suffering from the consequences today.

The third misleading assertion in the grand narrative of the triumph of Western democracy is the coupling of democracy to capitalism. Whatever Europe actually accomplished in the way of democracy was not due to the momentum of its economic system, but rather as a result of resistance to it.

The modern world-system was formed using massive violence against egalitarian movements, and the military and economic institutions that are still part of its basic structure were created to concentrate power in the hands of a few. Absolutism was a necessary phase in the formation of the new power structures. Only a concentration of physical violence under the control of a central government was able to collect taxes for the building of large armies and hold down resistance to the new system. Only a powerful central state could create the institutions, legal frameworks and infrastructures indispensable for the expansion of the modern economic system.

Absolutist organization, however, inevitably provoked disturbances and resistance from various sides, which, at worst, could have jeopardized the functioning of the system. More and more people were integrated into the economic and state machinery, both as workers and as higher officials, but with virtually no say in the political apparatus. For the vast majority of the population, integration into the new system meant radical disenfranchisement. Poorer peasants and workers were at the mercy of a central authority that forced them to pay taxes, drafted them into the army, made them work in factories through physical or structural violence, and inflicted harsh punishments for disobedience. This was accompanied by increasing impoverishment, which was reflected by a decline of real wages, a growing tax burden and the loss of the commons. Other sectors of the population, on the other hand, benefited economically from the new system, but were still not given appropriate weight in political decisions. This situation set the stage for the dawning "Age of Revolutions." While various groups of the economic elites fought for dominance in the political system (sometimes classified as "conservatives" and "liberals"), there were others—those who suffered the most from the system's injustices—who fought for a completely different order.

THE FILTERS OF DEMOCRACY

Faced with these explosive conflicts, the political and economic elites found themselves in a dilemma. To avoid the situation getting out of hand, they had to make certain concessions to rebellious parts of society. At the same time, however, the concessions had to be kept within limits. The functioning of the Great Machine logically excludes genuine democracy in the sense of self-determination and self-organization. Under the conditions of global competition, states and economic actors have always been forced to constantly increase the efficiency of their military and economic apparatuses. This requires that people will subordinate themselves as much as possible to the purposes of these systems. Choosing not to participate in this scheme has to be ruled out as an option. For example, it was intolerable that labor movements fundamentally rejected the principle of wage labor, which they persisted in doing well into the nineteenth century. It was likewise inadmissible to question the system of property ownership or the power of the metallurgical complex and the military. Whenever movements have attacked such systemically relevant institutions, states have resorted to massive physical violence, whether monarchy or democracy, conservative, liberal or even social-democratic. In this system, the limits of democracy have always been set not only by powerful individual interest groups, but also by the internal, autonomous logic of its institutions. If a functioning democracy were not to stop at the factory, barracks and school gates, it would amount to the dissolution of the entire operational structure of the modern world economy.

For this reason, the history of modern democracies must actually be written as a history of restricting democracy. For every freedom gained, there was a series of counter-measures aimed at undermining these freedoms in some other way.[4]

USA 1787: Republic or Democracy?
(The Filter of Representation)

At the founding of the United States of America—which was to become a model for modern republics—democracy was already being reined in. George Washington, Thomas Jefferson and James Madison, along with the other founding fathers, were not only busy liberating the country from the British colonial power, but were also working to keep egalitarian, grassroots democratic aspirations under control. In 1786 and 1787, shortly before the drafting of the American Constitution, "Shays' Rebellion" had rocked the political establishment. Small farmers, who had fought the British, often without pay, returned to their land to face heavy debt, foreclosures and imprisonment. Creditors tried by all means to force repayment with interest in order to pay off their own war debts to Dutch banks. They also insisted on reimbursement with gold and silver, which the farmers did not have. One farmer summed up the situation as follows: "The great men are going to get all we have and I think it is time for us to rise and put a stop to it, and have no more courts, nor sheriffs, nor collectors nor lawyers." The peasants occupied courthouses and eventually took up arms. It was only with great effort that the state of Massachusetts was able to rally 3000 men to put down the movement. In the face of such uprisings, the demand grew louder among major landowners, bankers and factory owners to establish a large federal state with a standing army to effectively counter unrest. The instrument to accomplish this was to be a new constitution.[5]

James Madison, the "father of the American Constitution" and fourth president of the United States, made a very clear distinction between *democracy*—which he saw as a breeding ground for instability and insurrection— and *republic*. According to Madison in 1787, the republic offered "a cure" against the evils of democracy: "The two great points of difference between a democracy and a republic are: first, the delegation of the government, in the latter, to a small number of citizens elected by the rest; secondly, the greater number of citizens, and greater sphere of country, over which the latter may be extended. The effect of the first difference is to refine and enlarge the public views, by passing them through the medium of a chosen body of citizens, whose wisdom may best discern the true interest of their country."[6]

What Madison dressed up with elegant words, John Jay, the first Chief Justice of the United States, set down in no uncertain terms: "Those who own the country ought to govern it."[7] As large landowners and slave owners, Madison, Jefferson and Washington were among the wealthiest citizens of the United States (although Washington later freed his slaves). In today's dollars, Madison was worth about $100 million; Jefferson, the "father of the Declaration of Independence," $210 million; and estimates for George Washington, the first US president, reach as high as $500 million.[8] It is therefore not surprising that these men created a political system that confined decisions to the smallest possible circle of people who were "not unduly attached" to the voters, as Madison put it.

The voters themselves were also a small, selected group. Neither women, blacks nor Native Americans had the right to vote, and white men were allowed to vote only if they possessed the required minimum level of wealth. Constitutionally, only about 15 to 20 percent of adults had any voting rights at all, but the founding fathers still saw too great a potential danger to the stability of the system. Therefore, voters had to be kept at a distance from political decisions through the filter of representation.

This filter unlinked the political decision-making process from the will of the people and introduced two separate time dimensions into the process: the time of elections that were to be held in intervals of two, four or six years; and the actual decision-making process, taking place at any time and with no possibility of being directly influenced by the voters. In this way, a protective wall was built between the space of the decision-makers and the public's space. As Madison correctly recognized: the bigger the state, the higher this protective wall would be. As the size of the territory increased, so did the distance between the representatives and their voters. It was for this reason that the founding fathers were so strongly committed to transforming the former confederation of states into a single large federal state. Its powerful central government was to dispose of a strong federal army to intervene in case the representatives failed to sufficiently "refine and enlarge the public views."

France 1789: The Filter of Money

In the French Revolution, it was even more difficult to keep egalitarian forces in check than in the American independence movement. There had been resistance and turmoil in France throughout the seventeenth and eighteenth centuries, but it was the impending bankruptcy of the French state (which before the Revolution had to raise half of its revenue to pay off war debts) that opened a window of opportunity. At first, it was predominantly wealthy citizens who confronted the financially checkmated king with demands for political participation, but increasingly, other voices were raised as well. In 1788, the extreme weather conditions of the "Little Ice Age" had led to massive crop failures in France and, subsequently, to a threefold increase in bread prices once the statutory price control had been lifted. Grain traders hoarded stores and speculated on further price increases. The hatred that had built up over generations due to state repression intersected with the economic hardship of both the peasants and the Parisian population to create an explosive mixture. Although the National Convention that was tasked with writing a new constitution consisted of mostly wealthy citizens—especially lawyers—some of them were receptive to the demands for economic justice by the wider population. Jacques Roux, the spokesman for the *Enragés* (the "angry ones"), announced to the session on June 25, 1793:

> *Freedom is nothing but a vain phantom when one class of men can starve another with impunity. Equality is nothing but a vain phantom when the rich, through monopoly, exercise the right of life or death over their like. The republic is nothing but a vain phantom when the counter-revolution can operate every day through the price of commodities, which three quarters of all citizens cannot afford without shedding tears. The laws have been cruel to the poor, because they were only made by and for the rich. Oh rage, oh shame.*[9]

Robespierre's Reign of Terror not only served to keep the royalists at bay, but also to prevent democracy from escalating to the system-threatening dimensions demanded by the Enragés. In April 1793, Robespierre declared to the National Convention, "equal distribution of property is a chimera." He reassured merchants and bankers: "I will not attack your treasures."[10] In September of the same year, he had Roux and the other Enragés arrested and sentenced to death. Most of them died by guillotine, and Roux by suicide. François Babeuf and his friends from the "Society of the Equals," who later held views similar to those of Roux, met the same fate under the rule of the "Directory" and were executed in 1797. This finally put an end to the anti-systemic dimension of the revolution. Napoleon's empire followed. But even though the revolution did not ultimately bring about a systemic change, it became a shining symbol of how it is possible to shake the political and economic system to its foundations.

Haiti 1804: The Filter of Debt

The call for freedom heard in France was echoed in the French colony of Saint-Domingue (now Haiti), where the majority black population rebelled in 1791 to free itself from slavery. In 1804, the Haitians finally managed to expel the French colonial masters and rid themselves of the *Code Noir* that Napoleon had reintroduced. However, this still did not result in real freedom, since the French government did not recognize Haiti and cut the country off from world trade. In 1825, France sent 14 warships to the Caribbean and made the government in Port-au-Prince an offer it could not refuse. Haiti would be recognized as an independent state if it paid 150 million francs (about $21 billion in today's currency) to compensate for the "expropriation" of the former plantation owners. These fictitious debts were an absurd contrivance, but turned out to be terribly real for Haiti. For the following 120 years, French gunboats were deployed whenever Haiti refused to service the debt. This extortion of Haiti by the French lasted up until 1947.[11] The extreme poverty and political violence that still prevail in the country today cannot be fully understood without acknowledging this history.

Haiti has become a model of how indebtedness can be used to destroy self-determination and self-organization, and debt still remains one of the most important tools of power for undermining the independence of former colonies.

The Filters of Voting Rights and Civil Rights

The French Revolution had been successful in spreading the concept across the globe that all people were citizens with equal rights. During the Revolution itself, however, a great deal was already being done to curb the consequences of this idea. Only six days after the Bastille was stormed, Abbé Siéyès, one of the most influential members of the National Assembly, proposed introducing a distinction between "active" and "passive" citizens. Only those who "contribute to public institutions," that is, exclusively wealthy white men, should be considered active citizens and granted voting rights. In October 1789, the National Assembly passed a law that defined the active citizen according to his tax contribution.[12] Women were completely excluded. The ideological justification for this two-class society was that women, the poor and also blacks were not able to act rationally and had to be educated to do so,[13] which was a variation on the Madison narrative that the irrational masses could not be trusted with any responsibilities.

In 1793, under pressure from the Enragés, the National Convention adopted the world's first constitution that provided for universal and equal suffrage—for men. In the end, however, it was never implemented. Olympe de Gouges was the first to call for women's suffrage in her *Declaration of the Rights of Woman and the Female Citizen*, but in 1793, she too was guillotined. It was not until 1944, more than 150 years later, that women were given the right to vote in France. Women had not only been systematically disenfranchised from voting, but in 1795, the

National Assembly also banned the participation of women in political assemblies. In 1804, the *Code Civil* came into force, which completely subjugated women to their husbands in legal and property matters, a regression to a legal status even worse than that under the Ancien Régime.[14]

Despite some partial victories, none of the social movements in nineteenth-century Europe, whether peaceful or militant, managed to establish universal and equal suffrage. Despite rallying millions of people in the streets, neither the Chartists in England nor the revolutionaries of 1848–9 in France, Germany, Italy or Hungary were successful in their battle for voting rights.[15] All across Europe, the right to vote was ultimately confined to wealthy male citizens, who made up less than 20 percent of the adult population. The stubborn resolve with which "conservatives" and most "liberals" alike tried to block the expansion of voting rights clearly shows that, at that time, suffrage for women and poorer people was seen as a serious threat to system stability. This was not to change until further filters were installed to prevent systemic issues from being debated in elections.

The Filter of "Public Opinion"

Since the invention of writing, both censorship and propaganda have been used to influence public opinion. With the advent of the printing press in the modern era, propaganda acquired previously unimagined possibilities. As was true of writing itself, however, the invention of the printing press proved to be a double-edged sword. Starting in the late seventeenth century, as the technology became less expensive, an upsurge in publishing activities increasingly provided space for critical voices. This occurred first in England and France, then later in Germany. Under certain circumstances, the competition between states made it possible to avoid censorship in one country by publishing in another. Aesthetes, revolutionaries and reactionaries alike eagerly published their magazines and leaflets, including authors such as John Locke, Jean-Jacques Rousseau, Friedrich Schiller, Heinrich von Kleist and Georg Büchner. It was the heyday of what the German sociologist Jürgen Habermas called the "bourgeois public sphere."[16]

Workers' and women's movements also took advantage of this public sphere. In the first half of the nineteenth century, for example, Great Britain experienced a veritable boom in the workers' press. One Member of Parliament was shocked to note that these papers "arouse passions and selfishness among the general population by contrasting their present situation with the future situation they aspire to, a condition as incompatible with human nature as it is with the immutable laws that Providence has created for the regulation of bourgeois society."[17] Although attempts to prevent such publications through restrictive laws and high taxes did not bear fruit, the workers' press still suffered a tremendous decline in the second half of the nineteenth century from which it never recovered.

The reason for this was primarily economic. In 1837, it only took a thousand British pounds to start a newspaper and the sale of 6000 copies to cover the costs. At the beginning of the twentieth century, however, it took 2 million pounds for a start-up and no less than 250,000 sold copies to cover costs.[18] The newly invented rotary printing press required a considerable investment, which usually only large companies could afford. As a result, newspaper ownership was increasingly concentrated in the hands of a small group of capital owners, who acquired enormous power to sway opinions. Thus, the logic of the market became an effective filter, allowing censorship to slowly fade into the background.

The narrowing of the spectrum is demonstrated, for example, by the fact that in the 1860s the *New York Tribune*, which was the most widely circulated newspaper in the world at the time, had authors such as Karl Marx and Friedrich Engels under contract as correspondents in England. By contrast, in the 1910s, it would have been unthinkable for someone like Rosa Luxemburg to have written for high-circulation newspapers in Germany, Great Britain or the US.

The increasing consolidation in the newspaper and news sector also gave birth to the modern media mogul. In 1851, the former carrier pigeon fancier Paul Julius Reuter founded the world's first news agency, Reuters, with his office on the London Stock Exchange. Reuters was to maintain a quasi-monopoly on international news for decades and is still the largest agency today.[19] Reuter, who was ennobled to the rank of Baron by the Queen, later tried his hand in Persian mining and founded the Imperial Bank of Persia.

A generation after Reuter, another Englishman, Alfred Harmsworth, Viscount Northcliffe, became the most powerful media magnate of his time. In addition to the largest British tabloids, the *Daily Mail* and the *Daily Mirror*, he also owned the world's leading "quality newspapers," *The Times* and *The Sunday Times*. History had never seen such power to sway opinion concentrated in the hands of a single private businessman before. Among other things, he used this power to massively mobilize for Britain's entry into the First World War. The competitor newspaper *Star* wrote: "Next to the Kaiser, Lord Northcliffe has done more than any living man to bring about the war."[20]

In the US, the multimillionaire William Hearst (upon whom Orson Welles's film character Citizen Kane was based) gained a similarly dominant position in the first third of the twentieth century. With the fortune of his father, who was co-owner of what was then the largest mining company in the US, in the background, he created an empire that culminated with 25 daily newspapers, 24 weekly newspapers, 12 radio stations and a film studio. It reached 40 million people across the country, which amounted to a third of all American newspaper readers.

Meanwhile, in Germany, Alfred Hugenberg, finance director of Krupp Steel and chairman of the company's supervisory board, was able to build up an equally comprehensive media empire with which he propagated right-wing nationalist ideas, especially National Socialism. With the support of the metallurgical complex (mining and heavy industry) and several major banks (above all Commerzbank and Deutsche Bank) he controlled roughly half of the German press in the 1920s and took over the UFA Film Studios in 1927.[21]

The concentration of media ownership by just a handful of individuals created a powerful filter for public opinion. And yet, there were limits to the power of the media tsars. In the first place, they had not yet taken control over all the newspapers; and secondly, there was still an engaged public that was not content with just media consumption, but also organized itself in political, artistic or scientific circles. Here, the information exchanged and the ideas that were developed often came from first-hand sources, and were based on personal observations, travel reports and information from delegates. The atomized television viewer, with a vision of the world outside the home and workplace mostly defined by prefabricated images from the tube, had not yet been conceived.

Ultima ratio regum: Cannons for the Status Quo[22]
When the filters of representation, money, limited civil rights and manipulated public opinion failed, governments, whether "conservative," "liberal," or even "social-democratic," resorted to open physical violence. Widespread police repression and even military action against workers' and women's movements were the order of the day throughout the nineteenth and early twentieth centuries—even to the point of open war, such as that waged against the revolutionaries of 1848–9.

In some instances, the violent crushing of egalitarian movements was actually the founding act of a newly created republic. A case in point is the birth of the Third Republic in France. In March 1871, while surrounded by Versailles government troops and German occupiers, the people of Paris had declared the city a self-governing commune. The Communards picked up where the 1789 Revolution had left off. They temporarily suspended the payment of rents, banned enforced debt collection and interest charges, handed over factories abandoned by their owners to workers' self-government, and created the beginnings of a public pension system. A response by the newly-founded Third Republic came quickly. In May, the Versailles army, supported by German troops, marched into Paris and shot tens of thousands of Communards, including thousands of women and children, often by summary execution. The "Bloody Week" massacres were not ordered by a monarch or a mad dictator, but by Adolphe Thiers, president of the Third Republic and, at the time, the leading historian of the French Revolution. The story of the Commune shows that the prospect of genuine democracy, having overcome the filters of representation and money, was fundamentally unacceptable from the perspective of the republic (in Madison's sense). We will see that this remains the case to this day.

THE ISSUE OF SYSTEM CONTROL

After more than 150 years of struggles across Europe, certain democratic rights were finally achieved, including universal and free suffrage. This was due to the remarkable perseverance and organizational efforts of workers', women's and civil rights movements. It is these organizations to which we owe today's minimal framework of rights that keeps state arbitrariness in check and provides us with certain freedoms — not to capitalism's supposed democratizing influence.

However, these achievements are not only due to the strength of the movements, but also to an inherent weakness of the Great Machine. Once the energy supply was switched from decentralized sources such as wind, water, wood and animal labor to fossil coal, the industrial system became increasingly vulnerable. A relatively small number of workers controlled enormous quantities of energy wherever the fossil fuel supply ran into bottlenecks: in large mines, at central railway lines and in ports. The supply of energy could not be allowed to fail, because the entire system of mass production was dependent on it. It did not take long for the labor movement to recognize this weakness. While the great English coal workers' strikes of 1842 were largely ineffective, by the end of the century the situation had changed dramatically. The strikes by coal, rail and port workers from the 1880s to 1910s, which shook virtually all major industrial nations, jeopardized the entire production and financial system of the global coal-based economy. In 1889, almost the entire coal workforce of the Ruhr District in Germany, some 90,000 people, declared a largely spontaneous strike. The army was sent in and 11 strikers were shot. Although the strike was suppressed, it altered the political landscape, and within a year the government had to withdraw its ban on trade unions and workers' parties. Similarly, in 1889, 260,000 coal workers in England and Wales went on strike, which, at the time, was the largest strike in the history of organized labor. The coal strikes increasingly expanded into general walkouts, for instance in Belgium in 1902, where workers demanded universal and equal suffrage. In 1914, a coal workers strike in Ludlow, Colorado, escalated to the level of a civil war, with the National Guard shooting down striking workers, their wives and their children with machine guns, and burning down their tent cities. John D. Rockefeller, who owned the mines, suffered considerable damage to his image and hired a certain Ivy Lee—who later became a co-founder of the modern public relations industry— to create positive press about the Rockefellers in the media. However, that was not the end of it. A report commissioned by Rockefeller in 1918 stated: "What might not happen, if upon a few days' or a few weeks' notice, the coal mines were suddenly to shut down, and the railways to stop running! Here is power which, once exercised, would paralyze the nation more effectively than any blockade in time of war."[23]

Left: The National Guard arriving in Ludlow, Colorado. Right: Strikers before their tent city (1914)

Against this backdrop, entrepreneurs and states were forced to either make certain concessions to workers, or face possible production losses that posed a risk to the system.[24] In the end, it was a choice between the devil and the deep blue sea. If they made too few concessions or none at all, they were in for further strikes and sabotage that threatened to paralyze the system. If the concessions went too far, there would be a threat of "real democracy" that might lead to dismantling the Great Machine. As the gap between these two poles became narrower and narrower, new strategies and methods had to be found to ensure that the Machine continued to function smoothly. A leap to a new level of control was needed.

The history of the twentieth century can only be understood if one realizes how urgent the search for a solution to this dilemma was for the economic and political elites. In principle, they had only two options: they could either formally embrace something like a representative democracy and then try to control it using various filters; or they could attempt to abolish the representative system and replace it with a totalitarian form of government. In the 1920s and 1930s, a large number of economic elites bet on this second option—not only in Germany and Italy.

Russia 1917

For a time, the First World War postponed the democracy problem for many states. A large armed conflict can temporarily put many internal conflicts on ice; it permits the suspension of democracy in the name of national security; and it creates the illusion of a community with a shared fate. In many countries, trade unions were willing to renounce the right to strike, and the state of emergency prompted an authoritarian takeover of the economy and politics. In the course of the war, however, the tables were turned, and the question of democracy ended up back on the agenda in an intensified form. Due to the unprecedented number of victims, ever larger sections of the population began to oppose the war, both covertly and openly. The longer it dragged on, the more that governments suffered a loss of legitimacy, especially in Germany and Russia.

In Russia, because of the extreme plight of the population and the weakening of the tsarist regime, the war had created a historical window of opportunity for revolution. First, the tsar fell, then the Bolsheviks rose to power in the October Revolution of 1917. For conservatives and liberals alike, their worst nightmare became reality as property owners were threatened with expropriation. By contrast, hopes rose among many peasants, workers and leftist intellectuals for something like a genuine democracy to emerge. In fact, Lenin had promised the Russian people that post-revolutionary power would come to the grassroots workers' and soldiers' councils that had already formed throughout the country after the February Revolution. But once Lenin's cadre party had seized power, it gradually pushed back on the councils until the dream of self-organization and self-administration evaporated.[25] Before seizing power,

Lenin had announced: "Socialism is not created by orders from above. Socialism is alive, creative—the creation of the popular masses themselves," while afterwards, he wrote: "The proletariat needs state power, the centralized organization of force, the organization of violence."[26] Nonetheless, it would be a mistake to simply see this as some sort of calculated deception. After the revolution, a four-year civil war had broken out with constant military interventions by foreign powers. Therefore, tightly controlled, centrally organized structures were necessary to keep the revolutionary government in power. The logic of war weakened the proponents of self-organization and strengthened authoritarian structures.

Even if Lenin's aims were clearly different, his understanding of democracy has certain parallels with Western mainstream "liberals" and the views of the US founding fathers. He considered the general population, whom he called the "masses," to be incapable of making rational decisions, and believed that they should be governed by a trained elite (a theory for which he was sharply criticized by Rosa Luxemburg, among others).

The astounding level of agreement on this question among such different political camps can be attributed to the mode of operation of the Great Machine, which Lenin and his comrades-in-arms wished by no means to dismantle, but merely to use in a different way. Lenin's idea of the future socialist society was inspired by the "Taylorist" industrial system and especially by the German war economy.[27] Under the leadership of the German industrialist Walther Rathenau (AEG), the war economy in Germany had become a highly effective, centrally planned megamachine. Lenin saw it as "the ultimate in modern, comprehensive capitalist techniques, planning and organization," and the model for a socialist society.[28] "Large-scale machine industry is the foundation of socialism," he explained, "it calls for absolute and strict *unity of will*, which directs the joint labors of hundreds, thousands and tens of thousands of people. But how can strict unity of will be ensured? By thousands subordinating their will to the will of one."[29]

This insight of Lenin's holds equally well for bourgeois industrial society. Large-scale technology that is based on the division of labor, whether capitalist or state-socialist, is incompatible with self-organization, in other words, with genuine democracy. The difference was that Lenin replaced the entrepreneur in charge of his employees with a party bureaucrat. This was certainly a huge step, for it meant the expropriation of the 1 to 2 percent of society that had owned most of the means of production. From the point of view of the Machine as a whole, however, the changes were far less dramatic than they might appear at first glance. In both systems, the most important functions were controlled by a layer of specialists who, in a developed industrial society, make up about 20 percent of the population.[30] The remaining 80 percent had to be kept as far as possible from decision-making and simply do what they were told. Either way, the entire purpose of the Machine was to accumulate capital for reinvestment in an endless cycle; or in Lenin's own words: "Socialism is merely state-capitalist monopoly which is made to serve the interests of the whole people."[31]

The Leninist system maintained the essential functions of the Megamachine (or, for the most part, created them in largely peasant-based Russia) in order to harness them for another goal—the redistribution of social wealth from top to bottom. Although there were actual successes, the system never broke away from the four tyrannies. Instead, the structural violence of the market was replaced by the direct rule of the bureaucracy; the tsarist police and military state was continued in another form; the metallurgical complex grew even stronger and a penal camp system was established to which, under Stalin, millions of people fell victim. Furthermore, the idea of man's boundless rule over nature reached unprecedented dimensions in the technocratic visions and large-scale projects of the Soviet Union, leaving post-apocalyptic landscapes in its wake from Chernobyl to Murmansk to Semipalatinsk.[32] During the early twentieth century, Lenin's propaganda apparatus proved to be groundbreaking in the development of ideological power, even though Western public relations techniques ultimately proved superior.

Despite these similarities, Leninism presented a frightful specter to large portions of the Western elite, who feared expropriation by such a revolution. Therefore the events in Russia heightened the urgency for them to find a way to steer the Great Machine between the Scylla of genuine democracy and the Charybdis of Leninism.

The "Guided Democracy"

While the image of a lever might suffice as a symbol for absolutism, or the exercise of linear power, the governance of a complex society might best be symbolized by the regulator on a steam engine. James Maxwell was the first to systematically investigate the *centrifugal governor* on steam engines in the 1860s, from which he developed the so-called control theory. This theory describes self-regulating systems that can be influenced from the outside by simple control variables (system inputs). Even though this scientific theory was not yet being translated directly into political practice, the ideas of economists and political thinkers revolved around similar questions and problems: how could the Great Machine be kept going as a self-regulating mechanism, and which control variables must be specifically influenced "from outside"?

One possible answer to these questions was the concept of "guided democracy." It was first formulated in the 1920s by the American journalist Walter Lippmann, the leading media theorist and one of the most influential intellectuals of his time. He had been an advisor to several US governments, and in

1921 was a founding member and later president of the Council on Foreign Relations, one of the first and, to this day, most prominent American think tanks.

Lippmann was of the opinion that in a modern democracy there are two kinds of people. On the one hand, there is the "bewildered herd," whose unqualified opinions are based on short-sighted self-interests. The complexity of modern societies is too much for them to cope with, so their participation in political life must be limited to choosing every four years between two competing factions of the "specialized class." The "specialized class," on the other hand, are the only ones who know how to control the complexities of the Megamachine in the interests of the general public. For this reason, it is necessary for the experts to steer the herd by specifically influencing public opinion, which Lippmann called the "manufacture of consent." He wrote in 1922:

> *The opportunities for manipulation [of public opinion] open to anyone who understands the process are plain enough. The creation of consent is not a new art. It is a very old one which was supposed to have died out with the appearance of democracy. But it has not died out. It has, in fact, improved enormously in technic, because it is now based on analysis rather than on rule of thumb. And so, as a result of psychological research, coupled with the modern means of communication, the practice of democracy has turned a corner. A revolution is taking place, infinitely more significant than any shifting of economic power.*[33]

Lippmann's views are in line with those of Madison and most of the other American founding fathers. His thoughts were further developed by Edward Bernays, who is considered the founder of public relations along with Ivy Lee. Bernays, a nephew of Sigmund Freud, used his uncle's theories about the unconscious in order to influence the wishes, feelings and thoughts of crowds.

He wrote in the introduction to his 1928 book *Propaganda*:

> *The conscious and intelligent manipulation of the organized habits and opinions of the masses is an important element in democratic society. Those who manipulate this unseen mechanism of society constitute an invisible government which is the true ruling power of our country. We are governed, our minds are molded, our tastes formed, our ideas suggested, largely by men we have never heard of. This is a logical result of the way in which our democratic society is organized. Vast numbers of human beings must cooperate in this manner if they are to live together as a smoothly functioning society [...] As civilization has become more complex, and as the need for invisible government has been increasingly demonstrated, the technical means have been invented and developed by which opinion may be regimented.*[34]

What Bernays wrote sounds like a full-fledged conspiracy theory with dark figures pulling the strings that society dances to. Of course, this image is misleading, and Bernays undoubtedly exaggerated the manipulative possibilities of his profession in order to do some advertising for his line of work. Yet, his analysis of the need to manage complex industrial societies is completely accurate, and the methods he developed have been extremely influential and successful, both for governments and for businesses. In 1917, he (like Lippmann) worked in the Committee on Public Information, a propaganda agency created by the US government that managed to make the nation's entry into the war palatable to a non-supportive public. The committee commissioned major Hollywood films and wrote up half-true and fake news stories to feed to newspaper editors (who, for a long time, accepted such "news" uncritically). They also sent out an army of volunteers who were trained to deliver "authentic" and positive-sounding four-minute statements for radio and all kinds of public events. Bernays later worked for various US presidents and became an important spin doctor for the tobacco, food, aluminum and auto industries. One of his greatest triumphs was selling the idea of women smoking as a symbol of freedom and independence. Joseph Goebbels studied Bernays' writings extensively to build his anti-Jewish propaganda machine—a macabre twist, since Bernays himself was a Jew.[35]

The ideas of Lippmann, Bernays and the Russian propaganda experts conjured up futuristic notions of total control over citizens' consciousness and emotions. Some found such a utopia with total social control to be appealing, while others saw it as a nightmare. It was during this period that the great dystopian novels such as *We* (1920), *Brave New World* (1932) and *1984* (1948) were written. In reality, however, it was evident that the idea of linear control did not really work. Even Goebbels found that he could not control public opinion unilaterally, but needed spies to tell him what people were secretly thinking and saying in order to fine-tune his propaganda.[36] Public opinion does not function linearly, but cybernetically, and system input must always be readjusted in order to achieve the desired system output.

"Guided democracy" was a response to the strength of social movements and the inevitable expansion of voting rights. One of its most important functions was to limit the scope of what can "reasonably" be discussed so that concepts that are threatening to the system do not gain traction. George Orwell described this phenomenon in his 1943 preface to *Animal Farm* that was censored by the British Department of Information:

> *At any given moment there is an orthodoxy, a body of ideas which it is assumed that all right-thinking people will accept without question. It is not exactly forbidden to say this, that or the other, but it is 'not done' to say it, just as in mid-Victorian times it was 'not done' to mention trousers in the presence of a lady. Anyone who challenges the prevailing orthodoxy finds himself silenced with surprising effectiveness.*[37]

To create such a "body of ideas which all right-thinking people will accept without question" is a very complex process in a world where there is neither a Vatican Council nor a Central Committee drawing the lines. Three subsystems play a decisive role here: the university system (as an apparatus of knowledge production and a filter for the "specialized class"), the party system (as part of the filter of representation) and the media. The limits placed on the spectrum of "reasonable" opinions are not primarily based on direct, linear influence by individuals, but on self-regulating mechanisms, of which the market itself is the most important. The way the commercial media function is a good example. As information turns into a commodity, those who have the most money will have the best chance to influence public opinion as they choose. Those with money cannot only place advertisements, but buy whole newspapers, television channels or news agencies and hire the best PR strategists to flood the market with information. They can also hire an army of lawyers to sue critical journalists, and influence the production of background information by commissioning scientific studies, financing university curricula (or even whole universities), as well as setting up NGOs, think tanks and foundations. Journalists who operate within this system inhale these manufactured worldviews daily until they become, at least in part, their own. The seemingly neutral rules of the market prove to be, on closer inspection, a means of systemic self-censorship. Even if this censorship often has gaps, it is still far more effective than state censorship, because *it does not appear to be censorship*.[38]

Nevertheless, this self-regulating system is far from perfect. It actually fails time and again, because, despite everything, people cannot be prevented from thinking for themselves. For this reason, "guided democracy" will always be vulnerable. Whenever it becomes fragile, whenever the "bewildered herd" breaks into the carefully confined realm of experts, then other, more radical methods of system control will be considered as options.

The German Revolution of 1918–19

The birth of fascism was a response to the massive anti-systemic movements that emerged at the end of the First World War, especially in Germany and Italy, and could no longer be held down by "guided democracy." In Germany, it began in October 1918 when sailors in Kiel, emaciated and disillusioned by a four-year war of annihilation, refused to fight in yet another senseless battle. The conscientious objectors formed councils, and despite a lack of central organization, within five days, the revolution had spread across the country from Hamburg to Munich, and Wrocław to Cologne. Companies and entire municipal administrations were taken over by councils, and in a very short time, simple workers and soldiers had managed to effectively self-organize. Despite its best efforts, the paralyzed empire had to watch helplessly as no more soldiers could be rounded up who were willing to shoot at their comrades. Unlike the Russian October Revolution, this revolution was not led by a Bolshevik elite, but by a predominantly social-democratic working class. It did not seek a "dictatorship of the proletariat," but the abolition of militarism and private capital through the self-administration of workers. Because the insurgents believed that the leaders of the social-democratic party also shared the same basic goals, they could not possibly imagine what was to take place a few months after the start of the revolution. Friedrich Ebert, the first social-democratic president of the German Reich, deployed a protofascist volunteer militia to shoot down the social-democratic revolutionaries. In early 1919, since the majority of soldiers who had fought in the war were still unwilling to fire on their compatriots, Ebert's only option was to use right-wing radical forces that his defense minister Gustav Noske (also a social democrat) hastily drummed up. In January of that year, the *Freikorps* marched into Berlin, and by March they had penetrated the working-class districts. In April they destroyed the Bavarian Soviet Republic that had been established in Munich. Thousands of mostly unarmed people were shot, and countless were tortured. Many of the Freikorps soldiers already wore swastika armbands; the nucleus of the fascist movement had been established.[39]

Left: Noske and Ebert who ordered the attacks. Right: The Freikorps in Bavaria (1919)

The Fascist Option

The official founding of the Italian fascist movement took place in Milan at about the same time. In the building of the Associatione degli Industriali Lombardi, the most powerful industrial association in Italy, Benito Mussolini and his partisans founded, on March 23, 1919, a militia-like organization called the Fasci Italiani di Combattimento—later to become the Fascist Party. This was done for many of the same reasons as in Germany. In northern Italy, workers' councils had occupied large factories and estates after the war, and in cities such as Turin, Genoa, Pisa and Livorno they had proclaimed a "workers' democracy." In response, many industrialists and landowners hired fascist goon squads, the *fasci*, to beat up or assassinate rebellious workers. Some factory owners also hired fascists to officially maintain "factory security." For two years, "Blackshirts" terrorized the land while officials mostly looked on and did nothing. In 1922, the fascists successfully smashed a nationwide general strike, which, in the eyes of the bourgeois elite, made them eligible to serve in government. In the same year, Mussolini was chosen as head of state.[40]

Mussolini's seizure of power gave rise to a new option: fascism as a method for controlling the Great Machine. At first, this alternative seemed repulsive to some liberal elites, who felt it was a step backwards to a time they thought they had already left behind. Wherever the filters of "guided democracy" no longer functioned, however, and where revolutionary tendencies among large portions of the public could not be kept in check, such extreme measures gradually became *Realpolitik* options.

This was not only true for Germany and Italy. Winston Churchill addressed the following to Mussolini at a press conference in Rome in 1927:

If I had been an Italian, I am sure I would have been entirely with you from the beginning to the end of your victorious struggle against the bestial appetites and passions of Leninism. Your movement has rendered service to the whole world. Italy has shown that there is a way of fighting the subversive forces.[41]

And as late as 1938, he asserted:

I have always said that if Great Britain were defeated in war I hoped we should find a Hitler to lead us back to our rightful position among the nations.[42]

Yet, Churchill believed that England did not have to resort to such extreme means because, as he put it, "it has its own way of doing things." In almost all other European countries, however, parliamentary systems were suspended in the 1930s and early 1940s, whether through elections, coups, civil war or due to Germany's military conquests. The fascist option was also by no means limited to Europe. Japan, by now highly industrialized, had experienced a severe economic crisis after the First World War and a massive upswing of anti-systemic movements. The response was the rise of "Tennō fascism," which like the

European variants, was very effective in neutralizing system-critical currents.

In the midst of this darkening world situation, during the Spanish Civil War of 1936–9, the inhabitants of Catalonia, Aragon and other regions made what was probably the most successful attempt to build a true democracy in early twentieth century Europe. George Orwell, who like many thousands of Britons, defied British law and fought as a volunteer for the Republic, wrote about his experiences:

> There was a feeling of having suddenly emerged into an era of equality and freedom. Human beings were trying to behave as human beings and not as cogs in the capitalist machine. And no one owned anyone else as his master.[43]

Almost all production in Catalonia was in the hands of the workers, from the tram factory to the hairdressing salon. The absence of bosses in no way led to a decline in production, and in many areas, especially agriculture, production actually increased. The workers were attacked not only by the fascists, but also by the Moscow-loyal Communist Party. Ultimately, with military support from the Germans, Franco's troops were able to put a brutal end to self-organization and the entire republic. The US government remained officially neutral, but Texaco supplied oil to the fascists, while General Motors and Ford provided them with more than 10,000 trucks. After the war, a senior official in the Franco government said: "Without American oil, American trucks and American loans, we would never have won the civil war."[44]

In most countries, fascism received enormous support from industrialists, bankers and large landowners.[45] In Germany, step by step, almost all of big industry and high finance came down on the side of the Nazis, even though not all considered National Socialism to be the most desirable solution. The economic elites in Germany largely abhorred parliamentary democracy, but they were also put off by the radical anti-Semitism and the partly anti-capitalist rhetoric of the NSDAP—at least initially. In his speech to a packed Industrial Club on January 26, 1932, Hitler tried to dispel these concerns and promised that private property would not be touched under his government. In November of the same year, some 20 industrialists wrote a letter to Reich President Hindenburg demanding Hitler's appointment as Reich Chancellor.[46] On February 20, 1933, Hitler and Göring held a secret meeting with leading business representatives and were successful in requesting support for the upcoming election campaign.[47] The help received also ensured that there would be no further elections for the following 15 years. AEG, Thyssen, Krupp, RWE, Daimler-Benz, Porsche, BMW, AFA (today Varta), Siemens, Borsig, Osram, Dr. Oetker, Wintershall, Unilever, Bertelsmann, Allianz, Merck, IG Farben (Agfa, BASF, Bayer and Hoechst), and leading bankers from Deutsche Bank, Commerzbank and Dresdner Bank supported the Nazis in a variety of ways and profited from them in two respects.[48] On the one hand, the militarized SS state suffocated trade unions and leftist movements more effectively than any parliamentary government could have done; on the other, it later contributed extremely inexpensive and disenfranchised labor to these companies in the form of millions of forced laborers.

The Nazis also received significant financial support from foreign sources of capital, including Vickers, the largest British arms company, Henry Deterding (General Director of Royal Dutch Shell) and the French Heavy Industry Association.[49] Louis Renault was an admirer of Hitler and met with him several times between 1935 and 1939.[50] Henry Ford, whose anti-Semitic writings were an inspiration to the Nazis and who received the highest award of the German Reich with personal congratulations from Hitler in 1938, sold equipment not only to Franco, but also to the German army well into the 1940s.

Despite this massive support from economic elites, however, it would be misleading to view fascism simply as a conspiracy engineered by the upper echelons. Unlike traditional military dictatorships, fascism was a *movement*. It was able to mobilize a society of traumatized, frustrated and disturbed people and rechannel their hatred of the system in a new direction, with the goal of saving this very system. It offered a "home" to the uprooted with the promise of a mythical national community; and it offered a vision of strength and power to the powerless who had returned traumatized from the battlefields of the Great War. Finally, to the victims of a monstrous economic system, it offered both simple explanations and a program for economic advancement.

From an overarching point of view, the ultimate function of fascism was to steer much of the anti-systemic impetus back onto a systemic path. To accomplish this, the primary technique that was used by fascism's most extreme form, German Nazism, was to define a group of culprits onto whom all evils could be projected—in this case, Jews. In doing so, the Nazis could exploit an almost 2,000-year history of anti-Judaism and anti-Semitism.[51] Building on this grim tradition, and equipped with the propaganda methods of modern public relations, the Nazis set in motion a gigantic mechanism for diverting and redirecting people's attention. Its purpose was to take the anger, desperation and hatred felt for a monstrous system and redirect it toward a particular group that had been chosen to be the scapegoat.

What happened next is well known. However, the horrors that were to sweep across Europe remain unfathomable. For six years, the Great Machine was transformed into a gigantic death factory, organized according to the Taylorist model of division of labor. It is often said that National Socialism was irrational, but in certain respects it was exactly the opposite: it was an excess—a running amok—of precisely the form of rationality upon which the Megamachine is based. Like perfectly functioning cogs, millions of people worked at full capacity in a mechanism that was quickly modified from the production of consumer goods to producing corpses. Fascism and National Socialism were not, as is repeatedly claimed, relapses into a "primitive barbarism," but phenomena of twentieth-century modernity.[52] The greatest murder in the history of humankind had its origins in the heart of "civilization."

Chapter 10

Metamorphoses

The Post-war Boom, Resistance Movements and the Limits of the System (1945–...)

Everything on this show is for sale.
FROM THE FILM THE TRUMAN SHOW

"Little Boy" was only 120 inches long and 28 inches in diameter, an object hardly bigger than a Christmas tree. In its metal casing, however, there was enough concentrated destructive energy to wipe out 80,000 people within seconds, radiate hundreds of thousands more and transform a large city into a lunar landscape. For the surviving Japanese and the rest of the world, the bomb was an epochal turning point. From now on, the extinction of humankind, indeed of all living things in nature, was a real possibility. It only took the push of a button, as effortless as operating a coffee machine.

The atomic bomb amassed all the accumulated power and destructive energy of the Great Machine. Long before, Leonardo da Vinci, the most innovative armaments engineer of his day, had written about the potential "to create coruscations and winds with dreadful thunder and lightning flashing through the darkness, and with impetuous storms to overthrow high buildings and to uproot forests."[1] The path from Leonardo da Vinci to the "father of the atomic bomb" Robert Oppenheimer reveals the explosive expansion of the metallurgical complex over 400 years. With as many as 100,000 people working on it, the production of the bomb was the largest scientific project of all time. It was also the beginning of industrialized large-scale research, the fulfillment of Francis Bacon's vision of "big science."

239

Left and middle: Uranium enrichment plant at Oak Ridge. Right: Atomic bomb explosion at Nagasaki

It was not just the size of the project that was extraordinary, but also its secrecy, both internally and externally. No working group was allowed to know what the others were doing, and the employees were ordered not to discuss their work with even their closest family members. The Manhattan Project developed into a kind of large technological parallel universe that was hermetically sealed off from the rest of society and removed from democratic control.

The atomic bombs dropped on Hiroshima and Nagasaki were by no means the only ones. Worldwide, the nuclear powers have detonated approximately two thousand atomic bombs for test purposes since 1945, with a cumulative explosive force of 34,000 Hiroshima bombs.[2] In the deserts of Nevada and Kazakhstan and in the oceans and on the atolls of the South Seas, those at the helm of the Great Machine were waging a world war against planet Earth that was mostly hidden from the public eye.

During this period, the fantasies of omnipotence harbored by engineers reached a high point, not only within the military, but also in civilian projects. In the Soviet Union, Stalin proposed his "Great Plan for the Transformation of Nature," which involved redirecting two of Russia's three largest river systems, with a length of more than 6000 miles, from the Arctic to the deserts of Central Asia. Meanwhile, the United States was working on a plan to use atomic bombs to create a second Panama Canal—the

"Pan-Atomic Canal"—through Central America. The German engineer Hermann Sörgel even proposed damming up the Straits of Gibraltar and draining most of the Mediterranean Sea.[3] Although these extreme projects were never realized, they were still typical of the thinking at the time. Nature became a malleable object in the hands of a god-like engineer who shaped it according to his fancy.

THE TRENTE GLORIEUSES

The 30 or so years that followed after "Little Boy" became known as the *trente glorieuses* (30 glorious years) or "The Golden Age of Capitalism." It was a time when the modern world-system experienced the greatest expansion in its history. Western Europe, North America and Japan developed into consumer societies with occasional double-digit growth rates that today are looked back upon with envy. The parliamentary system had been adopted by most of these countries and was supplemented by the establishment of welfare states. Like at the end of the film *Metropolis* (1927), labor and capital had apparently joined hands to make peace and advance human progress. Furthermore, this progress was finally to be transferred to the Global South in the form of "development." At last, it seemed that the monsters of modernity had been banished. The miracles of large-scale technology and the nearly inexhaustible energy supply from oil and nuclear fission would create a paradise on Earth in which past conflicts would disappear.

At least, this was the image drawn at the time by the public relations industry in countless commercials commissioned by governments and companies. By shifting the point of view, however, it is possible to tell radically different stories about this period. For example, from the perspective of indigenous populations, such as the Adivasi in India or the Penan on Borneo, this epoch was marked by a continuation and even acceleration of the colonial destruction of their cultures. The hunger for resources to feed industrial expansion increasingly robbed people of their habitats, with millions forcibly driven from their land for "development projects." Most ended up in the slums of the exploding megacities.

For colonial populations, however, this period was also associated with high hopes for political and economic self-determination. After decades-long struggles, almost all African and Asian countries finally achieved formal independence. These successes were nonetheless accompanied by enormous sacrifices. Between 1954 and 1962, in Algeria alone, roughly 300,000 people died fighting against the French colonial rulers, with additional millions being interned, tortured and severely traumatized.[4] In sharp contrast to their high-flown promises of "development" and peace, once colonies had gained independence, the former colonial powers continued to intervene in dozens of countries through covert operations in order to remove democratically elected governments and suppress independent development.

When this strategy failed in Vietnam, the US resorted to an open war, in which more bombs were dropped than during the entire Second World War,[5] and 3 to 4 million Vietnamese, Cambodians and Laotians lost their lives. Previously, the Korean War (1950–53) had already claimed at least as many victims. There, the US government waged what it called a "merciless" air war that eradicated about 20 percent of the population. Long before the Vietnam War, napalm had already been deployed against a civilian population on a large scale.[6]

If the camera's point of view shifts once again, this time to the perspective of Earth's non-human species, then this era looms as the beginning of one of the darkest ages in the history of the planet. Chainsaws wiped out forests at a previously unimaginable rate, heavy equipment ripped open the earth and turned entire regions into deserts, chemical factories poisoned rivers, and industrial agriculture transformed cultivated landscapes into pesticide-soaked monocultures.[7] The *trente glorieuses* mark the start of rapidly accelerating species extinctions that are now threatening to escalate into one of the greatest crises in the history of life on the planet.[8] At the same time, for farm animals such as cows, pigs and chickens, it was also the beginning of industrial livestock production and mass slaughter. For the animal world, this was like a macabre echo of gulags and concentration camps.

From the perspective of the Earth as an integrated living system, this epoch was also associated with a momentous atmospheric change. Driven by the exponentially increasing consumption of coal and oil, global greenhouse gas emissions tripled. In the three years from 1971 to 1973 alone, more CO_2 was pumped out than in the entire century and a half from 1750 to 1900.[9] With the post-war surge in expansion, the system finally achieved a level of power sufficient to change global meteorological forces: the weather conditions, the water cycle, as well as the air and ocean currents. Until then, such power had only been attributed to the gods. However, while a Poseidon in the Odyssey or a Yahweh in the story of the Flood were also able to call a halt to the deluges, the Great Machine has produced irreversible changes that are beyond anyone's control.

Constantly Moving Happiness Machines

Initially, the populations of North America and Western Europe were hardly aware of the boom's darker sides. Pressured by systemic competition with the Eastern Bloc, which also experienced considerable economic growth, and fearing eruptions of anti-systemic forces similar to those after the First World War, Western governments and companies opted to compromise with the workers. Never before in the history of the modern world-system had workers (at least in the Global North) been able to achieve such an increase in income. Never before had countries devoted so much of their financial resources to public welfare.

Although the economy was booming, the human realities were not always so glorious. Sixty million people had been killed in the war, and at least as many were seriously injured. For years, countless people had been surrounded by mass death, extreme violence and fear. The German philosopher Hannah Arendt, who traveled throughout Germany in 1950, diagnosed a "blind compulsion to constantly keep busy, and an insatiable desire to do something all day long":

> *This busywork has become their main weapon to defend against reality. It makes you want to scream that this nonsense is not what is real. The rubble is real; the past horrors are real; the dead that you try to forget are real. But these people are living ghosts who can no longer be touched by words, arguments, the look in a person's eye, or the sadness of the human heart.*[10]

In Europe, the US and Japan, the consumption of psycho-therapeutic drugs became a mass phenomenon. Questionable diagnoses such as "vegetative dystonia" and "dystrophy" suddenly became popular, which in the end were nothing more than euphemisms for post-traumatic stress disorders.[11]

In an insidious way, the disorientation and psychological disorganization of populations fit well with the needs of the economic system. The Second World War had produced a wide range of technological innovations that soon went into civilian mass production, including nuclear energy, jets, transistors and computers.[12] At the same time, a vast amount of capital, no longer needed for the war economy, was waiting to be utilized. The confluence of these factors was a wave of exponential growth in production, once more focused on the metallurgical complex; in particular the automobile industry. A largely traumatized and disoriented society was now lured by an enormous program of sedation and distraction, with Mickey Mouse waving from his Cadillac and Aunt Jemima serving up pancakes to create a world of anesthetizing amnesia.

The automotive industry played a central role in this expansion phase. Viewed objectively, individual transport by car is an extremely irrational concept when compared to the railway. It swallows up many times more energy, while enormous areas of land are dedicated to road construction that are no longer available for agriculture, housing, city life or nature. Every year, traffic accidents kill more than 1 million people worldwide (more than in armed conflicts), with another 40 million suffering severe injuries.[13] Ultimately, it leads to "hurry up and wait" for those stuck in endless traffic jams from Shenzhen, to Mumbai, to Los Angeles and across the globe. The cultural critic Ivan Illich once calculated that even if you are not sitting in stalled traffic, traveling by car is not faster than by bicycle if you factor in all the time it takes to earn the money needed to buy the car and pay for fuel, repairs, road construction taxes, insurance and traffic fines.[14] Despite the absurdity of the automotive system, after the Second World War virtually all governments from Washington and Paris to Moscow and Tokyo favored a "tout voiture" (completely automobile-based) strategy. In the US, car and tire manufacturers engaged in the systematic destruction of public transportation from the 1930s to the 1950s. General Motors, Standard Oil and Firestone bought public transportation companies under pseudonyms in 45 US cities, including New York and Los Angeles, in order to gradually shut down trams and commuter trains. The rail lines were then paved over with highways on which GM cars could drive using Firestone tires and fuel from Standard Oil.[15] Concurrently, the industry marketed the car as a symbol of freedom, independence and the embodiment of the American Dream.[16] The reason for this was simple: with the introduction of the automotive system, it was possible to sell each individual citizen a new car body, their own drive system and considerably more energy. At the same time, public investment in the highway network contributed a huge economic stimulus package to the construction industry—

another significant boost to the expansion of the Great Machine.

All the same, it was not easy to keep this machinery running for the long term. After a certain time, most households had a car, a television set and a refrigerator. In order to make more money from the accumulated profits, the newly created assembly lines had to keep running. Somehow, people needed to be persuaded to throw away their devices sooner and replace them with new ones. The solution was "planned obsolescence," the deliberate reduction of a product's lifespan. The principle had already been developed in the late 1920s, when General Motors put cars into circulation that were intentionally designed to last only a short time.[17] Other manufacturers followed suit, and after the war, this concept was applied in almost all industries. With the help of the booming advertising industry, the principle of *fashion*, which had previously been restricted to clothing, was now applied to all kinds of consumer goods, from sofas to built-in kitchens. Now, a new model was bought because it was new and "modern," not because the old one was broken. This was yet another point where the constraints of endless capital growth converged with an obsessive suppression of memory.

As early as 1928, US President Hoover had declared to a group of public relations experts: "You have taken over the job of creating desire and have transformed people into constantly moving happiness machines, machines which have become the key to economic progress."[18] Consumerism as a state religion was complemented by a new magic phrase in politics: "economic growth." The permanent expansion of the monetary economy (which is what "economic growth" means) has been a systemic necessity since the paradigm of endless capital accumulation emerged in the early modern era. But it was not until the period of the 1930s to 1950s that this growth was measured as GDP, and after the war officially elevated to the pinnacle of national priorities. At the time, the investiture of growth as a central political goal was attacked by many economists and politicians. Joseph Schumpeter, for one, felt that just a single parameter for measuring economic output was a "fiction created by statisticians" and a "meaningless pile of data."[19] A few months before he was assassinated in 1968, US presidential candidate Robert Kennedy gave a speech that summarized his criticism of growth ideology:

> Our Gross National Product counts air pollution and cigarette advertising, and ambulances to clear our highways of carnage. It counts special locks for our doors and the jails for the people who break them. It counts the destruction of the redwood and the loss of our natural wonder in chaotic sprawl. It counts napalm and counts nuclear warheads and armored cars for the police to fight the riots in our cities. It counts Whitman's rifle and Speck's knife, and the television programs which glorify violence in order to sell toys to our children. Yet the gross national product does not allow for the health of our children, the quality of their education or the joy of their play. It does not include the beauty of our poetry or the strength of our marriages, the intelligence of our public debate or the integrity of our public officials. It measures neither our wit nor our courage, neither our wisdom nor our learning and compassion, it measures everything in short, except that which makes life worthwhile.[20]

Nonetheless, despite all criticism, GDP growth eventually prevailed throughout the world as the most important indicator of progress and "development," not only within the economic community, but also in politics and international organizations such as the OECD (Organization for Economic Co-operation and Development).[21] When viewed from the perspective of the common good, this choice was just as irrational as the introduction of the automotive system, but in the logic of the Megamachine, which must expand in order to exist, it made perfect sense.

INDEPENDENCE MOVEMENTS IN THE GLOBAL SOUTH

The expansion of the system nonetheless met with considerable resistance in other parts of the world. Since the beginning of the century, strong anti-colonial movements had emerged in many African and Asian countries that were striving for independence and that often advocated alternative economic concepts. India was one of the first countries to take steps toward independence, in a way not yet seen in history. Mohandas "Mahatma" Gandhi had developed the concept of *satyagraha* ("holding onto truth," which is sometimes mistakenly referred to as "passive resistance") in South Africa at the beginning of the twentieth century. Gandhi perceived the principle of non-violence not as a weak fallback position, but as a powerful weapon. A tiny minority of British colonial rulers could only maintain their power over India if the Indians cooperated in some way. Gandhi therefore proposed a strategy of active non-cooperation that was aimed at the heart of the colonial machine. The goal was to break the international division of labor that had degraded India to a cheap supplier of raw materials and had destroyed its once highly developed textile production.

Millions of Indians boycotted British products, stopped paying taxes and tried to revive the tradition of village self-sufficiency, which had been devastated by forced market integration.

Being confronted with strategies of non-cooperation and civil disobedience, the British faced completely different challenges compared to armed uprisings. In 1930, for instance, the British army fired machine guns at a gathering of nonviolent protesting Muslims in Peshawar, who, despite the hail of bullets, maintained their inner calm: "When those in front fell down wounded by the shots, those behind came forward with their breasts bared and exposed themselves to the fire. Some people got as many as 21 bullet wounds in their bodies, and all the people stood their ground without getting into a panic."[22] Instead of stifling the resistance, such massacres only added fuel to the fire, and Great Britain had to withdraw from India in 1947. Formal independence had been achieved, but as we shall see, the struggle of Gandhi and his supporters was far from won.

"Development" as Internal Colonization

Two years after Indian independence, Harry Truman, in his inaugural speech as US president, split the Earth into two halves. There were the "developed" countries of the Global North and the "underdeveloped" countries of the South, which the North, with its superior civilization, was obliged to "free from their suffering."[23] In one fell swoop, 2 billion people and their cultures were branded as "underdeveloped." The division of humanity into the "developed" and the "underdeveloped" is easily recognizable as the modernization of older pairs of terms such as "Christians" and "pagans" or "civilized" and "savages," all of which served to justify the myth of superiority of the West and its missionary project.

In Truman's logic, history is one-dimensional. All of humanity is marching in a straight line toward the goal of Western industrial society as exemplified by the US. Anything else amounts to stagnation or regression, in short, "underdevelopment." The consequences of this logic would be the elimination of those cultures and forms of social organization that do not follow the straight line. The South African historian Jan L. Sadie described this situation in 1961:

Economic development of an underdeveloped people by themselves is not compatible with the maintenance of their traditional customs and mores. A break with the latter is a prerequisite to economic progress. What is needed is a revolution in the totality of social, cultural and religious institutions and habits, and thus in their psychological attitude, their philosophy and way of life. What is, therefore, required amounts in reality to social disorganization. Unhappiness and discontentment in the sense of wanting more than is obtainable at any moment is to be generated. The suffering and dislocation that may be caused in the process may be objectionable, but it appears to be the price that has to be paid for economic development; the condition of economic progress.[24]

The idea of "development" has dominated the minds of entire generations of politicians, economists and social planners, regardless of whether they were inspired by socialism or capitalism.[25] This is true not only in the immediate Western sphere of influence, but also in countries such as India and China, who had originally intended to set out on their own paths. In India, after Gandhi's assassination (1948), Jawaharlal Nehru's concept of large-scale, centralized development prevailed, which amounted to a complete departure from Gandhi's ideas. Abandoning the logic of the Great Machine had been Gandhi's goal, with the central pillars of his political philosophy being: *swaraj* (self-administration), *swadeshi* (local economy) and *sarvodaya* (the improvement of living conditions for all). Nehru, on the other hand, was determined to imitate the Western model of industrialization. The number of those who fell victim to this strategy was enormous. The Indian author Arundhati Roy estimates that, from the 1950s on, more than 50 million people were forcibly resettled for gigantic dam projects, most of whom ended up in the slums of rapidly expanding cities.[26] In large part, these people were members of the Adivasi, the "first people," who came from remote mountain and forest regions. Even today, there are still millions of Adivasi who are victims of displacement in the name of "development," especially due to dams and mining. The tremendous richness of their culture is now in danger of being eradicated once and for all. In China, the communists had achieved important successes in the first years after coming to power in 1949. Hunger and civil war were overcome, the mafia gangs defeated, foreign colonial powers expelled and the first pillars of a state social system established.

Left: Sardar-Sarovar dam in India. Right: A protest against flooding and expulsion

The "century of humiliation" was followed by an era of national unification and reconstruction that was based on a new social contract. Mao's goals were ambitious; he wanted to outdo the West by its own means, and in 1958 he announced the "Great Leap Forward." His intention was to reach the industrial level of Great Britain within a few years, with the steel industry seen as key to success. Unlike in the West, however, industrialization was to be organized on a decentralized basis in order to bridge the growing gap between urban and rural areas and to counteract the centralized state's concentration of power. What began as a meaningful initiative to strengthen rural self-organization took a misguided turn due to the fixation on metallurgical growth. In order to meet the government's excessive production quotas, people throughout the country were forced to use homemade ovens to melt down all objects made with iron—from shovels to bedframes—for conversion into steel. The result was mountains of useless metal scrap. Much worse was the fact that, due to the steel mania, farmers had neglected the harvest during a period of drought. This led to one of the most devastating famines in China's history with a death toll in the millions.[27]

Eight years later, Mao initiated the "Cultural Revolution" in order to counter the looming refeudalization and bureaucratization of society. This project, however, was also infected by a development concept that called for an abrupt break from all cultural and social roots. The struggle was directed at the "four ancients," which meant old ways of thinking, old cultures, old habits and old customs. Even if Mao had quite different economic and social goals, there were still obvious parallels to the capitalist ideology of development. Not only the party bureaucracy and intellectuals became the target of this campaign, but indigenous cultures as well. In Tibet, thousands of monasteries were destroyed, and Mongolians, Uighurs and the Dai in Yunnan were persecuted because their cultures were not "proletarian" enough.[28]

"Development" as Fata Morgana

In practice, "development" proved to be a kind of modern sacrificial cult, requiring a portion of the population and its culture to be sacrificed in order to pave the way for the nation's progress. The bitter irony of this story, however, is that the goal of this sacrifice, "progress," turned out to be a mirage for most countries. The sacrifices were made, but the development never took place. Wherever governments in the Global South seriously set out to undertake independent development—even if they followed Truman's straight and narrow pathway—they were attacked by the West using all available means, be it by violent overthrow of the government or with the structural violence of debt. The concept of "development" thus became a typical "double bind" trap: political thinking focused down to a single goal—to emulate the West—but precisely that goal was to remain out of reach for most countries.[29]

Truman had promised in his 1949 speech that "the old imperialism—exploitation for foreign profit—has no place in our plans. What we envisage is a program of development based on the concepts of democratic fair-dealing." However, while politicians like Truman kept making such promises, other elements within their governments were taking pains to quash genuine democracy and development in the Global South. A decisive role was played by the modern intelligence services, which had been created during the Second World War as paramilitary organs with tens of thousands of employees operating in the shadows of the official armed forces. A list of the violent coups they initiated would fill many pages, beginning with the overthrow of Mohammad Mossadegh and his democratically elected Iranian government in 1953.[30] The following are just a few examples.

In the early 1950s, the democratically elected government of Guatemala set out to transform the Central American state "from a backward country with a predominantly feudal economy into a modern capitalist state," as President Jacobo Arbenz Guzmán put it at the time.[31] As amenable to the system as this goal might sound, it was still unacceptable to the US, because it meant that the United Fruit Company (now Chiquita), which had previously controlled Guatemala as a "banana republic," must relinquish power. The Company hired none other than Edward Bernays to launch a PR campaign portraying Arbenz as a closet Stalinist who intended to set up a communist dictatorship. In 1954, the CIA staged a coup that toppled Arbenz from office and installed a puppet government, an event that was celebrated in virtually all Western media under the orchestration of Bernays' propaganda machine as a victory for democracy. For the next 30 years, Guatemala was ruled by various military regimes that reversed Arbenz's social reforms and waged a brutal war against the opposition that left more than 200,000 dead.[32]

In 1960, the efforts to achieve independence in the Congo had ensured that the Belgians finally left the country they had ravaged for nearly a hundred years. The first free elections brought Patrice Lumumba to power, who, like Arbenz and Mossadegh, sought an independent industrial development of the Congo and who even turned to the US for advice. For Western mining companies, however, this would have meant the end of their business model. Today, we know from the frank admissions of former Belgian and US secret service operatives that they had incited General Mobutu to first place Lumumba under house arrest and then ultimately murder him.[33] As confirmed by the US State Department and declassified CIA documents, the order came directly from President Eisenhower.[34] The international press and the UN mission on the ground looked on passively as Lumumba was mistreated by the military at Léopoldville airport and then bundled onto a plane for transport to the scene of his assassination. Mobutu's terrorist regime, which came to power in the following years and plundered the country until 1997, was recognized and actively supported by all Western governments. The result is a country that remains largely devastated to this day, marked by civil wars and extreme poverty.

In Indonesia, President Sukarno, a spokesman for the Non-Aligned Movement, who sought development that would be independent of both the West and the Soviet Union, was overthrown in a coup that led to a veritable genocide. Documents that were released a few years ago show that the CIA received instructions from the highest level to "liquidate Sukarno."[35] For this purpose, the man the Americans relied on was General Suharto. Using a CIA list of leading leftists as well as American weapons, Suharto sent out death squads in 1965 to murder several thousand people. The successes of the operation were regularly reported to the US embassy in Jakarta, and the CIA kept a careful record as the murders progressed. But Suharto went even further, recruiting tens of thousands of young men who were quickly trained to be murderers and sent out "to clean the country of Communists." Armed with machetes, clubs and pistols, they tortured and killed nearly 1 million people within a few months.[36] On the small island of Bali alone, which is now promoted as a South Seas paradise, around 100,000 people were murdered, which was 8 percent of the island's population.[37] Travelers gave reports of rivers that were literally blocked by corpses, making transport by water impossible. The result was a country paralyzed by shock and overwhelming fear among the population. Once Suharto took power, the so-called "Berkeley Mafia" economists—Indonesians educated in the US and sponsored by the Ford Foundation—turned economic policy on its head and opened the door to Western capital. Within only two years, virtually all of the country's natural resources, especially oil, copper, wood and rubber, had been divided up among transnational corporations.[38]

In one country after another, this was how the hopes for independent development were shattered, and how the Non-Aligned Movement, which had emerged between 1955 and 1961, was decisively crippled.

THE WORLD REVOLUTION OF 1968

After the Second World War, the second major challenge for the global Megamachine was the massive increase in civil rights protests and student movements that began in the 1960s. They were by no means limited to the US and Europe, but had spread around the world like wildfire, from Japan to Mexico and from Prague to Rio de Janeiro. The "world revolution of 1968" challenged the global system in a much more fundamental way than the now established "old left," which included communist and social-democratic parties as well as trade unions, who had little more to offer than another variation of system management. The new movements did not seek a mere redistribution of wealth, but a radically different way of life. They were inspired by a cultural movement, the global "counterculture" that encompassed music, theater, literature and film. Especially the young generation was in search of new forms of living together and a common economy beyond the nuclear family, the state and the market. Unlike the "old left" with its orientation toward state socialism, the 1968 movements posed a challenge to all four tyrannies: the tyranny of the market; the physical violence of the state; the ideological power of the media, schools and universities; and the tyranny of linear thinking, technocracy and the idea of total domination over nature. With the advent of the Vietnam conflict, for the first time in the history of the US, an ongoing war was openly rejected by large sections of the population. While the first anti-war events of the early 1960s took place in tiny rooms with barely a dozen participants, by 1965 there were hundreds of thousands out in the streets. Tens of thousands refused military service and publicly burned their draft cards, while musicals such as *Hair* and the plays of the "Living Theatre" became worldwide symbols of anti-military resistance.

Not only was the military called into question, but also all other disciplinary social structures that had developed in the modern era and become indispensable to the functioning of the system, such as schools, psychiatry, prisons and, last but not least, alienated wage labor. The "one-dimensional man" (Herbert Marcuse), who had been turned into a cog within the global mechanism, was to be liberated at all levels: economic, political, mental, physical and emotional.

The movements of the 1960s and early 1970s broke through the facade of a "guided democracy." Behind the shop windows of the brave new consumer world, they uncovered the bloodbaths being perpetrated around the globe in the name of "Western values." This was symbolized above all by Vietnam. The myth of a Western mission that promises salvation was publicly shattered, and the filters of representation that had guaranteed the stability of the system since Madison's time were no longer accepted. Grassroots democratic assemblies, teach-ins and sit-ins sprang up everywhere. Universities were transformed from institutions for producing "technocratically oriented intellectuals" (Samuel Huntington) into forums for open discussions about social change.

Particularly threatening was the fact that rebellious students joined together with other movements, bringing large sections of a previously marginalized population onto the streets, including the black civil rights movement, the indigenous peoples' movements and the women's movement. In 1968, the American Indian Movement was founded, which succeeded in bringing the voices of Native Americans to a wider public. In 1964, the black civil rights movement in the US achieved the abolition of legally institutionalized racist segregation. It then went a step further by joining the movements against the Vietnam War and for the pursuit of a post-capitalist society. A "second wave" of the women's movement rebelled against the patriarchal foundations of family, politics and economy and also joined with the peace movement and the "counterculture." Virtually all the institutions on which power and domination had been based in the last 500— or even 5000—years were now faced with enormous challenges.

The Response to 1968

The political and economic establishment was confronted with previously unknown forms of resistance. There had been successful strategies for containing the independence movements of the Global South; and, step by step, the "old left" in North America and Europe had also been tamed, especially by giving workers a greater share of the growing pie during the boom of the *trente glorieuses*. However, none of this was effective against the new movements. They could neither be overthrown by force nor bought off, and rather than a larger piece of the pie, they wanted the entire bakery. In addition, these movements were largely made up of students who were supposed to learn how to run the Great Machine and its countless subsystems, not to dismantle them. It was therefore necessary to put together a new tool kit that would combine old and "proven" instruments with new strategies.

Among such trusted devices was physical violence, although it was subject to certain limits in the "guided democracies" of the West. In Paris, during the barricaded battles of May 1968, the police deployed tear gas while arbitrarily arresting and beating protesters, thousands of whom were hospitalized. Meanwhile, tanks stood waiting for orders outside the gates of the city. In Mexico City, in October 1968, government snipers shot into a crowd of 10,000 unarmed protesters who had assembled. Hundreds died or were seriously injured. In Berkeley, California, Governor Ronald Reagan ordered the use of live ammunition against a peaceful crowd that had occupied a park, while helicopters dropped tear gas from overhead. The sheriff in charge later admitted that his people had fought "as if against the Vietcong."[39] In Ohio, the National Guard attacked unarmed students and shot four of them to death with dum-dum rounds from a distance of 100 yards. In Brazil, the US-backed military dictatorship arrested, tortured and murdered countless opponents of the regime, and in Czechoslovakia, hundreds of thousands of Warsaw Pact soldiers marched in to bring the "Prague Spring" to a violent end. However, violence was not always successful as a deterrent. After the Ohio massacre, 8 million students across the country went on strike, the largest student mobilization of all time. In France, prompted by police violence, workers showed solidarity with students and organized the most extensive spontaneous strike in French history.

As the use of open physical force caused public opinion to turn against governments and threatened to further destabilize the system, many states increasingly turned to covert violence. One example is the FBI's secret "Counterintelligence Program" (Cointelpro). Originally developed against alleged communists, it was now being used against the anti-war movement, Martin Luther King, the Black Panthers, the women's movement, the American Indian Movement, student groups and anti-war senators. Leaked in 1971, FBI-internal documents show that the program's purpose was to "discredit, destabilize and demoralize" critical movements, including those that were completely legal and peaceful. The methods ranged from dirty campaigns against movement leaders to the use of *agents provocateurs* and even to political murder. Anonymous phone calls and letters were used to deliberately incite paranoia among political activists. Martin Luther King, for example, was urged to commit suicide. FBI members planted false reports in the media, printed fake leaflets and organized pseudo-political groups to turn different factions of the movement against each other. The police and FBI broke into the residences of civil rights activists under flimsy pretexts and completely demolished them. Several members of the Black Panthers were shot to death in their own homes.[40]

Another example is the Italian "Gladio" network, uncovered in 1986 by the investigating magistrate Felice Casson. This was an organization run by neo-fascists and members of the Italian military intelligence service SISMI together with NATO and the CIA. The network perpetrated numerous terrorist attacks in Italy during the 1960s and 1970s with the explicit aim of placing the blame for the attacks on left-wing groups.[41] In response to a parliamentary enquiry, former Italian Prime Minister Andreotti confirmed Gladio's existence, adding that similar organizations existed in many other Western European countries.[42] In 1990, this led the European Parliament to demand an investigation into such secret paramilitary organizations in all EU states and to finally abolish them—but without significant success.[43] Today, the state-sponsored terrorism pursued by organizations such as Gladio, with the goal of enforcing repressive policies by creating a state of emergency, has become commonly referred to as the "strategy of tension."

The Ideological System is Shaken

In the early 1970s, especially due to increasing violence, the mood in many countries changed. To a degree, the climate of optimism and high hopes gave way to an atmosphere of fear. Many political groups splintered into conflicting factions, while others withdrew from the political arena to devote themselves to spiritual liberation. Still others opted for the "long march through the institutions" or fled to consumerism.

Although state violence had contributed to this fragmentation and intimidation, its success turned out to be limited. The ideological foundations of the system had been permanently shaken. With the exposure of American war crimes at Mỹ Lai in Vietnam (1969), and the unveiling of the "Pentagon Papers" (1971), large portions of the population came to realize that a brutal war of extermination had been waged in their name, under the masks of freedom and democracy. It turned out that the American people had been systematically lied to by four successive US governments about the goals of the war and the extent of the killing. The revelations about Cointelpro (1971) and secret CIA programs (1974) showed that the government was not above inflicting massive violence against its own people. Against this backdrop, Watergate (1972) was little more than a historical footnote.

These revelations shook not only the political establishment, but also the worldview of entire populations in the Western hemisphere. Now, it was no longer just a matter of misconduct by one government or another; the entire political and ideological system began to wobble, with the US at its epicenter. Confidence in state institutions, especially in the military, was permanently damaged.[44] This allowed the peace movement in the 1970s to become a strong anti-systemic force, which made warfare more difficult than ever before in the history of modern states. From then on, the military-industrial complex would remain at the center of public criticism and protest.

An additional new movement also emerged that was closely linked to resistance to the military—the modern ecology movement. Greenpeace was founded in 1970 in Canada as a protest organization against nuclear bomb testing in Alaska. At about the same time, Friends of the Earth was also formed as an anti-nuclear organization. "Earth Day" in 1970 brought 20 million

Americans onto the streets to demonstrate for environmental protection.

The ecology movement drew inspiration from a momentous and far-reaching upheaval in the sciences. In 1972, *The Limits to Growth,* a report to the Club of Rome, was published. Using computer models, scientists at the renowned Massachusetts Institute of Technology showed that continued industrial growth will lead to a global system collapse by the year 2100, a prognosis that has been repeatedly confirmed in many subsequent reviews and updates of the report.[45] In the realms of established physics, chemistry and biology, Ilya Prigogine's work on non-linear systems shook mechanistic notions of nature.[46] In economics, E. F. Schumacher, a former associate of John Maynard Keynes, developed the concept of a decentralized, ecological people's economy, strongly influenced by Gandhi. Schumacher's book *Small Is Beautiful* became an international bestseller. At about the same time, NASA scientist James Lovelock and biologist Lynn Margulis introduced the "Gaia hypothesis," the first scientific attempt to understand the Earth as a living, self-regulating system.

This new thinking was in turn reflected in the activities of countless "counterculture" communities that attempted to build a lifestyle beyond the destruction of nature, consumerism and competition (partly following older traditions of Romanticism and "life reform" movements). Yet another major break from the past was to emerge, the importance of which cannot be overestimated: the educational revolution. Since the early modern period, educational methods had prevailed at school and at home with the express aim of breaking the child's will in order to make it a smoothly functioning part of the family, military and economy.[47] Approaches to pedagogical reform that were based on respect for the child had existed for a long time. However, it was only in the period after 1968 that a movement began to develop in parental homes, daycare centers and independent schools that was capable of winning over a majority. Thus, another critical foundation of the disciplinary society was called into question.

The great political turnaround had failed to materialize in 1968 but the social changes were profound. A critique of the entire ruling structure of modernity and the Western concept of "civilization" was now on the agenda of a global "counterculture" that was penetrating ever deeper into the mainstream.

The "Moderation of Democracy"

In 1973, the Trilateral Commission was set up at the instigation of David Rockefeller to coordinate global system management between the US, Western Europe and Japan. Its members included leading politicians from all three regions, CEOs of corporations such as Exxon, Toyota, Fiat, Lehman Brothers and Coca-Cola, as well as union leaders and leading journalists, including the editors of *Time Magazine*, the *Financial Times* and the German weekly *Die Zeit*.

One of the first reports produced by the commission was entitled *The Crisis of Democracy*. In the report, Samuel Huntington and his co-authors from France and Japan diagnose an "excess of democracy" as a threat to the stability of the system. Huntington looks back wistfully to the 1950s, when "President Truman was able to govern the US with the cooperation of a relatively small number of Wall Street lawyers and bankers."[48] With remarkable openness, the authors note that "European democracies have been only partially and sometimes theoretically open. Their regulations were built on a subtle screening of participants and demands."[49] Huntington continues:

The effective operation of a democratic political system usually requires some measure of apathy and noninvolvement on the part of some individuals and groups. [...] Marginal social groups, as in the case of the blacks, are now becoming full participants in the political system. Yet the danger of overloading the political system with demands which extend its functions and undermine its authority still remains.[50]

Huntington also complains that advanced industrial societies have produced a layer of "value-oriented intellectuals, who devote themselves to the derogation of leadership, the challenging of authority, and the unmasking and delegitimation of established institutions."[51] The press posed yet another threat: "As a result of the increasing influence of the journalists vis-à-vis owners and editors, the press has taken an increasingly critical role toward government and public officials. In some countries, traditional norms of 'objectivity' and 'impartiality' have been brushed aside in favor of 'advocatory journalism'."[52] The new values that were spreading throughout society made it increasingly difficult for governments to "impose discipline and sacrifice upon its citizens."

The analyses in this report are some of the most accurate and forceful testimonies by "liberal" political elites about their fears regarding true democracy.[53] The report's final recommendations, however, remain relatively vague. For example, there is talk of restoring "an appropriate balance between the press, the government, and other institutions in society" or relating "educational planning to economic and political goals." The vagueness of these recommendations further underscores the helplessness that had befallen the establishment in the mid-1970s. The strategies of the "great rollback" were yet to be conceived.

THE GREAT ROLLBACK

The political and economic elites who tried to steer the Great Machine through turbulent times had to battle on at least two fronts during the 1970s. On the one hand, there was the challenge of counterculture and anti-systemic movements, and on the other, a global economic crisis. After three decades of boom and expansion, a period of stagnation and contraction began in 1973, heralded by a sharp rise in oil prices, a severe recession and the collapse of the world monetary system ("Bretton Woods System"), including the gold parity of the US dollar.

The answer to this turmoil was what later became known as the "neoliberal revolution," although in fact it was more of a conservative reaction. Its aim was to restart the stuttering accumulation machine, push back the counterculture and restore power to the dominant economic classes that had been significantly weakened in the 1960s.[54] This "revolution" had several pillars: one was politico-economic, another was ideological-propagandistic and (often overlooked) one was military.

The drama of the global economic downturn that began in 1973 is now almost forgotten. The US fell into a deep recession, and the price of oil quintupled at times, which not only called the automotive system into question, but the entire fossil-energy-based growth model. At the same time, Great Britain was experiencing a serious banking crisis. In 1976, the country faced insolvency and was forced to accept a loan from the International Monetary Fund on condition of a profound "structural adjustment." The city of New York also barely avoided bankruptcy in 1975.[55] As later in countless African, Asian and Latin American countries, these debt crises were to be exploited as an opportunity for a radical transformation within society. The prototype for this immediately followed the New York bankruptcy, when normal and low-income earners were expelled from Manhattan in order to transform it into an El Dorado for the super-rich.[56]

The Economy of Expropriation

In order to restart the money accumulation machine and restore its threatened power over society, owners of capital relied on a range of strategies typically used during phases of economic contraction. One of these was to make intensive efforts to reduce input costs, i.e. wages, taxes and resource expenditures. The various ways to reduce taxes and wages included: combating trade unions; lowering legal minimum wages and labor standards; relocating production to low-wage countries; financing campaigns to reduce corporate taxes; relocating company headquarters to tax havens; etc.[57] As we will see, the debt of the Global South would provide critical leverage for reducing resource prices.

A second reaction, also typical during contraction phases, was the expansion of speculative activity. Because investment in the so-called "real economy" was hardly worthwhile, capital owners increasingly invested in financial transactions that promised high short-term profits, while also pushing for the abolition of obstructive regulations. It is often said that speculation is ultimately a zero-sum game for all the players, but in practice, this is not quite the case. While profits flow into private hands during the expansion phase of a speculative bubble, once it bursts, the government is usually willing to offset a large portion of the losses and pass them on to the general population. A typical example is the major US banking and real estate crisis of 1982, known as the Savings and Loan Crisis. After the bubble burst, the public sector assumed as much as 124 billion US dollars of the costs, while private companies were only held liable for 29 billion US dollars.[58] This pattern has been repeated in countless banking and financial crises since the beginning of the 1980s, right up to the global financial crisis of 2008 and the subsequent "Euro crisis." In order to make speculation profitable in the long term, it is therefore not only crucial that obstructive regulations be abolished, but it is also necessary to ensure that speculation losses are not borne by the speculators themselves. Although this principle is incompatible with neoliberal *ideology*, it has occupied a crucial place in neoliberal *practice* from the outset.

The third strategy amounted to a kind of intra-systemic cannibalism. The system began to devour itself, starting with its own infrastructure. Areas that had, until then, wisely been

The End of the Megamachine

excluded from capital accumulation and were predominantly state-run or publicly organized were then privatized, such as the health, education and pension systems, transport infrastructure and water utilities. In order to pump up short-term profits, investors often trimmed back on the critical components of these infrastructures. Railway networks were dismantled, water pipe maintenance was neglected, personnel laid off, etc. Examples of such internal decay are legion, from the Argentine railway system, which has now almost disappeared, to the ailing London water supply.

All three strategies were very successful in generating high profits for individual companies and restoring class supremacy to the upper 1 percent. It was a veritable "coup d'état by transnational corporations" (John Ralston Saul), which rose to become the true sovereigns of the world. At the same time, however, these strategies produced enormous costs for the national economies. First of all, they ruined the infrastructure needed to maintain capital accumulation for the long haul. Secondly, these strategies can only work if more and more debt is accumulated somewhere within the system. When wages are lowered, consumers have to take on debt in order to continue buying up the output of production. If taxes are lowered, then states also have to borrow to continue providing infrastructure. Finally, if speculation is to pay off in the long run, then states will also have to borrow in order to offset losses. Therefore, over time, the neoliberal program will undermine not only the livelihoods of large sections of the population, but also the very foundations of the Great Machine itself.

Tanks and Propaganda
By its very nature, the implementation of such a socially destructive program was not an easy task, and it required varying mixtures of ideological, structural and physical violence, depending on the country and continent. The prototypical

266

case of military violence was Chile, where in 1973 the elected government of Salvador Allende was overthrown in a US-backed coup that was meant to pave the way for the shock program of the "Chicago Boys," followers of the radical free-market economist Milton Friedman. In the great stadiums of Santiago, which were converted into torture and execution arenas following the takeover, the military snuffed out any resistance to the coup in the name of "free markets."[59]

The Chilean model, however, would not transfer well to the North. The option of using tanks and torture was unthinkable here, so other means had to be employed. Thus, in the 1980s and 1990s, a propaganda battle of epic proportions began in North America and Western Europe. It started in the US and Great Britain, where the destruction of infrastructure and social security was sold to the public as personal liberation. The search for individual development and freedom from state intervention, which played an essential role in the "counterculture" of the 1960s, was reinterpreted as market-compliant self-optimization and consumer freedom. With billions of dollars from business interests, countless think tanks and foundations were set up to disseminate their "expertise" through political networks, universities and the mass media. The gospel they propagated was that if people finally took their fate into their own hands—free from the restrictions of the state, trade unions and stifling morals—then the invisible hand of the market would simply increase prosperity for all. Liberation from the state, however, was a fairy tale from the very beginning. While the program did indeed aim to do away with the welfare services that had been hard fought for by social movements, at the same time it relied on a massive expansion of the military, of "security technology" and surveillance, not least to maintain control over disintegrating societies.

In universities, the media, the arts and political parties, an ideological rollback occurred that Huntington and his co-authors could have only dreamed of. The commercialization and academic strictures placed on universities gradually pushed back critical thinking and promoted the "technocratic intellectual" that Huntington had always wished for.[60] A new wave of consolidation in the media sector and the privatization of television—in Germany and France in the portentous year 1984—made it harder than ever for committed journalists to assert themselves against publishers and owners. Sports events and casting shows took over more and more time slots and fulfilled an important ideological function by preparing viewers for a world of total competition. In cinema, monster and fantasy films, starting with *Jaws* (1975) and *Star Wars* (1977), replaced the more socially engaged movies of the 1960s and early 1970s.

Across the political landscape of the 1990s, the social-democratic parties finally abandoned their roots and became the most zealous executors of radical free-market politics, a development that has led to the virtual absence of real political alternatives at the ballot box.

The Great Rollback in the East

The globalization of the neoliberal program spared neither the countries of the Eastern Bloc nor China. When Mikhail Gorbachev began to slowly democratize the ossified authoritarian system of the Soviet Union in the late 1980s, he knew that he was initiating a risky process, but he had no idea what kind of floodgates he would be opening. His goal was a kind of social-democratic welfare state modeled on Sweden, but as we know, this would never be achieved. The economic downturns that followed the dissolution of the Soviet Union in 1991 were seen by Western advisors and lenders as an opportunity to push through their shock program and prepare the ground for one of the most remarkable exploitive raids in modern history. Western "investors" and local elites snatched the prime cuts of the disintegrating system and earned billions overnight. In 1993, when the Russian parliament refused to give Boris Yeltsin and his kleptocratic regime, which was supported by the International Monetary Fund and Western governments, dictatorial power and a blank check for radical structural adjustment programs, Yeltsin seized the "Pinochet Option." He had tanks and machine guns shoot at the parliament building until the elected deputies came out with their hands up. The headline of the *Washington Post* the day after the bloody coup d'état was, "A Victory for Democracy."[61]

In China, head of state Deng Xiaoping had been opening up the Chinese economy to foreign capital and increasing competition since the early 1980s, a process that would eventually lead to the Chinese boom in subsequent decades. Although China's balancing act between opening markets and state control produced impressive growth figures and raised the standard of living for many people, there were also considerable sacrifices right from the start. An estimated 70 million farmers were driven off their land, and ordinary workers lost virtually all social security benefits. Women, in particular, were forced to accept work under inhuman conditions in the sweatshops of the new special economic zones. Party cadres, on the other hand, appropriated the privatized state-owned enterprises and became multimillionaires within a few years.[62] This situation was one of the decisive factors that led to the 1989 Tiananmen Square protests. The Chinese leadership's reaction with tanks and mass shootings is well known. Deng Xiaoping stifled student and worker resistance, which paved the way for radical privatizations during the 1990s, and to China becoming one of the most socially divided nations on Earth.[63] It was not until the 2010s that the gap between rich and poor began to narrow somewhat once again.

However, the most extreme and violent form of neoliberal revolution took place in Iraq in 2003. After the US military had largely devastated the country, Paul Bremer, head of the

Provisional Authority, was the first to pass a package of laws that privatized all public institutions and handed Iraqi banks over to foreign control. Since then, the country has grown from one of the wealthiest in the Middle East into one of the poorest in the world. With its public infrastructure destroyed, the country has fallen apart and become prey to rival warlords and religious fanatics.[64]

The Power of Debt

In addition to military and ideological violence, there was yet another way to implement a neoliberal reorganization— the structural violence of debt. By the mid-1970s, enormous amounts of capital, including money from the Arab oil states, had accumulated in major financial centers, for which there were fewer and fewer profitable investment opportunities because of the global recession. One strategy for investing this capital safely and profitably was to offer "development" loans to countries in the Global South. Western bankers, economists and policy advisors fanned out across the southern regions to sell large infrastructure projects to the governments of former colonies that were financed by credits from the North and implemented by companies from the North. As a result, the countries of the Global South went into enormous debt to achieve "development" that, in most cases, was only a chimera. From 1970 to 2000, the indebtedness of the 60 poorest countries rose from 25 billion to 523 billion US dollars.[65] Many of the borrowers were dictatorships that had risen to power or were propped up with support from the West. Whether in Indonesia, the Philippines, Brazil, Uganda, Congo or Haiti, there was barely any accountability for how the money was used. Much of it disappeared into Swiss bank accounts and the rest went into oversized and absurd prestige objects, the countless ruins of which still blight the landscape today. Because of government guarantees, private investment risk was practically eliminated, which secured the flow of returns and interest. Countries such as Argentina, Zimbabwe and Mexico are still paying interest on these loans, although they have already repaid the borrowed sum several times over.[66] Due to the continuous flow of interest from the South, the poorest countries in the world have been subsidizing the accumulation of capital in the North, especially in the financial centers of New York and London.

The South's debt has not only made for profitable business, but it is also a means of political control. Those who take on debt also become susceptible to extortion. Thus, "dirty" military or paramilitary interventions could be replaced by "clean" economic coercion.

Between 1979 and 1981, the then chairman of the US Federal Reserve, Paul Volcker, shocked the world with radical increases in US key interest rates of up to 20 percent.[67] The consequences for the Global South were dramatic, and in a very short time the costs of debt service multiplied, with one country after another headed for bankruptcy. This debt crisis was the gateway for the rising power of the IMF, which was originally created to stabilize volatile currencies. Since the early 1980s, however, the Fund has taken on completely new tasks. Often in cooperation with the US Treasury, it has imposed "aid loans" on over-indebted countries in order to avert imminent national bankruptcy. In exchange for these loans, the IMF has then demanded far-reaching rights of intervention in the legislation and social structure of the borrowing countries. In this way, the IMF has become a kind of new colonial government in large parts of Africa, Asia and Latin America, undermining what had remained of the efforts for independent development after the covert operations of the 1950s to the 1970s. The debt crisis in the South proved to be extremely useful by ensuring a constant flow of capital to the banks, and also lowering the input costs of industries in the North. In return for emergency loans, the IMF required a strong focus on the export of industrial raw materials and agricultural products. The argument was, if you export more, then you can repay your debts faster. Since this prescription was assigned to many countries at the same time, the world market was literally flooded with wheat, rice, coffee, tobacco, sugar, copper, aluminium, coal and oil—and prices fell.[68] The crises in the South remained unsolved and further intensified, while processing industries in the North enjoyed lower input costs.

The Second Devastation of Mexico

These neoliberal shock therapies plunged most Latin American and African countries and much of Asia into a vicious cycle of debt, impoverishment and violence. A striking example is Mexico. When the national debt exploded as a result of the "Volcker Shock," the country faced bankruptcy in 1982. In exchange for an aid loan, the IMF and the US Treasury ordered an extensive structural adjustment program, which for the first time included a comprehensive privatization scheme in addition to massive cuts in public spending and deregulation of the financial system. Due to this program, the average real income of Mexicans fell by almost 50 percent. In Mexico City, spending on public services such as the water supply, waste collection and public health fell by about a quarter. In just 10 years, the city transformed itself from one of Latin America's most tranquil capitals into the continent's most dangerous metropolis.[69] Tenochtitlán had been wiped out by Hernán Cortés' troops more than 450 years earlier, and now the city was devastated once again; this time by the structural violence of the IMF regime.

The crisis worsened when Mexico signed onto the North American Free Trade Agreement (NAFTA) in 1994. Highly subsidized corn imports from the US now destroyed the livelihoods of small farmers, while US companies outsourced large parts of their production to Mexico. Tens of thousands of *maquilas* emerged on the US border. These were assembly and textile companies where impoverished women in particular worked for starvation wages. The cities of Ciudad Juárez and Tijuana increased their populations tenfold during this period, but when the industries migrated to even cheaper countries, especially China, the jobs dried up. The drug mafia and prostitution took their place. Twenty years earlier, Ciudad Juárez had been a quiet provincial town, and now it was the most violent city in the world with up to 4000 murders per year.[70] Today, one in ten of the city's residents is addicted to drugs. Meanwhile, Mexican entrepreneur and crisis profiteer Carlos Slim, later a co-owner of the *New York Times*, became the richest man on Earth.

The New "Others"

The neoliberal rollback tore up the social fabric and undermined social cohesion in the North, South, East and West. As in the radical free-market phase of the nineteenth century, many governments increasingly played the nationalist (or religious-fundamentalist) card to weld together society. The exuberant patriotism in Thatcher's Great Britain during the Falklands War, the Reagan era in the US, the rise of fascist Hindu nationalism in India, as well as the nationalist movements in many European countries are cases in point.

In order to forge an "us group," or imagined community, from a fractured society, an external enemy — "the other" — is necessary. Until 1989, communism had provided a passable foil for the West, but as soon as the Berlin Wall fell, a replacement was urgently needed. Ultimately, "Islamist terrorism" was tapped to fulfill this function. From 1993 on, the same Samuel Huntington who had promoted the "moderation of democracy" in 1975 had once again become extremely influential by spreading his theses on the "clash of civilizations."[71]

In the year of terror, 2001, ten times more people were murdered in the US by fellow citizens using firearms than by the attacks of September 11. Nonetheless, it was possible to stylize

"Islamism" as the greatest threat to mankind and thus justify subsequent wars and a massive dismantling of civil rights. Once again, the enemy of civilization could be located in the East (this time the Middle East). A 2000-year history of "Orientalism" which had set the wild, unpredictable Orient in opposition to the rational, civilized Occident provided a framework already deeply anchored in Western thinking, into which the new image of the enemy neatly fitted.[72] The various currents of political Islam, which were broadly subsumed under "Islamism," were quickly labeled "medieval," although they have absolutely nothing to do with the Middle Ages and are the product of modern colonial history.

The macabre point of this development is that the proclaimed enemy of civilization becomes a real one when the military is called in to fight it. Once again, Iraq provides the best example. While there was practically no Islamist-motivated terror there before the 2003 invasion, the alleged "war on terror" has led the country to subsequently fall prey to warlords and terrorist groups.

THE LIMITS OF THE SYSTEM

Since the early 1970s, the limitations of the global Megamachine have become increasingly apparent. During the oil crises of 1973 and 1979, people in industrialized countries experienced in concrete terms for the first time what the finite nature of fossil fuels means: fuel rationing, driving bans, panic buying and inflation. The ominous nuclear accidents in Harrisburg (1979), Chernobyl (1986) and finally Fukushima (2011) have severely shaken the idea that nature can be controlled through technology.

In the 1960s, large sections of the "specialized classes," from Los Angeles to Tokyo and from Paris to Brasilia, looked forward to a technocratic utopia in which cybernetically optimized humans could relax in quietly humming space gliders. These days, the only prospect remaining is that of a desolate dystopia: a planet torn between extreme wealth and abject misery, racing toward an ecological catastrophe with a huge arsenal of nuclear weapons, collapsing megacities and a dysfunctional financial system. While there are still some steadfast believers who turn their shining eyes toward the promise of large-scale technology and free markets, the collapse of optimism and progress ideologies that have shaped Western civilization for more than 200 years cannot be overlooked.

Economic Limits

Since the financial crisis of 2008, the instability of the global economic system has become abundantly clear to all. For large parts of the world's population, however, crashes and chronic crises have been part of everyday life for decades, from the Mexican crisis in 1982 to the Asian crisis in 1997 to the bankruptcies of Russia (1998), Brazil (1999) and Argentina (2000).

This increasing instability is not, as is often believed, caused by the unscrupulous behavior of a few leading bankers, but by the fact that the accumulation of capital based on the cycle of production, sales, profit and reinvestment has started to stall on a global scale. The most important reason for this is that the neoliberal rollback was very profitable for only a narrow group, and that it simultaneously weakened demand through wage dumping and job insecurity. People simply no longer have enough money in their pockets to buy up global production at profitable prices, while in the logic of the system, that production must continue to grow. This demand problem is exacerbated by the fact that more and more people have been laid off and are dropping out of the production system. Consequently, they no longer receive any wages with which to make purchases. The system is stifled by its own productivity. Large parts of the agricultural and industrial workforce have already been replaced by technology during the last hundred years, and with computerization, the trend is now spreading to the middle classes and the service sector.[73] The result is structural mass unemployment, which is becoming more and more acute, despite being hushed up by manipulated government statistics. While in the 1980s we were still talking about the "two-thirds society," in which one-third would become permanently excluded from gainful employment, today, on a global scale, we are moving toward a "one-fifth society" in which only 20 percent of the population is needed for production.[74] No one knows how the remaining 80 percent will end up nor how social peace and political stability can be possible under such conditions.

This structural crisis could theoretically be defused by a Keynesian program with extensive taxation of wealth, job creation in the public sector, wage increases, shorter working hours and much more. However, such a program of higher taxes and wages would significantly increase costs for capital owners, and severely cut into their potential profits. Therefore, they resist it with all means at their disposal and thus ultimately intensify the crisis. The more successful they are in accomplishing their short-term goals, the more they undermine the functionality of the economic system that sustains them. Even state actors can hardly be expected to solve this dilemma, because they are caught up in the logic of an intensifying global competition between regions.

For decades, this systemic crisis has been concealed by the rapidly growing indebtedness of companies, states and consumers. However, debt bubbles have the unpleasant tendency to burst at some point. In 2008, states were still able to cushion the near-collapse of the global financial system by billing themselves and their citizens for most of the costs of the crisis. Whether they can do this again is more than questionable, especially since not only their budgets are dwindling, but their legitimacy is as well.

The Regression of the State and the End of Loyalty

Since the 1990s, starting on the periphery of the world-system, more and more states have collapsed and are no longer able to maintain control over their own territories. In the meantime, a corridor of "failed states" about 10,000 kilometers long has formed, stretching from the Congo via Mali, Libya, Sudan and Somalia to Syria, Iraq and Afghanistan. Since the global financial crisis of 2008, the collapse of the state has also eaten its way to the edges of Europe. The civil war in Ukraine is a typical example. The categorization of "failed state" is partly arbitrary and is often used to justify "anti-terrorist" interventions, but the phenomenon behind it is real. A significant element in the collapse of states goes back to the debt crisis of the 1980s and 1990s. In many countries, such as Mali, after decades of structural adjustment there is no perspective for young people other than to join one of the rival militarized groups, be it the army, the jihadists or the drug smugglers.[75] The result is a war economy similar to the one in Europe during the Thirty Years' War.

As in Iraq, some states fail directly due to military intervention. What is striking in these countries is that, unlike in colonial times, the intervening power is no longer able or willing to establish stable state structures. In the case of the US, there are two obvious reasons for this: since the Vietnam War, the population is reluctant to permanently deploy ground troops abroad; and because of the enormous national debt, the US can no longer afford a long-term occupation and reconstruction program along the lines of the Marshall Plan.

State structures are eroding in certain sectors of industrialized countries as well. Almost the entire modern period up to the early 1970s was characterized by the centralization and state regulation of more and more functions of the system. The goal was to deepen control over populations and territories and optimize the capital accumulation apparatus. Nonetheless, the system has been developing backwards ever since, as clearly evidenced by the switch from conscription armies to mercenary troops and private military contractors, as was typical in the early modern era. In an increasing number of cases, corporations are also resorting to private mercenary armies in order to operate in an increasingly insecure world, just as the first public limited companies did in the seventeenth century.[76]

Another aspect of system regression is the disintegration of infrastructure. For centuries, centralized state power built roads, railways, bridges, electricity grids, water and sanitation systems, schools and administrative structures to provide the infrastructure necessary for the smooth functioning of the economy. Since the 1980s, this infrastructure has been disintegrating in many of the wealthiest industrialized countries, with that of the United States declining most rapidly. As early as 2003, the American Society of Civil Engineers stated that "the infrastructure necessary for the functioning of our economy and our quality of life is disintegrating."[77] For years, this organization has been calling for an investment program of over 2 *trillion* dollars, which, given the budget crisis, remains a pipe dream.

As the state withdraws from the maintenance of infrastructure and welfare services, it is evolving back to what it was from the start, a purely repressive military and police machine. The US is setting the example: while large sections of the population sink into poverty and struggle to survive amid a dysfunctional infrastructure, the government is concentrating on expanding surveillance systems, prisons and the military. As a result, citizens' loyalty to their state, which has been painstakingly nurtured since the nineteenth century, is waning. With the denunciation of the historical compromise between capital and labor, which culminated in the welfare states of the *trente glorieuses*, the possibilities of controlling the system within the framework of a "guided democracy" are dwindling. Citizens are turning away from established politics, options are becoming more radical, and the system is growing even more unstable.

The Return of Nationalism and Fascism

When the frustration and anger of the citizens crosses a certain threshold, and the "bewildered herd" (Walter Lippmann) breaks out of its pen and becomes uncontrollable, politics is left with two options. It can either make genuine concessions to the people and create more social justice; or it can protect the interests of the rich and powerful by distracting the herd and channeling their anger toward scapegoats. The scapegoat strategy works particularly well in times of crisis. Uncertainty, fear and latent paranoia are exploited to deliver vivid images of the terrorist Muslim, the criminal migrant, the belligerent Russian, the deceitful Chinese, the money-hungry Jew, the lazy Southern European, the dangerous drug addict, the parasitic welfare recipient and so on.

The list of such clichés is truly endless and varies from country to country. Political groups with vested interests use them adroitly to distract from systemic questions and distributional conflicts, while elements of the media volunteer to be megaphones for them. Since the 2000s, right-wing demagogues in many parts of the world have succeeded in coming to power by channeling the anger of their citizens toward demonized stereotypes. The fascist Jair Bolsonaro in Brazil, Donald Trump in the US, Matteo Salvini in Italy, Roberto Duterte in the Philippines and Victor Orbán in Hungary are just a few. As in the Europe of the 1920s and 1930s, it is becoming apparent that segments of big business are financing right-wing extremist networks and political parties because they see them as the last bastion for preserving their privileges. The consequences, however, are disastrous. The shift to the right intensifies all global crisis dynamics, including social divisions, the risk of wars, and a disruption of the natural foundations of life.

The Ultimate Limitation: The Planet

In order to function, the machinery of endless money accumulation needs a permanently increasing input of energy and raw materials. Patently, this also translates to an equally fast-growing output of waste and greenhouse gases. The link between economic growth and planetary destruction is so obvious that it only takes your five senses to grasp it. Whoever travels the devastated forests of Borneo or the Amazon, the oil-polluted coasts of Nigeria and the Gulf of Mexico, the contaminated regions around Fukushima and Chernobyl, the gigantic trash vortex in the Pacific Ocean, the regions poisoned by fracking in the US, the landscapes devastated by copper, gold, bauxite and uranium mining in Papua New Guinea, India, Ghana or Chile, or the islands of Puerto Rico and Jamaica, which have been destroyed by extreme hurricanes, does not really need to read all the scientific studies about the ruin of the biosphere that fill entire libraries. This small, random selection from the totality of planetary devastation is already sufficient to realize that a system that destroys its own life-supporting foundations at such a fast pace has no future. The end of cheap oil ("peak oil") and the foreseeable shortage of strategic raw materials such as copper and uranium also place material and energy limits on continued expansion.[78]

The repeatedly raised objections to these findings are that resource consumption and monetary growth are two very different things; that there has only been a false approach to growth so far; and that we just need to switch to a "green" and "sustainable" form of expansion. The magic word here is "decoupling." It means that as we continue to accumulate money, we must and can consume fewer and fewer resources per dollar earned. Decoupling has in fact been applied in all industrialized countries for centuries, simply because companies have always had an interest in reducing input costs, which also leads to conserving resources. In the logic of the Great Machine, however, companies never let savings disappear into a piggy bank, but reinvest them to expand production (or speculation). And for every dollar or pound saved by consumers, a purchase is made elsewhere, a phenomenon known as the "rebound effect."[79] Even those who do not spend all their money but deposit it in the bank will still end up reinvesting it in the cycle, because the bank "works" with it. In this way, the concepts of decoupling and resource efficiency are being reduced to absurdity.

Every human society, along with its economy, is a subsystem of planet Earth. It lives from a stream of substances provided by this superordinate system; from its ability to provide water, breathable air, food, minerals and somewhat stable weather conditions.[80] The Earth can easily do without human societies and economies, but these societies and economies cannot exist for a fraction of a second without the Earth's ultra-complex life-giving system. If the primary system breaks down, the subsystem will also collapse. For this simple reason, it is absurd to think that human economy and technology can dominate nature. A subsystem can never control the superordinate system on which it depends.

It is also impossible for a subsystem to infinitely grow within a superordinate system. If it exceeds certain critical thresholds, functions of the superordinate system collapse, which in turn undermines support of the subsystem. This has been experienced by many societies, from the inhabitants of Easter Island, who cut down their forests to the last tree, to the Maya and the Vikings.[81] The collapse of these cultures, however, has always been local. With the tremendous expansive and destructive power of the worldwide Megamachine, we have now reached global thresholds that affect virtually all systems critical to human life: soils, forests, seas, climate, biodiversity and fresh water cycles.

In the history of life on Earth, there have been five mass extinctions, also known as the "big five." Industrial civilization has set in motion the sixth mega-death, the largest since the dinosaurs were exterminated 66 million years ago. The UN warns that the dramatic loss of species is at least as dangerous as climate change, and also threatens human survival.[82]

Almost a third of all arable land has been lost since the Industrial Revolution; most of it during the last 40 years. Industrial agriculture erodes soils 10 to 100 times faster than they can regenerate, and on average, 1 percent of the world's arable land is lost every year.[83] In addition, there is a rapid increase in the amount of surface area being sealed over and in the poisoning of soils by pesticides, factory farming and heavy metals. The dwindling fertility of depleted soils can only be counteracted by artificial fertilizer. Its production using the Haber-Bosch process, however, requires considerable amounts of fossil oil, which is slowly becoming scarce and therefore expensive. Equally critical to the existence of agriculture is the supply of phosphorus. Progressive erosion is washing it out of the soil, and economically extractable deposits are dwindling, for example, in Europe.

The outlook for water is not any better. Only about 2 percent of the Earth's water volume consists of fresh water, of which a considerable part is still bound up in the ice masses of the polar regions. Portions of the ice are already melting. Industrial agriculture swallows up about 90 percent of the usable sources, not only from rivers and lakes, but also from underground water reservoirs (aquifers). The Ogallala aquifer in North America, for example, in which large reserves of fresh water were formed over millions of years, is being tapped by millions of pumps from Texas to South Dakota and will likely run out in the next 20 to 30 years. It is still unclear as to where the American Southwest will then obtain its water,[84] and the same problem applies to the large aquifers in Mexico, North Africa and the Middle East. In China, more than half of the groundwater is contaminated with industrial and agricultural residues.[85] The northern part of the country is already suffering from a structural water shortage, which is exacerbated by the Gobi desert's eastward advance toward Beijing. The Chinese government is trying to counter this crisis with one of the largest infrastructure projects in human history, a pipeline and canal system that pumps water from the Yangtze River over thousands of miles up to the north. However, if the water level in the Yangtze falls below a critical level, the flow will dry up.

These crises have been considerably aggravated by climate change. The large Himalayan glaciers are already melting, and when they disappear in a few decades, the major rivers, Huanghe (Yellow River), Yangtze, Brahmaputra, Indus and Ganges, will carry very little water during summer months to southern China, Bangladesh, Pakistan and northern India. No one knows how the 1.5 billion or so affected people will manage.

Nor can anyone predict what happens when governments are faced with the choice of turning off water and electricity to either their industries or their own people. In any case, under these conditions, between blackout, humanitarian catastrophe and revolt, stable system management is out of the question.

As life-giving fresh water threatens to disappear from the mountains, sea levels are rising. A quarter of the world's population lives in low-lying coastal regions, while the ice masses of Greenland and Antarctica are melting much faster than researchers assumed just a few years ago. A rise in sea-level of only 20–40 inches by the end of the century (a very optimistic estimate) would mean that megacities such as New York, Hong Kong, Shanghai, Calcutta, Dhaka, Mumbai, Jakarta or Lagos would no longer be sustainable for the long term. Not only is the average sea-level rising, but devastating storm surges such as Hurricane Sandy (2012), Typhoon Haiyan (2013) or Hurricane Harvey (2017) are increasing disproportionately and destroying infrastructures.[86] In Bangladesh, the rising salt water is already contaminating fresh water sources, causing entire regions to become uninhabitable long before they are permanently flooded.

When combined, these various factors—species extinction, loss of fertile land, dwindling fresh water sources, declining oil reserves, as well as climate-induced droughts and floods— may result in the collapse of global food production by 2040. This is indicated not only by the updated scenarios of the Club of Rome but also in a study commissioned by the insurer Lloyd's.[87]

The ecological limits of the system that we are about to reach cannot be separated from social and political limits. When more of the natural fundamentals of life are destroyed, then social conflicts intensify, which in turn can easily transform into political upheavals, from revolutions to authoritarian power grabs and wars. Ecological crises can also trigger major population migrations, which then exacerbate social conflicts and destabilize entire states. Moreover, ecological limits cannot be separated from economic limits. For example, it is possible for a blackout in Chinese industry to trigger a crash of the already unstable world financial system.

Ultimately, it is pointless to map out such scenarios, because unpredictability is precisely the decisive feature of the great systemic crisis into which we are moving ever more deeply. No one can say which subsystems will fail first, and in which part of the system, or when it will happen, or what the knock-on effects might be. We only know that the probability of such failures will increase rapidly if the Great Machine continues to operate. With every successful attempt to overcome a systemic limit and expand further, the impact on the next limit will be all the more calamitous.

Despite this fundamental unpredictability, security strategists and international think tanks have been obsessively hypothesizing various doomsday scenarios for years with the hope of still finding ways to control the system. It has not yet sunk in that the era of control is over. The vision of global system management—"global governance"—is disintegrating before our eyes and giving way to panicky ad-hoc measures. Here, it is military action taken against "rebels" and "terrorists," and there it is a rescue package for "zombie banks"; or perhaps there is jubilation about a new oil field in the melting Arctic, or an abstruse geoengineering plan from the files of Dr. Strangelove. The Great Machine is hitting a wall in slow motion, and those at the wheel are only making things worse by haphazardly yanking on all the levers. Ultimately, the only devices that could possibly help now were never installed in the first place—a brake and a reverse gear.

Chapter 11

Possibilities

Exit from the Megamachine

The stones on the Moldau's bottom go shifting
In Prague three emperors molder away
The top won't stay top, for the bottom is lifting
The night has twelve hours and is followed by day
BERTOLT BRECHT

The origins of people ruling over other people date back at least 5000 years. Whether this fateful invention will ever be banished from planet Earth is unclear, but we do know that all specific forms of domination have a limited life span. No social system is forever. This also holds true for the modern capitalist world-system that has conquered the Earth during the last 500 years. The growing instability and the possible disintegration of this system present an opportunity for change that has not existed for centuries. Under the right circumstances, the farther a complex system strays from equilibrium, the greater the impact that even small movements can have, just like the famous butterfly that triggers a tropical storm.

The transition from a complex, hierarchical social system such as the Megamachine to another that is either less or more hierarchical usually passes through a phase of disintegration followed by further phases of reorganization. Such a process can last decades or even centuries.[1] Disintegration, or collapse, often translates into chaos, but not necessarily an apocalypse. The often mourned "downfall of the Western Roman Empire," for example, was certainly not the end of the world, and it actually brought considerable relief to most of the population by ending slavery and freeing peasants from crushing taxes.

Compared to 1500 years ago, however, there are three reasons why present conditions are much more dangerous: first, we live in a world with approximately 15,000 nuclear warheads and 600 million small arms that threaten our survival; second, the rapid disintegration of planetary ecology is undermining the livelihoods of much of the world's population; and third, a globalized industrial society is more vulnerable to deteriorating supply mechanisms that threaten our existence. In Rome's agrarian society, reorganization was much easier. Therefore, today's transition strategies must not only deal with economic reorganization, but also with the question of how to respond to sudden system failures, supply bottlenecks and the spread of violence.

Essentially, it is impossible to predict where the coming changes will lead. What is certain, however, is that in the chaos looming on the horizon all our actions will count. The world-system theorist Immanuel Wallerstein puts it this way: that which occurs will be the result of an infinite number of individual decisions, made by an almost infinite number of people during an infinity of moments.[2] Even if we are often hit by feelings of ineffectiveness and powerlessness when faced by an overwhelming destructive system, everything that each of us thinks and does (or does not think or do) is of significance for how things will turn out in the future. Ultimately, whether new authoritarian systems, mafia syndicates, warlord networks or structures of democratic self-organization will get the upper hand, will depend on how we are prepared for the systemic ruptures that lie ahead. This means we must already begin our exit while the Great Machine is still operating.

There are two aspects regarding a breakaway from the current system. On the one hand, it is necessary to put up determined resistance against the destructive forces of the Megamachine, which even in its decline is trying to appropriate the last avail-able resources; on the other hand, new social and economic structures must be built that allow us to gradually live and operate outside the logic of the Machine.

The good news is that this exit has been in progress for quite some time, both in resisting the old and in building the new. All across the planet, thousands of battles are being fought daily against mining projects, oil drilling, fracking, pipelines, mega-dams, highways, nuclear power plants, land grabbing, privatization, expulsion, militarization and the power of the banks. These defensive struggles are just as important as building alternatives, for without them, even the best grassroots projects will ultimately be overrun by the voracious Megamachine or by chaotic violence.

There is more to defensive struggles than just putting up a defense. They bring isolated people together and overcome the barriers of education, class and background. This was the case, for example, when nurses, pensioners and students staged the occupation of Wall Street in New York, or when Native Americans are demonstrating with other environmental activists from all over the country against an oil pipeline at the Standing Rock Reservation in North Dakota. Resistance reinforces feelings of solidarity and self-efficacy, transforming people from powerless, isolated spectators of a global crisis drama into combative fellow citizens who organize and dare to oppose power.

Often, alternative forms of organization emerge from defensive struggles, such as the Zapatista movement, which began in 1994 in resistance to the North American Free Trade Agreement (NAFTA). In the past 20 years, despite considerable repression, the movement has established remarkable self-governing structures. A map of all these larger and smaller pockets of resistance shows that the seemingly impregnable system has long had countless holes and cracks into which other ways of life and economies have settled.[3]

These pockets also include, for example, new cooperative movements, solidarity economy networks, movements for free software and hardware, worker-run factories, transition towns, the "degrowth" movement and countless initiatives of peasant self-organization from India via Mali to Brazil. People all over the world are looking for new ways of life and new ways to work together outside of the destructive logic of global competition and endless growth.

All these movements and initiatives have drawn important lessons from the failure of state-socialist projects in the twentieth century: they do not believe in one-size-fits-all, drawing-board solutions, but in an organically growing variety of pathways; they seek forms of democratic self-organization instead of hierarchical cadre structures; and they have given up on the idea of dominating nature.

Revolution Without a Master Plan

It is often claimed that there are no well-developed alternatives to the existing system, but these innumerable movements and initiatives prove that just the opposite is true. People are perfectly capable of taking control of their own lives as a community if they are not hindered by the structural and physical violence of states, economic actors or criminal networks — or sometimes by their own conditioning. As we will see in this chapter, there are plenty of alternatives, whether in the areas of goods production, energy supply, transport, technology, agriculture and food, money or health care.

What does not exist, however, is a master plan for a single global system that will replace the old one. Not only is there no such plan, but most people do not believe that it is even a good idea to have one. This skepticism should not be confused, however, with the disappearance of utopias. On the contrary, for many people, their vision of utopia would be a garden-like world with an endless variety of biotopes rather than a manicured palace park in the style of Versailles. Instead of a master design, it is rather a mosaic; a patchwork of varying approaches that are adapted to local and cultural conditions. The exit from the Great Machine also means a departure from universalist thinking, which—from the Christian mission to the project of world communism—has laid claim to "the one truth" and "the one reason" (see Chapter 5). Therefore, the lack of a master plan is not a shortcoming, but an example of learning from the disasters of past centuries.

Nonetheless, this pluralism can also turn out to be a fatal weakness if it does not connect the various struggles at strategically critical points and occupy political spaces where systemic breaks appear. The World Social Forum, founded in 2001 as a counter-model to the World Economic Forum in Davos, was associated for a long time with the hope of being able to offer alternative forms of political organization. In recent years, however, it has suffered a noticeable loss in significance. Yet, at the same time, we do see the emergence of new structures, such as in the Arab Spring, the Occupy movement, the global climate movement and Black Lives Matter. The forms taken by the resistance currently resemble a constantly changing network with shifting nodes.

Despite fluid configurations and a diversity of approaches, however, there are core principles for change that can be identified. I will concentrate on four in this chapter: the exit from the logic of capital accumulation, the shrinking of the metallurgical-fossil complex, the search for genuine democracy, and the departure from the domination of nature.

Heads are Round so our Thoughts Can Change Direction

The exit from the Great Machine begins in our minds and imagination. Since childhood, we have been conditioned to assert ourselves against others in a competitive system. We are graded, evaluated, sorted into categories, and we must constantly compete for a place in the world. Our idea of life has been narrowed down to earning more points than others in the game of prestige and income. In this game, to be upgraded means that someone else must be downgraded. Therefore, the Great Machine creates artificial shortages, not only of goods and money, but also of attention and affection. Celebrities attract the attention of millions, while we don't give a second thought to the neighbors next door, even though they may be much more interesting people. We sit in partitioned cells and turn our eyes upward. An exit from the machine in our heads begins with unlocking our gaze, directing our attention beyond these cells, tearing down the cardboard walls and turning off our telescreens, so we can actually see those standing right next to us and stop staring up to "the top."

Once we have accomplished that, we can begin to imagine a society based on cooperation instead of competition. It could be a system that creates a good life for all, instead of affluence for few and scarcity for most; one that does not have to fill the emotional void with an ever-increasing amount of goods; and one in which people can unfold their personalities and their relationships with one another instead of driving the engines of accumulation.

It is only at first glance that the Great Machine appears to be a machine. The closer you get, the easier it is to see that it is actually made up of people who are disguised as machine parts, and of various small and big decisions that are masked as practical constraints. To leave the Machine, one must cease, step by step, to function as a cog and realize that, behind the facade of constraints, there are human decisions that can be changed. The machine will only run as long as we operate it. As Gandhi rightly recognized, even the mighty British Empire could not maintain control over India if its subjugated population simply ceased to participate.

Breaking Away from Capital Accumulation

In discussions about dealing with global crises, politicians, entrepreneurs and many NGO representatives have talked a lot in recent decades about "corporate responsibility," "green economy," as well as "win-win" and sustainability strategies. The idea has been to bring together business interests, environmental protection and social justice. While talking, however, they also carefully overlooked the enormous elephant in the room. It is an obvious fact that the principle of endless capital accumulation—making money just to make more money—is the primary reason that our economic system is on a crash course with the planet. However, every effort has been made to suppress this reality as much as possible, even by those with good intentions. Clearly, to remove the elephant has seemed too monstrous and unrealistic a task to undertake. The results of real (Soviet-style) socialism were too discouraging, and the radical free-market ideology that had prevailed since the 1980s was too dominant to even discuss abandoning capital accumulation. However, because fiddling about obviously yields no progress, and more than just a few extra "guard rails" are needed to truly transform the economy, the nearly forgotten elephant is slowly moving back to the center of attention. More and more people are starting to realize that a serious social-ecological turnaround can only happen once we begin to abandon the logic of capital accumulation.

If one tries to imagine this exit in the form of a major revolutionary event, however, it seems to be an unattainable fantasy. Where does one get a hold on such a beast? Which Winter Palace, which Bastille should be stormed? If the transition, however, is seen as a decentralized process that extends over decades and takes place in parallel at various locations around the world, it becomes apparent that work has already started on a global scale.

No society has ever been completely impregnated by the logic of accumulation. There have always been areas, large and small, that are characterized by solidarity and orientation toward the common good, from the family and neighborhood level, to non-profit associations, to providers of public health and water supplies. Large parts of humanity, who have been left behind by the world economy, are only able to survive with the help of solidarity networks.[4] Taking leave from capital accumulation means defending, expanding, reinventing and cross-linking these areas. It is a matter of gradually withdrawing society's production and supply systems from the Megamachine, which will make small grassroots initiatives just as important as major political struggles.[5]

The Battle over Property Rights

A central sticking point is the question of ownership. When people fight to prevent the privatization of their water and power plants, their public transport, their hospitals and universities, and when they occupy buildings to stop real estate speculators from hijacking their cities, they also work to contain the voracious accumulation machine and deprive it of sustenance. In Paris, Berlin, Naples, Budapest, Buenos Aires and many other cities, for example, citizens have achieved a remunicipalization of water utilities.[6] In Bolivia and Uruguay, the ban on privatizing public goods has even been enshrined in their constitutions. Around the world, thousands of smaller and larger struggles against the various forms of "accumulation through expropriation" are taking place every day. In dozens of countries from Peru to Madagascar, there is resistance to the purchase of large estates by transnational corporations ("land grabbing").[7] Cities have also become the scene of increasingly intense conflicts about whether private investors or citizens should own and control public spaces and residential areas. Since 2013, hundreds of thousands have taken to the streets of Brazil against the privatization and expulsions that were enforced in the context of major sporting events such as the soccer World Cup and the Olympic Games. Rapidly rising rents in many metropolitan areas provide constant fuel for protest. Hundreds of thousands of apartments are owned by global real estate funds such as Brookfield or Cerberus (also the name of the hellhound in Greek mythology). In many large cities, people now have to spend half of their income on rent, which is akin to working as serfs to ensure a return on the real estate agencies' investments. In order to jump off the absurd treadmill of wage labor and accumulation, it is therefore of crucial importance to separate housing from the money machine and put it in the hands of the residents themselves. Wherever this is accomplished, in the long run, an enormous amount of time and energy will be freed so that people can devote themselves to tasks other than feeding the Cerberuses of this world. One way to achieve this is the establishment of housing cooperatives that permanently withdraw real estate from the market. In order to provide the necessary funding, solidarity-based financing models such as the German *Mietshäusersyndikat* (Apartment-House Syndicate) are already being developed in many places.[8] However, the establishment of housing cooperatives will not be enough as long as large parts of our cities are still owned by real estate funds and other private owners who set the prices. In Berlin, this situation has prompted an initiative for a public referendum to expropriate around 200,000 apartments from large real estate companies and transfer them to common ownership.

The frontline of disputes over ownership and property rights also runs right through the world of science and genetics. When people take up the fight against the patenting of seeds and "biopiracy," or against international agreements on "intellectual property rights" (e.g. ACTA), the issue at stake is whether or not private companies will ultimately be granted total disposition over life and human culture.

Shrinking the Metallurgical and Fossil Fuel Complex

Mining and fossil fuels, together with their dependent enterprises (chemicals, automobiles, aircraft, armaments, nuclear power, cement, etc.), are, by far, the most destructive industries in the world. Whatever a social-ecological transformation may look like, it can only succeed if these industries are radically shrunk and portions of them are completely shut down. Since metallurgy and fossil energy have been the material backbone of the Great Machine for centuries and still are, it is not surprising that there is enormous resistance to downsizing them. There are nonetheless signs of hope. After decades of struggle, the German anti-nuclear-power movement has been pivotal in pushing through a program to phase out nuclear power—an indication that even such powerful institutions are vulnerable.

However, governments, which usually act in defense of their national industries, cannot be expected to take initiatives to shrink them. Even progressive governments like Bolivia's continue to rely on extractivism, especially when it comes to oil, gas and mining. To exit this process requires the citizens themselves to take matters into their own hands, and in many parts of the world they are already doing just that. A decisive role is played by the blockade of local resource grabbing. Whether in Ecuador, Nigeria, the US, Canada or Germany, people everywhere are resisting the destruction of their land caused by the expansion of opencast mining, oil drilling or natural gas production. In 2014, the citizens of Peru succeeded in stopping the opening of the world's largest copper and gold mine—at least temporarily—despite the government having declared a state of emergency to push through the project with military repression.[9] With great success, activists in Germany have been occupying a forest for years to halt the expansion of Europe's largest opencast lignite mines.[10]

With regard to the financing of extractivism, a global "divestment" movement has been founded, which calls on institutional investors such as pension funds, universities, churches, insurance companies and municipalities to withdraw their investments from fossil energy. Thousands of professors and tens of thousands of students in the US have already joined this campaign, and city councils, such as Oxford's, are starting to withdraw from financing fossil industries. The success of the movement lies not only in the divestment itself, but also in the discussions it triggers at universities, in religious communities and in political bodies.[11]

No less important than resistance to extractivism is the development of alternatives in the field of energy supplies and raw materials. The remunicipalization of power stations and their transfer to cooperatives that rely on local renewable energies is a very successful model, especially in Germany, which is already being emulated by many other countries. The crucial point here is that the generation of energy is being decentralized and will no longer be concentrated in the hands of large energy companies.[12]

The Fight Against the Structural Violence of Debt

Debt has been a primary means of "accumulation by expropriation" for 5000 years. Debtors often lose land, property and freedom to their creditors as soon as they have difficulties in making payments (see Chapter 1). The structural violence of debt has always been one of the decisive reasons for the concentration of property and power in the hands of a few. Since the capitalist world economy has been in a permanent crisis since the mid-1970s, there have been two ways that the debt economy has become a key method for continuing accumulation. First, the growing indebtedness of states and private households ensures a steady flow of money to property owners.[13] Second, debt provides a means of appropriating mortgaged goods from states and individuals. Whether in Greece, Ireland, Spain, Slovenia, Poland, Mexico, Egypt or Thailand, public debt has continually been used as leverage to force the sale of public goods to private investors (see Chapter 10). The expulsion of more than 10 million Americans from their homes since the 2008 financial crisis is another example of this modern form of "original accumulation."[14] Debts are also a means of exerting pressure for social conformity and obedience. High university fees, for example, require students to take on massive debts, so that, after graduation, they will have to take on work even under the most adverse conditions in order to service their creditors.[15]

In principle, there are two ways out of the debt trap, the most direct of which is to simply refuse to pay all or part of the debt. Ecuador, for example, has followed this path, with the government setting up a commission to review foreign debt in 2007. It concluded that 70 percent of the debt was "illegitimate," and creditors were subsequently forced to settle for an average of 30 cents on the dollar.[16] In the area of private debt as well, there are numerous initiatives to curb creditors' power, such as resistance to evictions in Spain and Greece, and the "Strike Debt" movement in the US. All these movements are striving to ensure that the human right to livelihood takes absolute precedence over debt servicing.

The second solution is to use the enormous assets of the wealthy—which are simply the reverse side of the mountains of debt—to relieve those debts, for example, through taxes or property levies. Naturally, owners of great wealth are resisting this as hard as they can, but the pressure on governments to resort to this obvious solution is growing.[17] In the 1930s, under massive pressure from the labor movement, the Roosevelt government did exactly this by raising income tax for the rich to as high as 79 percent and inheritance taxes to 77 percent. In 1933, Roosevelt even went so far as to confiscate private gold assets to finance his social programs. The wealthy had to stand by and watch as state inspectors opened their bank vaults and walked off with their gold bars.[18]

Exit from Below: New Ways of Self-Organization

The driving engine of the Great Machine is the use of money to make more money, regardless of whether the associated activities make sense, or not. To break out of this logic requires us to reintroduce the question of what purpose our economic endeavors serve. Instead of asking how we can stimulate the economy or create jobs, we need to reverse the point of view and ask, why are we making these things at all? What do we really need? And how can we produce and distribute those products that we really need? What can we do without? How should we go about making decisions about what and how we produce?

The founders of the Cooperativa Integral in Catalonia asked themselves precisely these questions and set out to find practical answers. The cooperative is a network of more than 5000 participants whose aim is to produce as many of the most vital necessities as possible in a self-organized manner. In contrast to traditional cooperatives, they focus not only on working together to organize specific areas such as housing or shopping, but also on building up an entire corresponding economic and social system. The cooperative is not built as a community in which everyone lives and works together, but as a network that extends geographically across Catalonia and also maintains numerous global links, for example, in software development. In order to facilitate the exchange between individual members and the various elements of the network, the cooperative has created its own "social currency," the *eco*. In addition, it is building networks for health care, education, transport and housing. The aim of all these undertakings is not to retreat into isolated self-sufficiency, but to transform society with social innovations.

The appeal of this approach also lies in the fact that it allows smooth transitions between wage labor outside the cooperative and collaboration within it. In this way, the network can grow and learn step by step without the burden of immediately providing a complete livelihood for all members.[19]

In Brazil, such approaches are even more advanced. The rapidly growing network of the "Solidarity Economy" currently comprises 22,000 initiatives with more than 1.6 million participants and a turnover equivalent to 4 billion dollars. This also includes approximately one hundred community banks that issue their own currencies. This network is based on self-governing groups and companies, with neither bosses nor employees, that have joined forces to organize the production, exchange and consumption of goods on the basis of solidarity and ecological principles. The pioneers of this "liberation economy" dream of a future when such structures will transform the entire economic system.[20]

The Rediscovery of the Commons

For at least 20 years, another remarkable example of self-organization has been observed in the field of software development. In a loose, low-hierarchy network of hundreds of thousands of volunteers, the open source movement has been successful in developing patent-free software. A good example is the Linux operating system, which is now used by such public institutions as the French Parliament.

Free software is an example of the rediscovery of a principle much older than markets and patents: the principle of the commons. Instead of competing against each other in the market and facing off over scarce goods, people cooperate to produce and use goods together, whether in agriculture or software development. In the case of computer codes or other intellectual inventions, this is relatively simple, because they are so-called non-rival goods. Even when already in use, other people may also use them. A banana can only be eaten once, but a computer program can be used an infinite number of times. Patents create an artificial shortage in the area of non-rival goods, which promotes the accumulation of capital in the hands of a few, while putting up unnecessary barriers to their access.

The situation is somewhat different when it comes to rivalrous (individual) usage, as in the case of land, fishing grounds, water sources or forests, since overuse can lead to shortages. Even in these areas, however, common ownership has been a tried and tested form of management for thousands of years, from pasture farming, as it is still found in Switzerland today, to the use of large river systems by neighboring residents or administrative entities. Commons should also not be falsely seen as providing unregulated access to resources.[21] On the contrary, as Nobel laureate Elinor Ostrom has pointed out, functional commons contain a whole series of rules and limitations.[22] Unlike with private property, however, it is the collective users who set down these rules for themselves in order to guarantee the fairest and most sustainable use possible. Therefore, commons are more than just goods in common possession, they are a form of human self-organization, of "commoning." This also distinguishes them from public goods, whose regulation and administration are usually delegated to bureaucracies.

Durable Products Instead of Disposable Goods

One of the most damaging and absurd consequences of the logic of endless capital accumulation is the ever-increasing production of goods that turn into mountains of rubbish in ever-shorter cycles. For decades, manufacturers of consumer goods, such as computers, mobile phones and other resource-intensive devices, have been designing their products to be more quickly thrown away and replaced by new ones (see Chapter 10). In the logic of competition and endless capital accumulation, this is inevitable to prevent their business model from coming to an abrupt end. However, if one takes a step outside this logic to ask, what is it that we really need (instead of how can we pump up growth, profit and jobs), then completely different perspectives open up. Disposable goods can be replaced by products designed for maximum longevity. Incomprehensible blueprints that are protected by patents can be replaced by open, modular designs that anyone can easily understand and maintain. Inspired by the successes of the open source software movement, a worldwide network for the development and manufacture of patent-free hardware has emerged that develops and produces exactly such construction plans to be freely available, from solar cells to tractors. As in the case of software development, this work is being carried out by volunteers who organize themselves in open networks around the world ("peer-to-peer production"). To ensure that P2P networks actually work for the common good, and that their ideas are not simply exploited by commercial providers, they must be integrated into cooperative structures with regulations that are oriented toward the common good and that set down corresponding usage rights.[23]

The average Central European or US citizen requires about 100 "energy slaves," owns an extensive array of machinery and travels more than 9000 person-miles per year. In view of these dimensions, it would be illusory to believe that a switch from throw-away goods to durable and easily reparable products would permit this current lifestyle to continue unchanged in a post-fossil-fuel future. The automotive system is one of the most obvious examples. Even extremely durable, energy-saving cars powered by electricity from renewable sources still manage to swallow up considerable resources for production and operation. They also require exactly the same road system as fossil fuel guzzlers.[24] Therefore, shrinking the metallurgical-fossil-fuel complex is about much more than repairing, saving and exchanging energy sources. It is also about reorganizing our social life, both in the city and the countryside. Bicycles, intelligent public transport and shorter distances to work do not necessarily require sacrifices, and may well lead to an increase in quality of life and "time prosperity."[25] The same applies to leisure activities. Consider fighting your way through rush-hour traffic with a two-ton paramilitary vehicle in order to jog on an electrically powered belt in the gym and watch commercials for even bigger cars on a 4K screen. It would be a lot healthier and more stress-free to bike a few laps through the streets of a car-free city. A comprehensive model for the ecological-social reconstruction of urban spaces has been developed by the initiative "Neustart Schweiz" (Restart Switzerland). The focus is on neighborhoods of about 500 inhabitants, where life and work are close together and transport costs are minimized. Nearby links to regional agriculture and local repair workshops also ensure an enormous reduction in the ecological footprint.

The Revival of Communities

In 2006, Rob Hopkins initiated an attempt at self-organization from below in the small English town of Totnes. His "Transition Town" movement now boasts more than 400 member communities worldwide. The idea is to find ways to free communities and municipalities from dependence on fossil fuels and global supply chains in the face of peak oil, climate change and financial crises. From a transition perspective, the current crises are not only threats, but may also be seen as opportunities for economic, social and cultural change that breathe new life into local communities. In Transition Towns, people can share their otherwise untapped knowledge and creativity with each other, whether to convert their city's energy supply to renewable sources, to jointly manage gardens or to build local trade networks with regional currencies.

A central principle of Transition Towns is to build resilience. In ecological terms, this means the ability of living systems to maintain their basic functions even in the face of changing environmental conditions or shock events. Applied to communities, this means, for example, producing as much as possible regionally so that any failures of supra-regional supply chains can be absorbed. It also means building social relationships based on solidarity that will enable a community to handle crises without falling apart. A decisive factor for this is diversity. Monocultures (in the broadest sense) easily break down under external stress, as shown by the history of forestry (see Chapter 8) or the collapse of industrial cities such as Detroit. Resilience comes from a broad diversity of life and economic forms, whether for social systems or ecosystems. Because systemic breaks are to be expected, resilience is of crucial importance for a successful socio-ecological transformation.[26]

The Role of Markets

As the British economist and growth critic Tim Jackson put it, the currently dominant economic system creates "a perverse set of incentives" for investment. It rewards all those who succeed in ruthlessly exploiting people and nature while externalizing their costs. At the same time, it hampers ecologically and socially meaningful investments, due to lower or non-existent private profits.[27] In order to reverse this, a number of initiatives are starting to work on changing the legal framework for entrepreneurial activity. These include, for example, the Austrian project Economy for the Common Good, which has gained the support of numerous companies worldwide. The idea is to shift the structure of legal incentives for companies away from competition and striving for profit toward cooperation and efforts on behalf of the public welfare. Instead of a financial balance sheet, companies present a Common Good Balance Sheet based primarily on social and ecological criteria. Those who do well in this respect receive legal advantages such as lower taxes, favorable loans or priority in public procurement. In the model, the ownership of an enterprise changes according to its size. The larger it is, the more workers and other stakeholders take over control. In order to function, however, this model requires comprehensive legal regulation and a fundamental about-turn in tax, economic and trade policies.[28]

The various approaches to leaving behind the logic of profit and accumulation suggest quite different views of the role that the market and money should play. While some are focused on completely and permanently doing away with the logic of markets and money, others lean toward giving markets and currencies new functions to perform. Despite these differences, a common denominator is emerging: the elements most essential to life must be freed from market control. For housing, food, water supply, energy, health, education, culture, communication and transport, it is a matter of creating forms of production and distribution that are based on solidarity. This might occur within cooperatives, nationwide networks or via public institutions. In this context, there are also a number of approaches to further develop and restructure public social security systems. Proposals for a solidarity-based citizens' insurance system that includes all people and income types are already being widely discussed, as are various concepts for a basic income.[29]

Ending Life Support for Transnational Corporations

All approaches to eliminating capital accumulation will sooner or later have to confront the power of large corporations that comprise the Megamachine. The 500 largest corporations on the planet now control a good 40 percent of the gross world product. They dominate a considerable portion of political decision-making processes, knowledge production and the media, and the trend is upward. Despite their obvious power, however, these giants have a weakness that is often overlooked—most could not exist without state support. The much-vaunted "free market" never really applied to them; on the contrary, their power and wealth are largely based on collusion with the state.

Large corporations and modern states have been interwoven and developed in a co-evolutionary manner since their inception in the early modern era (see Chapter 6). Even today, they remain closely intertwined. Key sectors such as coal, oil, automobiles and industrial agriculture are protected and substantially bankrolled by virtually all governments, whether through direct subsidies, tax breaks or trade privileges. According to the International Energy Agency, the oil, gas and coal industries alone receive 300 billion US dollars in subsidies every year.[30] There are additional subsidies for road construction, military safeguarding of pipelines and other transport routes. The global financial system, in turn, would have ceased to exist without trillions in government funding. Not only do big banks benefit directly from bail-outs and interest-free loans provided by central banks, but also from the implicit guarantee of immortality ("too big to fail") that affords them enormous competitive advantages.[31]

Additionally, there is a special form of subsidy that excuses large companies from liability, either partially or completely, in the case of ecological and social damages they have caused. The chemical disaster in Bhopal (1984), the fire at BP's Deepwater Horizon oil platform in the Gulf of Mexico (2010) and the Fukushima meltdown (2011) are typical examples. Climate chaos is probably the most dramatic form of this subsidy. Because states refuse to protect their citizens by setting serious limits on the burning of fossil fuels, many of the world's largest companies are free to continue with their business models.[32]

Even so-called free trade agreements usually contain hidden subsidies. In hundreds of international agreements, governments have granted private investors the right to sue them before private arbitration tribunals if these latter believe that environmental or consumer protection laws would deprive them of future profits.[33] Ultimately, this is nothing more than a mechanism created by states to subsidize investors.

There are various ways of cutting the corporate umbilical cord to state subsidies. In the case of another global financial crisis, it would mean no more unconditional bank rescues. Although good arguments can be made for counteracting another complete system crash in order to avoid consequences like those in 1929, this does not mean that the zombie banking system must continue to be fed. Legal options already exist for dismantling major banks that are failing; for securing existentially important deposits such as pensions and for sending certain creditors into well-deserved bankruptcy.[34] Whatever remains of such banks could then be transferred to alternative legal entities that are committed to the common good instead of shareholder profit.[35] These financial institutions could then provide funds for converting the energy system to one with decentralized renewable sources. Although civil society missed the opportunity for this kind of restructuring during the 2008 crisis, the situation might well change with the next crash. The people's appetite for financing further bail-outs is practically zero, which will put governments under considerable pressure.

There are also sharp conflicts in other cases that involve direct and indirect subsidization. In England, for example, hundreds of thousands of people have protested in recent years against the de facto tax-exempt status of many large companies.[36] At the same time, thousands of people around the world struggle daily to hold companies liable for the damages they cause. In Ecuador, where Texaco (a subsidiary of Chevron) has polluted large parts of the rainforest and is responsible for a huge increase in cancer rates, a court has already ordered the company to pay out 19 billion US dollars. Since Chevron refused to pay the sum, and the company had few assets in Ecuador that were vulnerable to seizure, the plaintiffs took their case to an Argentine court. In 2012, the court ordered the freezing of Chevron assets in Argentina worth exactly $19 billion—a unique historical occurrence.[37]

From a systemic perspective, all these struggles, which at first glance seem unconnected, do converge at a common vanishing point. They all throw sand into the gears of the accumulation machine. More importantly, they are crucial to preparing us for the inevitable systemic ruptures to come. Although a soft, controlled transformation from the current predatory system to an economy serving the common good is certainly desirable, it is also unrealistic. When massive economic collapses, large-scale bankruptcies with substantial job losses and political chaos do occur, everything will depend on how capable people are of organizing themselves, what arguments and discussions they have had in previous years and what visions for the future they may have already developed.

As long as the system functions fairly smoothly, many of the resistance activities may seem like tilting at windmills. However, as soon as the system enters chaotic phases, which is precisely what seems to be happening at the moment, the learning experiences from the "troubles of the plains" (Bertolt Brecht) become decisive. A society that for decades consisted of passive television viewers will not know what to do with a sudden power vacuum and will acquiesce to the next demagogue that comes along. On the other hand, politically alert and well-organized citizens have a real chance to use systemic crises as a starting point for social reconstruction that leads us out of the destructive logic of accumulation.

The Search for True Democracy

Representative systems, such as the one conceived by the founding fathers of the US, are now seen by an increasing number of people as a blockade to far-reaching socio-ecological change. There are various reasons for this. For one, the global system crisis reveals the fundamental deficiencies of a model that focuses on short-term goals such as elections and was designed from the start to keep systemic issues out of the debate (see Chapter 9). Secondly, the neoliberal rollback of recent decades has undermined many hard-won democratic achievements.[38] In the US, for example, the political system has now been largely eroded by the legalized corruption of elected representatives.[39] In Europe, non-elected institutions such as the EU Commission and the European Central Bank, which are permeated by industry lobbyists, determine a considerable part of the political agenda. The austerity programs they have imposed with an iron hand are well on their way to destroying the project of an integrated Europe.[40]

Representative democracy's loss of credibility has two faces. On the one hand, in many places, anti-democratic currents that rely on authoritarian solutions are gaining momentum. The rise of new right-wing extremist movements and political parties all over the world is a typical example; the triumph of theocratic fundamentalists is another. Calls for an eco-dictatorship or technocratic world government are also growing louder.[41] On the other hand, a search for new forms of democracy has also begun around the world in an effort to overcome the filters of representation, money, debt and manipulated public opinion. "Occupy," the Spanish "15-M movement," the "African Spring" and many Gandhi-influenced movements in India are cases in point.[42] Representative democracy is no longer seen by such groups as the ultimate goal, but as an intermediate step on the road to genuine self-determination and self-organization.

Going beyond representative democracy, however, does not mean giving it up. However imperfect and incomplete they may be, the rights fought for within the framework of the representative system for more than 200 years are a critical bulwark against forces that are eager to turn back the historical clock. It is therefore a matter of defending parliamentarism against authoritarian forces and the "corporate coup d'état," while also building new grassroot structures to gradually overcome the limitations of representative democracy. This dual strategy is all the more important because democratization from below is still in its infancy and will take time. Grassroots democracy is already being successfully practiced in many local structures, from self-organized daycare facilities to cooperatives. However, how such principles can best be transferred to larger forms of organization is for the most part still an open question.

Although there is a whole series of theoretical proposals, in the end, the question will not be answered on the drawing board, but in practice.[43] It is worth taking a cue from history, which shows that the representative system was by no means the only one that has been tried. In the Paris Commune, in the early days of the Russian Revolution, in the German Revolution of 1918–19, in the Spanish Republic, in the Prague Spring of 1968 and in Chile before the 1973 coup, workers organized themselves into councils. None of these council democracies failed because they were unworkable. On the contrary, it was precisely because they did work that they were all wiped out by military force.

The council concept is based on people organizing themselves and making decisions together in local units, such as production plants, universities, apartment blocks or urban districts. Where decisions are needed at a higher level, for example, for an entire city, the councils send delegates. Unlike representatives, these delegates are bound by a specific mandate and can be recalled at any time. An advantage to this approach is that the artificial divide between the economic and political spheres is eliminated at the root. Whenever people do or use something together, they also decide together.[44]

These historical models still inspire many initiatives today. Since 2013, for example, the predominantly Kurdish-speaking inhabitants in the northern Syrian province of Rojava have created autonomous administrative structures based on village, community and regional councils amid the turmoil of the civil war. The decisive factor here was a move toward economic democracy. Business enterprises in the region were reorganized in the form of production cooperatives in which workers determine the nature and content of their own activities.[45] This remarkable effort toward self-organization, however, is in severe danger. The Turkish army has already invaded the city of Afrin and threatens to overrun other parts of the province. The Syrian Kurds' situation exemplifies the ambivalence that occurs when central state structures disintegrate. The loss of control by the Syrian government has opened up new possibilities for Kurdish self-government, but this breakdown has also opened the door for warlords and religious fanatics. Central states are often one of the greatest obstacles to genuine democratization because of their authoritarian grip on territories and populations. Nevertheless, they can be indispensable in preventing the outbreak of chaotic violence or foreign invasions. Therefore, on the path to expanding and deepening democracy, both issues must be addressed: decentralized structures must be built from the bottom up, and centralized state structures must be transformed to permit more democracy.

Demilitarizing Society

The development of the modern world-system over the past 500 years has been marked by unprecedented militarization, which has also been used to overpower egalitarian movements. Today, more than 1.7 trillion US dollars are spent every year on the military worldwide (which corresponds roughly to India's total economic output), an increase of 70 percent since 1998.[46] The police are also expanding their armaments. New crowd control technologies such as observation drones, sound cannons and microwave weapons are in development, some of which are already in use.[47] In many countries, "SWAT" (Special Weapons And Tactics) teams that are similar to military combat units have also emerged in the last decades.[48] Police violence against peaceful protests is increasing at an alarming rate worldwide, according to a study by the International Network for Civil Liberties.[49]

Every prospective social transformation must confront the reality of a world jam-packed with weapons, since even the best initiatives can be quickly overrun by tanks or suffocated by tear gas. This was experienced up close by demonstrators in Cairo, Bahrain, New York's Zuccotti Park, Syntagma Square in Athens and in Istanbul's Gezi Park. The brutal smashing of the Occupy movement in New York and other US cities in autumn 2011 was, as leaks from internal FBI documents show, coordinated centrally by the FBI and the Department of Homeland Security with representatives from Wall Street banks.[50] Government agencies, intelligence services and local police functioned as the de facto enforcement arms of private corporations. This case shows that as soon as movements cross a certain threshold and become systemically relevant, they can very quickly be confronted with overwhelming paramilitary violence, even in formally democratic states.

On the physical level, activists and social movements usually have little with which to oppose such force. Therefore, their most important defensive weapon is the public delegitimization of violence, presuming that the public is made aware of the violence in the first place. In the 1960s and early 1970s, the disturbing images of the Vietnam War and police violence against students played a decisive role in delegitimizing governments and limiting the spread of violence. Since then, the Great Rollback in the media (see Chapter 10) has led journalists to curb their inclination "to side with humanity rather than with authority and institutions."[51] In this situation, a decisive role is being played by alternative media that document the abuse of power, such as the US channel "Democracy Now!" and organizations such as Wikileaks. By publicizing violence, they force governments to make concessions to public opinion and thus give emancipatory movements more breathing room. This is all the more important as modern surveillance systems have now created "all the ingredients for a turnkey totalitarian state," as Wikileaks founder Julian Assange put it.[52]

The Role of the Peace Movement

In the long run, peace, or at least the absence of war, is probably the most important prerequisite for the success of approaches to transformation that are described in this chapter. The peace movement therefore has a key role to play. In this context, a decisive question will be whether or not the US will peacefully give up its role as a global hegemon, a position that can no longer be sustained in the twenty-first century. For as long as the modern world-system has existed, the decline of one world power and the rise of another have always been fought out through decades of war. In times of crisis, conflicts were also often exploited as welcome opportunities to justify the authoritarian governance of the Great Machine and to put internal conflicts on ice (see Chapter 9). However, it is possible to prevent new outbreaks of such wars, and the chances for this might even be somewhat better than in earlier phases of the system.

One reason is that as the disintegration of the Megamachine begins, no new superpower has risen that can assume the role of the US. Instead, we might be heading for something like a multipolar world.[53] The economic weights are increasingly shifting toward China, which will become the world's largest economic power in the foreseeable future. But unlike Western countries, China does not rely on military conquest and dominance, but above all on trade, as it has done in past centuries.[54] One of the objectives of the largest infrastructure project in history, the "New Silk Road," which will connect China with Europe and Western Asia, is to prevent military confrontations with the US in the South China Sea. In addition, there are an increasing number of voices in the US calling for a reduction in the enormous amounts spent on arms. Giving up its imperial role could bring significant advantages to the broader US population, since the financial wherewithal would be freed up for a socio-ecological reconstruction, which is sometimes referred to as a "Green New Deal." To this end, the peace movements in the US can play a decisive role. Above all, there is an urgent need to dismantle the nuclear arsenals that pose an acute threat to our survival. In 2017, 122 of the 193 member states of the UN voted for a Treaty on the Prohibition of Nuclear Weapons. However, the nuclear states themselves did not participate in the negotiations, and nearly all NATO members boycotted the UN measure at the request of the Pentagon.

GIVING UP CONTROL OVER NATURE

From the outset, the emergence and expansion of the Megamachine was closely linked to the idea of man's domination of nature (see Chapter 7). Just as a king commands his subjects and an almighty God rules over his creatures, the modern *homo faber* controls nature and shapes it according to his wishes. Encouraged by the miracle technologies of the metallurgical-fossil complex, the misguided idea that we can manipulate the living world just like metals and hydrocarbons and make it bend to our will has become entrenched during the past centuries. The dreadful errors caused by this thinking are legion, from the "Green Revolution," to genetic engineering, to nuclear power and the idea that the Earth's ultra-complex climate system can be controlled by geoengineering.[55]

Since the 1970s, the devastating results from large-scale technology and linear thinking have inspired important new technological concepts that rely on cooperation with nature instead of control and domination. These approaches have been focusing on a variety of decentralized, small and medium-sized solutions adapted to local conditions ("appropriate technology").[56]

Technology not only deals with the relationship between humans and nature, but it also shapes interpersonal relationships and social structures. The cultural critic Ivan Illich coined the term "convivial" technology, which is suitable for enabling self-determined and resource-saving human communities and for freeing us from the alienating, destructive structures of large-scale technology.[57] However, a discussion about which technology to apply for which purposes can only be meaningful when we abandon the paradigm that increased productivity and efficiency are the only valid criteria for its development and use. Care robots may increase productivity in the care sector, but from a social perspective, there is certainly no gain. To escape the tyranny of efficiency, in turn, we need cooperative economic structures instead of competition. Under the conditions of competition in "free" markets, technologies that one-sidedly lean toward maximizing short-term output will always tend to prevail. Cooperation between people and cooperation with nature are, therefore, two sides of the same coin.

The Art of Cooperating with Complex Living Systems

One example of this dual cooperation is the irrigation system used by rice farmers on the Indonesian island of Bali. For more than a thousand years, it has guaranteed extremely efficient, socially just and ecologically sustainable water distribution.[58] The special feature of this system is that it functions neither through central planning nor through market mechanisms, but through a form of decentralized self-organization in which the people's social sphere is linked to ecological rhythms. All rice farmers, whose irrigation depends on a common source, are united in a *subak*, which roughly translates as "water network." The subaks are organized on a grassroots democratic basis, with leaders elected for a set period. Hierarchies that are based on caste affiliation or property are suspended in the subaks. The rhythm of the festivals held in subak temples serves at the same time to regulate the schedule of flooding and draining of the fields. The irrigation pattern produced in this way leads to the stabilization of a very complex local ecosystem and at the same time guarantees an equitable distribution of water.

In the 1970s, a group of Swiss engineers were contracted by the Indonesian government to convince the Balinese farmers that their system was inefficient and irrational, because it wasted too much time on pointless rituals and discussions and left the fields fallow for too long. They proposed that farmers should in future plant rice as often and as quickly as possible, regardless of the temple calendar, while using pesticides, artificial fertilizers and high-yielding varieties to maximize their harvest. The result was a disaster. Large portions of the crop were eaten by pests, soil fertility declined and chaos reigned. The government was eventually forced to return to the subak system.

This example shows the crucial role cultural practices can play in the vital regulation of human relations with nature. What the Swiss engineers dismissed as "religious," as illogical mumbo-jumbo, ultimately proved to be an indispensable part of an intricate, self-regulating system. This is precisely what the Balinese concept of *tri hita karana* (three causes of well-being) expresses, which underlies the subak system and has since been recognized by UNESCO as part of the world's cultural heritage. It is a dynamic equilibrium that connects ecosystems with the material and spiritual needs of human beings.[59]

From this perspective, the issue of technology goes far beyond technical questions. It is a matter of re-cultivating our economic practices and our social institutions, which in recent centuries have become severed from their cultural contexts. Understanding the entirety of social life as culture (not confined to just an evening concert or theater visit) means rediscovering work as a cultural activity that not only produces things, but also creates relationships and meaning. It also means understanding education as something that involves the development of the whole personality, not just the preparation of humans to become smoothly functioning parts within the economic machinery. There is actually no area of our life that does not urgently need re-cultivation. The quality of the alternative worlds we might create will not only be measured by whether they are ecologically sustainable and socially just, but also by the festivals we celebrate and the songs we sing.

Afterword

The Shadow of the Hydra

Pandemics and the Limits of Expansion

While the English and French editions of this book were being worked on, the corona pandemic spread across the earth. Many governments reacted to it with drastic measures: a massive restriction of basic rights, the decreed isolation of citizens and a shutdown of large parts of the economy. Only a good ten years after the world financial crisis of 2008/2009, the corona crisis has once again shaken the global megamachine to its foundations, with economic impacts that in some countries are more serious than those of the Great Depression of 1929. The long-term political consequences are not even foreseeable. Although the causes of these crises are very different, they have in common that they demonstrate the vulnerability and increasing instability of the modern world-system.

Pandemics and Biosphere Crisis

One aspect that has been little noticed so far is the connection between pandemics and the rapidly progressing destruction of the biosphere. Already since the 1970s, new and sometimes fatal pathogens have appeared with increasing frequency, spreading rapidly all over the world, thanks to globalized goods and passenger transport. These include HIV, the Ebola and Zika viruses, the causative agents of avian and swine flu, and various types of corona viruses, including the SARS virus and SARS-CoV-2, which is responsible for Covid-19. Around 75 percent of these new diseases originate from animals, of which about two thirds come from wildlife and one third from factory farming.

Since humans became sedentary and especially with the emergence of the first urban civilizations 5000 years ago, animal breeding brought a number of new diseases to our species, including measles and tuberculosis (from cows), whooping cough (from pigs) and influenza (from ducks). Vaccinations and antibiotics were able to contain some of these diseases during the 20th century. However, with the spread of industrial agriculture and the caging of billions of farm animals in a confined space, a breeding ground has developed for diseases that are increasingly beyond control. The attempt to regain control through the excessive use of antibiotics only leads in the long term to the spread of multi-resistant pathogens which are no longer manageable. In such an environment, viruses—against which antibiotics are not effective anyway—are given the opportunity not only to mutate very quickly, but also to transfer to the human organism and adapt to it. The H5N1 avian flu virus, for example, has occasionally already been transmitted to humans, where it developed an average mortality rate of around 60 percent— many orders of magnitude worse than the corona virus that caused the panic of 2020. Many epidemiologists assume that it is only a matter of time before such germs become much more easily transmissible through mutations than ever before.

Even more frequently than by farm animals, modern epidemics are caused by wild animals. The main reason for this is that the habitats of these animals are being destroyed more and more, for example by deforestation. Ebola, for instance, originates with bats, and in the 2017 epidemic, it occurred mainly in areas of Africa where deforestation was particularly rapid. As a result, homeless animals are moving closer and closer to human settlements, and their excrement is entering human food chains. The situation was similar at the end of the 19th century, when the Belgian colonial rulers cleared forests in the Congo, established rubber plantations and had railway networks built to transport copper from the mines to the ports. At that time, macaques driven from their habitat invaded human settlements, where they spread a certain Lenti virus that slowly adapted to the human body. Today we know it as HIV.

From this perspective, pandemics are a consequence of the colonial domination project of modern times. The attempt to subject nature to human control, and the entire planet to the logic of endless accumulation of capital, produces unforeseen reactions that can strike back at the system and ultimately even bring it down. Pandemics are an example of the short-sightedness of linear thinking (see Chapter 1), which is based on the misconception that the living world can be controlled by linear cause-and-effect chains, that is by the exercise of power through the pattern of command and obedience. But natural systems cannot be controlled and regulated like technical machines. They react like the Hydra in the Heracles saga: for every head cut off, many more grow back. Everything that lives is based on non-linear circular processes, in which every effect is at the same time the cause of countless other processes, most of which are incalculable. The pioneers of the timber industry experienced this in the 18th century, when, unaware of the complex cycles of forest ecology, they sought to maximize timber yields temporarily through monocultures, but some time later were confronted with the forest system's collapse (see Chapter 7). Similarly, industrial civilization as a whole is increasingly setting ecological chain reactions in motion in the 21st century. Sooner or later, these will cause yields to collapse, at first temporarily as in the Corona crisis, but eventually, as the rhythm of the crises becomes more intense, permanently. This is the typical fate of failing civilizations.

The term "ecological limits" is misleading in this context, because it suggests that, like a growing plant in a room, you would at some point bump into a ceiling that limits growth. But the "limits to growth" we are dealing with are of a completely different nature. They are more like a deeply sleeping dragon that you are confronting with noise. Up to a certain point, nothing will happen except maybe a sleepy growl or twitch. But once a certain tipping point is passed and the dragon awakes, there is no going back to the previous state.

Many of these tipping points are currently being reached — noticed by the general public at best only marginally — and are setting in motion long-term distortions that are many orders of magnitude more serious than the corona pandemic. The break-up of the West Antarctic ice sheet, for example, which alone will cause a long-term sea-level rise of about seven meters, may already be irreversible. The Amazon rainforest is on the verge of collapse due to deforestation, fires and global warming, and can rapidly transform itself from the world's most important CO_2 reservoir into a gigantic source of emissions. In the northern polar regions, the permafrost soils are melting and releasing more and more of the extremely powerful greenhouse gas methane. At a certain point, this process will become irreversible and can lead to "runaway climate change" that could make the planet largely uninhabitable.

The Structural Irrationality of the System

The corona crisis has revealed a structural schizophrenia in the system: While governments resorted to extreme means to contain Covid-19 — even a temporary shutdown of the economy — virtually nothing has happened in relation to the climate crisis for four decades. There are no binding reduction targets that are even remotely compatible with the two-degree target, nor is there a serious plan for the rapid restructuring of infrastructure and the economy. This is despite the overwhelming scientific consensus that accelerating climate chaos is many orders of magnitude more dangerous than the corona virus. Our political systems respond to short-term crises with panic and ad hoc measures, while long-term disruptions are de facto ignored — apart from occasional soapbox speeches. The highly praised "knowledge society" proves in this situation to be a chimera: for it is precisely here, where prognostic knowledge is the most relevant for the survival of humankind, namely in the climate issue, that it remains politically inconsequential. But how does this schizophrenic, irrational behavior come about?

The first answer to this question is relatively obvious: biosphere collapse is a long-term problem, while our political systems are short-term in nature. When a third of Bangladesh is flooded in a few decades, when large parts of the Middle East and Africa are no longer habitable due to overheating, and when European forests dry up completely, then almost all of the politicians who are setting (or not setting) the agenda today will have long since left office and most of them will already be dead.

The second answer lies in the structural racism of the system. The victims of climate chaos are above all the poorest people on earth, especially in the Global South. The corona virus, on the other hand, has not stopped at the barriers of class and nationality. Although poorer people have been hit much harder, the upper classes in the industrialized countries have also been at risk. While around the clock thousands of cameras sent pictures from corona intensive care units, giving us a doomsday feeling, hardly anyone cared about the many millions of inhabitants of the Mekong Delta, whose harvests are already being destroyed by the rising salt water.

However, the reasons for these very different reactions to the corona pandemic and the climate crisis reach even more deeply into the economic, political and ideological structures that form the foundation of the megamachine. The overarching principle of this system is the endless accumulation of capital. The most powerful economic institutions on earth, the large corporations that control around half of the world's economic output, all function according to this principle. They can exist only by constantly expanding and making more money from money, because that is their only purpose. Although the shutdown in the

Corona crisis also hit the balance sheets of these corporations, it very quickly became clear that the states would rescue them with aid packages worth billions, as governments had done in almost all previous crises. This is neither new nor surprising, for the modern world-system has never been based on free markets, but on a close intertwining of state and capital (see Chapter 6). Some corporations, such as Amazon, have even profited massively from the Corona crisis, because their competitors were swept off the market. Small and medium-sized companies, which employ by far the largest proportion of the world's workers, are disproportionately hard hit by the measures and are usually not rescued in the event of insolvency. The result is what economists euphemistically call a "market shakeout": The monopolistic or oligopolistic structures are further consolidated. The Corona crisis has also been successfully used by technology companies like Google and Microsoft to push for further digitalization of all areas of life, thereby considerably increasing surveillance possibilities as well as profits in this sector.

Against this background, it is clear why the economic lobbies' resistance to the corona shutdown was limited, despite occasional objections, and why states were able to take such massive action. The overall economic contraction was only temporary, the losses were more than royally compensated, and the basic structures of the megamachine were not only maintained, but in some cases even strengthened.

The situation is quite different, however, with the crisis in global life-supporting ecosystems. For if we take it seriously, it forces us to question the very foundations of our economic system: endless expansion and money multiplication. The business model, indeed the raison d'être of the most powerful economic players on earth, would inevitably be called into question if serious ecological restructuring were to begin. This also applies to the deeper causes of pandemics: in order to prevent their emergence and spread in the future, the economic expansion and the destruction of natural areas it causes would have to be halted. But that would mean questioning the foundations of the capitalist order. It is not surprising, therefore, that in recent decades all the stops have been pulled out to prevent these issues from being put on the agenda. This is quite consistent with the short-term self-preservation logic of the system. In the long run, however, this will only accelerate the path to global collapse.

The Worsening of Global Inequality

The Corona crisis has further exacerbated extreme social inequality both within most countries and between rich and poor nations. While corporations were provided with generous rescue packages, and the upper classes with their financial cushions were not existentially affected by the shutdown, millions of poor people, whether in India, southern Europe or the US, were struggling to survive. In addition, in many countries, broken and privatized health care systems were barely able to provide basic care for the population. Yet Covid-19 is not even a particularly dangerous virus compared to H5N1, for example.

For refugees, the closure of the borders to passenger traffic meant a further deterioration of their already miserable situation. On the Greek island of Lesbos, for example, 20,000 people had to languish in the misery of the Moria camp, which is designed for only 3,000 people. The other EU states were not even prepared to accept a few thousand of them. The situation of the refugees clearly shows how governments are gradually establishing a global apartheid system in order to prevent the victims of climate chaos, war and impoverishment from reaching those parts of the world that are still humanely inhabitable. Not only the USA and the EU seal themselves off from the South with massive military force. India has already built a four-meter high fence around Bangladesh—supposedly to curb the drug trade. But in the long term, the aim is to prevent people who will lose their land to rising sea levels from entering the country.

The global apartheid system, which bars the victims of the system from entering rich societies and locks them up in camps, generates despair and trauma, and finally anger and hatred. More and more people are left with no other possibility to survive than to join mafias and other armed organizations. The resulting violence destabilizes entire regions of the world and leads the system further and further into chaos.

The Corona Crisis as a Model of Authoritarian Control?

The more chaotic the system becomes due to social, economic and ecological upheavals, the more pressing the question becomes as to how to control the big machine in such turbulent times. The dilemma that the economic and political elites were already facing at the beginning of the 20th century (see Chapter 9) is reappearing in the 21st century in a more acute form. The option of authoritarian control is as obvious today as it was then. Indeed, the corona crisis and the social shutdown could be a foretaste of how governments will try to control an increasingly fragile system in the future: through a crisis mode that suspends democracy, initially temporarily, and eventually permanently.

In order to take back hard-won democratic rights from citizens, strong legitimacy is needed, and the best justification is always a powerful external enemy that must be fought with all means. Since 2001, the "war on terror" has served this purpose. Although every year in the EU about 1000 times more people die from car accidents or multi-resistant hospital pathogens than from attacks, some politicians and journalists have managed to frame terrorism—especially when it is attributed to "Islamists"—as the greatest threat to civilization. We were regularly admonished that we must defend "our Western values" by all means, including war and the restriction of our civil rights. This has made it possible to enforce comprehensive surveillance laws, to increase military budgets and militarization of the police—and last but not least, to further reduce the protection of refugees. The fear of terror has also been extremely useful in diverting attention from those far greater threats that do not come from imaginary barbarians from the Orient, but from the heart of Western civilization itself: the biosphere crisis and the growing danger of nuclear war.

In this respect, the Corona crisis and the biopolitical state of emergency have replaced the war on terror, which had already lost a great deal of its power of persuasion, as a reason for legitimizing authoritarian measures for a certain period of time. The rhetoric in both cases is astonishingly similar: Heads of government such as Emmanuel Macron (France), Pedro Sánchez (Spain), Giuseppe Conte (Italy) and Donald Trump have declared a "war against the virus". "The enemy", said President Macron, "is there, invisible, intangible, and it is advancing. This requires our total mobilization. We are at war." The pattern is familiar: The nation must pull together in the face of a treacherous and ruthless enemy, putting aside internal conflicts, civil rights and all other issues in general.

It is not a matter of questioning whether states should take protective measures in the face of a pandemic like Corona. However, it is obvious that, beyond sensible strategies to prevent infection, the crisis has been used by many governments to reinforce the already discernible tendency towards authoritarian structures. The measures in 2020 have made it clear to all citizens that their democratic rights can be very quickly withdrawn by the state. For many politically sensitive contemporaries, it was as if a window had suddenly been opened through which the icy wind of a rising dictatorship passed for a moment. Even if this window is successfully closed again: We now know what it could feel like when our rights are suspended overnight (an experience that people in many countries of the global South have already had more than enough). The enemy to be fought, the catastrophe which makes any means legitimate, will probably be different. But the mode of shutdown has already been practiced, including house arrest, bans on assembly and demonstration, total surveillance, control of social contacts and denunciation of dissenters.

The End of Truth and the Instability of Ideological Power

While it is evident that representative democracies in many parts of the world are becoming increasingly unstable, there is at the same time no reason to assume that the authoritarian structures that partly replace them would be any more stable in the long run. The constantly changing legitimations for the state of emergency also give them a certain volatility. Declaring war, sometimes against terror, sometimes against a virus, then again against migrants, wears off over time. Changing the enemy too frequently is irritating and exhausting—especially since for most people, fighting all those enemies in no way brings about any improvement in their own living conditions. On the contrary: the social downward spiral continues on. Permanent political stability can hardly be achieved in this way.

Added to this is the growing fragility of ideological power. Many authoritarian governments that have come to power since 2010 have propped up their rule on the targeted dissemination of fake news, both through social media and through major television stations and newspapers that are in line with their political ideology. Now, lying is nothing unusual for governments, even in relatively democratic countries. It is part of everyday political life, and it is always the task of a vigilant public and press to expose these lies. Dictatorships that violently suppress a critical public have always bolstered their power with propaganda. What is new about the current situation, however, is that the very concept of truth is being shaken. And this for several reasons. One is the established media's massive loss of credibility, and the other is the systematic attack on the sciences, especially climate research, by some governments and the lobby organizations behind them.

The relationship between power and science has always been ambivalent in the history of the modern world-system. On the one hand, capital owners and rulers needed science to develop new technologies for their economic and military expansion; for this reason, they massively funded a certain type of research. The birth of modern science in the 17th century cannot be understood without this connection (see Chapter 7). On the other hand, however, the sciences have also revealed some highly inconvenient truths, such as the fact that burning fossil fuels ruins the climate, that deforestation causes pandemics, or that the use of pesticides causes cancer. The strategy adopted so far to deal with these troublesome findings has been to ignore them for as long as possible. Where this was no longer possible, scientists were invited as advisors or, as in the case of climate conferences, elaborate meetings were held with them every year to give the impression that something was being done—only to continue business-as-usual without any change thereafter. This has been a way of formally preserving recognition of the sciences, while de facto, they were at best selectively acknowledged and often even completely ignored.

The preservation of this facade was and is crucial for the stability of the modern world-system for a specific reason: because the ideology which holds up the megamachine is based on the assertion that it is the most rational and in every respect superior system in human history. But if it becomes apparent that this supposedly rational civilization is completely blind to the most important information essential for survival, then the governors of this system face a serious dilemma: either they have to attack the sciences head-on and deny their findings, thus exposing rationality, one of the foundations of this civilization, as a myth. Or they react appropriately to the research and immediately begin a deep socio-ecological restructuring of society.

But since the second option seems too terrible, even unthinkable in the logic of the system, the only last resort is to sacrifice the claim of rationality. And this is exactly what the political leaders of the new Right, such as Jair Bolsonaro or Donald Trump, instinctively do. The success of their attack on scientific authorities is fed by the widespread feeling that the majority of people have long been systematically lied to by the "establishment". This impression cannot be dismissed: didn't neo-liberal economists spread false prognoses and promises with their pseudo-science for decades, thus exposing society to downright plunder? Have not many of the politicians and media who complain about fake news today themselves justified wars of aggression (for example against Iraq) with fake news? Hasn't mankind been steered into one economic and ecological crisis after the other by a self-adulating establishment that touts itself as having no alternative?

The deep insecurity that has arisen from these experiences in large parts of the population can easily be diverted into anger towards scapegoats. It is a politically extremely clever move by the new right to choose science for this purpose, because it kills two birds with one stone: on the one hand it can distract from systemic issues, and on the other hand it can remove obstacles to further expansion of the economic machinery. This is why scapegoating science is so attractive to powerful economic groups.

But this strategy also means that there is no longer any foundation for truth. With the rationality viewed as a facade, any lasting trust in a firmly established order collapses. We know from history that a certain ideological stability, with a frame of reference that is generally accepted and not called into question, is essential for social systems to endure. But where is this stability to come from when more and more people feel that order in the world is eroding and that there is no longer any criterion for truth—except the loudest megaphone?

Chances for Social Restructuring

In the disintegration of the current order, unexpected junctions are opening up again and again, where societies can take different paths. In the corona crisis, for example, there was certainly a window of opportunity not to channel the billions in rescue funding back into destructive sectors such as Wall Street and the aircraft and car industries, but instead into sustainable areas such as public transport and decent health care for all. But such conversion projects need very strong social movements that intervene in a coordinated and rapid manner in the political decision-making processes. Progressive civil society in most countries is too divided and weakened by decades of neoliberalism to be able to fulfill this function.

But this does not have to remain the situation in the long term. Crises can set long-term learning processes in motion. And there are indeed some important lessons to be learned from the corona crisis.

First, it has been shown that if they want to, states are quite capable of acting and can very quickly make far-reaching social decisions, including massive interventions in the economy and even in property structures. For decades, calls for effective climate protection measures have been dismissed with the argument that "free market forces" cannot or should not be interfered with. Ban short distance flights? Impossible! Ban SUVs in city centers? Unthinkable! Phasing out fossil fuels by 2030? Endangers jobs! Cut back on meat consumption? Eco-dictatorship! Convert car companies to build public transport? Communism! A trillion-dollar public investment program for social-ecological reconstruction? Too expensive!

But with the virus, suddenly almost anything was possible. Air traffic, for example, was simply shut down by decree. Money, which was supposedly never there for social-ecological restructuring, suddenly flowed in almost unlimited amounts. A sharp increase in national debt, which was inevitable as a result, was suddenly no longer a problem, whereas previously the dogma of austerity seemed untouchable. The myth of the weak, incapable state has finally collapsed, and one of the most urgent tasks of the global change movements is to translate this insight into political action and develop a comprehensive transformation program (see Chapter 11). In the long term, the historical task is to free the state from its interdependence with big business and to make it an institution obligated to serve the common good.

The second lesson is about how we deal with shrinking economies. Pandemics, financial crises and, above all, the collapse of life-sustaining ecosystems will inevitably force the economies of the rich countries of the North to contract in the long term. The corona crisis is an important learning experience for this: how must institutions be restructured, how must wealth, income and work be redistributed in order to make a dignified life possible for everyone? What is necessary to develop resilience and to detach the supply of vital goods and services from the global chains of capital valorization? How can resistance to state repression be organized in times of crisis? The need to ask these questions and test them in practice has become unmistakably clear to more and more people, due to the rapid succession of economic collapses since 2008 (financial crisis, "Euro crisis", corona crisis) and the escalating ecological catastrophes. The cumulation of crises that the megamachine is globally unfolding can no longer be watched on TV from a comfortable armchair, as has been the case in most Western countries up to now. It is breaking through into our reality.

Acknowledgments

I give special thanks to Andrea Vetter, Manfred Froh-Hanin and Matthias Schmelzer for their valuable suggestions and literature references, their critical readings of the text and for our many conversations. Manfred Froh-Hanin was also tremendously helpful as a copy editor of both the German and the English versions of this book. I would also like to thank the translator, Bill C. Ray, as well as Penelope Pinson, who translated the afterword, for their important contributions.

Sincere thanks must also be given to those with whom I had the pleasure to conduct extensive interviews for the newscast Kontext TV, and whose works have provided important inspiration for this book, including: Immanuel Wallerstein, Silvia Federici, Noam Chomsky, Maude Barlow, Pat Mooney, Vandana Shiva, Nnimmo Bassey, Saskia Sassen, Ugo Bardi and Johan Galtung. Additionally, the works of Giovanni Arrighi, Gregory Bateson, Mike Davis, David Graeber, Michel Foucault, Naomi Klein, Carolyn Merchant, Lewis Mumford, Ilya Prigogine, Wolfgang Sachs and James C. Scott have decisively enriched the content of this book.

I would especially like to thank GEA/Waldviertler and Heinrich Staudinger, as well as Ronald Thoden, for their generous financial support of the English translation. I am also grateful for the contributions of Michael Sadtler and Edith Sadtler. For the first steps in the translation process, I am greatly obliged to Cecile Rossant and Christian Niemitz-Rossant.

Endnotes

Introduction

1. Oxfam: *Reward Work, Not Wealth*, Oxfam Briefing Paper, January 2018, www.oxfam.org/en/research/reward-work-not-wealth; Crédit Suisse: *World Wealth Report 2018*, www.credit-suisse.com/corporate/en/research/research-institute/global-wealth-report.html.

2. TNIS-Emnid poll by the Bertelsmann Foundation, Gütersloh 2010.

3. According to a 2017 Harvard poll, 51 percent of 18–29 year-old US citizens are against a capitalist economy, which is a 10 percent increase over the previous year. (Bloomberg, November 6, 2017).

4. See the study by the Rodale Institute: *Regenerative Organic Agriculture and Climate Change*, Kutztown (PA) 2014, http://rodaleinstitute.org/reversing-climate-change-achievable-by-farming-organically;   see also Vandana Shiva in a discussion with *Democracy Now*, July 8, 2010.

5. The British Center for Alternative Technology, for example, has calculated that it is possible with only existing technologies, and no further innovation, to make an industrial country such as Great Britain free of CO_2 by 2030. Alice Hooker-Stroud (ed.): *Zero Carbon Britain: Rethinking the Future*, Machynlleth (Wales) 2013.

6. About inherent system inequality, see Thomas Piketty: *Capital in the Twenty-First Century*, Cambridge (MA) 2014. About the history of Western universalism, see Immanuel Wallerstein: *European Universalism: The Rhetoric of Power*, New York 2006.

7. Lewis Mumford also uses the term "Megamachine" for hierarchically structured societies such as the ancient Egyptian or Roman Empire (Lewis Mumford: *The Myth of the Machine*, 2 volumes, New York 1967/1970). In this book, however, I use the term exclusively in reference to the modern world-system.

8. André Gorz: *Ecologica*, Calcutta 2010, Chapter 5.

Chapter 1

1. About the economy of hunter-gatherers and the transition to agriculture, see Marshall Sahlins: *Stone Age Economics*, New York 1972.

2. Michael Mann: *The Sources of Social Power, Volume 1: A History of Power from the Beginning to AD 1769*, Cambridge 1986, p. 41.

3. See the exhibition catalog: Badisches Landesmuseum Karlsruhe (ed.): *Vor 12.000 Jahren in Anatolien. Die ältesten Monumente der Menschheit*, Darmstadt 2007.

4. James C. Scott: *Against the Grain. A Deep History of the Earliest States*, New Haven 2017, p. 57.

5. A transition to the Bronze Age also occurred in the Harappa culture along the Indus River. It is still controversial among researchers today whether or not and to what degree there was social stratification and forms of authoritarian governance. In any case, compared to Mesopotamia, metallurgy played a much smaller role. See Brett Hoffmann, Heather Miller: "Production and Consumption of Copper-base Metals in the Indus Civilization," in: *Journal of World Prehistory*, vol. 22, 2009, pp. 237–264.

6. See David Wengrow: *What Makes Civilization? The Ancient Near East and the Future of the West*, New York 2010, pp. 81–85.

7. James C. Scott: *Against the Grain. A Deep History of the Earliest States*, New Haven 2017, pp. 128–137.

8. *The Epic of Gilgamesh*, translated by Andrew George, London 1999, standard version, tablet 1, p. 3f.

9. See Michael Mann: *The Sources of Social Power, Volume 1*, Cambridge 1986, pp. 63f.

10. "Macht soll heißen jede Chance, innerhalb einer sozialen Beziehung den eigenen Willen auch gegen Widerstand durchzusetzen. [...] Herrschaft soll heißen die Chance, für einen Befehl bestimmten Inhalts bei angebbaren Personen Gehorsam zu finden." ("Power means a situation where one actor within a social relationship will be in a position to carry out his own will despite resistance. [...] Rule [or domination, or authority] means a situation where a command with a given content will be obeyed by a given group of persons.") Max Weber: *Wirtschaft und Gesellschaft: Grundriss der verstehenden Soziologie*, Leipzig 2005 [1922], p. 32.

11. Thomas Hobbes: *Leviathan*, London 1651, p. 62.

12. Michael Mann: *The Sources of Social Power, Volume 1,* Cambridge 1986, p. 48. That an increase in violence results when states are formed is denied by evolutionary psychologist Steven Pinker in his popular book, *The Better Angels of Our Nature: Why Violence Has Declined* (New York 2011). However, leading anthropologists, statisticians and historians have shown that Pinker's argument is based on "cherry-picked cases with high casualties, clearly unrepresentative of history in general." See Richard Brian Ferguson: "Pinker's List: Exaggerating Prehistoric War Mortality," in: D. P. Fry (ed.): *War, Peace, and Human Nature: The Convergence of Evolutionary and Cultural Views,* Oxford 2013, pp. 112–131. The statisticians Nassem Talib and Pasquale Cirillo proved that Pinker's theory of reduced violence during the civilizing process is untenable and built on erroneous methodology. See Nassim Taleb, Pasquale Cirillo: "The Decline of Violent Conflicts: What Do the Data Really Say?" in: *Nobel Foundation Symposium 161: The Causes of Peace,* Stockholm 2016, pp. 1-26. The publisher of a set of historiographical volumes about Pinker's theories has arrived at the following conclusion: "The overall verdict is that Pinker's thesis [...] is seriously, if not fatally, flawed. The problems that come up time and again are: the failure to genuinely engage with historical methodologies; the unquestioning use of dubious sources; the tendency to exaggerate the violence of the past in order to contrast it with the supposed peacefulness of the modern era; [...] and its extraordinarily Western-centric, not to say Whiggish, view of the world." Marc Micale, Philip Dwyer: "Introduction," in: *Historical Reflections,* Volume 44, Issue 1, New York 2018, pp. 1–5.

13. David Graeber: *Debt: The First 5,000 Years,* New York 2011, p. 201; Richard E. Mitchell: "Ager Publicus. Public Property and Private Wealth during the Roman Republic," in: Michael Hudson (ed.): *Privatization in the Ancient Near East and Classical World,* Cambridge (MA) 1996, pp. 253–276.

14. James C. Scott: *Against the Grain. A Deep History of the Earliest States,* New Haven 2017, p. 120f.

15. See Johan Galtung: "Violence, peace and peace research," in: *Journal of Peace Research*, vol. 6, no. 3 (1969), p. 167–191.

16. See Leften Stavros Stavianos: *A Global History: From Prehistory to the Present*, Upper Saddle River (NJ) 1994, pp. 9–15.

17. Our modern concept of property is composed of a series of rights of disposal, which historically have not always been linked to each other: the use of a thing (Lat.: *usus*); the returns that a thing makes possible (*usus fructus*); how a thing is altered, including its damage or destruction (*abusus*); the exclusion of its use by others; the transfer of ownership of the thing; and its use as collateral. See also Chapter 3.

18. Dietz-Otto Edzard: "Private Land Ownership and its Relation to 'God' and the 'State' in Sumer and Akkad," in: Michael Hudson (ed.): *Privatization in the Ancient Near East and Classical World*, Cambridge (MA) 1996, p. 111.

19. The Center for the Study of Institutional Diversity, co-founded by Elinor Ostrom, has produced a list of case studies documenting different ways of dealing with commons: https://asu.pure.elsevier.com/en/organisations/institutional-diversity-center-for-the-study-of-csid.

20. Little is known about how exactly this occurred. It is possible that the families of the first rulers (lugal) were at the heart of privatization. Dietz-Otto Edzard: "Private Land Ownership and its Relation to 'God' and the 'State' in Sumer and Akkad," in: Michael Hudson (ed.): *Privatization in the Ancient Near East and Classical World*, Cambridge (MA) 1996, p. 110.

21. Gaius Plinius Secundus: *Natural History*, book 18, section VII, available online at: web.archive.org/web/20161229101439/http://www.masseiana.org/pliny.htm. The African province was composed of today's Tunisia and portions of Libya.

22. David Graeber: *Debt: The First 5,000 Years*, New York 2011, p. 79.

23. R. K. Englund: "*Texts From the Late Uruk Period,*" in: P. Attinger and M. Wafler (ed.): *Mesopotamien: Späturuk-Zeit und Frühdynastische Zeit*, Freiburg (Switzerland) 1998, pp. 176–81.

24. Guillermo Algaze: *Ancient Mesopotamia at the Dawn of Civilization*, Chicago 2008, p. 129.

25. The first debt forgiveness is documented in the year 2400 BC under King Enmetena of Lagash. David Graeber: *Debt: The First 5,000 Years*, New York 2011, p. 216.

26. The covenant with God, to which Moses and the Old Testament prophets referred, said that the land belonged to no one but God Himself, who gave it to the Israelites to use in equal parts, which means that the private accumulation of land was illegal.

27. Claude Lévi-Strauss: *Tristes Tropiques*, New York 1974, p. 294.

28. David Wengrow: *What Makes Civilization? The Ancient Near East and the Future of the West*, New York 2010, p. 82.

29. Samuel N. Kramer: *History Begins at Sumer: Thirty-Nine Firsts in Man's Recorded History*, Philadelphia 1981, pp. 3–13.

30. The historian Flavius Josephus (37–100 AD) describes, for example, that at the beginning of the Jewish War in 66 AD the insurgents destroyed debt documents as one of their first acts: "They carried the fire to the place where the archives were reposited, and made haste to burn the contracts belonging to their creditors, and thereby to dissolve their obligations for paying their debts; and this was done in order to gain the multitude of those who had been debtors, and that they might persuade the poorer sort to join in their insurrection." Flavius Josephus: *The Jewish War*, book II, chapter 17, section 6, in: *The Works of Flavius Josephus*, translated by William Whiston, http://penelope.uchicago.edu/josephus.

31. See Ina Wunn: *Die Religionen in vorgeschichtlicher Zeit*, Stuttgart 2005.

32. Quote from: Samuel N. Kramer: *History Begins at Sumer: Thirty-Nine Firsts in Man's Recorded History*, Philadelphia 1981, pp. 90–92.

33. Michael Mann: *The Sources of Social Power, Volume 1*, Cambridge 1986, p. 158.

34. Gregory Bateson: *Mind and Nature*, New York 1979, p. 101.

35. Elias Canetti: *Crowds and Power*, London 1962 (original German title: *Masse und Macht*, Hamburg 1960).

Chapter 2

1. Hesiod: *Works and Days*, 143–153, translated by H. G. Evelyn-White, available online at: www.ellopop.net/elpenor/greek-texts/ancient-greece/hesiod/works-dayp.asp?pg=5.

2. Guillermo Algaze: *The Uruk World System*, London 2005.

3. Clemens D. Reichel, "Excavations at Hamoukar, Syria," in: *University of Chicago Oriental Institute, Fall 2011 News and Notes*, no. 211, Chicago 2007, pp. 1–9.

4. Jer 50:17. Jeremiah refers to the destruction of the northern kingdom of Judah in 722 BC, as a result of which ten of the 12 tribes of Israel disappeared from history. (All Bible quotes are from the *New International Version* [NIV]).

5. Keith Roberts: *The Origins of Business, Money, and Markets*, New York 2011, p. 217.

6. R. F. Tylecote: *A History of Metallurgy*, Midland 1992, p. 62.

7. Theodore A. Wertime: "The Furnace versus the Goat: The Pyrotechnologic Industries and Mediterranean Deforestation in Antiquity," in: *Journal of Field Archaeology*, vol. 10, no. 4 (1983), p. 452.

8. See also J. Donald Hughes: "Environmental Impacts of the Roman Economy and Social Structure," in: Alf Hornburg, J. R. McNeill, Joan Martinez-Alier (ed.): *Rethinking Environmental History: World-System History and Global Environmental Change*, Lanham (MD) 2007, p. 37.

9. See R. Krause et al.: „Prähistorische Siedlungen und mittelalterlicher Bergbau im Montafon, Vorarlberg", in: *Archäologie Österreichs Spezial 4*, Vienna 2012, pp. 147–166.

10. Ugo Bardi: *Extracted: How the Quest for Mineral Wealth Is Plundering the Planet*, White River Junction (VT) 2014, p. 109.

11. *The Natural History of Pliny*, translated by John Bostock and H.T. Riley, vol. 6, Sydney 2016 [London 1857] Book 33, Ch. 21, pp. 101–102.

12. Extensively described in the documentary film, *Le sable: enquête sur une disparition* by Denis Delestrac, France/Canada 2013.

13. This figure only refers to the period 1950–1990. See: Bogumil Terminski: *Mining-Induced Displacement and Resettlement: Social Problem and*

Human Rights Issue (A Global Perspective), Warsaw University, 2012. Download: papers.ssrn.com/sol3/paperp.cfm?abstract_id=2028490.

14. Vandana Shiva in an interview on Kontext TV, July 11, 2011, www. kontext-tv.de/en/node/2438.

15. Chris Hedges: *Days of Destruction, Days of Revolt*, New York 2012, p. 152 f.

16. Ugo Bardi: *Extracted: How the Quest for Mineral Wealth Is Plundering the Planet*, White River Junction (VT) 2014, p. 176.

17. These were in the *2014 Forbes Fortune Global 500*: Royal Dutch Shell, Sinopec, China National Petroleum, ExxonMobil, BP and Glencore (commodity trading).

18. Mircea Eliade: *The Forge and the Crucible*, London 1962, p. 173. Eliade writes that the legacy of alchemy is to be found above all "in the systems of political economy, whether capitalist, liberal or Marxist, in the secularized theologies of materialism, positivism and infinite progress—everywhere, in short, where there is faith in the limitless possibilities of homo faber."

19. The first systematic use of fossil coal took place in English iron production in the eighteenth century. This gave the British arms industry a decisive advantage over the Spanish. See Ugo Bardi: *Extracted: How the Quest for Mineral Wealth Is Plundering the Planet*, White River Junction (VT) 2014, p. 103–105.

20. See Pat Mooney: *Next Bang. Wie das riskante Spiel mit Megatechnologien unsere Existenz bedroht*, Munich 2010, p. 111 f.

21. Rv 21:5.

Chapter 3

1. See Adam Smith: *The Wealth of Nations*, New York 1994 [1776], p. 14.

2. "No example of a barter economy, pure and simple, has ever been described, let alone the emergence from it of money; all available ethnography suggests that there never has been such a thing." Caroline Humphrey, quoted from: David Graeber: *Debt: The First 5,000 Years*, New York 2012, p. 29.

3. Ibid., p. 3ff.

4. Michael Mann: *The Sources of Social Power, Volume 1*, Cambridge 1986, p. 194.

5. Erica Schoenberger: "The Origins of Market Economy," in: *Comparative Studies in Society and History*, no. 50 (3), Cambridge 2008, p. 66f.

6. See Geoffrey Ingham: *The Nature of Money. New Directions in Political Economy*, London 2004.

7. In Lydia, it was not states but rich families that first minted coins. Bearing the seals of these families, they were used to strengthen client relationships and thus political power. Thus, coins did not originate, as classical theory contends, from the barter trade, but primarily from a political motive. In long-distance trade and local economies, coins were to play only a minor role for a long time to come.

8. Keith Roberts: *The Origins of Business, Money, and Markets*, New York 2011, p. 66.

9. Erica Schoenberger: *The Origins of Market Economy*, op. cit. p. 670.

10. Ibid., p. 675; see also R. Duncan-Jones: *Money and Government in the Roman Empire*, Cambridge 1994.

11. Erica Schoenberger: *The Origins of Market Economy*, op. cit. p. 672.

12. In Athens and Rome, this concerned primarily those who did not have full civil rights (the majority of the population) and the inhabitants of subjugated provinces.

13. Michael Mann: *The Sources of Social Power, Volume 1*, Cambridge 1986, p. 138.

14. Erica Schoenberger: *The Origins of Market Economy*, op. cit. p. 671.

15. Siegfried Lauffer: *Die Bergwerkssklaven von Laureion*, Wiesbaden 1979, p. 25.

16. Ibid., p. 5ff.

17. David Graeber: *Debt: The First 5,000 Years*, New York 2011, p. 229.

18. Mt 20:1–16.

19. Keith Roberts: *The Origins of Business, Money, and Markets*, New York 2011, p. 185.

20. Diodorus: *World History*, book 5, chapter 38, Loeb Classical Library, English translation by C. H. Oldfather, Cambridge (MA) 1967, http://

penelope.uchicago.edu/Thayer/E/Roman/Texts/Diodorus_Siculus/
home.html.

21. Ibid.

22. See David Graeber: *Debt: The First 5,000 Years,* New York 2011, p. 223ff.

23. Keith Roberts: *The Origins of Business, Money, and Markets,* New York 2011, pp. 245–249.

24. "Shares of ownership, called *particulae* (little parts), were traded in the Forum, making it perhaps the world's first stock exchange." Keith Roberts: *The Origins of Business, Money, and Markets,* New York 2011, p. 204.

25. Lk 2:1–20. About the resistance to taxes, see Flavius Josephus: *The Jewish War,* book II, chapter 8, section 1 in: *The Works of Flavius Josephus,* translated by William Whiston, http://penelope.uchicago. edu/josephus; also: Richard A. Horsley: *Jesus and Empire. The Kingdom of God and the New World Disorder,* Minneapolis 2003, p. 41.

26. The relationship between market actors and state actors, both in antiquity and today, is much more complex than can be described here. The juxtaposition of world empire and world market is intended to show the shift in weight within this relationship. See also Immanuel Wallerstein: *World-Systems Analysis. An Introduction,* Durham 2004.

27. Max Weber: "Die protestantische Ethik und der Geist des Kapitalismus," in: *Gesammelte Aufsätze zur Religionssoziologie,* Tübingen 1988, p. 51.

28. "Roman law gave publican societies perpetual life and the ability to own property, make contracts and hire employees; it divided rights of ownership from a managerial authority, creating new entities, corporations, with powers that surpassed those of individuals and partnerships." Keith Roberts: *The Origins of Business, Money, and Markets,* New York 2011, p. 204.

29. See David Graeber: *Debt: The First 5,000 Years,* New York 2011, pp. 198–203; also Richard E. Mitchell: "Ager Publicus. Public Property and Private Wealth during the Roman Republic," in: Michael Hudson (ed.): *Privatization in the Ancient Near East and Classical World,* Cambridge (MA) 1996, pp. 253–276.

30. Ibid., p. 206.

31. Serfdom in the Middle Ages differed from slavery in at least one essential point: serfs could not be sold. Nonetheless, slavery in the narrower sense still existed in some places, especially in Spain. See Christian Delacampagne: *Une histoire de l'esclavage: de l'Antiquité à nos jours*, Paris 2002, pp. 101ff. and 111f.

32. However, the legal situation varies considerably from country to country. In Anglo-Saxon countries such as Great Britain and the US, landowners actually have the full right to dispose of their property, *ad coelum*, i.e., theoretically, to the center of the earth. All the same, the state reserves rights of appropriation (purchase rights) for strategic raw materials such as oil and coal. In Germany, on the other hand, landowners only hold ownership rights to "grundeigene" resources such as sand and gravel, but not to "bergfreie" resources. These include coal or metals for which only the state can grant concessions. Therefore, landowners in Germany can be forced to give up their land if raw materials are to be mined from it. This still occurs on a large scale, for instance, in opencast lignite mining.

33. The first patent on a living being was granted in the US in 1988 for the so-called "oncomouse." Researchers at Harvard University incorporated a cancer-causing gene into the genetic material of the mouse, whose name is now a registered trademark of DuPont. The European Patent Office finally recognized this patent in 2004, paving the way for European patents on life.

Chapter 4

1. In the historiography of the past 40 years there have been intensive efforts to correct this picture with an alternative historiography. Important contributions have been made by the *Alltagsgeschichte* (history of everyday life), the history of mentalities, feminist historiography as well as economic and social history. An example of such historiography "from below" is Howard Zinn's *A People's History of the United States*. However, these studies continue to have difficulty penetrating the public consciousness and the political sphere.

2. Jean Delumeau: *La Peur en Occident (XIVe–XVIIIe siècles)*, Paris 1978.

3. Mk 5:1–10.

4. The historians John D. Crossan and Richard Horsley explain that naming the demon "Legion" is not only another expression for "multitude," but probably refers directly to Roman armies. See e.g. Richard Horsley: *Jesus and Empire. The Kingdom of God and the New World Disorder*, Minneapolis 2003, p. 107.

5. Flavius Josephus: *Antiquities of the Jews*, book 17, chapter 10, section 10, in: *Complete Works of Josephus,* vol. 3, New York, p. 65.

6. Tacitus: *Agricola*, Chapter 30.

7. Judith Herman: *Trauma and Recovery. The Aftermath of Violence—from Domestic Abuse to Political Terror*, New York 1992, p. 20.

8. Ibid., p. 51.

9. Angela Kühner: "Kollektive Traumata," *Berghof Report,* no. 9, Berlin 2002, p. 34.

10. Ibid., p. 36.

11. Francis Fukuyama: *The End of History and the Last Man*, New York 1992. An excellent overview of the continuity of apocalypticism in Western civilization is provided by Walter Sparn: "Chiliastische Hoffnungen und apokalyptische Ängste. Das abendländische Erbe im neuen Jahrtausend," in: Bernd U. Schipper, Georg Plasger (ed.): *Apokalyptik und kein Ende?*, Göttingen 2007.

12. Dan 3:1–97. For an interpretation of the book of Daniel, see also Klaus Koch: "Daniel und Henoch – Apokalyptik im antiken Judentum," in: Bernd U. Schipper, Georg Plasger (ed.): *Apokalyptik und kein Ende?*, Göttingen 2007.

13. Dan 7:19.

14. Dan 7:9–11.

15. The author of the book of Revelation is not, as old church tradition would have it, identical with either the disciple John or with the author of the Gospel of John.

16. Tacitus: *Annals*, book 15.44, translated by Alfred John Church and William Jackson Brodribb, https://en.wikisource.org/wiki/The_Annals_(Tacitus).

17. The style in which the Revelation of John is written indicates a Palestinian author. The city of Ephesus, where John lived before his exile to Patmos, was a refuge for many of the Jews who fled Judea after the catastrophe in the year 70.
18. Rv 21:1–2.
19. Rv 21:2.
20. Rv 20:15.
21. Rv 21:15–18.
22. Rv 21:4.
23. See Walter Sparn: "Chiliastische Hoffnungen und apokalyptische Ängste. Das abendländische Erbe im neuen Jahrtausend," in: Bernd U. Schipper, Georg Plasger (ed.): *Apokalyptik und kein Ende?*, Göttingen 2007, p. 211.
24. See also Walter Benjamin's *Engel der Geschichte*: "A storm is blowing from Paradise; it has got caught in his wings with such violence that the angel can no longer close them. The storm irresistibly propels him into the future to which his back is turned, while the pile of debris before him grows skyward. This storm is what we call progress." Walter Benjamin: "Theses on the Philosophy of History," in: *Illuminations*, translated by Harry Zohn, New York 1969, p. 249.
25. John D. Crossan: *Who Killed Jesus? Exposing the Roots of Anti-Semitism in the Gospel Story of the Death of Jesus*, San Francisco 1995, Chapter 5.
26. To date, the most comprehensive scientific project for reconstructing the practices and views of the Jesus movement is the "Jesus Seminar" at the Westar Institute (US). More than 200 researchers from all over the world have been participating since 1985, and their results have been summarized in the following books: Robert W. Funk: *The Five Gospels. What Did Jesus Really Say?*, San Francisco 1996; Robert W. Funk: *The Acts of Jesus. What Did Jesus Really Do?*, San Francisco 1998. An excellent overview can be found in John D. Crossan: *The Historical Jesus: The Life of a Mediterranean Jewish Peasant*, San Francisco 1993.
27. Flavius Josephus: *The Jewish War*, book II, chapter 13, section 4. However, it is questionable whether Jesus himself ever took the title

of Messiah. In the earliest sources about the Jesus movement, the logia-source Q and parts of the Gospel of Thomas (GT), there are no references to the Messiah title at all.

28. See Richard A. Horsley and John P. Hanson: *Bandits, Prophets, and Messiahs: Popular Movements in the Time of Jesus*, Harrisburg 1999.

29. See also the extensive discussion of this point by John D. Crossan: *Who Killed Jesus? Exposing the Roots of Anti-Semitism in the Gospel Story of the Death of Jesus*, San Francisco 1995, Chapter 6.

30. This is discussed in detail in the following: Richard A. Horsley: *Jesus and Empire: The Kingdom of God and the New World Disorder*, Minneapolis 2003; John D. Crossan: *The Historical Jesus: The Life of a Mediterranean Jewish Peasant*, San Francisco 1993.

31. The apocalyptic portions of the gospels all have later dates. In the earliest sources that date back to the time before the destruction of Jerusalem, such as the logia-source Q, used by Matthew and Luke, and also the very early parts of the apocryphal Gospel of Thomas, no apocalyptic speeches by Jesus appear. See Robert W. Funk: *The Five Gospels. What Did Jesus Really Say?*, San Francisco 1996.

32. Compare these independent passages: Lk 17:21 "The kingdom of God is in your midst." and GT 113.4, "Rather the kingdom of the Father is spread out across the earth, and men see it not."

33. Richard Horsley: *Jesus and Empire. The Kingdom of God and the New World Disorder*, Minneapolis 2003, p. 108.

34. See also Karen L. King: *The Gospel of Mary of Magdala. Jesus and the First Woman Apostle*. Santa Rosa 2003, and Elaine Pagels: *Adam, Eve and the Serpent: Sex and Politics in Early Christianity*, New York 1988, as well as the PBS series, *Frontline, "From Jesus to Christ"*: www.pbp.org/wgbh/pages/frontline/shows/religion/first/women.html.

Chapter 5

1. Gal 1:8.

2. The Mont Pèlerin Society was founded in 1947 on the initiative of Friedrich von Hayek as an association of liberal economists. It quickly advanced to become one of the most important think tanks for the

dissemination of radical free-market thinking. About the London Missionary Society, see Chapter 8.

3. At first glance, Buddhism seems to be an exception. By the third century BC the Indian ruler Ashoka had sent emissaries in all directions to spread the message of Buddha. However, this "mission" differed in some essential points from the later Christian efforts. First, this mission was not violent. Both the practice and message of the emissaries were based on the concept of radical non-violence, to which Ashoka had committed himself as repentance for waging years of cruel imperial wars. The second and deeper reason for the absence of violence is that Buddhism makes no absolute claim to truth, nor does it promote the idea of dividing people into believers and unbelievers. Therefore, there was no ideological foundation for forced conversions.

4. See Mary Boyce: *A History of Zoroastrianism*, vol. 1, Leiden 1996.

5. The Church has long invoked the so-called mission command of the resurrected Jesus. The earliest source ("Go into all the world and preach the Gospel to all creation. Whoever believes and is baptized will be saved, but whoever does not believe will be condemned." Mk 16:15–16), however, is a later addition to the Gospel according to Mark. Also, corresponding passages in Matthew (Mt 28:16–20), Luke and John are dated relatively late. They are missing completely from the earliest sources: Q, Mk (without the later addition) and the earliest parts of the Gospel of Thomas.

6. Gal 1:13.

7. Although Paul's letters are the earliest preserved Christian texts of all, they reveal almost nothing about Jesus's life and the nature of his movement.

8. See also Hyam Maccoby: *The Mythmaker: Paul and the Invention of Christianity*, New York 1987. Central to Pauline theology, the myth of a God who dies and is resurrected is also found in the Mithras, Attis and Osiris cults, which were very popular in the Roman Empire during Paul's lifetime. God having a physical son is a Greek idea and was alien to the realm of Jewish thinking in which Jesus and his

followers were active. The same goes for the idea of an original sin that must be atoned for by human sacrifice.

9.   John D. Crossan, Jonathan L. Reed: *In Search of Paul. How Jesus's Apostle Opposed Rome's Empire with God's Kingdom*, San Francisco 2004. Crossan also points out that the often-quoted statements by Paul against the equality of women and slaves are found in the so-called pseudepigraphic letters, which were not written by Paul himself. They are also found as later insertions into authentic letters. The Epistles to the Ephesians and Colossians, the Second Epistle to the Thessalonians and the Epistles to Timothy and Titus are not considered to have been written by Paul (ibid., p. 105).

10.   See also: Wolfgang Sachs (ed.): *The Development Dictionary: A Guide to Knowledge as Power*, London 1992, p. xviii.

11.   Quote by Johannes Fried: *Aufstieg aus dem Untergang*, Munich 2001, p. 31.

12.   1 Cor 1:23.

13.   "In person he is unimpressive and his speaking amounts to nothing." 2 Cor 10:10.

14.   Quote from: Immanuel Wallerstein: *European Universalism. The Rhetoric of Power*, New York 2006, p. 5.

15.   Reinhold Rau (ed.): *Briefe des Bonifatius: Willibalds Leben des Bonifatius*, Darmstadt 1968, pp. 493–495.

16.   In 772, Charlemagne had the Saxons' World Tree (Irminsul) destroyed. For the Saxons, who lived between the northern Rhine and the Elbe rivers, the Irminsul represented the axis of the world that connected heaven and earth. This desecration and humiliation led to open revolt. Charlemagne responded with a war that lasted 32 years. According to a contemporary source, he had 4500 men executed in the Massacre of Verden alone. In the same year he passed a law that punished resistance to baptism with death: ("If any one of the race of the Saxons hereafter concealed among them shall have wished to hide himself unbaptized, and shall have scorned to come to baptism and shall have wished to remain a pagan, let him be punished by death." ((*Capitulatio de partibus Saxoniae*).

17. See Hartmut Boockmann: *Deutsche Geschichte im Osten Europas. Ostpreußen und Westpreußen*, Munich 2002, pp. 75–115; Beate Szillis-Kappelhoff: *Prußen – Die ersten Preußen. Geschichte und Kultur eines untergegangenen Volkes*, Schnellbach 2014.

18. See Immanuel Wallerstein: *Historical Capitalism*, London/New York 1983, p. 81: "The belief in universalism has been the keystone of the ideological arch of historical capitalism."

Chapter 6

1. From a nightmare Leonardo described in his notebook; quote from Lewis Mumford: *The Myth of the Machine. Technics and Human Development*, New York 1967, p. 334.

2. In a relatively small area such as the archbishopric of Treves (Germany) alone, 368 women were burned to death from 1587–1595. See Jean Delumeau: *La Peur en Occident (XIVe–XVIIIe siècles)*, Paris 1978, p. 351.

3. See also the first German criminal code, the *Constitutio Criminalis Carolina* (1532), also known as Charles V's "Peinliche Halsgerichtsordnung" (meticulous procedure for the judgment of capital crimes).

4. Before applying torture, the *Constitutio Criminalis Carolina* required serious grounds for suspicion as well as witnesses. In practice, however, especially during witch trials, these requirements were mostly ignored. The reason given was that it was a *crimen exceptum*, an exceptional crime, or a *crimen atrocissimum*, a crime of the most terrible kind, in which the normal rules did not apply.

5. Jean Delumeau: *La Peur en Occident*, pp. 202, 210f., 237–242. It is no coincidence that depictions of apocalyptic scenes always appear precisely in the places and times where the money-military complex is expanding: the "Triumph of Death" in Northern Italy in the fourteenth century; Dürer's "Apocalypse" in Nuremberg around 1511 (a city which was decisively influenced by the Augsburg mining entrepreneurs and bankers Fugger and Welser); and Bosch's visions of hell in Flanders about a decade earlier.

6. Jean Delumeau: *La Peur en Occident*, p. 215.
7. Subsistence means that communities produce for their own needs; commons are common goods shared by various people under rules they have negotiated among themselves (see Chapter 11).
8. Richard Cowen: *Exploiting the Earth*, ch. 7 (publication in preparation). Source for the working version: http://mygeologypage.ucdavis.edu/cowen//~GEL115/.
9. See Silvia Federici: *Caliban and the Witch: Women, the Body and Primitive Accumulation*, New York 2004, p. 26.
10. James C. Scott: *Seeing Like a State. How Certain Schemes to Improve the Human Condition Have Failed*, New Haven 1998, pp. 25–29.
11. See Lynn White: "The Historical Roots of Our Ecological Crisis," in: *Science*, vol. 155, New York 1967, pp. 1203–1207.
12. Joachim of Fiore divided history into three ages: the age of the Father (the epoch of the "Old Testament"), the Son (the Church at the time) and the Holy Spirit. This third age had not yet come and would bring the heavenly Jerusalem to earth. In it, the church would relinquish its possessions and be restored to its original form. However, Joachim did not imagine a society of equals, but instead, a rigid hierarchy based on the structures of Benedictine monasteries.
13. Jean Delumeau: *La Peur en Occident*, p. 114.
14. Ibid., p. 108.
15. Silvia Federici: *Caliban and the Witch*, pp. 43–47. Federici quotes a contemporary who takes the point of view of the nobility: "The peasants are too wealthy and do not know what obedience is. They ignore the law and wish for a world without nobility." (p. 45)
16. This uprising was called "Jacquerie," a reference to the nobility's mocking name for farmers, "Jacques Bonhomme." According to contemporary sources, the peasants reduced hundreds of castles and manor houses to rubble and ashes—events that have left a deep impression on the memory of the French nobility.
17. See also Murray Bookchin: *The Third Revolution. Popular Movements in the Revolutionary Era*, vol. 1, London 1996, pp. 23–37.
18. See Silvia Federici: *Caliban and the Witch*, p. 21–22: "Capitalism was

the response of the feudal lords, the patrician merchants, the bishops and popes, to a centuries-long social conflict that, in the end, shook their power, and truly gave 'all the world a big jolt.' Capitalism was the counter-revolution that destroyed the possibilities that had emerged from the anti-feudal struggle."

19. Amalfi and Pisa were other powerful maritime republics, but eventually lost their importance, while Venice and Genoa became hegemonic in the Mediterranean.

20. See Janet Abu-Lughod: "Discontinuities and Persistence," in: André Gunder Frank and Barry K. Gills: *The World System: Five Hundred Years or Five Thousand?*, London 1996, pp. 247–277.

21. An essential component of the Venetian business model was to offer protection to the militarily weak Byzantine Empire. For the use of its war fleet, Venice received trade privileges in return, which further promoted Venice's economic and military strength.

22. Lewis Mumford: *The Myth of the Machine. The Pentagon of Power*, New York 1970, p. 149. Dante immortalized the arsenal in the 21st song of the *Inferno*.

23. Frederic Chapin Lane: *Venice: A Maritime Republic*, Baltimore 1973, p. 337.

24. See Robert S. Lopez: *The Commercial Revolution of the Middle Ages 959–1350*, Englewood Cliffs (NJ) 1971, p. 69.

25. Jürgen Kocka writes in *Geschichte des Kapitalismus* (Munich 2013, p. 31): "In the last two centuries of the first millennium, the rudiments of a merchant capitalist bourgeoisie emerged in some parts of Arabia, more clearly here than anywhere else in the world at that time. Yet the merchant capitalists had no share in the political power exercised by the traditional elites, noble landowners, and military leaders. The bourgeoisie that was emerging here in a sporadic and rudimentary fashion was not a ruling class."

26. During the "dress rehearsal" for the first crusade in 1087, Genoa, together with Pisa and Amalfi, had already participated in the looting of Mahdia, the Muslim capital of the region of "Africa" (*Ifriqiya* in Arabic), located in present-day Tunisia. This ensured the maritime

sovereignty of Genoa in the western Mediterranean and paved the way for the First Crusade. Much of the booty was used to build Pisa's famous cathedral.

27. William of Tyre: *A History of Deeds Done Beyond the Sea*, vol. II, New York 1943, p. 371.

28. The Treaty, *Partitio terrarum imperii Romaniae,* provided that three-eighths of the Byzantine Empire would go to Venice, three-eighths to other participants in the Crusade and one-quarter to the Emperor of the newly created "Latin Empire."

29. See Immanuel Wallerstein: *World-Systems Analysis: An Introduction*, Durham 2004, p. 2f.: "The totally free market functions as an ideology, a myth, but never as a day-to-day reality. One of the reasons it is not a day-to-day reality is that a totally free market, were it ever to exist, would make impossible the endless accumulation of capital. [...] In a perfect market, it would always be possible for the buyers to bargain down the sellers to an absolutely minuscule level of profit, and this low level of profit would make the capitalist game entirely uninteresting to producers." See also Fernand Braudel: *Civilization and Capitalism, 15th–18th Century*, vol. 2, New York 1982, p. 229. Braudel distinguished between three levels of economy: subsistence, market and capitalism, referring to capitalism as an "anti-market."

30. In *The Long Twentieth Century. Money, Power and the Origins of Our Times* (London/New York 2010), Giovanni Arrighi describes in detail the interdependence of state and capital with the emergence of the modern world-system. The first systemic accumulation cycle was marked by the connection of the Genoese banks with the Spanish and Portuguese military states, which together formed an "amphibious" system of rule. (The title *The Long Twentieth Century* is misleading, however, because the book covers a period from the thirteenth to the twentieth centuries).

31. Janice E. Thomson: *Mercenaries, Pirates and Sovereigns*, Princeton 1996, p. 27.

32. See Georges Duby: *Rural Economy and Country Life in the Mediaeval West*, London 1968, pp. 226–259. See also: Erica Schoenberger, "The Origins

of Market Economy," in: *Comparative Studies in Society and History*, no. 50 (3), Cambridge 2008, p. 683: "As in Rome, the monetization of the tax system forces commercialization. The surplus must now be sold in order to obtain the cash demanded for state obligations. Nonetheless, as in the case of Rome, the state obligations are overwhelmingly concerned with territorial conquest and control, so the needs of waging war continue to play a leading role in this process."

33. Erica Schoenberger: "The Origins of Market Economy," p. 681.

34. Immanuel Wallerstein: *The Modern World-System, vol. I: Capitalist Agriculture and the Origins of the European World-Economy in the Sixteenth Century*, New York 1974, p. 21. See also Giovanni Arrighi: *The Long Twentieth Century*, p. 109.

35. Immanuel Wallerstein quotes the historian Michael Postan, who described the English nobility's reaction to the loss of income as "gangsterism." Immanuel Wallerstein: *The Modern World-System, vol. I*, p. 46f.

36. These figures are based on data provided by the contemporary banker and chronicler Giovanni Villani. However, the historian Edwin S. Hunt has questioned these figures. ("A New Look at the Dealings of the Bardi and Peruzzi with Edward III," in: *The Journal of Economic History*, vol. 50, no. 1, 1990, pp. 149–162). But even if the sums were smaller, they represented a considerable contribution, without which the Hundred Years' War might never have begun.

37. See Emmanuel Ladurie: *The French Peasantry 1450–1660*, Berkeley 1987.

38. Janice E. Thomson: *Mercenaries, Pirates and Sovereigns*, Princeton 1996, p. 28.

39. Fernand Braudel also described the period from 1350–1454 as the "Hundred Years' War of Italy." Jakob Burkhardt spoke of the Italian Renaissance as a "war of all against all" (Arrighi: *The Long Twentieth Century*, p. 92).

40. Henry Naeve et al.: *Private Militärunternehmen: Geschichte, Verfassungsmäßigkeit, internationale Regulierung und aktuelle Rechtsfragen*, Hamburg 2013, p. 30.

41. Janice E. Thomson: *Mercenaries, Pirates and Sovereigns*, Princeton 1996, p. 27f.

42. Hans Christian Huf: *Mit Gottes Segen in die Hölle. Der Dreißigjährige Krieg*, Berlin 2003, p. 31.

43. See Robert Rebitsch: *Wallenstein: Biographie eines Machtmenschen*, Vienna 2010, p. 132.

44. Quote from Ulrich Zimmermann: *Mittelalterlicher Bergbau auf Eisen, Blei und Silber*, Institut für Ur- und Frühgeschichte der Universität Freiburg, online publication: www2.ufg.uni-freiburg.de/d/publ/zimm1.html.

45. This mine was also the basis for the power of Duke Otto of Saxony, who later became known as Emperor Otto the Great, founder of the Ottonian dynasty. See Richard Cowen: *Exploiting the Earth*, loc. cit. ch. 7.

46. In turn, this mine formed the power base of "Otto the Rich," who founded the dynasty of the later Saxon kings. S. Richard Cowen: *Exploiting the Earth*, loc. cit. ch. 7.

47. The different stages of the silver rush in Central Europe, especially in Saxony and Bohemia, are known in German as "Berggeschrey" ("mining clamor").

48. Wolfgang König (ed.): *Propyläen Technikgeschichte, vol. 2: Metalle und Macht*, Berlin 1997, p. 221.

49. See Jürgen Kocka: *Geschichte des Kapitalismus*, p. 66.

50. Eduardo Galeano: *Open Veins of Latin America*, London 1973, p. 17.

51. Egon Friedell: *Kulturgeschichte der Neuzeit*, vol. 1, Munich 1991, p. 240f.

52. Neslihan Asutay-Effenberger, Ulrich Rehm (ed.): *Sultan Mehmet II: Eroberer Konstantinopels – Patron der Künste*, Vienna 2009, pp. 211–219.

53. Richard Cowen: *Exploiting the Earth*, loc. cit. ch.10.

54. With the introduction of cannons, old fortifications had become useless, they could be destroyed in a single day and had to be replaced by much more complex constructions. Antwerp's seven-kilometer long fortress alone, which was built to withstand cannons, needed thousands of workers and cost 1 million guilders. By today's

purchasing power, this would equal roughly 60 million euros. In addition to the armies and metal production, such fortifications formed decisive "hot spots" in the expanding money and market economy. See: Robert Kurz: "Vater Staat und Mutter Krieg. Die Geburt des Geldes," in: *Blätter für deutsche und internationale Politik*, 9/2012, p. 106.

55. See Jason W. Moore: "Silver, Ecology, and the Origins of the Modern World, 1450–1640," in: Alf Hornburg, J. R. McNeill, Joan Martinez-Alier (Hg.): *Rethinking Environmental History: World-System History and Global Environmental Change*, Lanham (MD) 2007, pp. 123–137.

56. Ibid., p. 103.

57. See Jürgen Kocka: *Geschichte des Kapitalismus*, p. 43f. and p. 53: According to Kocka, competition between warring states was one of the decisive driving forces behind the development of European capitalism. Conversely, forced capital accumulation was a prerequisite for the formation of powerful territorial states.

58. Richard Cowen: *Exploiting the Earth*, loc. cit. ch.10.

59. Georgius Agricola: *De Re Metallica*, London 1912 [1556], p. 8 f.

60. Ibid., p. 11f.

61. Ibid., p. 12.

62. In Old English, the word *weald* originally meant dense forest, but in today's dictionaries it is defined as "open landscape." In fact, today the entire southeast of England is largely free of forests.

63. In many ways, the Swedish system was similar to the Greek and Roman systems in antiquity. Mining made it possible to acquire silver and produce weapons with which to build a large army and capture prisoners of war. In turn, they were used as slaves in the mines, so that still more new weapons could be produced and prisoners of war captured.

64. The Banco di San Giorgio was founded as an association of creditors from the Republic of Genoa. In the following years, it gained complete control of public finances and was "more effective than any other institution until the creation of the Bank of England," which

also came into being as an association of creditors just 300 years later (Giovanni Arrighi: *The Long Twentieth Century*, pp. 93, 102, 104).

65. See Mark Häberlein: *Die Fugger. Geschichte einer Augsburger Familie (1367–1650)*, Stuttgart 2006, p. 47. The Fuggers dominated the Slovak, Hungarian and Alpine copper trade, which together accounted for 80 percent of the total European market.

66. Fugger also had by far the largest mercury mines in the world in Almadén, Spain. Since mercury was mainly used for silver production, this put him in control of yet another part of the value chain.

67. See also Giovanni Arrighi: *The Long Twentieth Century*, p. 126.

68. Together with Genoese bankers, the Augsburg bankers Fugger and Welser provided 70 percent of the total loans to the Spanish crown between 1521 and 1555. Mark Häberlein: *Die Fugger. Geschichte einer Augsburger Familie (1367–1650)*, Stuttgart 2006, p. 77.

69. Howard Zinn: *A People's History of the United States*, New York 2003, p. 1.

70. Ibid., pp. 1–5.

71. See David E. Stannard: *American Holocaust. The Conquest of the New World*, New York 1992, and David E. Stannard: "Uniqueness as Denial: The Politics of Genocide Scholarship," in: Alan S. Rosenbaum (ed.): *Is the Holocaust Unique? Perspectives on Comparative Genocide*, Philadelphia 2009, pp. 295–340.

72. Bartolomé de las Casas: *A Short Account of the Destruction of the Indies*, translated by Nigel Griffin, London/New York 1992, p. 11.

73. Ibid., p. 15.

74. See David Graeber: *Debt: The First 5,000 Years*, New York 2012, p. 317 ff., also Jürgen Kocka: *Geschichte des Kapitalismus*, p. 48.

75. Silvia Federici: *Caliban and the Witch*, p. 111.

76. Eduardo Galeano: *Open Veins of Latin America*, London 1973, p. 18.

77. Extensive material about Potosí can be found in Alice Creischer et al.: *Das Potosí-Prinzip. Bildproduktion in der globalen Ökonomie*, exhibition catalog, Cologne 2010.

78. Ibid., p. 39f.

79. Ibid., p. 39.

80. Silvia Federici: *Caliban and the Witch*, p. 29.

81. The real wage of an English carpenter shrank by 70 percent from 1450 to 1650. See Immanuel Wallerstein: *The Modern World-System, vol. I: Capitalist Agriculture and the Origins of the European World-Economy in the Sixteenth Century*, New York 1974, p. 80; Silvia Federici: *Caliban and the Witch: Women, the Body and Primitive Accumulation*, New York 2004, p. 76–81.

82. In some regions, witches were referred to as "herege" (heretics). See Silvia Federici: *Caliban and the Witch*, p. 179

83. Jean Delumeau: *La Peur en Occident*, pp. 208–211; 237–242.

84. Ibid. pp. 210–216.

85. *Constitutio Criminalis Carolina*, also known as Charles V's "Peinliche Halsgerichtsordnung" (meticulous procedure for the judgment of capital crimes).

86. Karl Marx: *Capital. Volume I: The Process of Production of Capital*, translated by Samuel Moore and Edward Aveling, edited by Friedrich Engels, London 1887 [German edition: 1867], ch. 24.

87. Martin Luther: "Wider die mörderischen und räuberischen Rotten der Bauern" [1525], in: *Martin Luther: Werke*, vol. 18, Weimar 1888ff., pp. 357–361. (English: *Against the Murderous, Thieving Hordes of Peasants*.)

88. In his letter to the Romans, Paul wrote: "Let everyone be subject to the governing authorities, for there is no authority except that which God has established. The authorities that exist have been established by God. Consequently, whoever rebels against the authority is rebelling against what God has instituted, and those who do so will bring judgment on themselves." Rom. 13:1–2.

89. Martin Luther: *Ob Kriegsleute in seligem Stande sein können* [1526] (English: *Whether Soldiers, Too, Can Be Saved*). Ibid. also: "Christians, do not fight against your lord or tyrant." And: "A mad mob is a desperate, accursed thing; no one can rule it as well as tyrants. They are the club tied to the dog's neck. If there were a better way to rule them, God would have set some other ordinance over them than a sword and tyrants. [...] Herefore, I advise everyone who would act in this matter with a good conscience and do what is right, that he be

satisfied with the worldly rulers and make no attack upon them[...]
And it is better for the tyrants to wrong them a hundred times than
for the mob to treat the tyrant unjustly but once." (Translation by C.
M. Jacobs).

90. *Confessio Augustana* (Augsburg Confession), article 16, en.wikisource.
org/wiki/Augsburg_Confession. This document was written under
the direction of Philipp Melanchthon. He is regarded as the founder of
the German *Gymnasium* (secondary school) and has had a considerable
influence on the development of the school and university system.

91. Quoted from: Thomas Seifert: *Die Täufer zu Münster*, Münster 1993, p.
42.

92. See Jürgen Kocka: *Geschichte des Kapitalismus*, p. 40f.

93. Robert S. Lopez: *The Commercial Revolution of the Middle Ages 959–
1350*, Englewood Cliffs (NJ) 1971, p. 93.

94. Ibid., p. 97 and p. 108.

95. In the case of *societas* and *compagnia*, all partners were liable for any
losses. In the case of *commenda*, the life of the company was limited
to one trading trip. Robert S. Lopez: *The Commercial Revolution of the
Middle Ages 959–1350*, Englewood Cliffs (NJ) 1971, p. 75 ff.

96. There were earlier stock exchanges in Italy and elsewhere, but they
were not lasting institutions. The Amsterdam Stock Exchange was the
first permanent stock exchange, and its trading volume far exceeded
that of its predecessors. See also Giovanni Arrighi: *The Long Twentieth
Century*, p. 142.

97. The emergence of companies as legal entities separate from the personal
budgets of their shareholders is a phenomenon that only existed in
Europe and not in the commercial cultures of China and Arabia. See also
Jürgen Kocka: *Geschichte des Kapitalismus*, p. 35f. The "disembedding"
of the economy from society is a term that was coined by the economic
historian Karl Polanyi. However, he did not see the beginnings of this
process until the early nineteenth century. See Karl Polanyi: *The Great
Transformation*, New York 1944. For criticism of Polanyi's dating, see
Robert Kurz: "Vater Staat und Mutter Krieg. Die Geburt des Geldes," in:
Blätter für deutsche und internationale Politik, 9/2012.

98. Daron Acemoğlu, James A. Robinson: *Why Nations Fail: The Origins of Power, Prosperity, and Poverty*, New York 2012, pp. 248–249.

99. The term "City upon a hill" was first conceived in 1630 by John Winthrop in his sermon "A Model of Christian Charity." The term is taken from Mt 5:14, "A town built on a hill cannot be hidden." The apocalyptic connotations were unmistakable. Winthrop was one of the first governors of Massachusetts Bay Colony. The "City upon a hill" was often quoted by leaders such as John F. Kennedy and Ronald Reagan to underline the world-historical mission of the US.

100. Howard Zinn: *A People's History of the United States*, New York 2003, p. 15.

101. These companies included the Virginia Company of London, the Plymouth Company and the Massachusetts Bay Company.

102. In the first volume of *Capital,* Marx had already pointed out the important role played by national debt in the emergence of capitalism. See also Giovanni Arrighi: *The Long Twentieth Century*, p. 13f.

103. See also Immanuel Wallerstein: *The Modern World-System, vol. I: Capitalist Agriculture and the Origins of the European World-Economy in the Sixteenth Century*, New York 1974. Wallerstein distinguishes between two types of world-systems: the world empires and the modern world economy. His primary criterion for this distinction is the question of whether, in case of doubt, the logic of capital accumulation takes precedence in decision-making processes or not.

104. The violence in this war was no less brutal than the sadism of the Conquista, as an eyewitness account of the conquest of Heidelberg shows: For three days there was "massacre, plunder and larceny; thumb screws, gagging, beating, tormenting, drilling into fingernails, burning of privates, hanging, and burning the soles of feet" (Hans Christian Huf: *Mit Gottes Segen in die Hölle. Der Dreißigjährige Krieg*, Berlin 2003, p. 248). In one day, at least 20,000 people were killed in the devastation of Magdeburg. One survivor reports that the bodies were then dismembered, and the heads and breasts of murdered women were cut off (ibid., p. 153).

105. Ibid., p. 103.

Chapter 7

1. The seventeenth and early eighteenth centuries in Europe are often regarded as a time of crisis due to low economic growth and incessant wars, and indeed this phase was associated with a massive increase in exploitation and misery for the majority of the population. However, this was not caused by a crisis of the system itself but, on the contrary, it was a result of its stabilization. See Immanuel Wallerstein: *The Modern World-System, vol. II: Mercantilism and the Consolidation of the European World-Economy, 1600–1750,* Cambridge (MA) 1980, p. 33f.

2. See Immanuel Wallerstein: *Historical Capitalism,* London 1983.

3. "Scientism" is an ideology claiming that all meaningful questions can be answered by scientific methods. About criticism of scientism, see Jürgen Habermas: *Technik und Wissenschaft als "Ideologie,"* Frankfurt/M. 1969; Karl Popper: *The Poverty of Historicism,* London 1957.

4. Giovanni Fontana: *Bellicorum instrumentorum liber,* online at: http://bibliodyssey.blogspot.de/2010/01/bellicorum-inst rumentorum-liber.html.

5. See Immanuel Wallerstein: *European Universalism,* New York 2006, p. 51.

6. See Chapter 1.

7. The 50-member board of this corporation represented about 650 investors. Wesley Frank Craven: *The Virginia Company of London, 1606–1624,* Williamsburg 2009 [1957], p. 19.

8. Francis Bacon: *The Wisdom of the Ancients,* ch. 17 [1609].

9. Quote from Carolyn Merchant: *The Death of Nature: Women, Ecology, and the Scientific Revolution,* New York 1980, p. 171.

10. Francis Bacon: *On the Dignity and Advancement of Learning,* quoted from: Carolyn Merchant: "The Scientific Revolution and the Death of Nature," in: *Isis,* ed. 97, 2006, p. 529.

11. *Works of the Honorable Robert Boyle,* Whitefish (MT) 2003, p. 740.

12. The text is from Galileo's book *Il Saggiatore,* published in 1623. An English translation can be found in: Stillman Drake: *Discoveries and Opinions of Galileo,* New York 1957, p. 237f. See also Lewis Mumford:

The Myth of the Machine. The Pentagon of Power, New York 1970, p. 65.

13. This statement refers to the "father of Behaviorism," John B. Watson, in his book *Behaviorism* (Chicago 1961). The level of influence Watson's school still has in our time is shown by the fact that Burrhus Skinner, Watson's most famous successor, was named the most important psychologist of the twentieth century by the American Psychological Association in 2002.

14. Ilya Prigogine, Isabelle Stengers: *Order Out of Chaos: Man's New Dialogue with Nature,* New York 1984, p. 32.

15. René Descartes: *Traité de l'homme,* Paris 2018 [1664].

16. "God has laid down these laws in nature just as a king lays down laws in his kingdom." René Descartes: Letter to Mersenne, April 15,1630, in: *Descartes' Philosophical Letters,* Oxford 1970, p. 11.

17. Many Renaissance philosophers such as Tommaso Campanella, Agrippa von Nettesheim and Giordano Bruno referred to Plato's concept of a world soul. See Carolyn Merchant: *The Death of Nature.*

18. Quote from Carolyn Merchant: *The Death of Nature,* p. 286.

19. See Gregory Bateson: *Mind and Nature,* New York 1979, p. 101.

20. On self-organization and non-linear processes, see the work of Ilya Prigogine, e.g.: Ilya Prigogine, Isabelle Stengers: *Order Out of Chaos: Man's New Dialogue with Nature,* New York 1984. Prigogine and Stengers investigate non-linear processes in inanimate and animate nature.

21. Michael Mann has compiled figures on the military expenditure of European states from the sixteenth century to 1815. If direct military expenditure and debt repayments, which nearly always are due to military operations, are added together, the military's share of the national budget in practically all European countries, whether England, France, Russia or Prussia, is 80–90 percent. This ratio tends to be maintained even in peacetime. The enormous increase in national budgets since the seventeenth century is almost exclusively due to the expansion of the military. Mann concludes: "As yet the functions of this state—a 'constitutional' state, let it be remembered— are overwhelmingly military. Other functions largely spin off from

its wars." Michael Mann: *The Sources of Social Power, Volume* 1, p. 486–490. For the time after 1760 see Michael Mann: The *Sources of Social Power, Volume 2, The Rise of Classes and Nation-States, 1760–1914,* Cambridge 1993, pp. 371–375.

22. See Immanuel Wallerstein: *The Modern World-System, vol. I: Capitalist Agriculture and the Origins of the European World-Economy in the Sixteenth Century,* New York 1974, p. 218.

23. Jürgen Kocka: *Geschichte des Kapitalismus,* München 2013, p. 27.

24. Max Weber had already remarked in his *History of Science* (1923) that the fierce competition of European city states—and later territorial states—for mobile capital was the central cause behind the development of capitalism in Europe. See also Giovanni Arrighi: *The Long Twentieth Century. Money, Power and the Origins of Our Times,* London/New York 2010, p. 12f.

25. German forestry later became a model for the conversion of forest management in England, France, the US and many other countries.

26. James C. Scott: *Seeing Like a State. How Certain Schemes to Improve the Human Condition Have Failed,* New Haven 1998, p. 15.

27. Ibid., p. 20.

28. Ibid., p. 56.

29. Ibid., p. 60f.

30. Ibid., p. 63.

31. The French anthropologist Marc Augé describes places where history, relationships and identities have been erased as being "non-places." See Marc Augé: *Non-Lieux, introduction à une anthropologie de la surmodernité,* Paris 1992.

32. The idea for the Orange Army Reform was inspired by the "humanist" Justus Lipsius (1547–1606).

33. Michel Foucault: *Discipline and Punish: The Birth of the Prison,* New York 1995, p. 166.

34. Ibid., p. 150.

35. Ibid., p. 167.

36. Quote from Lewis Mumford: *The Myth of the Machine. The Pentagon of Power,* New York 1970, p. 103.

37. See Ken Robinson: *Out of Our Minds. Learning to be Creative*, Hoboken 2011; Manfred Spitzer: *Lernen. Gehirnforschung und die Schule des Lebens*, Heidelberg 2007.

38. Christian Delacampagne: *Une histoire de l'esclavage: de l'Antiquité à nos jours*, Paris 2002, p. 181f. See also Marcus Rediker: *The Slave Ship. A Human History*, London 2008.

39. Christian Delacampagne: *Une histoire de l'esclavage: de l'Antiquité à nos jours*, p. 175.

40. Louis Sala-Molins: *Le Code Noir ou le calvaire de Canaan*, Paris 2007, p. VIII.

41. Code Noir, par. 44.

42. Ibid., par. 38.

43. See Sidney W. Mintz: *Sweetness and Power: The Place of Sugar in Modern History*. New York 1985.

44. Jürgen Kocka: *Geschichte des Kapitalismus*, München 2013, p. 68.

45. See Karl Marx: "The Division of Labour in Manufacture," in: *Capital. Volume I: The Process of Production of Capital*, translated by Samuel Moore and Edward Aveling, edited by Friedrich Engels, London 1887 [German edition: 1867], ch. 14.

46. See Robert Kurz: "Die Diktatur der abstrakten Zeit. Arbeit als Verhaltensstörung der Moderne," in: Robert Kurz, Ernst Lohoff, Norbert Trenkle (Hg.): *Feierabend! Elf Attacken gegen die Arbeit*, Hamburg 1999.

Chapter 8

1. Anthony D. Barnosky et al.: "Has the Earth's sixth mass extinction already arrived?", in: *Nature*, vol. 471, March 3, 2011, pp. 51–57.

2. The first steam engine, the *aelopile*, was described by Heron of Alexandria in the first century BC, but it had no practical application.

3. Werner Sombart: *Der moderne Kapitalismus*, vol. 2, München/Leipzig 1928, pp. 1137–1151. As to the scope of the wood shortage there is still an academic debate. See Joachim Radkau, Ingrid Schäfer: *Holz. Ein Naturstoff in der Technikgeschichte*, Reinbek 1987. Critical to this topic, however, is not the question of whether there really was an absolute

shortage of wood, or if there might have been only temporary, local shortages. The important issue is that, in some places, the prices for wood and charcoal rose sharply due to the heavy use of forests by the arms industry, shipbuilding and housing construction. Because of the competitive pressure between iron producers such as England and Sweden, such price increases played a significant role in the search for alternative energy sources. See also Chapter 2 of this book.

4. In astronomy, a *nova* is a thermonuclear explosion within a double star system in which matter and energy are transferred from one star to another.

5. Wolfgang König (ed.): *Propyläen Technikgeschichte, Band 3: Mechanisierung und Maschinisierung*, Berlin 1997, p. 25.

6. To this day, monetary growth and energy consumption are still closely linked worldwide. Although relative decoupling is possible, it is limited. In the region of the 15 primary EU countries, for example, material and energy output stagnated at a high level from the mid-1970s onwards, while GDP grew slowly. See Wuppertal Institut für Umwelt, Klima, Energie: *Zukunftsfähiges Deutschland in einer globalisierten Welt*, Frankfurt/M. 2008, p. 101. See also the chapter: "The myth of decoupling," in Tim Jackson: *Prosperity Without Growth: Foundations for the Economy of Tomorrow*, London 2009, pp. 84–102. A discussion about decoupling can also be found in Chapter 10 of this book.

7. Karl Polanyi: *The Great Transformation*, New York 1944.

8. However, "proletarization" and the uprooting it entailed also had limits, since the institution of the family was needed to guarantee the reproduction of the labor force. Wallerstein notes that the "semi-proletarian" household was the norm in historical capitalism and remains so today, because it offers the best conditions for the exploitation of labor. Those living in households in which a portion of the necessities of life are provided by subsistence activities (especially by women) tend to accept work at wages that by themselves would not be enough to survive. Immanuel Wallerstein: *Historical Capitalism*, London 1983, pp. 26–28.

9. Silvia Federici: *Caliban and the Witch: Women, the Body and Primitive Accumulation*, New York 2004, p. 135.

10. Joseph Townsend: "A Dissertation on the Poor Laws" [1786], quoted in Karl Polanyi: *The Great Transformation*, New York 1944, p. 113. One of the most influential advocates of abolishing state welfare for the poor, along with Joseph Townsend, was the economist Thomas Malthus, who claimed that all living beings were in a constant struggle for survival. Malthus's ideas would later become decisive for Charles Darwin's concept of "survival of the fittest."

11. Friedrich Engels: *The Condition of the Working Class in England*, New York 1987 [1844/1887].

12. Flora Tristan: *Promenades in London*, in Doris Beik, Paul Harold Beik: *Flora Tristan, Utopian Feminist: Her Travel Diaries and Personal Crusade*, Bloomington 1993, pp. 67–73.

13. See also Edward Palmer Thompson's epoch-making study of the English working class: *The Making of the English Working Class*, New York 1966.

14. Quoted from: *Chomsky on Democracy and Education*, ed. Carlos Otero, London 2012, p. 29.

15. About the Luddites, see: Edward Palmer Thompson: *The Making of the English Working Class*, New York 1966, pp. 484–496.

16. Benedict Anderson: *Imagined Communities*, New York 1983.

17. Eric Hobsbawm: *Nations and Nationalism Since 1780: Programme, Myth, Reality*, Cambridge 1991, pp. 19f., 102ff.

18. Heinrich Heine: "Über Ludwig Börne," in: *Heines Werke in 5 Bänden*, vol. 4, ch. 4, Berlin 1974, Online at: http://gutenberg.spiegel.de/buch/373/4.

19. Immanuel Wallerstein: *The Modern World-System, volume IV: Centrist Liberalism Triumphant, 1789–1914*, Berkeley 2011, p. 144.

20. Eric Hobsbawm: *Nations and Nationalism Since 1780*, p. 74.

21. Ibid., p. 116.

22. This declaration was signed by over 3000 professors from 53 universities. It continues: "Our belief is that for the whole culture of Europe, salvation depends on the victory which German 'militarism'

will fight for." de.wikisource.org/wiki/Erkl%C3%A4rung_der_
Hochschullehrer_des_Deutschen_Reiches.

23. Wallerstein also quotes Gareth Jones (*Languages of Class*, Cambridge 1984): "One of the most striking features of the social movements between 1790 and 1850 had been the clarity and concreteness of their conception of the state[...]It had been seen as a flesh and blood machine of coercion, exploitation and corruption." *The Modern World-System, volume IV: Centrist Liberalism Triumphant, 1789–1914*, p. 173.

24. See also: Rosa Luxemburg: *Die Akkumulation des Kapitals*, Berlin 1975 [1913].

25. See Immanuel Wallerstein: *The Modern World-System, vol. III: The Second Era of Great Expansion of the Capitalist World-Economy, 1730–1840s*, San Diego 1989, pp. 127–189 (Wallerstein includes Russia as well as the other regions mentioned).

26. Norman Lewis: *The Missionaries: God Against the Indians*, New York 1988, Chapter 1.

27. Norbert Elias: *The Civilizing Process*, Oxford 1994 [1939/1969], p. 43.

28. Inscription on the Livingstone Memorial at Victoria Falls.

29. Quoted from the BBC: *The Story of Africa*, www.bbc.co.uk/worldservice/specials/1624_story_of_africa/page26.shtml.

30. Immanuel Kant: *Physische Geographie,* part 2, section 1, par. 4, Königsberg 1802. See also Emmanuel Chukwudi Eze: "The Color of Reason: The Idea of 'Race' in Kant's Anthropology," in: Emmanuel Chukwudi Eze (ed.): *Postcolonial African Philosophy. A Critical Reader*, Cambridge (MA) 1997.

31. The genocide of the Herero and Nama in today's Namibia from 1904–07 cost the lives of about 80,000 people. See Medardus Brehl: "Der Völkermord an den Herero 1904 und seine zeitgenössische Legitimation," in: Micha Brumlik, Irmtrud Wojak: *Völkermord und Kriegsverbrechen in der ersten Hälfte des 20. Jahrhunderts*, Frankfurt (Main) 2004, pp. 77–98. At about the same time, the German colonial troops conducted a war of extermination in East Africa against the local population, known as the "Maji-Maji War." The Germans responded to the uprising against forced labor and oppressive

taxation with a scorched earth policy. They burned villages and fields to starve the population, and devastated large parts of the country. In this "war" only 15 Europeans died, but at least 75,000 Africans perished. A comprehensive collection of essays on the subject is found in: Felicitas Becker, Jigal Beetz (eds.): *Der Maji-Maji-Krieg in Deutsch-Ostafrika 1905–1907*, Berlin 2005.

32. See David Renton, David Seddon, Leo Zeilig: *Congo: Plunder and Resistance*, London/New York 2007, ch. 1; Adam Hochschild: *King Leopold's Ghost: A Story of Greed, Terror and Heroism in Colonial Africa*, Boston 1998.

33. Mark Twain: *King Leopold's Soliloquy*, Philadelphia 1905.

34. Immanuel Wallerstein: *The Modern World-System, vol. III: The Second Era Great Expansion of the Capitalist World-Economy*, pp. 157–160.

35. Mike Davis: *Late Victorian Holocausts: El Niño Famines and the Making of the Third World*, London/New York 2002, p. 7.

36. Ibid., p. 31f.

37. Ibid., pp. 26, 45.

38. Ibid., pp. 31, 48.

39. Ibid., pp. 39f.

40. Ibid., p. 38ff.

41. See Jean Ziegler: *Das Imperium der Schande*, München 2005, pp. 100–127.

42. Mike Davis: *Late Victorian Holocausts*, p. 12.

43. Giovanni Arrighi: *Adam Smith in Beijing. Lineages of the 21st Century*, London 2009.

44. Julia Lovell: *The Opium War: Drugs, Dreams and the Making of China*, London 2011.

45. United Nations: *World Drug Report 2011*.

46. Alfred W. McCoy: *The Politics of Heroin: CIA Complicity in the Global Drug Trade*, New York 2003.

47. Hong claimed to be the younger brother of Jesus Christ. See Jürgen Osterhammel: *Die Verwandlung der Welt*, München 2009, p. 784.

48. The term "Boxer Rebellion" was coined in England and refers to the martial arts skills of the insurgents. They called themselves the

Yihetuan movement, which means something akin to "League for Justice and Harmony."

49. Minqi Li: *China and the 21ˢᵗ Century Crisis*, London 2016, p. 16. For example, the British and French secret services, together with the now legally operating opium corporations in Shanghai, established powerful mafia organizations: the so-called Red and Green Gangs. They would later prove useful in the fight against the Communists, fueling a civil war that would not end until after the Second World War.

50. Unfortunately, the devastating consequences of Western intervention in China are also played down in the most comprehensive book yet on the Opium Wars: Julia Lovell: *The Opium War: Drugs, Dreams and the Making of China*, London 2011. Lovell argues that Chinese historiography would overrate the importance of the Opium Wars in the collapse of the empire in order to create a national myth. While it is true that some Chinese scholars and politicians use the history of interventions to divert attention from internal crises, it is also obvious that Lovell serves the long Western tradition of minimizing colonial crimes by setting one of the most momentous colonial wars into the realm of mythology.

51. Much has been written about the "enthusiasm for war" in August 1914. As recent research has shown, however, it is largely a myth produced after 1918 by war supporters, among them Social Democrats who were seeking to justify their unconditional support for the war. While some in the bourgeoisie, including personalities such as Thomas Mann and Max Planck, actually were enthusiastic, those in the working class were mostly reserved or hostile. Tens of thousands even took part in anti-war demonstrations. See Wolfgang Kruse: "Die Kriegsbegeisterung im Deutschen Reich," in: Marcel van der Linden, Gottfried Mergner (eds.): *Kriegsbegeisterung und mentale Kriegsvorbereitung*, Berlin 1991, pp. 73–87; Tillmann Benidowski: *Sommer 1914: Zwischen Begeisterung und Angst – wie Deutsche den Kriegsbeginn erlebten*, München 2014.

52. The relationship between chemistry and metallurgy can be traced back to the time of alchemy. Both emerged as methods for mastering

and transforming matter in order to make it usable for the purposes of the Great Machine.

53. Karl Kraus: *Die letzten Tage der Menschheit*, preface, Berlin 1971 [1926]. (English: *The Last Days of Mankind*, New York 1974).

Chapter 9

1. Quoted from Richard Hofstadter: *The American Political Tradition*, New York 1948, pp. 15–16.

2. *Weißbuch. Vorgelegt dem Reichstage in der 3. Session der 9. Legislatur-Periode. Vierzehnter Teil*, Berlin 1895, p. 175.

3. Swedish Prime Minister Olof Palme was one of the few politicians who clearly stated that schools and the world of work are undemocratically organized. In 1968, he wrote: "If you want to change society and democratize it, school is without doubt one of our best instruments. However, we should not have high expectations for democracy in the classroom if we are not also prepared to make democracy a reality in workplaces outside of school." (Quote from: Thomas Meyer: *Praxis der Sozialen Demokratie*, Wiesbaden 2006, p. 65).

4. Wallerstein comments: "The specter that haunted the notables was that of democracy. The distinction between the liberal state and democracy was, in Max Beloff's words, 'the most important distinction in nineteenth-century politics.' Democracy, in nineteenth century usage, meant taking popular sovereignty seriously. The notables were not, and have never been, ready to do that[...] The problem for the notables, therefore, was how to construct a structure that would seem to be popular and in fact was not, but would nonetheless retain the support of a significant proportion of the 'people'." Immanuel Wallerstein: *The Modern World-System IV: Centrist Liberalism Triumphant, 1789–1914*, Berkeley 2011, p. 22f. Hobsbawm sees this similarly: "Democracy and liberalism looked more like opponents than allies." (Quote from Wallerstein, ibid., p. 77).

5. Howard Zinn: *A People's History of the United States*, New York 2001, p. 91ff.

6. James Madison: *Federalist Paper number 10* [1787].

7. Quote from Richard Hofstadter: *The American Political Tradition*, New York 1948, pp. 15–16.

8. See "The Net Worth of the American Presidents: Washington to Obama", 24/7 Wall St., May 17, 2019 https://247wallst.com/banking-finance/2010/05/17/the-net-worth-of-the-american-presidents-washington-to-obama/2/.

9. A complete English translation of the *Manifesto of the Enragés* can be found online: www.marxists.org/history/france/revolution/roux/1793/enrages01.htm.

10. Speech given on April 26, 1993. Quote from George Henry Lewes: *The Life of Maximilien Robespierre*, London 1849, pp. 291–292.

11. France reduced the debt in 1838 to 90 million francs (including the portions already paid), and in 1883 Haiti paid off the last amount, but this formal repayment was secured by borrowing from private Parisian banks. About the history and debts of Haiti, see Jan Rogozinski: *A Brief History of the Caribbean: From the Arawaks and Carib to the Present*, New York 1995.

12. Immanuel Wallerstein: *The Modern World-System, volume IV: Centrist Liberalism Triumphant, 1789–1914*, Berkeley 2011, p. 145.

13. Ibid., p. 7.

14. Ute Gerhard: *Frauenbewegung und Feminismus. Eine Geschichte seit 1789*, München 2012, p. 27.

15. In France, the revolution of 1848 was able to win universal suffrage for men, but two years later it was once more massively curtailed.

16. Jürgen Habermas: *Strukturwandel der Öffentlichkeit. Untersuchungen zu einer Kategorie der bürgerlichen Gesellschaft*, Frankfurt/M. 1990.

17. Quote from: Edward S. Herman, Noam Chomsky: *Manufacturing Consent. The Political Economy of the Mass Media*, New York 1988, p. 3.

18. Ibid., p. 4.

19. *The London Times* was the only newspaper with an international network of correspondents. All others relied on Reuters. See Jürgen Osterhammel: *Die Verwandlung der Welt. Eine Geschichte des 19. Jahrhunderts*, München 2009, p. 75.

20. Quote from Adrian Bingham: "Monitoring the Popular Press: An Historical Perspective," in: *History and Policy*, May 2, 2005, www. historyandpolicy.org/policy-papers/papers/monitoring-the-popular-press-an-historical-perspective.

21. The purchase of the UFA studios was mainly financed by Deutsche Bank. Heinrich Witthoefft, Chairman of the Supervisory Board of Commerzbank, was a member of the "Wirtschaftsvereinigung zur Förderung der geistigen Wideraufbaukräfte," the umbrella company of the Hugenberg Group.

22. "Ultima ratio regum" translates as "the last resort of kings." Many regents had this inscription imprinted on their cannons, including Frederick II of Prussia.

23. Timothy Mitchell: *Carbon Democracy. Political Power in the Age of Oil*, London 2011, p. 25.

24. Ibid., pp. 19–27.

25. James C. Scott: *Seeing Like a State. How Certain Schemes to Improve the Human Condition Have Failed*, New Haven 1998, p. 159.

26. Ibid., p. 161.

27. Eric Hobsbawm: *Nations and Nationalism Since 1780: Programme, Myth, Reality*, Cambridge 1991, p. 132.

28. James C. Scott: *Seeing Like a State. How Certain Schemes to Improve the Human Condition Have Failed*, New Haven 1998, p. 100.

29. Ibid., p. 163.

30. Michael Albert calls these 20 percent the "coordinator class." See Michael Albert: *Parecon. Life after Capitalism*, New York 2004.

31. Vladimir Ilyich Lenin: "The Impending Catastrophe and How to Combat It" [1917], in: *Lenin's Collected Works*, Moscow 1977, vol. 25, p. 362. English translation online: www.marxists.org/archive/lenin/works/1917/ichtci/11.htm#v25zz99h-360.

32. Rusted out Russian nuclear submarines can be found lying about on the ground near the northern port city of Murmansk. Semipalatinsk in Kazakhstan was a nuclear weapons testing ground for decades.

33. Walter Lippmann: *Public Opinion*, New York 1965 [1922], p. 158. Available online at: www.gutenberg.org/ebooks/6456.

34. Edward Bernays: *Propaganda*, New York 2004 [1928], p. 37.

35. About Edward Bernays and the history of public relations, see Stuart Ewen: *PR!: A Social History of Spin*, New York 1987, as well as the BBC television series *The Century of the Self* by Adam Curtis (GB 2002).

36. See also Gregory Bateson: *Steps to an Ecology of Mind*, San Francisco 1972, pp. 484–493.

37. George Orwell: "The Freedom of the Press," in: *Animal Farm*, London 1976.

38. See Edward S. Herman, Noam Chomsky: *Manufacturing Consent. The Political Economy of the Mass Media*, New York 1988. The "propaganda model" developed by Herman and Chomsky for the functioning of mass media in "democracies" describes a series of economic and ideological filters that ensure that certain kinds of information are widely disseminated and others are not. In addition to the filters of property, revenue structure and news sources, there is also what Herman and Chomsky call "flak," in other words, the attacks by powerful interest groups that journalists fear, whether in the form of lawsuits, campaigns or calls to the editor-in-chief. Those who wish to avoid receiving "flak" prefer to write that which has always been accepted without contradiction.

39. An excellent portrayal of these events can be found in Sebastian Haffner: *Failure of a Revolution: Germany 1918–1919*, San Francisco 1973 (German: *Der Verrat. 1918/19 – als Deutschland wurde, wie es ist*, Berlin 1993 [1968]).

40. See Gerhard Feldbauer: *Wie Italien unter die Räuber fiel. Und wie die Linke nur schwer mit ihnen fertig wurde*, Cologne 2011.

41. Press conference in Rome, January 1927, quote from Martin Gilbert: *Winston S. Churchill, Vol. 5: The Prophet of Truth, 1922–1939*, Hillsdale (MI) 2009, p. 226.

42. *The London Times*, November 7, 1938.

43. George Orwell: *Homage to Catalonia*, London 1938, ch. 1, online version at: www.telelib.com/authors/O/OrwellGeorge/prose/HomageToCatalonia/catalonia_ch_1.html

44. Anthony Beevor: *The Battle for Spain: The Spanish Civil War 1936–1939*, London 2006, p. 138. The quote is by José Maria Doussinague, an undersecretary in the foreign office.

45. In Italy, for instance, the fascists were supported by Giovanni Agnelli (Fiat), Guido Donegani (Banca Italiana Commerciale) and the tire manufacturer Alberto Pirelli. See Gerhard Feldbauer: *Wie Italien unter die Räuber fiel. Und wie die Linke nur schwer mit ihnen fertig wurde*, Cologne 2011.

46. The "Industrielleneingabe" (industrial petition) was signed by, among others, former (and later) Reichsbank President Hjalmar Schacht, Fritz Thyssen as well as leading representatives of Commerzbank, AEG, Wintershall and Merck.

47. The invitation was accepted by Günther Quandt (AFA/Varta, founder of the Quandt-Klatten empire, which owns about half of BMW), Fritz von Opel, Gustav Krupp von Bohlen und Halbach, Friedrich Flick, Hugo Stinnes Jr. (Reichsverband der Deutschen Industrie) and leading representatives from IG Farben, Allianz AG, Siemens AG and Hoesch AG. This meeting was quite successful for the NSDAP, with some 2 million Reichsmarks flowing into its account from, among others, AEG, Telefunken, Osram, IG Farben and the mining sector. Goebbels then noted: "We are raising a very large sum for the election, which will relieve all of our money worries in one fell swoop. I will immediately notify the entire propaganda apparatus, and an hour later the rotary presses will be rattling away. We will now operate at full capacity. If there are no unexpected breakdowns, then we have already won all across the board." (Elke Fröhlich: *Die Tagebücher von Joseph Goebbels*, part 1, vol. 2, Munich 1987, p. 380).

48. Among the "Circle of Friends of the Economy," also known as "Freundeskreis Reichsführer SS" or "Freundeskreis Himmler," were, for example: Karl Blessing (Unilever, from 1958–1969 head of the Deutsche Bundesbank), Rudolf Binge (Siemens-Halske), Friedrich Flick (Mitteldeutsche Stahlwerke), Karl Ritter von Halt (Deutsche Bank), Richard Kaselowsky (Dr. Oetker), Karl Lindemann (Dresdner Bank), Friedrich Reinhart (Commerzbank), Hellmut Röhnert

(Rheinmetall-Borsig), Heinrich Bütefisch (IG Farben). AEG, Thyssen, AFA (today's Varta) and Osram had contributed funds to the NSDAP already in February and March of 1933, as had Kurt Schmitt, board member of Allianz AG (documented in lists from the IG Farben trials). Heinrich Mohn (Bertelsmann) was a "supporting member of the SS." Franz Josef Popp, general director of BMW, became an NSDAP member in 1933. Ferdinand Porsche and Günther Quandt (BMW) were "Wehrwirtschaftsführer" (leading war-effort industrialists). About the role played by Daimler-Benz, see the extensive study by Karl-Heinz Roth: *Das Daimler-Benz-Buch. Ein Rüstungskonzern im "Tausendjährigen Reich,"* Nördlingen 1987.

49. Note by Undersecretary Pünder on the financing of the NSDAP, April 16, 1932, from the files of the Reich Chancellery, www.bundesarchiv. de/aktenreichskanzlei/1919–1933/1021/bru/bru3p/kap1_1/para2_208. html.

50. Annie Lacroix-Riz: "Louis Renault et 'la fabrication de chars pour la Wehrmacht'," in: *Le Grand Soir,* March 12, 2011.

51. The origins of anti-Judaism and anti-Semitism can be traced back to the Gospel of Matthew ("His blood is on us and on our children!", Mt 27:25). See John Dominic Crossan: *Who Killed Jesus? Exposing the Roots of Anti-Semitism in the Gospel Story of the Death of Jesus,* San Francisco 1995.

52. See also: Zygmunt Bauman: *Modernity and the Holocaust,* Ithaca (NY) 1989.

Chapter 10

1. Lewis Mumford: "The Premonitions of Leonardo da Vinci," in: *New York Book Review,* December 29, 1966.

2. Arms Control Association: *The Nuclear Testing Tally,* www. armscontrol.org/factsheets/nucleartesttally.

3. Joachim Radkau: *Nature and Power: A Global History of the Environment,* Cambridge (MA) 2008, p. 258.

4. During the Algerian struggle for independence, approximately 2 million Algerians were forcibly interned by the French occupying

forces, countless numbers of whom were tortured (Martin Evans: *Algeria: France's Undeclared War*, Oxford 2012, pp. 249–255). The systematic "disappearance" of political opponents, their torture and secret murder later became collectively known as the "French Doctrine" and was used as a model by many Latin American dictatorships. (About the practice of torture at sea: Pierre Vidal-Naquet, *Les crimes de l'armée française. Algérie 1954–1962*, Paris 2001, and Frantz Fanon: *Les damnés de la terre*, Paris 2002 [1961].) Since 2000, French officers have publicly admitted to their involvement in torture and mass executions (see the interview with General Paul Aussaresses in *Le Monde*, September 13, 2000).

5. Adam Jones: *Genocide: A Comprehensive Introduction*, Oxford 2010, p. 46.

6. General Curtis LeMay, then head of the Strategic Air Command during the Korean War, said on the record: "Over a period of three years or so, we killed off 20 percent of the population." Dean Rusk, a war hawk and later Secretary of State, added: "We bombed everything that moved in North Korea, every brick standing on top of another." When the cities had all been wiped out, and the US could no longer find any more to bomb, they began to blow up dams and flood the fields, which led to massive famine. See: Blaine Harden: "The US war crime North Korea won't forget," *Washington Post*, March 24, 2015.

7. About the consequences of industrial agriculture, see the epoch-making book *Silent Spring* by the biologist Rachel Carson, which in 1962 provided a decisive impulse for the emergence of the environmental movement in the US. Carson pointed out that the widespread use of "biocides" such as DDT was eradicating a significant portion of the flora and fauna.

8. Anthony D. Barnosky et al.: "Has the Earth's sixth mass extinction already arrived?", in: *Nature*, vol. 471, March 3, 2011, pp. 51–57.

9. World Resources Institute.

10. Hannah Arendt: *Besuch in Deutschland*, Berlin 1993 [New York 1950].

11. Ibid., p. 48ff. and p. 217.

12. The first purely electronic universal computer, the ENIAC, was commissioned by the US Army in 1942 and was used to calculate ballistic tables. Harvard Mark I, developed by IBM, went into operation in 1944 and, among other applications, was used in the Manhattan Project to calculate implosions. Meanwhile, Konrad Zuse built the first European computers in Germany, the Z3 and Z4. The bipolar transistor was developed for use in radar equipment.

13. WHO: *Global status report on road safety*, Geneva 2013.

14. Illich writes: "The model American male [...] spends four of his sixteen waking hours on the road or gathering his resources for it. [...] In countries deprived of a transportation industry [...] people allocate only 3 to 8 per cent of their society's time budget to traffic instead of 28 per cent" (*Energy and Equity*, London 1974, pp. 30–31).

15. In 1950, a court found the companies to be guilty of a "criminal conspiracy," but they came away with a ludicrous fine of only 5000 dollars. See Stephen B. Goddard: *Getting There: The Epic Struggle Between Road and Rail in the American Century*, Chicago 1996.

16. See Wolfgang Sachs: *Die Liebe zum Automobil. Ein Rückblick in die Geschichte unserer Wünsche*, Reinbek 1984.

17. About "planned obsolescence" see the documentary film *Prêt à jeter* by Cosima Dannoritzer (France/Spain 2010), also Giles Slade: *Made to Break: Technology and Obsolescence in America*, Cambridge (MA) 2007.

18. Quote from the BBC documentary series *The Century of the Self* by Adam Curtis (GB 2002).

19. Joseph A. Schumpeter: *Business Cycles: A Theoretical, Historical, and Statistical Analysis of the Capitalist Process*, New York/London 1939, p. 484.

20. Robert F. Kennedy: *Remarks at the University of Kansas*, March 18, 1968, quote from the John F. Kennedy Library, online at: www.jfklibrary.org/learn/about-jfk/the-kennedy-family/robert-f-kennedy/robert-f-kennedy-speeches/remarks-at-the-university-of-kansas-march-18-1968.

21. Matthias Schmelzer: *The Hegemony of Growth: The OECD and the Making of the Economic Growth Paradigm*, Cambridge 2017.

22. Gene Sharp: *Gandhi Wields the Weapon of Moral Power: Three Case Histories*, with a foreword by Albert Einstein, Ahmedabad 1960, pp. 128–129.

23. Harry S. Truman: *Inaugural Address*, January 20, 1949, online at: https://avalon.law.yale.edu/20th_century/truman.asp. See also Arturo Escobar: *Encountering Development. The Making and Unmaking of the Third World*, Princeton 1995, p. 3f.

24. J. L. Sadie: "The Social Anthropology of Economic Underdevelopment," in: *The Economic Journal*, no. 70, London 1961.

25. About the history and criticism of the ideology and practice of "development," see Arturo Escobar: *Encountering Development. The Making and Unmaking of the Third World*, Princeton 1995; Majid Rahnema (ed.): *The Post-Development Reader*, Dhaka 1997 and Wolfgang Sachs, Gustavo Esteva: *Des ruines du développement*, Paris 1996.

26. Arundhati Roy: "The Greater Common Good," in: *The End of Imagination*, Chicago 2016, pp. 107–150.

27. See Yang Jisheng: *Tombstone: The Untold Story of Mao's Great Famine*, London 2012.

28. A differentiated (in some places also apologetic) analysis of the Cultural Revolution, which addresses both destructive and constructive aspects, is offered by Mobo Gao: *The Battle for China's Past. Mao and the Cultural Revolution*, London 2008.

29. According to Gregory Bateson, "double bind" describes a communicative situation in which a "sender" sends out contradictory demands that put the "recipient" in an existential dilemma. If he fulfills requirement #1 he cannot fulfill requirement #2, and vice versa, which in any case results in a penalty.

30. In 2009, with the release of the relevant archive materials, President Obama officially admitted US participation in the 1953 coup. In 2013, the CIA also admitted its involvement after denying it for 60 years (Malcolm Bryne: *CIA Admits It Was Behind Iran's Coup*, Foreign Policy, March 18, 2013).

31. Naomi Klein: *The Shock Doctrine: The Rise of Disaster Capitalism*, New York 2007, p. 59.

32. The Comisión para el Esclarecimiento Histórico, appointed by the UN, stated in its final report on the Guatemalan civil war in 1999 that the military government was responsible for 93 percent of the more than 200,000 war victims.

33. After Lumumba was elected, the Belgians' first step was to occupy the Katanga mining region with a mercenary force and proclaim it an independent state. When Lumumba asked the UN and US for military aid, he was refused. He then turned to the Soviet Union, which finally sent military advisors and weapons, prompting the US government to work with Belgian intelligence to assassinate Lumumba. See Leo Zeilig: *Lumumba: Africa's Lost Leader*, London 2015; David Renton, David Seddon, Leo Zeilig: *Congo: Plunder and Resistance,* London/ New York 2007; as well as the documentary film *Mord im Kolonialstil* by Thomas Giefer (Germany 2000).

34. http://history.state.gov/historicaldocuments/frus1964-68v23. Already in 1975, the former minute-taker of the White House, Robert Johnson, revealed in an interview by staff of a Senate intelligence committee, that Eisenhower had ordered the assassination of Patrice Lumumba in August 1960 (The Guardian, August 10, 2000)..

35. Naomi Klein: *The Shock Doctrine: The Rise of Disaster Capitalism*, p. 67.

36. See also the documentary film: *The Act of Killing* by Joshua Oppenheimer (Denmark/Norway/GB 2012).

37. Vijay Prashad: *The Darker Nations. A People's History of the Third World*, New York 2007, p. 154 f.

38. Naomi Klein: *The Shock Doctrine*, p. 69

39. *Time Magazine*, February 16, 1970.

40. Brian Glick: *War at Home: Covert Action Against U.S. Activists and What We Can Do About It*, New York 1989.

41. See Dario Azzellini: "Bomben für das System – Die 'Strategie der Spannung'," in: *Italien. Genua. Geschichte, Perspektiven*, Berlin 2002, as well as the ZDF documentary film: *Stay behind: Die Schattenkrieger der NATO* by Ulrich Stoll (Germany 2014).

42. Gunther Latsch: "Die dunkle Seite des Westens," in: *Der Spiegel* April 11, 2005.

43. *Official Journal of the European Communities* no. C 324 from December 24, 1990, p. 202.

44. According to surveys, 41 percent of the US population still expressed "great confidence" in their government in 1966, compared with only 19 percent in 1973. In the same period, confidence in large companies fell from 55 to 29 percent, and confidence in the army from 62 to 27 percent. By contrast, confidence in the media rose from 25 to 41 percent. Almost two-thirds of young people believed that parties must be fundamentally reformed or even abolished. Michel J. Crozier, Samuel Huntington, Joji Watanuki: *The Crisis of Democracy. Report on the Governability of Democracies to the Trilateral Commission*, New York 1975, p. 83.

45. Donella Meadows, Dennis Meadows, Jørgen Randers: *Limits to Growth: The 30-Year Update*, White River Junction (VT) 2004; Ugo Bardi: *The Limits to Growth Revisited*, New York 2011.

46. The deterministic and mechanistic notions of nature had already been shaken by quantum physics since the 1920s. It was not until the 1970s, however, that such ideas found interest in wider circles.

47. About "black pedagogy" see Katharina Rutschky: *Schwarze Pädagogik. Quellen zur Naturgeschichte der bürgerlichen Erziehung*, Berlin 1977, as well as Alice Miller: *For Your Own Good: Hidden Cruelty in Child-Rearing and the Roots of Violence*, New York 1980.

48. Michel J. Crozier, Samuel Huntington, Joji Watanuki: *The Crisis of Democracy. Report on the Governability of Democracies to the Trilateral Commission*, New York 1975, p. 98.

49. Ibid., p. 12.

50. Ibid., p. 114.

51. Ibid., p. 7.

52. Ibid., p. 181.

53. Huntington was close to the Democratic Party and was a security advisor in the government of Jimmy Carter (1977–1981). A substantial portion of the Carter administration was recruited from members of the Trilateral Commission. The Commission's work does not reflect any extreme right-wing positions, but rather the "liberal" mainstream.

54. In the 1920s, the income of the richest 0.1 percent of the population in the USA and Europe accounted for about 8 percent of the gross domestic product, compared with only 2 percent in the mid-1970s. The share of national wealth among the super-rich had also fallen from 50 to almost 20 percent. The neoliberal reaction succeeded in restoring pre-war conditions by the end of the 1980s. David Harvey: *A Brief History of Neoliberalism*, Oxford 2005, p. 15ff.

55. *New York Times*, December 31, 2006.

56. David Harvey: *A Brief History of Neoliberalism*, Oxford 2005, pp. 45–48.

57. See Immanuel Wallerstein: "Structural Crisis, or Why Capitalists May No Longer Find Capitalism Rewarding," in *Does Capitalism Have a Future?*, Oxford 2013, pp. 21–31.

58. Timothy Curry and Linn Shibut: "The Cost of the Savings and Loan Crisis," in: *FDIC Banking Review*, vol. 13, no. 2, Arlington 2000.

59. Allende had been elected with a program that provided for the nationalization of the mining sector and central infrastructures, many of which were in the hands of US companies such as ITT. A US Senate report later revealed that ITT then drew up an 18-point plan for President Nixon, advising him to "get to reliable sources within the Chilean military, build up their planned discontent against Allende, thus, bring about necessity of his removal." Naomi Klein: *The Shock Doctrine: The Rise of Disaster Capitalism*, p. 65.

60. About the neoliberal reconstruction of higher education, see Henry A. Giroux: *Neoliberalism's War against Higher Education*, Chicago 2014.

61. Naomi Klein: *The Shock Doctrine: The Rise of Disaster Capitalism*, p. 229.

62. See also David Harvey: *A Brief History of Neoliberalism*, pp. 121–151.

63. Ibid., pp. 257–267.

64. Ibid., p. 6; Naomi Klein: *The Shock Doctrine: The Rise of Disaster Capitalism*, p. 325–340.

65. Vijay Prashad: *The Darker Nations. A People's History of the Third World*, New York 2007, p. 276.

66. For credits totaling 540 billion US dollars, the 60 poorest countries in the world paid 530 billion US dollars in interest and loan repayments between 1970 and 2000. Nevertheless, the total amount owed from

these loans remains 523 billion US dollars—a case of true financial "alchemy," as Vijay Prashad (ibid.) notes.

67. David Harvey: *A Brief History of Neoliberalism*, p. 23.

68. By 2000, world market prices for food, tea, coffee and tobacco had fallen to only one-sixth of their peak value in 1975 and those for industrial raw materials had fallen to one-third. See: Bundeszentrale für politische Bildung: www.bpb.de/nachschlagen/zahlen-und-fakten/globalisierung/52664/rohstoffpreise. However, this trend has been reversed since the beginning of the new millennium.

69. David Harvey: *A Brief History of Neoliberalism*, p. 100.

70. Charles Bowden: *Murder City. Ciudad Juárez and the Global Economy's New Killing Fields*, New York 2011.

71. Samuel Huntington: "The Clash of Civilizations," in: *Foreign Affairs*, Summer 1993; about Huntington's role, see also Michael Hardt, Antonio Negri: *Multitude: War and Democracy in the Age of Empire*, New York 2004, p. 33–35.

72. See Edward Said: *Orientalism*, New York 1968, as well as Immanuel Wallerstein: *European Universalism*, New York 2006, pp. 31–49.

73. See Randall Collins: "The End of Middle-Class Work," in: *Does Capitalism Have a Future?*, Oxford 2013, pp. 37–69.

74. Hans-Peter Martin, Harald Schumann: *The Global Trap: Globalization and the Assault on Prosperity and Democracy*, London 1997, p. 14. Today, only a quarter of the world's working population has what we would call a permanent job, i.e. a stable employment relationship, and the trend is downward. In most African countries, only 20 percent of people who are capable of working have any sort of employment. (ILO: World Employment Social Outlook 2015: *The Changing Nature of Jobs*, Executive Summary, p. 3).

75. See the Kontext TV interview with the former Malian minister of culture Aminata Traoré: *Der Fall Mali: Wie 30 Jahre Neoliberalismus den Boden für den Krieg bereiteten*, www.kontext-tv.de/en/node/2551.

76. See Jeremy Scahill: *Blackwater: The Rise of the World's Most Powerful Mercenary Army*, New York 2007; Peter W. Singer: *Corporate Warriors: The Rise of the Privatized Military Industry*, Ithaca (NY) 2004.

77. *Der Standard*, September 13, 2003.

78. See Ugo Bardi: *Extracted: How the Quest for Mineral Wealth Is Plundering the Planet*, White River Junction (VT) 2014.

79. Tilman Santarius et al. (ed.): *Rethinking Climate and Energy Policies: New Perspectives on the Rebound Phenomenon*, New York 2016.

80. See Joan Martinez-Alier: *Ecological Economics, Energy, Environment and Society*, New York 1987.

81. Jared Diamond: *Collapse: How Societies Choose to Fail or Succeed*, New York 2005.

82. *The Guardian*, November 6, 2018.

83. David Montgomery: *Dirt: The Erosion of Civilizations*, Berkeley 2007, p. 236.

84. About the global water crisis, see Maude Barlow, Tony Clarke: *Blue Gold: The Battle Against Corporate Theft of the World's Water*, Toronto 2002, as well as Maude Barlow: *Blue Covenant: The Global Water Crisis and the Fight for the Right to Water*, Toronto 2007.

85. *Die Zeit*, April 23, 2014, citing the annual report by the Chinese Ministry of the Environment.

86. Stefan Rahmstorf, head of the Earth System Analysis Department at the Potsdam Institute for Climate Impact Research (PIK), in an interview with Fabian Scheidler, Kontext TV, June 14, 2018, www. kontext-tv.de/de/node/2894.

87. Graham Turner: *Is Global Collapse Imminent? An Updated Comparison of The Limits to Growth with Historical Data*, University of Melbourne, research paper no. 4, August 2014; Lloyd's Emerging Risk Report 2015: *Food System Shock. The Insurance Impacts of Acute Disruption to Global Food Supply*, London 2015.

Chapter 11

1. See Joseph A. Tainter: *The Collapse of Complex Societies*, Cambridge 1988.

2. Interview with Immanuel Wallerstein on Kontext TV, June 29, 2011, www.kontext-tv.de/en/broadcasts/immanuel-wallerstein-limits-capitalism.

3. See John Holloway: *Crack Capitalism*, London 2010.
4. See also J. K. Gibson-Graham: *The End of Capitalism (as we knew it)*, Hoboken 1996; and *Postcapitalist Politics*, Minneapolis 2006.
5. See also the concept of "interstitial transformation" in Eric Olin Wright: *Envisioning Real Utopias*, London/New York 2010.
6. A worldwide overview of remunicipalization in the water sector is online at: www.remunicipalisation.org
7. Successful initiatives against land grabbing are documented in: "GRAIN," Joan Martinez-Alier et al.: *The Many Faces of Land Grabbing*, EJOLT Report No. 10, 2014.
8. Mietshäusersyndikat (apartment-house syndicate): www.syndikat. org/en/.
9. Lynda Sullivan: *Peru's Conga Mine Conflict: Cajamarca Won't Capitulate*, http://upsidedownworld.org/main/peru-archives-76/4823-perus-conga-mine-conflict-cajamarca-wont-capitulate, May 1, 2014.
10. The occupation protests in the German lignite mining areas are organized by the international network "Ende Gelände," among others: www.ende-gelaende.org/en/.
11. Naomi Klein: *This Changes Everything. Capitalism vs. the Climate*, New York 2014, pp. 337–366.
12. Ibid., p. 97ff.
13. Japan, for example, now spends more than half of its tax revenues on debt servicing (*Neue Zürcher Zeitung*, January 29, 2013).
14. Laura Gottesdiener: "The Great Eviction. The landscape of Wall Street's creative destruction," in: *The Nation*, August 1, 2013. See also Saskia Sassen: *Expulsions. Brutality and Complexity in the Global Economy*, Cambridge (MA)/London 2014.
15. In Europe, the structural violence of debt is strikingly evident in the case of Greece. With the open threat to collapse the banking system and thus the country's entire economy, creditors have put the left-wing government, elected in 2015, in a hopeless situation. Its only choice was between immediate collapse and a total sell-out of the country. As was the case in numerous African, Latin American and Asian countries in the 1980s and 1990s, debt is being used by creditors

to eliminate political self-determination and destroy hard-won social rights.

16. See the interview with Ecuador's former foreign minister Ricardo Patiño on Kontext TV, November 4, 2011: www.kontext-tv.de/node/2429. The government-appointed National Debt Commission classified a portion of the debt as "illegitimate" because it had been acquired under a military government that was not democratically legitimate. Furthermore, the debt conditions were extremely disadvantageous and the money was not used for the benefit of the citizens. Although, since 2004, Argentina had already chosen a similar path to Ecuador, so-called "vulture funds" later bought up parts of this debt at junk prices and are currently trying through court action to be paid the full amount.

17. Even the IMF and the EU Commission are considering a wealth levy. See IMF Fiscal Monitor: *Taxing Times*, October 2013, p. 49. The management consultancy Boston Consulting also advocates a drastic debt cut through taxation of large assets. A third method of debt reduction would be controlled inflation, but so far there have been few advocates for this.

18. US President Franklin D. Roosevelt's corresponding decree is known as Executive Order 6102, dated April 5, 1933.

19. The cooperative's website URL is: http://cooperativa.cat. See also the interview with Ariadna Serra on Kontext TV: www.kontext-tv.de/node/2687. Cooperatives have a long tradition in Spain. The world's largest cooperative, Mondragón, with around 80,000 members, is located in Basque Country. For a (partly critical) discussion on Mondragón see J. K. Gibson-Graham: *Postcapitalist Politics*, Minneapolis 2006, pp. 101–126.

20. See the interview with Euclides Mance of the Brasilian network Solidarius on Kontext TV: www.kontext-tv.de/node/2687.

21. The much-quoted essay "The Tragedy of the Commons" by Garret Hardin is based on this error ("The Tragedy of the Commons," in: *Science* no. 162, 1968, pp. 1243–1248).

22. Elinor Ostrom: *Governing the Commons: The Evolution of Institutions*

for Collective Action, Cambridge 2015; here is a summary of core principles for successful commons management provided by Silke Helfrich et al.: *The Wealth of the Commons: A World Beyond Market & State*, Amherst (MA) 2013.

23. Michel Bauwens, Franco Iacomella: "Peer-to-Peer Economy and New Civilization Centered Around the Sustenance of the Commons," in: Silke Helfrich et al.: *The Wealth of the Commons: A World Beyond Market & State*, Amherst (MA) 2013, pp. 323–330.

24. See Bernhard Knierim: *Essen im Tank. Warum Biosprit und Elektroantrieb den Klimawandel nicht aufhalten*, Vienna 2013.

25. About the future of mobility, see: *Zukunftsfähiges Deutschland in einer globalisierten Welt*, a study by the Wuppertal Institut für Klima, Umwelt, Energie, Frankfurt (Main). 2008, pp. 586–597; Harald Welzer, Stephan Rammler: *Der Futurzwei Zukunftsalmanach 2013*, Frankfurt/M. 2012, pp. 305–350.

26. Rob Hopkins: *The Transition Handbook. From Oil Dependency to Local Resilience*, Dartington (Devon) 2008, p. 55f. Among other things, the transition movement is based on the concepts of permaculture. An introduction is offered by: Rosemary Morrow: *Earth User's Guide to Permaculture*, East Meon (Hampshire) 2006.

27. See the interview with Tim Jackson on Kontext TV: www.kontext-tv.de/en/node/2358; also Tim Jackson: *Prosperity Without Growth: Economics for a Finite Planet*, London/New York 2009.

28. Christian Felber: *Change Everything: Creating an Economy for the Common Good*, London 2015. The Economy for the Common Good also provides for a change in the ownership and decision-making structures of companies. Profits may only be reinvested for the promotion of the common good or distributed to employees, but not to shareholders. Beyond a certain size, companies become the property of their employees.

29. The French décroissance movement puts forth an interesting proposal for an infrastructural basic income, which is partly provided in the form of free municipal services and allows people to become participants in self-organized structures. See Vincent Liegey et al.:

Un projet de Décroissance, Manifeste pour une Dotation Inconditionnelle d'Autonomie, Paris 2013.

30. www.worldenergyoutlook.org/resources/energysubsidies/.

31. About subsidizing major banks, see the report of the New Economics Foundation: *Quid pro Quo. Redressing the Privileges of the Banking Industry*, London 2011. For British big banks alone, the NEF arrives at a subsidy total of 46 billion pounds *per year*.

32. About the so-called "carbon bubble," see: Bill McKibben: "Global Warming's Terrifying New Math," in: *Rolling Stone*, July 19, 2012; Carbon Tracker Initiative: *Unburnable Carbon — Are the World's Financial Markets Carrying a Carbon Bubble?*, London 2012, www. carbontracker.org/report/carbon-bubble.

33. Uruguay, for example, has already been sentenced to pay millions to the tobacco company Philip Morris because the local government has enacted strict anti-smoking laws. See Lori Wallach: "TAFTA/TTIP — die große Unterwerfung," in: *Le Monde diplomatique*, November 8, 2013.

34. Paul Tucker, vice-governor of the Bank of England, and Martin Gruenberg, head of the US deposit insurance fund FDIC, presented a concept for the orderly insolvency of major banks in 2012. See the documentary film *Staatsgeheimnis Bankenrettung* von Harald Schumann (Germany 2013).

35. Philipp Hersel and Axel Troost drafted a concept for the German Left Party in 2010 for the socialization of German banks that was based on the two pillars "public savings banks" and "cooperative banks": *Den Bankensektor neu ordnen und mit der Vergesellschaftung beginnen*, www. axel-troost.de.

36. Activists from the organization UK Uncut, for example, occupied branches of companies such as Vodafone, which de facto do not pay taxes (*The Guardian*, June 15, 2014). In 2011, several hundred thousand people took to the streets in London against social cuts and tax evasion: www.kontext-tv.de/en/node/2365.

37. BBC, November 7, 2012, www.bbc.com/news/world-latin-america-20246295. Since then, the legal dispute has continued before various courts.

38. See Colin Crouch: *Post-democracy*, Cambridge 2005.

39. In various rulings, the Supreme Court relaxed the limits on campaign contributions by individuals and companies to the extent that companies can de facto buy off congressmen and entire campaigns. See *New York Times*, April 2, 2014, and Noam Chomsky's comment on the "Citizen United" ruling, in: *In These Times*, January 21, 2010. Oil Change International documents the flow of campaign contributions from the oil, gas and coal industries and the associated voting behavior of MPs: dirtyenergymoney.org.

40. In the Greek crisis, these institutions, together with the IMF, blatantly established a dictatorship of creditors and downgraded Greece to a neo-colonial protectorate whose government and parliament have only one function: to execute orders from Berlin, Brussels, Frankfurt and Washington. See the interview with Yanis Varoufakis on Kontext TV, February 15, 2016: www.kontext-tv.de/en/node/2768.

41. See David Shearman, Joseph Wayne Smith: *The Climate Change Challenge and the Failure of Democracy*, Santa Barbara 2007; James Lovelock, known for the co-development of the Gaia hypothesis, said in an interview that "it may be necessary to put democracy on hold for a while" in order to enforce climate protection (*The Guardian*, March 29, 2010).

42. About India, see Aseem Shrivastava, Ashish Kothari: *Churning the Earth. The Making of Global India*; Vandana Shiva: *Earth Democracy: Justice, Sustainability, and Peace*, New York 2005. About the "African Spring" (which was overshadowed by the "Arab Spring" and widely disregarded by the Western media) see the interviews with Aziz Fall and Firoze Manji on Kontext TV: www.kontext-tv.de/en/node/2549.

43. About the theoretical proposals for a reorganization of democracy, see, for example, David Van Reybrouck: *Against Elections: The Case for Democracy*, London 2016; Takis Fotopoulos: *Towards an Inclusive Democracy. The Crisis of the Growth Economy and the Need for a New Liberatory Project*, London/New York 1997.

44. On the topicality of the council principle, see Michael Albert: *Parecon: Life After Capitalism*, London/New York 2004.

45. Both the imprisoned Kurdish leader Abdullah Öcalan and the Kurds of Northern Syria refer conceptually to the works of Murray Bookchin. See, for instance, Janet Biehl, Murray Bookchin: *The Politics of Social Ecology: Libertarian Municipalism*, Montreal 1997; Murray Bookchin: *The Next Revolution: Popular Assemblies and the Promise of Direct Democracy*, London/New York 2015.

46. The figures for the increase are adjusted for inflation. Stockholm International Peace Research Institute, 2013.

47. Sonic cannons have apparently already been used in the evacuation of Occupy camps in Oakland and New York City (see Adam Martin: "Occupy Oakland's Tent City is Gone," in: *The Wire*, October 25, 2011).

48. About the arming of police in the US, see Radley Balko: *The Rise of the Warrior Cop. The Militarization of America's Police Forces*, New York 2013.

49. International Network of Civil Liberties Organizations: *Take Back the Streets. Repression and Criminalization of Protest around the World* (2013), download at: www.aclu.org/sites/default/files/assets/global_protest_suppression_report_inclo.pdf.

50. *The Guardian*, December 29, 2012. The documents have been published online by the organization *Partnership for Civil Justice Fund* at: www.justiceonline.org/commentary/fbi-files-ows.html.

51. Michel J. Crozier, Samuel Huntington, Joji Watanuki: *The Crisis of Democracy. Report on the Governability of Democracies to the Trilateral Commission*, New York 1975, p. 99.

52. *The Guardian*, December 7, 2012.

53. Immanuel Wallerstein: "Structural Crisis, or Why Capitalists May no longer Find Capitalism Rewarding," in *Does Capitalism Have a Future?*, Oxford 2013, p. 31.

54. See Giovanni Arrighi: *Adam Smith in Beijing: Lineages of the 21st Century*, London/New York 2009; Fabian Scheidler: *Chaos. Das neue Zeitalter der Revolutionen*, Vienna 2017.

55. About the consequences of the "Green Revolution" and genetic engineering, see Christoph Then, Runa Boeddinghaus: *Industrielle*

Landwirtschaft in der Sackgasse, a study commissioned by the Green Party/Europäische Freie Allianz, Wiesbaden 2014. About geoengineering, see Naomi Klein: *This Changes Everything. Capitalism vs. the Climate,* New York 2014, pp. 256–291; Pat Mooney: *Next Bang! Wie das riskante Spiel mit Megatechnologien unsere Existenz bedroht,* Munich 2010, pp. 145–159.

56. See E. F. Schumacher: *Small is Beautiful. Economics as if People Mattered. 25 Years Later,* Vancouver 1999.

57. Ivan Illich: *Tools for Conviviality,* London/New York 1973.

58. Stephen Lansing: *Perfect Order: Recognizing Complexity in Bali,* Princeton 2012; also *Priests and Programmers. Technologies of Power in the Engineered Landscape of Bali,* Princeton 1991.

59. whc.unesco.org/en/list/1194.

Selected Bibliography

1. Power

Guillermo Algaze: *Ancient Mesopotamia at the Dawn of Civilization*, Chicago 2008.

Karen Armstrong: *The Great Transformation. The World in the Time of Buddha, Socrates, Confucius and Jeremiah*, London 2007.

Johan Galtung: "Violence, peace and peace research," in: *Journal of Peace Research*, vol. 6, no. 3 (1969).

The Epic of Gilgamesh, translated by Andrew George, London 1999.

Michael Hudson (ed.): *Privatization in the Ancient Near East and Classical World*, Cambridge (MA) 1996.

Samuel N. Kramer: *History Begins at Sumer: Thirty-Nine Firsts in Man's Recorded History*, Philadelphia 1981.

Michael Mann: *The Sources of Social Power, Volume 1: A History of Power from the Beginning to AD 1760*, Cambridge 1986.

Marshall Sahlins: *Stone Age Economics*, New York 1972.

James C. Scott: *Against the Grain. A Deep History of the Earliest States*, New Haven 2017.

Leften Stavros Stavianos: *A Global History: From Prehistory to the Present*, Upper Saddle River (NJ) 1994.

Max Weber: *Wirtschaft und Gesellschaft: Grundriss der verstehenden Soziologie*, Leipzig 2005 [1922].

David Wengrow: *What Makes Civilization? The Ancient Near East and the Future of the West*, New York 2010.

Ina Wunn: *Die Religionen in vorgeschichtlicher Zeit*, Stuttgart 2005.

2. Metal

Ugo Bardi: *Extracted: How the Quest for Mineral Wealth Is Plundering the Planet*, White River Junction (VT) 2014.

J. Donald Hughes: "Environmental Impacts of the Roman Economy and Social Structure," in: Alf Hornburg et al. (ed.):

Rethinking Environmental History: World-System History and Global Environmental Change, Lanham (MD) 2007.

Pat Mooney: *Next Bang. Wie das riskante Spiel mit Megatechnologien unsere Existenz bedroht*, München 2010.

Theodore A. Wertime: "The Furnace versus the Goat: The Pyrotechnologic Industries and Mediterranean Deforestation in Antiquity," in: *Journal of Field Archaeology*, vol. 10, no. 4 (1983).

3. Market

Christian Delacampagne: *Une histoire de l'esclavage: de l'Antiquité à nos jours*, Paris 2002.

David Graeber: *Debt: The First 5,000 Years*, New York 2012.

Geoffrey Ingham: *The Nature of Money. New Directions in Political Economy*, London 2004.

Keith Roberts: *The Origins of Business, Money, and Markets*, New York 2011.

Erica Schoenberger: "The Origins of Market Economy," in: *Comparative Studies in Society and History*, nr. 50 (3), Cambridge 2008.

Richard Seaford: *Money and the Early Greek Mind*, Cambridge 2004.

Adam Smith: *The Wealth of Nations*, New York 1994 [1776].

4. Powerlessness

John D. Crossan: *The Historical Jesus: The Life of a Mediterranean Jewish Peasant*, San Francisco 1993.

—*Who Killed Jesus? Exposing the Roots of Anti-Semitism in the Gospel Story of the Death of Jesus*, San Francisco 1995.

Judith Herman: *Trauma and Recovery: The Aftermath of Violence— from Domestic Abuse to Political Terror*, New York 1992.

Richard A. Horsley: *Jesus and Empire. The Kingdom of God and the New World Disorder*, Minneapolis 2003.

Flavius Josephus: *The Works of Josephus*, Peabody (MA) 1987.

Book of Revelations (The Bible: New International Version [NIV])

Bernd U. Schipper, Georg Plasger (ed.): *Apokalyptik und kein Ende?*, Göttingen 2007.

5. Mission

John Dominic Crossan, Jonathan L. Reed: *In Search of Paul. How Jesus's Apostle Opposed Rome's Empire with God's Kingdom*, San Francisco 2004.

Hyam Maccoby: *The Mythmaker: Paul and the Invention of Christianity*, New York 1987.

Paul's Epistles, especially: *Galatians, Corinthians 1, Romans* (The Bible: New International Version [NIV])

Immanuel Wallerstein: *European Universalism: The Rhetoric of Power*, New York 2006.

6. Monsters

Georgius Agricola: *De Re Metallica*, London 1912 [1556].

Giovanni Arrighi: *The Long Twentieth Century. Money, Power and the Origins of Our Times*, London/New York 2010.

Francis Bacon: "The New Atlantis" [1625], in: *Francis Bacon: The Major Works*, Oxford 2008.

Murray Bookchin: *The Third Revolution. Popular Movements in the Revolutionary Era*, vol. 1, London 1996.

Fernand Braudel: *Civilisation matérielle, économie et capitalisme, XVe–XVIIIe siècles*, 3 volumes, Paris 1979.

—*La dynamique du capitalisme*, Paris 1985.

Bartolomé de las Casas: *A Short Account of the Destruction of the Indies*, translated by Nigel Griffin, London/New York 1992.

Richard Cowen: *Exploiting the Earth*, chs. 8 and 10, http://mygeologypage.ucdavis.edu/cowen//~GEL115/.

Jean Delumeau: *La Peur en Occident (XIVe–XVIIIe siècles)*, Paris 1978.

Silvia Federici: *Caliban and the Witch: Women, the Body and Primitive Accumulation*, New York 2004.

Eduardo Galeano: *Open Veins of Latin America*, London 1973.

André Gunder Frank, Barry K. Gills: *The World System: Five Hundred Years or Five Thousand?*, London 1996.

Stuart Hall: "The West and the Rest," in: Stuart Hall et al. (ed.): *Formations of Modernity*, Oxford 1992.

Hans Christian Huf: *Mit Gottes Segen in die Hölle. Der Dreißigjährige Krieg*, Berlin 2003.

Jürgen Kocka: *Capitalism: A Short History*, Princeton 2017.

Wolfgang König (ed.): *Propyläen Technikgeschichte, Band 2: Metalle und Macht*, Berlin 1997.

Robert Kurz: "Vater Staat und Mutter Krieg. Die Geburt des Geldes," in: *Blätter für deutsche und internationale Politik* 9/2012.

Robert S. Lopez: *The Commercial Revolution of the Middle Ages 950–1350*, Englewood Cliffs (NJ) 1971.

Michael Mann: *The Sources of Social Power, Volume 2: The Rise of Classes and Nation-States, 1760–1914*, Cambridge 1993.

Karl Marx: "Die sogenannte ursprüngliche Akkumulation," in: *Capital*, vol. 1, ch. 24.

Jason W. Moore: "Silver, Ecology, and the Origins of the Modern World, 1450–1640," in: Alf Hornburg et al. (ed.): *Rethinking Environmental History: World-System History and Global Environmental Change*, Lanham (MD) 2007.

Lewis Mumford: *The Myth of the Machine*, 2 volumes, New York 1967/1970.

David E. Stannard: *American Holocaust: The Conquest of the New World*, New York 1992.

— "Uniqueness as Denial: The Politics of Genocide Scholarship," in: Alan S. Rosenbaum (ed): *Is the Holocaust Unique? Perspectives on Comparative Genocide*, Philadelphia 2009.

Janice E. Thomson: *Mercenaries, Pirates and Sovereigns*, Princeton 1996.

Immanuel Wallerstein: *The Modern World-System, vol. I: Capitalist Agriculture and the Origins of the European World-Economy in the Sixteenth Century*, New York 1974.

—*World-Systems Analysis. An Introduction*, Durham 2004.

Lynn White: *"The Historical Roots of Our Ecological Crisis,"* in: *Science*, vol. 155, New York 1967, pp.1203–1207.

Howard Zinn: *A People's History of the United States*, New York 2015 [1980].

7. Machine

Marc Augé: *Non-Lieux, introduction à une anthropologie de la surmodernité*, Paris 1992.

Gregory Bateson: *Mind and Nature*, New York 1979.

Christian Delacampagne: *Une histoire de l'esclavage: de l'Antiquité à nos jours*, Paris 2002.

René Descartes: *Traité de l'homme*, Paris 2018 [1664].

Stillman Drake (ed.): *Discoveries and Opinions of Galileo*, New York 1957.

Michel Foucault: *Discipline and Punish: The Birth of the Prison*, New York 1995 [1977].

Jürgen Habermas: *Technik und Wissenschaft als "Ideologie,"* Frankfurt (Main) 1969.

Robert Kurz: "Die Diktatur der abstrakten Zeit. Arbeit als Verhaltensstörung der Moderne," in: Robert Kurz et al.: *Feierabend! Elf Attacken gegen die Arbeit*, Hamburg 1999.

Karl Marx: "Teilung der Arbeit und Manufaktur," in: *Capital*, vol. 1, ch. 12.

Carolyn Merchant: *The Death of Nature: Women, Ecology, and the Scientific Revolution*, New York 1980.

Ilya Prigogine, Isabelle Stengers: *Order Out of Chaos: Man's New Dialogue with Nature*, London 2018 [1984].

Marcus Rediker: *The Slave Ship. A Human History*, London 2008.

Katharina Rutschky: *Schwarze Pädagogik. Quellen zur Naturgeschichte der bürgerlichen Erziehung*, Berlin 1977.

James C. Scott: *Seeing Like a State. How Certain Schemes to Improve the Human Condition Have Failed*, New Haven 1998.

Otto Ulrich: *Technik und Herrschaft. Vom Handwerk zur*

verdinglichten Blockstruktur industrieller Produktion, Frankfurt (Main) 1979.

Immanuel Wallerstein: *The Modern World-System, vol. II: Mercantilism and the Consolidation of the European World-Economy, 1600–1750*, Cambridge (MA) 1980.

8. Moloch

Benedict Anderson: *Imagined Communities: Reflections on the Origin and Spread of Nationalism*, London/New York 1983.

Giovanni Arrighi: *Adam Smith in Beijing: Lineages of the 21st Century*, London/New York 2009.

Micha Brumlik, Irmtrud Wojak: *Völkermord und Kriegsverbrechen in der ersten Hälfte des 20. Jahrhunderts*, Frankfurt (Main) 2004.

Mike Davis: *Late Victorian Holocausts: El Niño Famines and the Making of the Third World*, London/New York 2002.

Eric Hobsbawm: *Nations and Nationalism Since 1780: Programme, Myth, Reality*, Cambridge 1991.

Wolfgang König (ed.): *Propyläen Technikgeschichte, Band 3, Mechanisierung und Maschinisierung*, Berlin 1997.

Karl Kraus: *Die letzten Tage der Menschheit*, Berlin 1971.

Norman Lewis: *The Missionaries: God Against the Indians*, New York 1988.

Rosa Luxemburg: *Die Akkumulation des Kapitals*, Berlin 1913.

Karl Polanyi: *The Great Transformation*, New York 1944.

David Renton, David Seddon, Leo Zeilig: *Congo: Plunder and Resistance*, London/New York 2007.

Edward Palmer Thompson: *The Making of the English Working Class*, New York 1966.

Flora Tristan: *The London Journal*, London 1982 [1842].

Mark Twain: *King Leopold's Soliloquy*, Philadelphia 1905.

Immanuel Wallerstein: *Historical Capitalism*, London 1983.

—*The Modern World-System, vol. III: The Second Era of Great Expansion of the Capitalist World-Economy, 1730–1840s*, San Diego 1989.

9. Masks

Zygmunt Bauman: *Modernity and the Holocaust*, Ithaca (NY) 2001.

Edward Bernays: *Propaganda*, New York 1928.

Noam Chomsky, Edward S. Herman: *Manufacturing Consent. The Political Economy of the Mass Media*, New York 1988.

Stuart Ewen: *PR!: A Social History of Spin*, New York 1987.

Jürgen Habermas: *Strukturwandel der Öffentlichkeit. Untersuchungen zu einer Kategorie der bürgerlichen Gesellschaft*, Frankfurt (Main) 1990.

Sebastian Haffner: *Failure of a Revolution: Germany 1918–1919*, San Francisco 1973.

Walter Lippmann: *Public Opinion*, New York 1922.

James Madison: *Federalist Paper Number 10* [1787].

Timothy Mitchell: *Carbon Democracy. Political Power in the Age of Oil*, London 2011.

George Orwell: *Homage to Catalonia*, London 1938.

— "The Freedom of the Press," in: *Animal Farm*, London 1945.

Jürgen Osterhammel: *The Transformation of the World: A Global History of the Nineteenth Century*, Princeton 2015.

Immanuel Wallerstein: *The Modern World-System, volume IV: Centrist Liberalism Triumphant, 1789–1914*, Berkeley 2011.

Jean Ziegler: *L'Empire de la honte*, Vanves 2007.

10. Metamorphoses

Ugo Bardi: *The Limits to Growth Revisited*, New York 2011.

Maude Barlow: *Blue Covenant: The Global Water Crisis and the Fight for the Right to Water*, Toronto 2007.

Charles Bowden: *Murder City. Ciudad Juárez and the Global Economy's New Killing Fields*, New York 2011.

Michel J. Crozier, Samuel Huntington, Joji Watanuki: *The Crisis of Democracy. Report on the Governability of Democracies to the Trilateral Commission*, New York 1975.

Jared Diamond: *Collapse: How Societies Choose to Fail or Succeed*, New York 2005.

Arturo Escobar: *Encountering Development. The Making and Unmaking of the Third World*, Princeton 1995.

Frantz Fanon: *The Wretched of the Earth*, New York 1963.

Henry A. Giroux: *Neoliberalism's War against Higher Education*, Chicago 2014.

Michael Hardt, Antonio Negri: *Multitude: War and Democracy in the Age of Empire*, New York 2004.

David Harvey: *A Brief History of Neoliberalism*, Oxford/New York 2005.

Chris Hedges: *Days of Destruction, Days of Revolt*, New York 2012.

Ivan Illich: *Energy and Equity*, Cuernavaca 1974.

Adam Jones (ed.): *Genocide, War Crimes & the West: History and Complicity*, London 2004.

— *Genocide: A Comprehensive Introduction*, New York 2010.

Naomi Klein: *The Shock Doctrine: The Rise of Disaster Capitalism*, New York 2007.

Donella Meadows, Dennis Meadows, Jørgen Randers: *Limits to Growth: The 30-Year Update*, White River Junction (VT) 2004.

David Montgomery: *Dirt: The Erosion of Civilizations*, Berkeley 2007.

Vijay Prashad: *The Darker Nations. A People's History of the Third World*, New York 2007.

Joachim Radkau: *Nature and Power: A Global History of the Environment*, Cambridge (MA) 2008.

Majid Rahnema (ed.): *The Post-Development Reader*, Dhaka 1997.

Arundhati Roy: *The End of Imagination*, Chicago 2016.

Wolfgang Sachs (ed.): *The Development Dictionary: A Guide to Knowledge as Power*, London 1992.

Edward Said: *Orientalism*, New York 1978.

Tilman Santarius et al. (ed.): *Rethinking Climate and Energy Policies: New Perspectives on the Rebound Phenomenon*, New York 2016.

Giles Slade: *Made to Break: Technology and Obsolescence in America*, Cambridge (MA) 2007.

Immanuel Wallerstein, Randall Collins, Michael Mann et al.: *Does Capitalism Have a Future?*, New York 2013.

Leo Zeilig: *Lumumba: Africa's Lost Leader*, London 2015.

11. Possibilities

Colin Crouch: *Post-Democracy*, Cambridge 2004.

Giacomo D'Alisa, Federico DeMaria, Giorgos Kallis: *Degrowth: A Vocabulary for a New Era*, New York 2015.

Christian Felber: *Change Everything: Creating an Economy for the Common Good*, London 2015.

J. K. Gibson-Graham: *Take Back the Economy: An Ethical Guide for Transforming Our Communities*, Minneapolis 2013.

André Gorz: *Ecologica*, Calcutta 2010.

Silke Helfrich et al.: *The Wealth of the Commons: A World Beyond Market & State*, Amherst (MA) 2013.

John Holloway: *Crack Capitalism*, New York 2010.

Rob Hopkins: *The Transition Handbook: From Oil Dependency to Local Resilience*, White River Junction (VT) 2014.

Ivan Illich: *Tools for Conviviality*, New York 1973.

International Network of Civil Liberties Organizations: *Take Back the Streets. Repression and Criminalization of Protest around the World* (2013), download at: www.aclu.org.

Naomi Klein: *This Changes Everything. Capitalism vs. the Climate*, New York 2014.

Stephen Lansing: *Perfect Order: Recognizing Complexity in Bali*, Princeton 2012.

Joan Martinez-Alier: *Ecological Economics, Energy, Environment and Society*, New York 1987.

Elinor Ostrom: *Governing the Commons: The Evolution of Institutions for Collective Action*, Cambridge 2015.

Saskia Sassen: *Expulsions: Brutality and Complexity in the Global Economy*, Cambridge (MA) 2014.

E. F. Schumacher: *Small Is Beautiful: Economics as if People Mattered*, London 1973.

Vandana Shiva: *Earth Democracy: Justice, Sustainability, and Peace,* New York 2005.

Joseph A. Tainter: *The Collapse of Complex Societies,* Cambridge 1988.

Eric Olin Wright: *Envisioning Real Utopias,* London/New York 2010.

Afterword

David Quammen: *Spillover: Animal Infections and the Next Human Pandemic,* New York 2012.

Sonia Shah: *Pandemic: Tracking Contagion from Cholera to Ebola and Beyond,* New York 2016.

Image Sources

P. 15: Mistreated prisoners: Reconstruction of a roll seal from Uruk/Warka (Iraq), ca. 3300 to 3000 BC: Vorderasiatisches Museum Berlin. Photo by the author.

P. 34: Left: Fantasy of the sword Excalibur. Public Domain.
Right: Artillery shell XM932 Excalibur.
© www.globalsecurity.org.

P. 38: Left: Sandro Botticelli: *Hell* (from the Dante Cycle, c. 1485), Vatican Library. Public Domain.
Right: Udachnaya mine, Russia 2004. Photo: Alexander Stapanov, GNU license 1.2.

P. 40: Left: Wagner, Dr. Faust's assistant with homunculus, copper engraving, nineteenth century. Public Domain.
Right: Vision of a test tube baby. © www.imagepoint.biz.

P. 49: Left: Slaves in the Laurion mines, Greece, fifth century BC. Public Domain.
Right: Lydian coin, sixth century BC. Photo: © Andreas Pangerl, www. romancoins.info.

P. 64: Left: Vision of the Celestial Jerusalem, copper engraving, sixteenth century. Photo: Philipp Medhurst, Creative Commons (CC BY-SA 3.0).
Right: Le Corbusier: Plan for a new Paris ("Plan Voisin"), 1925. Photo: SiefkinDR, CC-BY-SA-4.0.

P. 69: Left: Businessman in Houston, Texas. Photomontage by the author.
Right: Worker in a sulfur mine, Java (Indonesia). Photo: Jean-Marie Hullot, Creative Commons (CC BY-SA 2.0).

P. 81: Left: Missionary with the Ibo people (Nigeria), Public Domain.
Right: US military in Haiti, 2010. Photo: Fred Baker/US Army, Public Domain.

P. 87: Left: Hans Memling: *The Last Judgment*, National Museum Gdańsk, Public Domain.
Right and center: Hieronymus Bosch: *The Garden of Earthly Delights* (details), Museo del Prado, Madrid. Public Domain.

P. 106: Left: Cavalry, sixteenth century, Metropolitan Museum of Art, New York. Photo: Kowloneese, Creative Commons (CC BY-SA).
Right: Cyborgs. Photomontage by the author.

P. 123: Left: Execution of Anabaptists in Münster, contemporary pen drawing by Georg Berger. Public Domain.
Right: Execution on the breaking wheel: Jaques Callot (1592–1635): *Les misères et les malheurs de la guerre* (No. 14). Public Domain.

P. 138: Left: Model of a combat robot based on drawings by Leonardo da Vinci. Photo: Erik Möller. Public Domain.
Left: US Marines. Photo: US Army, Public Domain.

P. 157: Historical city maps of Bruges (fourteenth century) and Karlsruhe (seventeenth century). Public Domain.

P. 164: School based on the Monitorial System, France, lithograph by H. Lecomte, 1818. Public Domain.

P. 193: Left: Matabele War, Shangani battle on October 25, 1893, painting by Richard C. Woodville, Jr.. Public Domain.
Right: Electricity Pavilion, Chicago World's Fair, 1893. Public Domain.

P. 198: Left: London Stock Exchange, ca. 1873, British Library. Public Domain.
Right: Famine victims, Madras Province (India), 1877. Public Domain.

P. 223: Left: National Guard soldiers arriving in the strike area near Ludlow (CO), 1914. Public Domain.
Right: Striking coal workers in Ludlow, 1914. Public Domain.

P. 233: Left: Reich Chancellor Friedrich Ebert (right) with Gustav Noske, 1919. Public Domain.
Right: The Freikorps in Bavaria (1919). Public Domain.

P. 240: Left: Operators of the uranium enrichment plant in Oak Ridge, Tennessee, the center of US nuclear bomb production between 1943 and 1945. The operators did not know what they were working on. Photo: Ed Westcott/American Museum of Science and Energy Center. Public Domain. Middle: Billboard at the exit of the nuclear weapons production facilities in Oak Ridge, Tennessee. Photo: James E. Westcott, Public Domain.
Right: Atomic bomb explosion, Nagasaki, August 9, 1945, taken from Charles Levy's B-29 bomber. Public Domain.

P. 251: Left: Sardar-Sarovar Dam, Gujarat, India, 2006. Photo: Vijayakumarblathur, Creative Commons (CC BY_SA 4.0).
Right: Activist Medha Patkar protests with local residents against the flooding of a village following dam construction. Photo: International Rivers Network.

Timeline A: The Four Tyrannies
(Chapters 1–5)

Ca. 9000 BC: First sedentary cultures in Anatolia, Syria and Palestine

7400–6000 BC: Settlement of Çatal Höyük in Anatolia

3500–3000 BC: Beginning of the Bronze Age; first hierarchically organized city states in Sumer

Ca. 3200 BC: Development of writing as a logistical technique in Sumer and Egypt

Ca. 3100 BC: First royal dynasty in Egypt

2800–1800 BC: Urban Indus Civilization

Ca. 2700 BC: King Gilgamesh of Uruk (oldest sources of the epic by the same name: ca. 2300 BC)

2334–2200 BC: Akkadian Empire: first centrally administered territorial empire with a standing army

2200–1500 BC: Beginning of the Bronze Age along the Yellow River in China; first dynasties

Ca. 1200 BC: Beginning of iron smelting in Anatolia

911–609 BC: Neo-Assyrian military empire from the Persian Gulf to Egypt

Eighth century BC: Time of the earliest biblical prophets (Amos and others)

Ca. 650 BC: First coins minted in Lydia and Greece, shortly afterwards in India and China

Between 563 and 400 BC: Lifetime of Siddhartha Gautama (Buddha)

500–148 BC: Greatest power of the Greek-Hellenistic money-war complex in the eastern Mediterranean region and in the Near East

164 BC–90 AD: The climax of ancient apocalypticism in the eastern Mediterranean region

146 BC–235 AD: Greatest power of the Roman money-war complex, from Palestine to the North Sea

6 BC–31 AD: Lifetime of Jesus of Nazareth

46–57: Paul's missionary travels

66–70: Jewish War; destruction of Jerusalem by Roman troops

Ca. 70–100: Origin of the four gospels of the New Testament

235–284: Crisis and partial disintegration of the Roman Empire

380: Christianity becomes the state religion of the Roman Empire

Fifth century: final decline of the (western) Roman money-war complex; coinage, slavery and large armies largely disappear from Europe

570–632: Lifetime of Mohammed

632–1258: Expansion and height of the Islamic caliphate from Spain, across North Africa to the Indus River

716–755: Bonifatius's missionary travels through Frisia, Hesse, Thuringia and Bavaria

772–804: Violent Christianization of the Saxons between the Rhine and Elbe rivers

1147: Crusade against the Vends between the Elbe and Oder Rivers; forced Christianization

1234–1283: War of the Teutonic Order against the Prussians; forced Christianization

Timeline B: Formation of the Global Megamachine (Chapter 6)

1099: First crusade, co-financed by Genoese merchants; massacre in Jerusalem

1168: Silver discoveries in Freiberg (Saxony); revival of the coinage system

Twelfth century (and beyond): Taxes are gradually changed over from in-kind goods to coinage

Twelfth and thirteenth centuries: Poverty movements; beginning of the church inquisition

1204: Crusade against Byzantium financed by Venice; plundering of Constantinople

1260: End of the world, according to Joachim of Fiores's prediction

Ca. 1300: First firearms in Europe

1320–1321: Beginning of the "Little Ice Age"; Great Famine in Europe

1337–1453: Hundred Years' War: mercenary armies, expansion of the money economy

Ca. 1340: Invention of double-entry bookkeeping in Venice and Genoa

1348–1349: Black Plague epidemic in Europe, starting in Venice and Genoa

1358: Insurgents in France set fire to hundreds of castles ("Jacquerie")

1378: Textile workers take over the government in Florence ("Ciompi Uprising")

1379–1382: Occupation of Ghent and large parts of Flanders by insurgents

1381: Insurgent peasants occupy the Tower of London ("Peasants' Revolt")

1407: Foundation of the Banco di San Giorgio in Genoa

1410–1439: Hussites conquer large parts of Bohemia and Silesia;

Hussite Crusades

From 1450: First large cannons lead to an arms race in Europe

1450–1550: Mining and arms boom in Europe

1453: Ottomans conquer Constantinople; beginning of a search for a sea route to Asia ("India")

1492 (and beyond): Conquest and genocide in Central and South America, financed by banks in Genoa, Augsburg and Antwerp

1495–1560: The Fuggers are the most powerful financial and mining entrepreneurs in the world

Sixteenth century: High point of land privatization and expulsions in England

1500–1700: Falling real wages in Europe; impoverishment of large parts of the population

1525: The German peasant movement is crushed, with the support of Fugger and Luther

1532: End of the world according to Martin Luther's prediction

1532: First German criminal code legalizes torture, the Wheel, burning alive, quartering

1532–35: Anabaptists take over the government of Münster; the Anabaptist movement is crushed

1545: Discovery of the silver mines of Potosí (Bolivia); inflation in Europe follows

1550–1650: High point of witch hunts in Europe

1590–1607: Orange army reform in the Netherlands: first modern standing army

1602: Foundation of the Dutch East India Company (VOC)

1612: The first stock exchange is established in Amsterdam; Amsterdam is the center of the world economy

1618–48: Thirty Years' War; Wallenstein's mercenary army is the largest company in the world

1620: Beginning of colonization and genocide in North America, driven by corporations such as the Virginia Company

1621: Genocide of Banda Islanders (Indonesia) by the VOC

Timeline C: Consolidation, Expansion and Crises (Chapters 7–9)

1600–1800: Establishment of large standing armies and disciplinary institutions in Europe

1623: Galileo Galilei: "The book of the universe is written in the language of mathematics."

1627: *Nova Atlantis* by Francis Bacon: a vision of a technocratic society

1632/1662: *Traité de l'homme* by René Descartes: a mechanistic description of life

1650–1800: Transatlantic slave trade booms, run by joint stock companies such as the Royal Africa Company; Caribbean, North America and West Africa become part of the world economy

1651: *Leviathan* by Thomas Hobbes: "The war of all against all"

1670: English East India Company is granted the right to wage war and mint coins.

1687: *Principia Mathematica* by Isaac Newton: deterministic laws of motion

1712: First steam engine used in a coal mine in northern England

1760–1840: Early phase of industrialization, beginning in England

1776: *The Wealth of Nations* by Adam Smith; founding of classical economics

1776/1787: Independence and Constitution of the US; approximately 15 percent of the population has the right to vote

1789–1799: French Revolution; a constitution with universal suffrage is not implemented

1791–1804: Revolution in Haiti; abolition of the Code Noir and independence

1803–1814: Napoleonic wars, in which about 5 million die

1803–1842: Reign of terror by the London Missionary Society on

Tahiti

1804–1847: Genocide of the Tasmanians by the British colonial power

1809–1822: Decolonization of large parts of Latin America

1815–1914: Great Britain global hegemonic power

1834: New poor laws in England: total deregulation of the labor market; mass misery and slums

1834–80: High phase of classical economic liberalism ("laissez-faire")

1839–42/1856–60: Opium wars; Great Britain forcibly integrates China into the world economy

1840–1918: High industrialization; metallurgical complex boom (coal/steel/railway)

1848–49: Europe-wide revolutionary movements are defeated

1851: Foundation of Reuters, the world's first news agency, on the London Stock Exchange

1858: Anti-colonial uprising in India; British Crown takes over colony from British East India Company

1871: Commune of Paris, smashed by the "Third Republic" with the help of German troops

1876–78/1896–1902: Catastrophic famine in India, China, East Africa and Brazil due to the El Niño climate phenomenon and forced integration into the world market

1879–1914: Violent integration of Africa into the world market ("Scramble for Africa"), Zulu war 1879; genocide in Congo

1888–1908: Wars of extermination against the Ndebele in British South Africa 1893–97; genocide of the Herero and Nama in "German South West Africa" 1904; war of extermination against the inhabitants of "German East Africa" (Maji-Maji War) 1905

From 1880: Electrification in Europe, North America and Japan

1881–1934: US military interventions in Latin America and "Banana Wars"; US hegemony in the region

1885: Invention of the machine gun

1886: First commercial production of motor vehicles with internal combustion engine

1889–1914: Wave of mass strikes in Europe and the US (especially coal, railway and port workers)

1900: Anti-colonial "Boxer Rebellion" in China; defeated by Western armies, Japan and Russia

1900–1914: Alongside coal, crude oil becomes the most important source of energy for the expanding Megamachine

1900–1914: Arms race in Europe

1903–1940: Climax of Alfred and Harold Harmsworth's media empire in Great Britain

1914–18: First World War with approximately 10 million dead

1917: October Revolution in Russia followed by four years of civil war

1918/20: For the first time, women gain universal suffrage in Germany, Great Britain, US

1918/19: November Revolution in Germany, defeated by fascist "Freikorps"

1919–21: Revolutionary movements in Italy, put down by fascists

1919–37: Peak of the media empire of the Hugenberg Group in Germany

1920–51: Climax of William Hearst's media empire in the US

1922: Benito Mussolini becomes head of government in Italy

1922: *Public Opinion* by Walter Lippmann; theory of "guided democracy"

1922–1975: Fascism in Europe, most recently in Portugal (until 1974) and Spain (until 1975)

1926–1945: "Tennō Fascism" in Japan

1927–1953: Stalin's dictatorship in the USSR; camp system (Gulag) with millions dead

1928: *Propaganda* by Edward Bernays: the foundation of modern public relations

1929–33: World economic crisis; New York takes over the role of world financial center from London

1933: Election victory of the NSDAP, with campaign support from German industry and German banks

1933–38: "New Deal" in the USA; massive government stimulus packages

1936–39: Spanish Civil War; destruction of the republic and the social revolution

1939–45: Second World War and genocide of Jews, Sinti and Roma; approximately 65 million dead

Timeline D: The Boom and Limits of the Megamachine (Chapters 10–11)

1945: Atomic bombs dropped on Hiroshima and Nagasaki; US becomes global hegemonic power

1945–73: Largest economic expansion in the history of the modern world-system

1945–76: Decolonization of Southeast Asia, India (1947), China (1948) and Africa

1946–54: War by France against the independence movement in "Indochina"

1949: First successful atomic bomb test by the Soviet Union; nuclear arms race begins

1949: US President Truman's inaugural speech: division of the world into "developed" and "underdeveloped" countries

1950–53: Korean War; 5 million Koreans and Chinese and 40,000 US soldiers die

1953–today: series of military coups and interventions under the auspices of Western secret services (including Iran 1953, Guatemala 1954, Congo 1960, Brazil 1964, Indonesia 1965, Honduras 1972, Chile 1973, Argentina 1976, Haiti 1991)

1954–62: Algerian War; at least 300,000 Algerians die in the fight for independence

1955–65: Climax of the Non-Aligned Movement

1955–68: Civil rights movement in the US seeking equal rights for African Americans

1955–75: Vietnam War ("Second Indochina War"); 3 to 4 million Vietnamese, Laotians and Cambodians die

1965–73: "World Revolution of 1968"/movement against the Vietnam War

1969/70: Founding of Greenpeace against atomic bomb tests; growth of the modern environmental movement

1969–85: "Strategy of tension": terrorist attacks by the Gladio organization in Italy

1972: Report to the Club of Rome: *The Limits to Growth*

1973: Oil crisis; start of a global recession; end of the Bretton Woods monetary system

1973–today: Neoliberal rollback, starting with the military coup in Chile

1977: Great Britain almost bankrupt; IMF structural adjustment programs launched

1981–today: Media empire of Rupert Murdoch (The Times, Fox, News Corp. and others)

1982: Beginning of the Savings and Loan Crisis in the US

1982: Mexico crisis; first extensive privatization programs under the direction of the IMF; start of the debt crisis in the Global South

1984/85: Beginning of the privatization of broadcasting in Germany and France

1989: Suppression of the Chinese opposition to political repression and deregulation of the economy

1989–95: Collapse of the USSR and neoliberal shock programs in Eastern Europe

1994: North American Free Trade Agreement; beginning of the Zapatista Movement in Mexico

1997–2000: Series of financial crises (Asian crisis 1997/98, Russia 1998/99, Argentina 2000, Dotcom 2000)

1999: Mass protests against World Trade Organization; start of the "anti-globalization movement"

1999–2017: Left-leaning governments in Latin America; partial emancipation of the region from the IMF and the US

2001: First World Social Forum in Porto Alegre (Brazil)

2001: Attacks on New York and Washington; declaration of the "War on Terror"

2003: Iraq war ("Third Gulf War") under US leadership; Iraq subsequently becomes "failed state"

2007–2009: World financial crisis; since 2009: "Eurocrisis"/ neoliberal shock programs in Southern Europe

2009: Foundation of the BRIC Group (Brazil, Russia, India, China)

2010/11: Arab and African Spring; revolutions against authoritarian regimes

2011/12: Occupy Wall Street; mass protests against austerity programs in Southern Europe

2013: Foundation of the Belt and Road Initiative („new silk road") by the Chinese government.

Since 2014: Right-wing nationalist and fascist governments come to power in many countries (India 2014, Poland 2015, USA 2017, Brazil 2018, Great Britain 2019).

2014–2019: About 20,000 people die in the Mediterranean while trying to reach the „Fortress Europe".

2019: The movement "Fridays for Future" organizes climate strikes which mobilize millions of people around the world.

2020: Covid-10 pandemic („Corona"); shutdown of parts of the economy with the consequence of a grave recession.

Index

1848 (revolution) 157, 168, 185, 217, 220, 355
1968 (revolution) 255–259, 310
1984 (novel) 230

A

Absolutism 145, 156, 208
Adivasi 241f.
African Lakes Corporation 189
Agricola, Georgius 108f.
Acre (city in Galilee) 96
al-Andalus (Islamic Iberia) 115
Al-Aqsa Mosque 96, 116
Alchemy 40f., 107, 325, 354
Algeria (War of Independence) 242
Alienation 165f., 169, 256, 314
Allende, Salvador 267, 365
American Dream 245
American Indian Movement 257
Amsterdam 9, 128, 343
Amsterdam Stock Exchange 127, 160, 392
Anabaptists 63, 122–124, 392
Anthropocene 173f.
Antiochus IV 65–67
Anti-Semitism 185, 236f., 359
Antwerp 103, 115, 117, 392
Apocalypse 63–73, 87, 287, 334
Arendt, Hannah 244

Argentina 271, 275, 307, 369
Armagnacs (mercenaries in the Hundred Years' War) 101
Armaments industry 105–109, 154, 176, 203, 236, 239f., 288, 313
Arms race 107f., 203f., 240
Assyrian Empire (Aššur) 36, 389
Athens (antiquity) 47
Atomic bomb 21, 239–241, 247, 261, 313f., 397
Augsburg Confession 122f., 343
Automotive industry 245f., 302f.
Automatons 30, 136–138, 145, 161, 246

B

Babeuf, François 215
Bacon, Francis 63, 139, 140–142, 240
Bali 255, 315f.
Banco di San Giorgio 110, 340
Banda Islands 128
Bank of England 340, 371
Banks 45, 101, 106, 110f., 113–115, 151, 174, 211, 220, 272, 306f., 312, 334, 337, 355, 368, 371
Bardi (Italian banker family)

101, 110, 338

Bateson, Gregory 30, 362

Behaviorism 143, 346

Belle Époque 193

Bernays, Edward 228–230, 253, 357

Biosphere 7, 41, 173, 280

Black Panthers 259

Black pedagogy 364

Black powder 106f., 204

Black Prince (Edward, the) 101f.

Blackwater (company) 53

Bonifatius 79, 390

Book of Revelation 41, 64, 67, 69, 71, 129, 329f.

Bosch, Hieronymus 87, 334

Boyle, Robert 142

Brave New World (novel) 230

Brazil 39, 167f., 196, 258, 271, 275, 279, 290, 294, 300, 394, 397, 399

British East India Company 127, 189, 195, 199, 200, 393f.

British South Africa Company 192

Bronze Age 13f., 35, 320, 389

Bruges (medieval revolt) 92

Bundschuh movement 121

Byblos 96

Byzantium (Byzantine Empire) 94, 97f., 107, 336f., 391

C

Cadastral land register 155

Calvinism 68, 128f.

Campanella, Tommaso 63, 346

Camposanto (Pisa) 87

Capital accumulation 9, 53, 85, 98, 108, 111, 118, 120, 125f., 131, 135, 144, 151, 174, 177–180, 246, 264–266, 271, 275, 278, 280, 291–301, 305, 307f., 337, 340, 344

Carthage 51f.

Çatal Höyük 13f., 22, 27, 389

Cathars 90

Chaplin, Charlie 178

Charcoal 36f., 109f., 176f., 349

Charlemagne 80, 333

Charles V (Holy Roman Emperor) 111, 334, 342

Charles VII (of France) 102

Chartist movement 217

Chemical industry 40f., 204, 242, 296

Chernobyl 227, 275, 280

Chevron 307

Chicago Boys 267

Chile 39, 267, 280, 310, 365, 397f.

Chilperic I (Frankish king) 88

China 14, 94, 98, 107, 131, 151, 189, 196f., 199–202, 250–252, 268f., 273, 283, 313, 343, 353, 362, 389, 394f., 397–399

Christianity 5, 8, 28, 59, 64, 67, 71–74, 75–81, 97, 122f., 132,

190f., 249, 291, 332, 390

Churchill, Winston 234

CIA 253f., 259f., 362

Citizen Kane (movie) 219

Ciudad Juárez 273

Civil rights movement (USA)
257–259, 397

Climate change 5, 7, 110, 192,
199, 303, 306

Club of Rome 261, 284, 398

Coal (fossil fuel) 36, 39f., 110,
168, 173–179, 222f., 243, 272,
305f., 325, 328, 372, 394f.

Code Civil 217

Code Noir 167f., 215, 393

Code of Hammurabi 26

Coinage 34, 47–52, 65, 100, 104,
127, 132, 326, 389–393

Cointelpro (FBI program) 258,
260

Colonialism 9, 61, 124, 140, 144

Coltan 4, 39

Columbus, Christopher 79, 98,
112f., 116

Comenius, Johann 164

Commercialization 47, 50, 56,
65, 268, 338

Commerzbank 220, 236, 356,
358

Commons 118f., 132, 210, 300f.,
335

Congo 4, 39, 109, 194f., 253f.,
271, 277, 394, 397

Conquista 112–117, 149, 193,

344

Constantinople 94, 97, 107, 112,
391f.

Constitutio Criminalis Carolina
(German penal code) 334, 342

Consumerism 64, 246, 260

Cook, James 190

Cooperatives 106, 124, 183, 289,
295, 297, 299, 305, 309f., 369

Copper 34–40, 104f., 109, 111,
176, 192–194, 255, 272, 280,
296, 341

Corporations 6, 27, 39, 45,
52–54, 56f., 75, 106, 124–128,
141, 183f., 189, 194f., 199f.,
208, 255, 262, 266, 278, 294,
305–308, 312, 327

Cortés, Hernán 115f., 272

Council on Foreign Relations
228

Counterculture 255, 257, 261f.,
264, 267

Crimea 98, 110

Crowd Control 311

Crucifixion 61, 68, 72

Crusades 9, 95–98, 116, 336f.,
391f.

Cultural Revolution (China)
252, 362

D

Daniel (Old Testament book)
65–67, 73, 329

de Witte, Hans (Dutch banker)

103, 111

Debt 6, 23–26, 50f., 60, 65, 89, 110f., 115, 118, 131f., 152, 196f., 211, 215f., 221, 252, 264–266, 270–272, 277, 297f., 309, 323, 344, 346, 355, 368f., 398

Debt relief 24, 50f.

Decoupling (energy use) 281, 349

Degrowth 290

Democracy
— Council democracy (soviet republics) 224, 232f., 310, 373
— Guided democracy 227–231, 256, 258, 279, 395
— Representative democracy 208f., 223, 309
— Republic 211f., 214, 221

Deng Xiaoping 269

Descartes, René 137, 145, 393

Deutsche Bank 220, 236, 356, 358

Development 5, 241f., 247, 249–255, 270, 272, 274

Devil 67, 87, 120

Dickens, Charles 182

Disciplinary institutions 9, 162–171, 204, 208, 256, 262, 393

Disenchantment of the world 158

Dominium (Roman law) 55f.

Dutch East India Company (VOC) 126–128, 160, 167, 392

Dystopia 230, 275

E

Easter Island 281

Ebert, Friedrich 232f.

Ecological limits 7, 176, 280–284

Ecology movement 260f.,

Economic growth 175, 243, 246f., 280

Ecuador 298, 307, 369

Educational revolution 261

Edward III 101

Eisenhower, Dwight D. 34, 254

El Niño (climate phenomenon) 196, 199

Electrification 192, 194, 394

Embriaco (Genoese family) 96

Enclosure of the Commons 118f., 131f., 169, 181

Engels, Friedrich 182, 218f.

European Central Bank (ECB) 309

Extractivism 296f.

F

Failed states 201, 277

Famine 91, 99, 196–198, 251, 360

Fascism 188, 232–238, 279, 395

Faust 40

FBI 258f., 312

Feudalism 92f., 99, 101, 184, 335f.

Financial crises
— Asian crisis 275
— Euro crisis 265
— Global financial crisis (1929)
306f., 395
— Global financial crisis (2008)
265, 275–277, 298, 307
— Mexico crisis (1982) 272f.,
398
— Savings and Loan Crisis 265
Financial system 2, 5, 34, 222,
272, 275f., 284, 306
Fiore, Joachim of 90, 335
Firearms 20, 107, 273, 391
Flanders 102, 118, 334, 391
Florence 92, 102f., 110, 391
Ford (company) 235f.
Ford Foundation 255
Forestry 155, 347
Founding fathers (USA) 211,
213, 225, 228, 308
Fracking 280, 289
Francis of Assisi 90
Frankenhausen (battle of) 121,
193
Freikorps (fascist troops) 232f.,
395
French Revolution 185, 213–
216, 393
Friedman, Milton 267
Fugger, Jakob 111, 121, 334,
341, 392
Fukushima 274, 280, 306
Fukuyama, Francis 64

G
Gaia hypothesis 261
Galilei, Galileo 96, 137, 142–
145, 393
Gandhi, Mahatma 248f., 261,
292, 309
Gauntlet (running the) 160
Gaz de France 195
General Motors 235, 245f.
Genetic engineering 41, 140,
314
Genoa 9, 91, 94f., 98, 110f., 115,
117, 125, 233, 336, 340, 391
Genocide 3f., 79, 86, 111, 113f.,
117, 127f., 193, 195, 198, 254,
351f., 392, 394, 396
Geoengineering 141, 285, 314
Ghent (medieval city) 92, 391
Gilgamesh 16, 389
Gladio (secret organization)
259, 397
Gold 33f., 37–39, 45, 47, 70, 97,
112f., 115f., 176, 192, 211f.,
264, 280, 296, 298
Gorbachev, Mikhail 268
Gospels 59f., 72, 75f., 78, 330–
332, 359
Gouges, Olympe de 216
Greece (antiquity) 37, 46–48,
208, 389
Greece (financial crisis) 297f.,
368, 372
Green economy 293
Greenpeace 260

Guatemala 4, 253
Guilds 118

H
Haber-Bosch process 282
Habsburg (dynasty) 111
Haiti 81, 113, 215f., 270, 355,
   393, 397
Hamoukar (ancient Syrian city)
   35
Harappa 320
Harmsworth, Alfred
Haussmann, George Eugène
   157
Hawkwood, John 102
Hearst, William 219
Heavenly Jerusalem 63, 68–70,
   73, 335
Heine, Heinrich 185
Hell 38, 75, 87, 117, 120, 129,
   334
Herero (ethnic group in
   Sothern Africa) 193, 208,
   351f., 394
Heretics 76, 90, 118f., 342
Hispaniola 113
Hobbes, Thomas 18, 124, 132,
   135, 137, 145f., 149
Homo faber 314, 325
Hoover, J. Edgar 246
Hugenberg, Alfred 220, 356,
   395
Huntington, Samuel 256, 262f.,
   267f., 273, 364

Hussites 93, 391

I
Illich, Ivan 245, 314, 361
Imagined communities (B.
   Anderson) 184f.
India 189, 195–199, 241, 248–
   251, 273, 283, 292, 309, 332,
   389, 394
Indonesia 39, 69, 127f., 189,
   254f., 270, 315f., 392
Inflation (early modern era)
   118f., 392
Inquisition 86, 90, 93, 119f.,
   141f., 391
Intelligence services 253–255,
   259, 312
International Monetary Fund
   (IMF) 75, 264, 269, 271–273.,
   369, 372, 398
Iraq 4, 201, 269f., 274, 277
Iron Age 34–37
Islamism 273f.

J
Japan 200, 202, 234f., 239, 255,
   262, 368, 396
Jay, John 207, 212
Jefferson, Thomas 140, 211f.
Jerusalem 63–65, 68f. 72f., 96f.,
   123, 129, 140, 331, 335, 390,
   391
Jesus of Nazareth 59–61, 71–74,
   76f., 122, 129, 330f., 332, 390

Joachimsthal (silver mines) 109
Joint-stock company 52, 124–128, 167

K
Kafka, Franz 204f.
Kant, Immanuel 191
Kennedy, John F. 344
Kennedy, Robert 247
Kent State massacre (Ohio) 258
King, Martin Luther 258f.
Kipling, Rudyard 80
Knights 96, 99, 101, 106
Kraus, Karl 204f.
Krupp (corporation) 36, 220, 236, 358
Kutná Hora (silver mines) 105

L
Labor market 47, 60, 179–182, 394
Labor movement 183f., 210f., 222f., 298
Land grabbing 60, 289, 294
Las Casas, Bartolomé de 114
Lascaux 27
Laurion (Greek silver mines) 49–51
Le Corbusier 63f., 157
Lee, Ivy 222, 228
Lenin, Vladimir Ilyich 224–227
Leviathan (book by Thomas Hobbes) 124, 135, 145f.
Liberalism 128, 167, 181, 188, 210, 217, 224, 331, 354
Lippmann, Walter 227–230
Living Theatre 256
Livingstone, David 190
Livingstonia Central Africa Company 189
Locke, John 167, 218
London Missionary Society 189f. 393
Lord Lytton 197
Louis XIV 150
Lowell Mill Girls 183f., 208
Luddites 184
Ludlow, Colorado (massacre) 222f.
Lumumba, Patrice 253f., 363
Luther, Martin 87, 121–123, 342, 392
Luxemburg, Rosa 219, 225

M
Machine gun 192f., 203, 222, 248, 269, 394
Madison, James 211–213, 216, 228, 256
Mali 277
Mao Tse Tung 251f.
Marx, Karl 120f., 218f., 344
Matabele Wars 192f.
Maxim, Hiram 192f., 203
Maxwell, James 227
Mbuti (people in Central Africa) 78
Mechanistic worldview 29–31,

135–149, 314–316
Medici (Italian family) 110
Medieval Warm Period 89–91
Mercenaries 50, 52, 102–104,
    121, 127f., 130f., 168f., 193,
    195
Mesopotamia 14–16, 20, 23f.,
    26, 28, 35, 50
Messiah 72, 330f.
Metallurgy 40f., 104–110, 141,
    296f., 320, 353f.
Metropolis (movie) 241
Mexico 106, 113, 192, 255, 258,
    271, 272f., 282, 398
Midas 47
Militarization 50, 65, 94f.,
    98–104, 150, 311–314
Military service 47, 150, 256
Mining 33–39, 104–111, 176–
    178, 191, 194, 219f., 250, 253f.,
    280, 289, 296, 328, 354, 363,
    392
Mission 5, 75–81, 95–97, 116,
    129f., 149, 189–192, 199, 201,
    207, 249, 256, 291, 332, 390,
    393
Mobutu, Sese Seko 254
Moctezuma II 106
Monitorial system (schools)
    163f.
Monopolies 95f., 98, 103f., 111,
    126, 128, 141, 214, 219, 226
Mont Pèlerin Society 75, 331
Morel, Edmund 194

Mountaintop removal 39
Mussolini, Benito 233f., 395
My Lai (massacre) 260

N
NAFTA (North American Free
    Trade Agreement) 272, 289
Nanotechnology 41
Napoleon I 190, 215, 393
National Socialism 220, 234–
    238
Nationalism 184–188, 273, 279
Native Americans 191, 213, 257,
    289
Natural sciences 40f., 138–149,
    295
Neoliberalism 3, 263–275, 308,
    365, 398
New York (bankruptcy) 264
Newton, Isaac 137, 146, 167,
    393
Noske, Gustav 232f.
Nuclear energy 241, 244, 275,
    289, 296

O
Occupy movement 291, 309,
    312, 373, 399
October Revolution (Russian
    Revolution) 224–227, 232, 395
Oil industry 39, 41, 56, 179, 235,
    243, 245, 255, 270, 274, 280,
    282, 289, 296, 303, 305f., 372
Omnipotence (theological and

technocratic) 28f., 41, 66, 141, 240

Orwell, George 230, 235

P

Palestine (antiquity) 36, 51, 65, 95, 97, 389

Palestine (modern era) 69

Palladio, Andrea 156

Paris Commune 158, 221, 310, 394

Patriarchy 19, 55f., 140, 257

Paul (apostle) 75–78, 121, 332f., 342, 390

Pax Augusta 61

Pax Britannica 188

Peasants' Revolt (medieval) 92, 391

Peer-to-peer production (P2P) 302

Penan (Southeast Asian people) 241

Pentagon papers 260

Pequot (North American people) 129

Peru 113, 117, 294, 296

Plague (late Middle Ages) 67, 86, 91f., 101f., 131, 391

Planned obsolescence 246

Polanyi, Karl 180, 343

Potosí (Bolivian silver mines) 116–118, 392

Prague Spring 258, 310

Prigogine, Ilya 144, 261

Primitive (original) accumulation 120, 298

Propaganda 119, 187, 202, 217, 227, 229f., 237, 253, 266f., 357f.

Property 6, 13, 17, 22–24, 26, 54–57, 89, 120, 122f., 141, 153, 156, 194, 211, 215, 217, 224, 236, 294–298, 301, 315, 322, 327f., 370

Prophets (Old Testament) 26, 57, 68, 72f., 323, 389

Prussia 80, 149f., 160f., 346, 356, 390

Puritans 68, 129

R

Racism 187, 190–192, 257

Railways 105, 177, 196f., 203, 222f., 245, 266, 278, 394f.

Rammelsberg (silver mines) 104

Rathenau, Walther 225

Rationality 136f., 237

Reagan, Ronald 258, 273

Rebound effect 281

Reformation 63, 121–123

Religion 5, 25f., 28, 72, 74–76, 103, 135f., 168, 190f., 246

Rembrandt 128

Renaissance 86, 116, 141, 146, 338, 346

Renault, Louis 236

Reuter, Paul Julius 219, 355, 394

Rhodes, Cecil 173, 191f.
Robespierre, Maximilien de 214f.
Rockefeller, David 262
Rockefeller, John D. 222f.
Rojava (Syria) 310
Roux, Jacques 214f.
Royal African Company 167
Royal Dutch Shell 236
Royal Society 142
Rubber 194, 255
Russia 201f, 224–227, 240, 268f., 275, 346, 356

S
School 161, 162–166, 186, 208, 211, 256, 261, 278, 343, 354, 395, 399
Schumacher, E. F. 261
Scientism 18, 29, 138–149, 345
Self-organization 9, 147, 183, 210, 216, 224–226, 235, 251, 288, 290, 299–301, 303, 309f., 315, 346
Senegal Company 167
Sforza (Milanese dynasty) 102, 137
Siéyès, Abbé 216
Silver 34, 37, 45, 49–53, 65, 97, 99f., 104f., 106, 109, 111, 116–118, 211, 339, 340, 341, 391f.
Slavery 8, 24f., 46, 49, 55f., 60, 67, 88, 120, 166–170, 183f., 215, 288, 328, 390

Smith, Adam 45, 393
Social democracy 211, 220, 232, 255, 353
Socialism 224–226, 255, 293
South Sea Company 167
Soviet Union 224f., 241, 254, 268, 363, 397
Spain 37, 51f., 88, 112–117, 119, 297f., 328, 341, 369, 390, 395
Standing army 65, 102, 150, 159, 212, 389, 292
Steam engine 173f., 177, 227, 348, 393
Stock exchange 43, 45, 126, 160, 198, 219, 327, 343, 392, 394
Strategy of tension 259, 397
Strike 222–224, 233, 258, 298, 395
Structural adjustment programs (IMF) 264, 269, 272, 277, 398
Structural violence 17f., 21–24, 175, 180, 195, 226, 252, 270, 297, 368
Subak system (Bali) 315f.
Subsidies 98, 271f., 306f., 371
Suez Lyonnaise des Eaux (corporation) 195
Suffrage 216f., 221f., 355, 393, 395, 395
Suharto, Haji Mohamed 254f.
Sumer 14–17, 22–27, 389
Swift, Jonathan 167
Synthetic Biology 41, 140

T
Tábor (Czech city) 93
Tacitus 61, 67
Taylorism 225
Tenochtitlán 106, 272
Terrorism 259, 274
The Weald (iron industry)
 107–110
Thirty Years' War 86,103, 109f.,
 131, 277, 392
Torture 60, 86, 90, 114f., 119–
 123, 141f., 233, 242, 254f., 258,
 267, 334, 359f., 392
Transition towns 290, 303
Trauma 59–74, 79f., 91f., 116,
 131f., 182f., 205, 237, 242,
 244f.
Trilateral Commission 207,
 262f.,
Tristan, Flora 181f.
Truman, Harry 249, 252f., 262
Twain, Mark 194
Tyre, William of 96f.

U
Ukraine 277
United Fruit Company
 (Chiquita) 253
Universalism (Western) 75–81,
 97, 139, 149, 334
Uranium 34, 39, 240, 280
Uruk 24, 35
Utopia 63f., 68–70, 119, 130,
 230, 275, 290

V
Varus (Roman governor) 61
Venetian arsenal 94–98
Venice 91, 94–98, 102, 110, 126,
 336f., 391
Vickers (armaments producer)
 36, 236
Vietnam War 200, 242, 256f.,
 260, 277, 312, 397
Vinci, Leonardo da 85, 102,
 137f., 239
Virginia Company 141, 344f.,
 392
Volcker shock 271

W
Wage labor 21, 47, 108, 120,
 166f., 168–171, 183, 211, 256,
 295
Wage slavery 183
Wallenstein 103f.
Wallerstein, Immanuel 6, 288,
 317, 334, 337, 344, 349, 354,
 366, 402
War entrepreneurs (condottieri)
 102, 132, 150, 174
War on Terror 274
Warlords 137, 150, 202, 270,
 274, 311
War economy 99–112, 131, 225,
 244, 277, 288
Washington, George 211f.
Water crisis, global 282–284
Welfare state 241

William the Conqueror 100f.

Witch hunts 119f., 392

Women's movement 216, 218, 220, 257, 259

Workhouses 162, 169

World Social Forum 291

Writing (origins of) 14, 18, 25–27, 389

Y

Yeltsin, Boris 269

Z

Zapatists 289

Zoroastrianism 75

Zwingli, Huldrych 122

About the Author

Fabian Scheidler, born in 1968, studied history and philosophy at the Freie Universität Berlin. He lives and works in Berlin as a writer for print media, television and theater. In 2009, he co-founded the independent newscast Kontext TV (**www.kontext-tv.de/en**), which is dedicated to global justice issues. In 2009, he received the Otto Brenner Media Award for Critical Journalism. He has also worked as a dramaturg and playwright for the renowned Grips Theater in Berlin for several years. In 2013, his opera *Death of a Banker* (music by Andreas Kersting) premiered at the Gerhart Hauptmann Theater in Görlitz (Germany). *The End of the Megamachine* was released in German in 2015. A French translation is to be published in autumn 2020 by Les Éditions du Seuil. In 2017, Fabian Scheidler published *Chaos. Das neue Zeitalter der Revolutionen* (*Chaos. The New Age of Revolutions*).

For more information about the book, including videos, reviews, lecture tours and Fabian's blog, please visit: **www.end-of-the-megamachine.com.**

For more information about the author and for contact requests, please visit **www.fabianscheidler.com.**

CULTURE, SOCIETY & POLITICS

The modern world is at an impasse. Disasters scroll across our smartphone screens and we're invited to like, follow or upvote, but critical thinking is harder and harder to find. Rather than connecting us in common struggle and debate, the internet has sped up and deepened a long-standing process of alienation and atomization. Zer0 Books wants to work against this trend. With critical theory as our jumping off point, we aim to publish books that make our readers uncomfortable. We want to move beyond received opinions.

Zer0 Books is on the left and wants to reinvent the left. We are sick of the injustice, the suffering, and the stupidity that defines both our political and cultural world, and we aim to find a new foundation for a new struggle.

If this book has helped you to clarify an idea, solve a problem or extend your knowledge, you may want to check out our online content as well. Look for Zer0 Books: Advancing Conversations in the iTunes directory and for our Zer0 Books YouTube channel.

Popular videos include:

Žižek and the Double Blackmain

The Intellectual Dark Web is a Bad Sign

Can there be an Anti-SJW Left?

Answering Jordan Peterson on Marxism

Follow us on Facebook
at https://www.facebook.com/ZeroBooks and Twitter at https://twitter.com/Zer0Books

Bestsellers from Zer0 Books include:

Give Them An Argument
Logic for the Left
Ben Burgis
Many serious leftists have learned to distrust talk of logic. This is a serious mistake.
Paperback: 978-1-78904-210-8 ebook: 978-1-78904-211-5

Poor but Sexy
Culture Clashes in Europe East and West
Agata Pyzik
How the East stayed East and the West stayed West.
Paperback: 978-1-78099-394-2 ebook: 978-1-78099-395-9

An Anthropology of Nothing in Particular
Martin Demant Frederiksen
A journey into the social lives of meaninglessness.
Paperback: 978-1-78535-699-5 ebook: 978-1-78535-700-8

In the Dust of This Planet
Horror of Philosophy vol. 1
Eugene Thacker
In the first of a series of three books on the Horror of Philosophy,
In the Dust of This Planet offers the genre of horror as a way of
thinking about the unthinkable.
Paperback: 978-1-84694-676-9 ebook: 978-1-78099-010-1

The End of Oulipo?
An Attempt to Exhaust a Movement
Lauren Elkin, Veronica Esposito
Paperback: 978-1-78099-655-4 ebook: 978-1-78099-656-1

Capitalist Realism
Is There no Alternative?
Mark Fisher
An analysis of the ways in which capitalism has presented itself
as the only realistic political-economic system.
Paperback: 978-1-84694-317-1 ebook: 978-1-78099-734-6

Rebel Rebel
Chris O'Leary
David Bowie: every single song. Everything you want to know,
everything you didn't know.
Paperback: 978-1-78099-244-0 ebook: 978-1-78099-713-1

Kill All Normies
Angela Nagle
Online culture wars from 4chan and Tumblr to Trump.
Paperback: 978-1- 78535-543-1 ebook: 978-1-78535-544-8

Cartographies of the Absolute
Alberto Toscano, Jeff Kinkle
An aesthetics of the economy for the twenty-first century.
Paperback: 978-1-78099-275-4 ebook: 978-1-78279-973-3

Malign Velocities
Accelerationism and Capitalism
Benjamin Noys
Long listed for the Bread and Roses Prize 2015, *Malign Velocities*
argues against the need for speed, tracking acceleration
as the symptom of the ongoing crises of capitalism.
Paperback: 978-1-78279-300-7 ebook: 978-1-78279-299-4

Meat Market
Female Flesh under Capitalism
Laurie Penny
A feminist dissection of women's bodies as the fleshy fulcrum of
capitalist cannibalism, whereby women are both consumers and
consumed.
Paperback: 978-1-84694-521-2 ebook: 978-1-84694-782-7

Babbling Corpse
Vaporwave and the Commodification of Ghosts
Grafton Tanner
Paperback: 978-1-78279-759-3 ebook: 978-1-78279-760-9

New Work New Culture
Work we want and a culture that strengthens us
Frithjoff Bergmann
A serious alternative for mankind and the planet.
Paperback: 978-1-78904-064-7 ebook: 978-1-78904-065-4

Romeo and Juliet in Palestine
Teaching Under Occupation
Tom Sperlinger
Life in the West Bank, the nature of pedagogy and the role of a
university under occupation.
Paperback: 978-1-78279-637-4 ebook: 978-1-78279-636-7

Ghosts of My Life
Writings on Depression, Hauntology and Lost Futures
Mark Fisher
Paperback: 978-1-78099-226-6 ebook: 978-1-78279-624-4

Sweetening the Pill
or How We Got Hooked on Hormonal Birth Control
Holly Grigg-Spall
Has contraception liberated or oppressed women?
Sweetening the Pill breaks the silence on the dark side of hormonal
contraception.
Paperback: 978-1-78099-607-3 ebook: 978-1-78099-608-0

Why Are We The Good Guys?
Reclaiming your Mind from the Delusions of Propaganda
David Cromwell
A provocative challenge to the standard ideology that Western
power is a benevolent force in the world.
Paperback: 978-1-78099-365-2 ebook: 978-1-78099-366-9

The Writing on the Wall
On the Decomposition of Capitalism and its Critics
Anselm Jappe, Alastair Hemmens
A new approach to the meaning of social emancipation.
Paperback: 978-1-78535-581-3 ebook: 978-1-78535-582-0

Enjoying It
Candy Crush and Capitalism
Alfie Bown
A study of enjoyment and of the enjoyment of studying. Bown asks what enjoyment says about us and what we say about enjoyment, and why.
Paperback: 978-1-78535-155-6 ebook: 978-1-78535-156-3

Color, Facture, Art and Design
Iona Singh
This materialist definition of fine-art develops guidelines for architecture, design, cultural-studies and ultimately social change.
Paperback: 978-1-78099-629-5 ebook: 978-1-78099-630-1

Neglected or Misunderstood
The Radical Feminism of Shulamith Firestone
Victoria Margree
An interrogation of issues surrounding gender, biology, sexuality, work and technology, and the ways in which our imaginations continue to be in thrall to ideologies of maternity and the nuclear family.
Paperback: 978-1-78535-539-4 ebook: 978-1-78535-540-0

How to Dismantle the NHS in 10 Easy Steps (Second Edition)
Youssef El-Gingihy
The story of how your NHS was sold off and why you will have to buy private health insurance soon. A new expanded second edition with chapters on junior doctors' strikes and government blueprints for US-style healthcare.
Paperback: 978-1-78904-178-1 ebook: 978-1-78904-179-8

Digesting Recipes
The Art of Culinary Notation
Susannah Worth
A recipe is an instruction, the imperative tone of the expert, but this constraint can offer its own kind of potential. A recipe need not be a domestic trap but might instead offer escape – something to fantasise about or aspire to.
Paperback: 978-1-78279-860-6 ebook: 978-1-78279-859-0

Most titles are published in paperback and as an ebook. Paperbacks are available in traditional bookshops. Both print and ebook formats are available online.
Follow us on Facebook
at https://www.facebook.com/ZeroBooks
and Twitter at https://twitter.com/Zer0Books